New Towns in the New World

D1161386

The Columbia History of Urban Life
KENNETH T. JACKSON, GENERAL EDITOR

The Columbia History of Urban Life

KENNETH T. JACKSON, GENERAL EDITOR

New Towns
in the New World

Images and Perceptions of the

Nineteenth-Century Urban Frontier

DAVID HAMER

COLUMBIA UNIVERSITY PRESS

NEW YORK

Columbia University Press
New York   Oxford
Copyright © 1990 Columbia University Press
All rights reserved

Library of Congress Cataloging-in-Publication Data
Hamer, D. A. (David Allan)
New towns in the New World / David Hamer.
p.   cm.—(The Columbia history of urban life)
Includes bibliographical references.
ISBN 0-231-06620-1
1. Urbanization—History—19th century.   2. Urbanization—United
States—History—19th century.   3. Urbanization—Australia—
History—19th century.   4. Urbanization—Canada—History—19th
century.   5. Urbanization—New Zealand—History—19th century.
I. Title.   II. Series.
HT361.H35   1990
307.76'09—dc20   89-27777
CIP

Printed in the United States of America
c 10 9 8 7 6 5 4 3 2 1

Book design by Ken Venezio

Contents

v

Contents

Illustrations appear as a group following pages 84 and 148

Preface and Acknowledgments

M Y interest in the urbanization of "new countries" began about ten years ago when I was searching for explanations of the marked division between "town" and "country" which appeared in New Zealand politics in the late nineteenth century. I discovered that there had as yet been little attempt to assess the significance of towns and cities in relation to New Zealand's development as a "new society." Although New Zealand has become a highly urbanized country, the urban dimension of its development had impinged very little on popular and scholarly perceptions of that process. Urban history was then a very new area of interest and academic research in New Zealand. In endeavoring to contribute to its promotion, I was led to look to the histories of other "new societies" of the nineteenth century for ideas and methodologies that might guide my work. I discovered situations there that were not too dissimilar from those which characterized my own country—a recent development of urban history following a long neglect of the role of towns and cities in the shaping of the "new country" and the formation of myths of national identity. This book is the outcome of my efforts to make sense of this state of affairs by going back into the nineteenth century to analyze how some of the people who founded these "new societies" perceived the relationship of urbanization to this process.

During my research for this book I have accumulated many debts, and I now gratefully acknowledge these. Although none of those whose help I have received have any responsibility for the final outcome of my labors, I hope that they will regard this acknowledgment and the book itself as some small recompense for the support they have given me.

In the first place, I would like to thank my own university, the Victoria University of Wellington, for twice granting me the opportunity to pursue my researches into urban history on leave. I am also grateful to my colleagues in the History Department for their interest and encouragement.

My research while on leave was greatly aided by my tenure of several awards. In 1979 I was fortunate to obtain a Fulbright travel grant which enabled me to spend seven months in the United States. Among the institutions which offered me facilities for my work during that period of leave were the Charles Warren Center at Harvard University, the History and Geography Departments at the University of Wisconsin–Madison, and the Wisconsin State Historical Society. I do, however, wish to make special acknowledgment of the support I received from the Huntington Library, which granted me a Visiting Fellowship in August and September 1979.

During 1979 I was able to lay the foundations of my project by studying the history of the urban frontier in the American West. In the ensuing years my focus became more precisely defined as I concentrated on the study of contemporary perceptions of the urbanizing process and broadened my research to take in trends in Australia and Canada.

I used a further period of leave in 1987 to visit Australia and Canada, to undertake additional research in the United States, and to complete the present book. I am grateful to the Humanities Research Centre at the Australian National University, Canberra, for awarding me a Visiting Scholarship, and to the Newberry Library, Chicago, for a Library Fellowship.

During the course of my work for this book I was helped by the staff of many libraries. Without their guidance and knowledge of the relevant materials a book of this type could not be written. I would like to record my appreciation in particular of the assistance I received from staff at the Widener Library, Harvard; the Huntington Library, San Marino; the libraries of the University of Wisconsin–Madison; the Wisconsin State Historical Society Library, Madison; the libraries of the Australian National University, Canberra; the National Library of Australia; the Mitchell Library, Sydney; the Washington State Library, Olympia; the Montana Historical Society Library, Helena; the Western History Department, Denver Public Library; the Public Archives of Canada; the library of Carleton University, Ottawa; the Regenstein Library at the University of Chicago; the Newberry Library, Chicago; the Alexander Turnbull Library, Wellington; and the Victoria University of Wellington Library.

I received assistance from numerous institutions in my search for relevant illustrative material. I acknowledge in particular the help given by the Mitchell Library, Sydney; National Library of Australia; National

Gallery of Victoria; Alexander Turnbull Library, Wellington; Washington State Library, Olympia; Montana Historical Society; Glenbow Archives, Calgary; Western History Department, Denver Public Library; Royal Ontario Museum, Toronto; National Gallery of Canada; Public Archives of Canada; Hamilton Public Library, Ontario; Amon Carter Museum, Fort Worth; and the Minnesota Historical Society. I am also grateful for the assistance of Mr. John Casey, photographer at Victoria University of Wellington.

Many people helped with advice and encouragement at various stages of my research. In Australia, Ian Donaldson, Graeme Clarke, and Mary Theo were generous with their support during my stay at the Humanities Research Centre. I was grateful also for the hospitality and interest of Graeme Davison, Max Neutze, and Derek Schreuder. Among those who helped me during my visits to North America I would like to thank in particular John and Annette Bellamy, Geoffrey and Judith Briggs, Richard Brown, David and Pat Buisseret, Roger Lotchin, John Long, Sandra Myres, Alison Reyner-Hooson, David Ward, and Rosalind and Jonathan Wood.

I have greatly appreciated the encouragement I have received from Kenneth Jackson. I would also like to mention the detailed and thoughtful advice supplied at a critical stage in the formulation of my plans by an anonymous reader for Columbia University Press. At the Press Kate Wittenberg has been an unfailing source of guidance and sound advice.

I have two special debts that I must acknowledge. One is to the secretaries in the History Department at Victoria University—Gloria Biggs, Kristin Downey, and Alisa Hogan—who have coped so capably and uncomplainingly with successive drafts of this book.

However, my deepest debt is owed to Bea, my wife, who has borne with more patience than I deserved my lengthy absences from home while undertaking the research for this book. Without her support I could not possibly have completed such an ambitious, continent-spanning project. It was a delight to us both that we were able to share part of the experience of my 1987 quest for the American urban frontier.

New Towns in the New World

Introduction

THE opening up of "new societies" in the nineteenth century has traditionally been associated with the settlement of the land, and it was certainly so described in the emigration literature of the time. Yet it was also a process of urbanization. Powerful myths later prevented this aspect of colonization from being given its full and proper weight. Only relatively recently have historians in the United States, Canada, and Australia begun to pay serious attention to the existence during the initial settlement periods in their countries of an "urban frontier." They have shown that this "urban frontier" had a substantial influence over the process of settlement and that many of the "nonurban" forms of occupation and exploitation of the land and its resources owed much to the organizing and support facilities which towns provided. The insight that this was so, although it may appear to us to have derived from a dramatic new trend in frontier historiography—corresponding with the publication of Richard C. Wade's *The Urban Frontier* in the United States and Norman Harper's paper on "The Rural and Urban Frontiers" in Australia [1]— is in fact a reversion to a major nineteenth-century perception of the process of frontier settlement. Among the many influences which helped to overlay and obscure this perception from the late nineteenth century onward were Frederick Jackson Turner's famous 1893 essay, "The Significance of the Frontier in American History," which makes minimal references to towns and cities; the cult of the cowboy in the United States; and in Australia the popularity in art and literature and in Australians' perception of their national identity of what has come to be called "the Australian legend," the ingredients of which have been almost entirely nonurban. [2]

The purpose of this book is to get back to contemporary perceptions and to discover what people who were observing or trying to influence the process at the time thought about the role which towns were playing or ought to play in the settlement of their "new countries." I shall be emphasizing to what extent the "urban frontier" was a contemporary theme rather than one devised for the first time by historians of our own time. Indeed, historians have been led to adopt the theme to a large extent because it has been so forcefully suggested to them by the materials that they have used. If anything, those materials, especially when derived from what might be called "booster" sources, tend to exaggerate the place of towns in the "frontier" processes. Some historians have argued—from analysis of the process of founding of towns—that the actual sequence of settlement, in the United States at least, did often conform more to the "Turnerian" model than to the "spearhead" thesis favored by Richard Wade and others.[3] Historians who insist on a central role for the urban component in the "frontier" have undoubtedly been influenced by the prominence of this theme in contemporary booster literature and in newspapers, which often had a primarily boosterish purpose in presenting the relationship between towns and the frontier. But what this book is about is not what "really" happened but what people thought was happening or should happen, and the contemporary records which may have misled some historians are its principal object of investigation.

The evidence that is used and examined in this study relates to contemporary perceptions of, reactions to, and debates concerning urban development in certain "new countries" of the nineteenth century. The purpose is to see what happened from the contemporary perspective. In trying to find out what "really" happened, historians often move far away from that perspective and fail to appreciate adequately the contribution to what "really" happened of the particular ways in which people living at the time saw and interpreted what was going on. To take an example relevant to the subject of this book, much modern writing on urban history is based to a large extent on statistical data of which the people whose urban lives are thereby being described had and could have had little or no knowledge. During the 1970s urban history, especially in North America, became increasingly quantitative. Phenomena such as social stratification, social mobility, geographical mobility, persistence and transience, were measured and correlated with ever greater sophistication. The processing of census and other data by computers has vastly expanded the horizons of social and urban history but also takes historians a long distance from the perceptions of contemporaries. Then again there has been a strong reaction against the old-fashioned type of "urban biography." Yet in some important respects, such as the personalizing of urban identities and the perception of processes of "growth" and "maturing" in the "life" of a city, such works were a good deal closer to—were indeed to a substantial extent derivative from—nineteenth-century modes of interpretation of urban development and change.

A relatively new subdiscipline, urban history developed rapidly for a time and attracted many to claim to be its practitioners. It eventually suffered from what might be termed a bandwagon effect. A great deal of research activity became categorized as "urban history." In one sense that was accurate, but the sense was very broad indeed. Across the whole spectrum of publications in "urban history" the only common factor seemed to be that they all dealt with some aspect of life in urban communities. Given the character of modern society, this made "urban history" a notably capacious umbrella. Under it sheltered much material that might in other times or circumstances have been labeled "social history" or "labor history" or "economic history." The subject, new as it was and with its theoretical and methodological underpinnings and disciplinary boundaries by no means firmly established, began to collapse under the weight of its own popularity. It became about everything and therefore about nothing. G. M. Trevelyan described social history as history with politics left out. Urban history seemed to be social history with rural areas left out.[4]

When books and journals of "urban history" were published, it was sometimes not easy to tell what the contributions had in common. The title of the published proceedings of a major conference, *The Pursuit of Urban History,* had an ambiguity that may have been intentional.[5] This conference was seen as a sequel to one organized ten years earlier by the English urban historian H. J. Dyos.[6] He had recently died, and there was much nostalgic writing about him, which appeared to suggest that a major cohering influence in the study of urban history had been his personality and drive.[7] All this has indicated that there is something of a crisis of confidence among those who have "pursued" urban history.

It could be argued that the main problem is really nothing more substantial than an excessive preoccupation with labeling. Why should historians feel inhibited about doing research just because they are unable to find some convenient category into which to slot their work? If the concept of "urban history" is felt to be meaningless, why not just discard it, rather than allow debate over what it does or should mean to paralyze our work as historians?

3

But "urban history" achieves an extra dimension if it not only describes something that happened within an urban setting but also defines the significance of that in relation to more general issues concerning the character of towns or cities as an environment within which people live and work. One way to approach this is to write urban history as the history of ideas and perceptions, making the town or city itself the object of perception and commentary. One does not have to discard the more detailed study of aspects of life within towns. Rather one finds that the history of these is more easily explained if understood in relation to broader ideas held at the time of what towns were or ought to be like as communities.

The framework for the study of urban history is often provided by the "models" of geographers, economists, or sociologists. These may have very little to do with the ways in which contemporaries perceived urban communities. An example is "central place" theory, which presents a model of the evolution of hierarchies among towns from an assumed starting point of almost complete absence of differentiation in the frontier situation. Ironically, exclusive reliance on this theory to "explain" urban development is reminiscent of the geographical determinism of nineteenth-century boosters. But if it does have any such ancestry, this has gone unacknowledged. What is overlooked is that the nineteenth-century people who established and built towns had their own ideas about the process, ideas that are, by our standards, hopelessly unscientific and crude but that nevertheless played a major role in shaping the course of town creation and development. What this book seeks to offer is an alternative, or rather supplementary, set of ideas about urbanization in "new societies," the ideas that contemporaries themselves believed in and used.

What is analyzed here should also be of interest to historians who write or try to use *local* histories. Such histories abound in all the countries being surveyed in this book. But "local history" has, in spite of some outstanding practitioners, acquired rather a bad reputation. Many "local histories" are no more than ill- or indeed nondigested compilations of information about local life—churches, schools, hospitals, prominent personalities. Organizing ideas are often conspicuous by their absence. The authors often fail to make connections between what they describe and what was going on in other comparable communities or in society at large or in the wider region or nation. In this respect at least their work is clearly directly descended from earlier histories of towns which, as shall

4

be explained in a later chapter, often had a strong boosting purpose and reflected the typical preoccupation of boosters with the "destiny" of one town. The directness of this descent has been strengthened by the fact that historians rely so much on evidence that was originated in, and collected and preserved by, agencies such as newspapers and historical societies which were strongly influenced by boosting motivations. The particular value of local histories can begin to be defined and unlocked if we see them as purveyors and perpetuators of local traditions, the origins and meanings of which may be only dimly understood by the authors of more recent histories. One purpose of this book is to uncover some of the original perceptions and ideas which led to the forming of these traditions.

Another feature of local histories which impresses historians—such as myself—who work their way through them in search of material to support broad generalizations is the similarity, almost the uniformity, of their structure. The same phenomena and institutions seem to be under review over and over again. The similarity of the events selected as worthy of commemoration is very evident. One way of understanding the recurrence of these patterns of presentation of the "life" of a community is to trace the underlying structure of ideas and assumptions as to significance. This book seeks to offer an analysis of certain sets of ideas as a contribution to this process. An example is the occurrence of fires, very common in young towns. In chapter 7 I discuss the significance of responses to fires and the use of the "phoenix" theme in relation to contemporary ideas about social evolution and the connections between "old" and "new" in the development of towns.

In studying the ideas which underlay the development of towns in "new societies" and examining the ways in which people at the time perceived and reacted to what was going on, I shall necessarily be confining myself to those who left some kind of record of their thoughts, ideas, and responses—writers of travel accounts and emigrants' guidebooks, intellectuals, politicians, artists, journalists, diarists. These constitute, of course, only a tiny minority of the people who were involved in the processes being commented on. The opinions and perceptions of the vast mass of migrants, settlers, and townspeople went unrecorded and will be forever unknown. Whether the majority of people ever would have engaged in the kinds of broad reflection on the character and course of urban development which are cited in this book is very doubtful. They would have had no time or need or desire to. Letters and diaries written by "ordinary" townspeople are, not surprisingly, filled with details of and comments on everyday happenings, the problems of their business lives, reactions to their immediate situations. Sustained, generalized commentary on social developments is rare and when it does occur, is more often than not expressed in the clichés which are to be found in the booster publications described in this book.

This is therefore an account of the views on urbanization in "new societies" of those people who have left a record of their thoughts. Of course, most of them did not just leave this record for the benefit of posterity. They had purposes in publishing their interpretations, and one of the aims of this book is to suggest what these were. Boosters, for instance, were very much into the business of manipulating perceptions, of encouraging townspeople to "see" not the depressing and primitive present of a town's early stages of development but the "future greatness" which awaited it. Although some intellectuals who sought to make an objective analysis of the trends will appear in this story, nearly everyone who is quoted had some sort of axe to grind. There were towns to be promoted, there was real estate to sell, there was emigration to be encouraged, there was "moving on" to be deterred. Many of the people who are quoted were people whose views mattered in the sense that they influenced the making of decisions about the founding and physical development of towns. Although there are examples of debate—in journals of opinion or among politicians—about the trends in urban development, this book is to a large extent about image-making, how and why certain predominant perceptions or images of the town in the process of formation of "new societies" emerged, and what influence these images can be found to have had.

I have left the subject of the book to be in large part determined and defined by the course which the debates took and the literature suggested. Basically it concerns perceptions of and reactions to the development of towns and cities in certain "new societies" of the nineteenth century. The focus is placed on Australia and New Zealand and on those areas of Canada and the United States which were opened up for intensive occupation and settlement by Europeans in that century. In particular, I shall be looking at ideas concerning what is now known as "the urban frontier," a subject conceived in two broad senses—the process of founding and building new cities which can be seen to have been a form of

6

"frontier," developing separately from and paralleling, preceding, or following other forms of initial occupation of newly opened up regions, such as agriculture, mining, and pastoralism; and the relationship between the total "frontier" process and the growth of towns.

The treatment of four "new societies" raises a wide range of issues of comparability. In many ways, of course, they were not at all alike. European settlement of Australia began with the convict colony at Botany Bay in 1788, although it was not until well into the next century that settlement developed in any other part of the country. Adelaide, for instance, was not founded until 1835–36, and Melbourne followed two years later. Essentially, therefore, Australia was a "new society" of the nineteenth century. Of its cities only Sydney had any sort of pre-nineteenth-century past, and most vestiges of that era soon disappeared. New Zealand was not annexed by Britain until 1840. Even in the 1830s only a few thousand Europeans lived there, mostly in scattered whaling and mission settlements along the coasts. Auckland was founded as the capital in 1840, and Wellington was established in the same year by the New Zealand Company. Colonization companies were responsible over the next decade for the foundation of Christchurch, Dunedin, Nelson, and Wanganui.

The history of American westward expansion belongs, of course, largely to the nineteenth century. But it is complicated by the fact that there was already the experience of two centuries of settlement on the eastern seaboard, and that experience created strong traditions both of subduing "the wilderness" and of establishing and building towns. The continuities from these into the expansion of the nineteenth century were substantial, for example, in the extremely significant New England contribution to the settling of the West and the founding of its towns.[8] Perceptions of the cities of the East varied constantly. Were they too part of the New World, to be distinguished from those of the Old World, and associated with the cities of the West as part of a continuum of American achievement in creating a New World form of urban society? Or were the new cities of the West to be distinguished from them too as they were perceived to have acquired certain Old World urban characteristics?

Canada appears to fall somewhere in between. From Ontario west, its settlement by Europeans was almost entirely a post-1800 phenomenon, and, as in Australia, much of the initial founding of towns was done by colonial authorities responsible to the Colonial Office in London. But, like the United States, although to a much lesser extent, Canada had a history of town development that preceded 1800. Organized largely by the French, this was much less of a precedent for subsequent Canadian expansion than was Puritan colonization for what happened in the United States in the nineteenth century.

The differences, however, were not always as clearcut as might be imagined. For instance, Australia and New Zealand may have been a *tabula rasa,* but the forms of urban settlement which were imposed on them derived from the long evolving traditions of British imperial policy and assumptions about the ways in which a colony should be organized. The mixed feelings of Western Americans toward their Eastern cities were paralleled by the complex combinations of awe, pride, revulsion, and desire to emulate with which Australians of the nineteenth century contemplated London and other English cities.

This is a comparative study insofar as and to the extent that contemporary discussions of the development of towns in these "new societies" had a comparative dimension. Often they did. The comparing of one country with another was frequently done by travelers and became an important contributor to the evolution of myths of national identity. However, the predominant mode of comparison was between Old World and New World. Chapter 3 will be devoted to this theme, and references to it appear regularly in the other chapters.

But to proceed entirely by way of a comparison between one nation and another would do considerable violation to the reality of nineteenth-century perceptions. Modern historical writing has become strongly national in its orientation, reflecting the twentieth-century reality of nations with clearly defined boundaries and strongly developed national identities. But in the nineteenth century the situation was far more fluid. Each of these new countries underwent a lengthy and complex process of evolution into the nation-state which exists today, and there were many points at which there could have been radically different outcomes. Throughout the century Australia was a continent of colonies founded and settled at different times and governed separately. It was not until 1901 that these colonies federated into the Australian Commonwealth, and even then they retained their own state governments. As for New Zealand, it began its existence as a nation only in 1840 (when it was briefly part of the colony of New South Wales) and had a system of provincial governments until 1876. In the nineteenth-century perspective

8

New Zealand was one of a series of "Australasian" colonies. The United States underwent a massive expansion across the continent, absorbing vast territories that at the beginning of the century belonged to Spain and France, and transforming out of all recognition the cluster of colonies along the eastern seaboard that had won independence from Great Britain and made itself into a union of states. In the 1860s the very existence of the nation was challenged in the Civil War. Canada too underwent vast changes in its structure as a nation.

All this has two major implications for the study of contemporary perceptions and perspectives. The first is that it means that contemporaries were not nearly as accustomed as we are to comparing these countries with one another as monolithic entities. They were more inclined to compare one region with another and to see a rapidly evolving situation in which it was not at all easy to discern and generalize about national characteristics. Second, there was awareness of a process of migration and of settlement of "new countries" which transcended national boundaries. This study is based on an assumption that the histories of the "urban frontiers" of the nineteenth century, and the ways in which contemporaries interpreted and reacted to their development, had much in common. It is therefore in part an exercise in comparison and in part a survey of shared ideas and influences.

In the nineteenth century Canada, Australia, New Zealand, and the western parts of the United States were commonly referred to as "new countries" or "new societies" or collectively "the New World."[9] They were often analyzed as such, for example by Edward Gibbon Wakefield, who was deeply involved in the affairs of Canada, Australia, and New Zealand and wrote extensively about the United States. His ideas ranged widely across the whole spectrum of experience in the settling of these lands and he engaged in extensive and very influential generalizing about the character of "new societies."[10]

There was a common stock of ideas and assumptions about social evolution. Expectations as to what would, and beliefs as to what should, happen in a "new society" were very similar. This is discussed in chapter 4. Deviations from these expectations and these models and "laws" of social evolution were frequent, but to a large extent there was a shared yardstick for measuring these and worrying about them as "unhealthy" and "unnatural."

One feature which distinguished the "new countries" was that their

European populations grew from being minimal or even nonexistent through migration, mostly from Britain and Europe but also, in the case of the United States, from the earlier settled regions of the East and South. The migrants were people who were faced with a vast range of choices—among countries, regions, towns, and cities. There was a great deal of competition among interested agencies—governments, cities, colonization, steamship, and railroad companies—to influence these choices. Australia, the United States, Canada, New Zealand were rival "emigration fields," and within each country colonies, provinces, regions, and cities vied with one another to divert to themselves as much as possible of the migratory flow. The publicity that was issued made very similar kinds of promises. Abstractions were offered which had little to do with the reality of the place to which migrants were being invited but referred to universally shared perceptions of the New World—as utopia, as Arcadia, as El Dorado. For what many migrants wished to go to was not so much a specific geographical location as an ideal concept of "a better world." Emigration and booster literature endeavored to plant in their minds appropriate images. We shall see the role which images of towns played in this regard.

Nor was it only migrants that countries and states and towns needed to attract. Also sought was capital, and here too imagery was important. Towns sought to project the appearance of being not just profitable but also safe places in which to invest, while countries used the state of their cities as proof that they were no longer primitive frontier societies.

In many ways the towns which developed on the "urban frontiers" of the nineteenth century resembled one another very closely and were perceived in this light by commentators at the time. High levels of transience were characteristic of all new towns and reduced the extent to which marked local variations were able to emerge. Commitment to improvement of one's own or one's family's prospects rather than to the subordination of self-interest involved in "building a community" was regarded as characteristic of the frontier. The history of the urban frontier is littered with the records of hundreds and hundreds of failed or abandoned towns. The most extreme manifestation of the community of transients was the mining town whose suddenly swollen population could vanish just as suddenly. The term "instant city" has been used to describe communities of this type where vast numbers of people from many different places were thrown together, unified only by their desire to find gold or other precious metal or to provide services for those who were engaged in this quest.[11] This was an international type of "urban frontier" settlement, for the series of "gold rushes" in the United States, Australia, New Zealand, and Canada brought miners flooding again and again across national boundaries.

Another feature that all "urban frontiers" had in common was speculation, both in the creation of town sites—frequently only on paper—and in the subsequent buying and selling of town lots. Much of the work of forming the urban frontier was done by speculators who created far more towns than would be needed and then set about vigorously competing with one another to attract settlers and investment. Which towns succeeded depended often much less on the existing features of the location than on the promotional and entrepreneurial skills of the people who came to set up business there and worked to obtain assets such as railroad connections and government institutions.

This means that boosterism too was a characteristic of urban development in "new countries." It has been written about explicitly mainly in connection with the United States and the Canadian prairie provinces,[12] but it was a universal phenomenon, peaking in intensity at certain places and periods when competitiveness among towns was most marked and subdued at others, for instance, where the preeminence of one city was so clear that the ambitions of others were cramped.

The process of settlement of new countries was universally described as "conquering the wilderness." The rise of towns always offered the most dramatic proof that this goal was being accomplished. We shall find that celebration of it was often associated with very negative attitudes toward "nature." One frequently criticized feature of the new towns of the nineteenth century was the way in which their plans ignored, and indeed involved the obliteration of, attractive aspects of the natural landscape. Of great influence here were ideas of social evolution which assumed the banishment from the urban scene of all indications of the original, "primitive" condition of the site. Included in this were the indigenous peoples of the territories being settled. Although towns played a major role in policies of subjugating and controlling indigenous peoples—many towns in the west of the United States originated as forts—the Maori, the aborigines, and the North American Indians were increasingly treated as not "belonging" in this European form of community, and, through a variety of processes, their presence in towns became more and more marginal and ghostly.

It is necessary to describe and emphasize the boundaries within which I have confined this study. In the first place, it examines only certain types of perception of urbanization, those which relate to themes of "newness," of the contrast between "Old World" and "New World," of the relationship of urban growth to theories and assumptions concerning social evolution, and of the replacement of "savagery" and "wilderness" by this more "civilized" form of settlement of the land. These themes will be found to interlock with one another, indeed to overlap at numerous points. What will not be discussed, except insofar as they are relevant to the above mentioned themes, are perceptions of what might be referred to as ordinary processes and problems of urban growth—local government, sanitation, transportation, street improvements.

Second, the study is confined to those places where, and eras when, there was vigorous and sustained discussion of the new towns along the lines indicated above. This means an emphasis on the early and mid-nineteenth century and on the American Midwest, on Ontario in the case of Canada, and on Australia and New Zealand. To a large extent the shape of the book has been determined by the character and quantity of the nineteenth-century literature about urbanization on "the frontier," and that has resulted in a fairly marked bias in favor of the American West and Australia. There are several reasons why the contemporary discussion of urban development was particularly lively and abundant there. Wherever large numbers of towns were founded, often for speculative reasons, and it was clear that there were far more than a region would require for many years to come but there seemed no overwhelming reason why some of these towns should grow and others come to nothing, a very competitive situation resulted. This was certainly the case throughout the American Midwest from the 1790s to the 1870s. Wherever there was this competitiveness, there was also the phenomenon known as boosterism. All sorts of persons with an interest in a town's development and predominance over its rivals—newspaper editors, businessmen, real estate agents, politicians, speculators—worked to boost the town. The words and images that they employed in doing so made reference not just to the claimed merits of their particular town but also to an ideal of urban community in the circumstances of the new country. This happened in part because they were attempting to disparage the claims of rival towns and to furnish proof of their own town's inevitable destiny as the metropolis of its region. Into this type of activity could enter all sorts of arguments and theories about the role of towns in a new society. The literature of midwestern boosterism is vast and often rich in analysis of urbanizing trends.

In eastern Canada, some of the Australian colonies, and New Zealand large numbers of towns were founded. But there were not the expectations of metropolitan destiny to justify and produce a comparable outpouring of boosting propaganda. By American standards, boosting in the new towns and cities of these countries was decidedly low-key and unimpressive. Boosting was subdued also because so many of the towns were founded by governments or by companies given a monopolistic control over the initial settlement of a region. These creations often imposed a *pattern* of urban relationships at the outset, thus allowing little of the American midwestern fluidity and uncertainty about future developments.

Where large cities did develop, they generated their own species of celebratory literature, and much boosting continued to be needed to sustain confidence in growth. At times in the United States rivalries at this level led to a good deal of discussion of goals of urban development, most notably in the cases of Chicago, St. Louis, and Cincinnati. In Australia such rivalry appeared most strongly, and persists to this day, in the relationship between Sydney and Melbourne. But in Australia the rise of large cities—these two in particular—set off a debate, which has no real parallel in any of the other countries, about the significance of this for the development of the nation. As a result, one chapter in the book is devoted largely to an analysis of this debate.

The book surveys in turn the major themes which emerge from an analysis of the literature relating to the development of towns in "new countries" of the nineteenth century. Although there is not space for a detailed description of the history of these countries and of their towns and cities, chapter 1 provides some background by analyzing the general characteristics of the "urban frontier" in each country, with particular reference to the first half of the century. Within this chapter there is extended comment on what appeared to be a major difference between the "urban frontier" in the United States, where the founding and development of towns seemed to be left mainly to private enterprise, and urbanization in colonial societies which seemed to be much more under the control of the government.

Chapter 2 examines the literature in which perceptions of new towns in the New World were most commonly formulated and recorded—travel books and guidebooks, written to inform people in the Old World who might be thinking of emigrating to or investing in a new country, and booster publications, many of which were written to promote the claims of towns. The limitations of travel and guidebooks as sources of evidence about actual contemporary conditions in towns are acknowledged and explained, but the emphasis is on their value as sources of insight into contemporary perceptions of those conditions. The chapter leads into a discussion of boosterism through an argument about the awareness of town promoters that their towns were in this way constantly being evaluated and described and so particular attention needed to be paid to those aspects of towns that would be most likely to impress visitors and observers. Since booster publications are one of the main sources of knowledge of contemporary ideas about urbanization in the New World, the chapter concludes with an examination of the aims of boosting and the extent to which it can be taken seriously as a mode of expression of these ideas.

In chapter 3 the urbanization of new countries is considered within the context of prevailing notions about the differences between the Old World and the New. Visitors certainly did try hard to define what was new and distinctive about the new societies in general and about the cities which grew within them. Naturally there was fascination in discovering what happened to people from Old World societies when they were transplanted into this new environment. Did it transform them into a "new people"? Were they enabled to implement ideals of a new society which people in the Old World could still only dream about? Such questions were of particular interest to those who wished to discover the bounds of adaptability of Old World institutions and social structure. As regards towns, they discovered much that was different. But they themselves were agencies in the offsetting or narrowing of these differences in that they regularly compared New World towns with those of the Old and measured out praise of the former in proportion to the extent to which they matched up to the standards derived from the latter. Much of this chapter is indeed about migration and concerns the influences over the responses of migrants to the towns to which they came for the purpose of starting a new life. Finally, there is analysis of the efforts made to eliminate, counter, or obscure "frontier" or "colonial" aspects of new towns.

The reactions of contemporaries to New World urbanization are explicable to a large extent by reference to their assumptions concerning social evolution. They believed that the development of human society was controlled by certain "laws" which meant that the New World would, once settled by Europeans, commence a course of evolution similar to that which had occurred in the Old World. Initially, therefore, it was expected that society in the New World would be a good deal more "primitive" than that in the Old. However, argument then revolved over whether the New World environment would enforce a lengthy period of "catching up" as the process of social evolution unwound or whether what we now call the "cultural baggage" brought with them by settlers would enable them to accelerate or short-circuit the process and arrive rapidly at the same level of social development as that already attained in Britain and Europe. Either way, however, the evolutionary model prevailed. Chapter 4 discusses its application to the analysis of the place of towns within new societies and refers to the efforts of commentators to cling to the concept of evolution as they became aware, for example in mid-nineteenth-century America, of a process of settlement so rapid as to leave distinctions among "stages" within it barely discernible. There was a particular dilemma for those, such as the colonial authorities in Canada, Australia, and New Zealand, who embarked on the planning of schemes of colonization and, for a variety of reasons, believed that it was necessary to provide towns at or near the outset of settlement rather than wait for processes of social evolution to bring them into being "naturally." Chapter 4 explores how they responded to the interpretation which contemporary thinking inevitably imposed on their policies, namely that they were defying the laws of social evolution and must expect as a result an "unhealthy" and "unbalanced" type of community.

Chapter 5 examines the implications of two clichés which came to predominate in descriptions of New World urbanization. One concerned rapidity of growth, and the other explained this by reference to "magic." There was a growing feeling that Old World "laws" were not adequate, and perhaps not even relevant, to describe what was happening in the new countries. One reflection of the vacuum which resulted from this collapse of faith in the old ideas was increasingly frequent recourse to the "magic" explanation. The chapter explores the connections between perceptions of rapidity in growth of cities and the tendency to "personalize" the growth process as one of "maturing" and "aging." A major problem here was the association between theories about social evolution and belief in the cyclical or rise-and-fall character of the history of human civilizations. Must there be, then, not only a remarkably rapid rise of New World societies but also an equally rapid and dramatic fall? Cities had a key role to play in the answering of this question because their emergence was believed to mark the arrival of an advanced stage in the evolution of a society. The chapter considers the significance in this regard of the jettisoning of cyclical theories and the attempt to replace them by new evolutionary laws which provided for an indefinite expansion of urban civilization. Some of these did not even stop short of prophesying the emergence of one great dominating "world city."

As indicated already, chapter 6 concentrates on one country, Australia, where the inversion of the "natural" sequence of social evolution was observed to have occurred in a most extreme form. This gave rise to much discussion of the causes of the trend and of its implications for the social well-being of Australia's population, "abnormally" concentrated as it appeared to be within a few large cities. We shall see that there were those in Australia who argued that such concentration was beneficial to the development of a new country.

Chapter 7 looks at the perceived relationship of the towns of the "urban frontier" to the "future" element of the temporal continuum of their development. It was frequently observed that townspeople, particularly but by no means exclusively on the American "urban frontier," appeared preoccupied with the future to the extent that they did not notice the present or at least were remarkably tolerant of its uncomfortable and unattractive aspects. Faith in the certain development of a great urban future was something which boosters worked very hard to foster. This chapter will explore the implications of this preoccupation for perceptions of the present and the past.

Chapters 8 and 9 consider the significance of towns as a replacement for and counter to "primitivism." The first deals with the perceptions of the relationship between towns and the natural environment or "wilderness," as it was commonly styled. The second focuses on the identification of indigenous peoples with the "primitive" initial stages of social evolution which a town-based "civilization" was "destined" to supersede. Towns became increasingly uncomfortable places for indigenous peoples to live in, and there was a widespread belief among townspeople that it was inevitable that there should be no place for them within a type of community which belonged to a more advanced phase of the evolution of "civilization."

A final chapter addresses the question of the relationship between the urban frontier and the development of myths of national identity.

CHAPTER ONE

Urban Frontiers

I N the United States at the start of the nineteenth century there was
considerable settlement activity along the Ohio River and in the lands
of the Western Reserve and John Cleves Symmes' Miami Purchase.
Cincinnati had been founded in 1788 at what seemed a strategic place for
commanding river traffic. The site of Cleveland was chosen in 1796,
although by 1810 the town had only 57 inhabitants. For many years
tensions between the United States and the British authorities in Canada
remained high, erupting into war in 1812, and towns on the lakes assumed great military and strategic significance. Detroit, scene of frequent
conflict and on the very cutting edge of conflict among Indians, Americans, British, and French, had a population of 2,500 by 1800 and was
chosen in 1805 to be the political center of the new Michigan Territory.
Settlement of Kentucky had begun in the revolutionary era (Danville was
founded in 1775), but it now went ahead much more rapidly. Lexington
developed as an important trading center and had a population of around
1,500 by the turn of the century. There was also considerable development of settlement in western Tennessee.

In the first decade of the century a major new impetus for western
expansion came from the Louisiana Purchase of 1806. During the later
part of the eighteenth century several small French towns and villages
had been founded along the Mississippi and Missouri rivers. Largest of
these was St. Louis with a population of about 1,000 in 1800. Others
included Sainte Genevieve, Cape Girardeau, and Kaskaskia. After the
Purchase American settlement began to inundate this region, expanding
into Indiana and over the Wabash as far as the Mississippi. In 1809 a new
Territory of Illinois was organized. At this stage the main towns of
Illinois were in the south. Chicago was as yet unheard of, its site the
location of Fort Dearborn where occurred a massacre by Indians in 1812.

The settlement of Upper Canada (Ontario) had hardly begun. The
main settlements west of Montreal were still forts and fur-trading depots.

York—later Toronto—was a garrison town, controversially planted by Lieutenant-Governor John Graves Simcoe in what then seemed to be the wilderness. Simcoe looked even further west for what he hoped to be the capital of this new region at London, on the banks of "the Thames."[1] Closer to the American border, on the Niagara frontier, military tensions remained high. Settlements of United Empire Loyalists—refugees from revolutionary America—were begun but were slow to produce towns.

In Australia at the turn of the century the only urban settlement of any significance was at Sydney, the site since 1788 of a penal settlement to which were sent convicts from Britain. In addition to the convicts Sydney had a large population of administrators and soldiers as well as a growing number of emancipated convicts and "ticket-of-leave" men. In 1804 an additional town called Hobart was founded on Van Diemen's Land (later Tasmania).

During the next decade, 1810–20, the new towns of the American trans-Appalachian West attracted growing attention from travelers who came to see what kind of society was emerging in this region.[2] Because travel was so difficult—by coach or riverboat—they passed through many towns, and the impression to be gained from their accounts was of large numbers of small towns appearing "like mushrooms." Of the larger towns Lexington impressed in particular as a focus of cultural life. By 1820 its population had reached 5,200. Many new river towns were laid out in this decade, and some became very prosperous, as the fine homes surviving to the present day in towns such as Madison, Indiana, testify. Steubenville in Ohio, and New Albany, Richmond, and Evansville in Indiana are just a few of the river-located towns that date from this era. There was already much speculation in town-sites as promoters tried to calculate which would be the likeliest focal points for commerce in the rapidly developing and changing transportation networks of the interior regions of the continent. New transportation connections could transform the significance and size of a town. Cleveland, still with a population of only 150 in 1815, began to go ahead dramatically when it was linked by road to the Ohio River and became an important port for Great Lakes steamboat traffic. Another significant urban development was the beginning of serious analysis by locally based "boosters"—as distinct from travelers—of the place of the town in "the West" with the publication in 1815 of Daniel Drake's *Natural and Statistical View* of Cincinnati. This inaugurated a series of works by Drake, B. and E. D. Mansfield, Charles

Cist, and others which "boosted" Cincinnati and helped to establish a format for this kind of literature. His theme, that Cincinnati was to be "the future metropolis of the Ohio," was to be echoed in countless works over the next half-century by boosters who sought to prove that their particular midwestern city was "destined" to be the great "central city" of the American continent.

The War of 1812 also gave a boost to urban development in Upper Canada. Kingston became an important naval, military, and ship-building and -repairing center, while in the country to the north officers on half-pay settled in or near new towns such as Perth. Otherwise the Canadian side of the Great Lakes and the Niagara frontier remained very undeveloped by American standards.

In Australia this became known as the "Macquarie era." Lachlan Macquarie, governor of New South Wales from 1810 to 1821, paid particular attention to town founding and improvement. He founded numerous new towns in the vicinity of Sydney, notably Windsor and Richmond, and made great efforts to "improve" Sydney, which had a population of 6,000 in 1810 and had grown to double that by 1821. By then its population was about half that of mainland New South Wales.

In 1825 the Erie Canal, under construction since 1817, was completed. By linking New York and the East to the Great Lakes it had a profound impact on urban development in the American Midwest. The 1820s and 1830s were an era of massive canal construction throughout the region. In 1825, for instance, the Ohio legislature launched a large-scale internal improvements program. Town rivalries played a major role in the implementation of this, in the pattern of canals which was created, and in the very high cost of it.[3] A canal was built to link Cleveland to the Ohio River, and by 1830 the population of that town had reached 1,000. Few towns attracted more interest and publicity in this era than Louisville.[4] It was located on what had been a most strategic site where rapids prevented further navigation up the Ohio River. Goods which reached this point consequently had to be transshipped. However, in the 1820s a canal was built to bypass the rapids. This was not done without much controversy and anxiety in Louisville, but for a time the city flourished in a different capacity as a major port and trading center on a vast canal-river system that extended all the way from the Great Lakes to New Orleans at the mouth of the Mississippi. The era from the 1820s to the 1830s was the golden age of steamboat traffic on the major American rivers and of the river towns which assumed a characteristic form with their levees, Front and Water Streets, and fine "antebellum" mansions overlooking the rivers. However, these towns were vulnerable on many scores. There were too many of them, as there was intense speculation in river-front town sites; disease wreaked havoc in their low-lying districts, which were also subject to frequent inundation; and eventually the rail-road was to destroy their economic *raison d'être*.

During the 1820s settlement extended into interior Indiana away from the major rivers. Indianapolis was selected to be the capital of the new state of Indiana in 1821 at a location whose essential feature was central-ity, not proximity to a major river. Here was a site the potential of which awaited the advent of the railroad for its realization. Anderson was laid out in 1827. Towns also began to appear along the Missouri west of St. Louis: Lexington and Liberty in 1822, Independence in 1827. Apart from the old French settlements (Dubuque, Prairie du Chien), and some forts, there was as yet little penetration of the upper Mississippi region. However, an extensive lead-mining district was opened up in northwest-ern Illinois, and the town of Galena began to grow on the Fever River.

Canals made an impact in Canada too. The completion of the Erie Canal was one reason for the dramatic rise in the population of York— from 1,200 in 1820 to 9,200 in 1834, when the town was renamed Toronto. In 1829 a ship canal was dug from Lake Ontario to Lake Erie, enabling shipping to bypass the Niagara Falls. New towns such as St. Catharines sprang up along this canal. As speculative town founding became rampant in the American regions to the south and west, the lack of such activity in Upper Canada became very noticeable and caused increasing comment. One writer, John Howison, expressed the view that there just was not enough enterprise or energy in Canada to make town-site speculation successful.[5] However, the 1820s are interesting in the history of Canadian urban development because of the efforts of the British-based Canada Company to settle vast tracts in western Ontario in the region between York and Lake Huron. The towns of Guelph, God-erich, Cambridge, and Galt were founded, and the company's chief agent in Canada in the late 1820s, John Galt, was a Scottish novelist who wrote about the experience of town-founding.[6]

The 1830s saw the foundation of Chicago—in 1831 on the site of Fort Dearborn and where a river flowed into Lake Michigan—and the first Chicago boom-and-bust cycle. There was rapid growth and much speculation in real estate. Values soared, only to come tumbling down in the "crash" of 1837. Another midwestern town that originated in this decade was Kansas City, 1838.

Much of the urban development in the West in this decade took place around the Great Lakes. Michigan was rapidly settled, and a string of new towns appeared in the southern regions between Chicago and Detroit whose population rose from 2,200 in 1830 to 9,102 in 1840. Eastern capitalists financed the founding of towns on Lake Michigan such as Green Bay and Milwaukee. John Jacob Astor, who founded Green Bay, had a hotel built there, financed the establishment of a bank, and employed as his agent James Duane Doty, one of a new breed of western town-site promoters.[7] Doty was shortly to play a major role in the founding of Madison, made the capital of Wisconsin in 1836 in an interior location, and, like Indianapolis, endowed with a plan of streets radiating out from a central area that was reserved for the capitol.[8]

Migrants were soon pouring into Milwaukee, which at this stage grew faster than its rival to the south, Chicago.[9] Several other ports developed and grew rapidly on Lake Erie, for example, Toledo, which by 1840 had a population of 1,112. In the same decade Cleveland, stimulated by the completion of the Ohio Canal from Portsmouth in 1833, rose from 1,000 to 6,000.

The 1830s saw the peak of the "internal improvements" craze. The policy of federal support for canals—and road—construction in the West became a subject of intense political controversy, being espoused by Henry Clay and opposed by Andrew Jackson in his Maysville Road veto of 1830. In the later part of the decade railroads also began to be involved. There was promotion of local lines such as the one that ran north to Vernon from Madison on the Ohio River. Urban rivalries influenced greatly what happened. In the words of Harry R. Scheiber, the struggle for internal improvements "became the cause of the most vigorous and persistent rivalries among western urban communities," rivalries which were "marked by intense ambitions, deeply rooted fear of failure, and ingenious employment of the instruments of political and economic leverage at the disposal of urban leaders."[10] In the preceding decades in the Ohio Valley many small towns and villages had been founded. Now the fates of all of them were at stake. Each tried to secure its own road and canal and, later, railroad. The Ohio debt soared as a result, and the state came to the verge of default. There was no overall strategy or planning.

Every town required appeasement with its own feeder canal or branch line. In these political struggles the community consciousness of many towns was forged around the theme of rivalry with other towns. This was a theme that was to be repeated throughout the experience of American westward expansion, as was also the incessant striving to become a county seat—or perhaps even the capital—and to retain that status against the challenges of rival towns.

There was as yet no idea of system and interdependence in the relationship of towns to one another. Each town's leaders envisaged it as having its own self-contained hinterland or "country behind it." The struggle was to make that as large as possible. Byron Kilbourn, founder of Milwaukee, wrote in 1836: "There are no conflicting interests between Green Bay, Milwaukee, and Chicago; each has its own appropriate country; and that *naturally* united to Milwaukee by common interest is at least equal in extent and fertility, and I hesitate not to add, will sustain a *more* dense population than either of the others."[11] It was only gradually that there emerged the concept of towns being subordinate to and dependent on larger cities in a hierarchical and integrated relationship.

It was at this time that Americans were beginning to get a reputation —and to perceive themselves—as great city-builders. As settlement spread rapidly in regions that had long been under Spanish or French influence, there were many contrasts drawn between Yankee vigor in this respect and the French and Spanish villages that seemed to have remained scarcely changed for centuries. In 1839 Alphonse Dubois de Saligny, French chargé d'affaires to the Republic of Texas, went on a tour of the coastal towns of Texas, such as Galveston, and wrote in amazement:

Familiar as I have been for some time with the sight of the marvels brought forth each day by the activity of the Americans, and although I am accustomed to seeing on every side the flourishing towns spring from the earth, as if by magic, in places where even yesterday rose thick forests which were impenetrable to man and occupied only by wild animals, I swear . . . that I have never seen anything comparable to the sights which were offered to me on the trip that I have just made. I did not yet know what prodigious feats could be accomplished by the audacious industry of this American race, by their tireless perseverance, and by their energetic spirit of enterprise. This magnificent land, owned for several centuries by the Spanish race, was even two years ago only a vast solitude where the traveler scarcely found, here and there, a few poor villages, some miserable huts of fishermen. Today, one finds towns everywhere, all located with a rare wisdom and, as in most American towns, built on a large plan.[12]

There was speculation in abundance, and vast numbers of towns that were laid out never came to anything. Failures did not check optimism and the urge to speculate. In 1837 a New York newspaper urged its readers not to be deterred by the slump in western urban real estate. It urged them to look at Illinois and Wisconsin and to acknowledge that in a comparable region in the East one would find thirty or forty populous towns. "We find in these regions of unsurpassed fertility but a single village peeping out amidst a wide circuit of country full of every productive quality in soil, minerals, river and lake navigation. . . . A country settling with such unparalleled rapidity must have its great central commercial points, its manufacturing villages, its agricultural towns, and all these will rise under the magical wand of emigration." [13]

Three western cities attracted particular attention in this decade. One was Cincinnati. Mrs. Trollope's *Domestic Manners of the Americans* (1832) caused great offence there by its adverse comments on society in that "Porkopolis." [14] A second was Cairo, a town which appeared to have the best site of all—at the junction of the Ohio and Mississippi rivers. There was a brief but intense wave of enthusiasm for Cairo, and its population reached 2,000 by 1840. But appearances were deceptive. The site was very low-lying and frequently inundated. Decline set in rapidly and by 1850 the population was only 242. Charles Dickens visited it in 1842 and through his account of Cairo in *American Notes* (1842) immortalized it as the epitome of the American mania for speculation in town sites on western rivers. [15] He reinforced this with his satirical account of Eden in *Martin Chuzzlewit* (1844). A third city to arouse interest was St. Louis, which many predicted would become *the* great central city of the Mississippi valley. St. Louis' population was over 6,000 by 1830 and rose to 35,390 in 1840.

In Canada the rapid growth of Toronto was one of the main talking-points of the 1830s. But settlement progressed only slowly in other parts of Upper Canada. A few new towns were founded in the west—Brantford in 1830, the Scottish settlement at Fergus in 1833—but there was much adverse comment on the poor showing made by Canada when its towns were contrasted with their American counterparts across the border (see below).

The 1830s were a decade of explosion in Australian urban development following four decades in which urban settlement had been confined to Sydney and its immediate vicinity and Van Diemen's Land. In the southeast of the continent lay a territory called "Australia Felix" by the explorer and surveyor Thomas Mitchell. Prior to the 1830s only one attempt had been made to establish a settlement in this region, and it had failed. However, it now began to attract the attention of pastoralists who crossed over from Van Diemen's Land in 1835 and established a primitive port settlement at the mouth of the Yarra river. Technically they were illegal trespassers on Crown land, but the New South Wales governor, Richard Bourke, decided to extend Crown control rather than attempt to expel them. The colonial secretary in London authorized the marking out of, and sale of allotments in, a township at Port Phillip. In March 1837 Bourke visited the site and initiated the laying out of the town of Melbourne.[16] Its growth as trade and administrative center for such a vast region does not now seem surprising, but by Australian standards down to this time the emergence within two years of a population of 3,000 was astounding. To the south another port, Geelong, was laid out soon after, while Portland, sections in which were first offered for sale in 1840, became the principal port for the squatters—pastoralists occupying but not owning Crown land—of the western districts of what in 1850 separated from New South Wales as the colony of Victoria.

The second major urban development of the decade was the founding of the city of Adelaide as principal town of the new colony of South Australia which was organized by a British colonization company.[17] The choice of its site by Colonel William Light was controversial because it was six miles inland. Hitherto all of Australia's major urban sites had been ports—Sydney, Hobart, Newcastle, Melbourne. However, Light had to choose a site with enough land to provide 1,000 acres of town lots and 2,000 acres of parkland. The site having been surveyed in 1837, holders of 437 Preliminary Land Orders selected their town acres in order determined by lot, and the sections remaining were sold cheaply at auction. Unfortunately, the surveying of the rural sections took far longer, and for two years settlers had to stay in Adelaide, which thus assumed a population much greater than would have been the case had the rural land been immediately available. Intensive speculation in town acres ensued, and the town became even larger in area as laborers dispersed to "villages" on cheaper land outside the parkland. It was well into the 1840s before a healthier balance between city and country emerged in the

South Australian settlement, but what happened in those early years stamped an indelible impression on the distribution of population in South Australia.

Colonial authorities had long assumed, and acted on the assumption, that a major part of their responsibility was to establish towns. In Canada most towns were founded by the government. Towns were regarded as very important agencies for facilitating the settlement of the land. They provided local markets which farmers needed in the early stages when bad roads hindered access to more distant localities. If government did not provide towns, the process of settlement was certain to be slowed down. "Government," writes D. N. Jeans about New South Wales, "saw the town as an essential part of its planning effort to encourage the emergence of a settled civilized community."[18]

Governments in Australia, New Zealand, and Canada were involved in particular in the creation of "capitals," towns that were to be the location of national, regional, or provincial administration. Even in the United States, at least in the early nineteenth century, the founding of "capitals" was a major exception to the otherwise strong disposition to leave town promotion to private enterprise, and much effort was put into devising plans for such cities as Indianapolis, Detroit, and Madison to make them "capital"-like in style and layout—although in the implementation of these plans many of the fancier features were usually discarded.[19] Austin, Texas, is an example of the creation of a capital in the United States by a government for the promotion of settlement and the "protection of the frontier."[20]

Some colonial governors took their responsibilities very seriously and tried to make their new capitals as elegant as possible. Felton Mathew, New Zealand's first surveyor-general, bestowed on the new capital, Auckland, a plan similar to that of his native city of Bath in England, a supreme example of Georgian urban style.[21] John Graves Simcoe had the grandest of designs for his capital of York (Toronto), like Austin deliberately planted on the fringes of settlement. He sought to implement this through minutely detailed regulations and very close supervision of their administration.[22] Notable among the Australian governors who manifested this kind of attitude to their capitals was Lachlan Macquarie, Governor of New South Wales from 1810 to 1821. He was not in the same position as Simcoe had found himself in, of being able to found a city. Sydney had been established more than two decades earlier as the location of a convict settlement. But Macquarie wished to transform the town and make it look like the capital that it was supposed to be. Like Simcoe he proposed doing this through the issuing and enforcing of detailed regulations. "It will be my particular Study," he informed the colonial secretary, "to have Edifices of All Descriptions within the Town built on a regular Plan, so as to Combine Convenience with Ornament, and preserve the Regularity of the Streets and Houses."[23] Over the next decade, with the assistance of a notable convict architect, Francis Greenway, Macquarie did indeed do much to give Sydney the appearance of a capital. He also tried to improve the appearance of Hobart, the chief town of Van Diemen's Land, and even took seriously the work of creating "secondary" towns, which would later be assigned to private enterprise. He invested the determination of sites for these towns—Windsor and the other "Macquarie towns" near Sydney, and Bathurst across the Blue Mountains—with elaborate ritual.[24] Perhaps the last governor who was interested in, and capable of, involving himself so closely in the creation and planning of towns was Ralph Darling.[25]

The grand visions of the colonial governors were seldom realized. At Toronto there was an inevitable conflict between Simcoe's dreams of an elegant waterfront and the value for commerce of this part of the city. Commercial and residential buildings were soon interspersed, and the scenic potential of the waterfront was sacrificed—as was to happen in so many other cities on rivers or lakes.

Some governors attempted to control the disposal and use of land in their capitals, but it was usually a losing battle against the pressure of commercial and speculative interests. Speculation in urban real estate was particularly intense in towns whose survival and growth seemed to have been guaranteed by their creation or selection as capitals. Attempts were made to protect capitals. For example, the new governor of the Swan River colony in Western Australia, James Stirling, was instructed in 1832 to reserve "a square of three Miles (or, 1,910 acres)" around his capital and to make land within this area available only on Crown leases not exceeding twenty-one years.[26] But gradually the colonial authorities lost control over urban development as they were forced to sell land to raise revenue and to share power with settler representatives whose principal concern was to maximize scope for commercial development.

Improvements were all very well, but they were expensive. There was a reaction against what was perceived as the "extravagance" of the Macquarie era. In New South Wales the influence of Surveyor-General Thomas Mitchell was felt into the 1830s. Mitchell has been described as "a man of forthright vision, planning for what he saw as the good of the public." He created "impressive public space" in the towns that he created as regional "capitals," such as Goulburn, Maitland, and Port Macquarie. But, after he went on leave in 1837, government planning policy became much more limited, aiming principally at providing scope for capitalists to make over new towns to their own uses. There was little provision from now on of decorative public space in the plans given to towns.[27]

A common criticism of government policy with regard to the creation of new towns in the 1830s and early 1840s in Australia and New Zealand was that it was primarily motivated by greed for revenue which resulted in its making available for sale only limited amounts of land in order to raise its price. This fostered speculation with all sorts of harmful consequences for the interests of the community—interests that had been given the highest priority in the urban designs of Macquarie and Mitchell. A series of episodes, at Brisbane, Melbourne, and Auckland, did much to discredit government control of the process of creation of new towns.

New South Wales was a colony which had developed, because it was a penal settlement, under particularly strict government control. But, on the other hand, by the 1830s its great potential as a field for capitalist enterprise was becoming obvious and was advertised as an incentive for migrants and investors. In Britain there was at this time an intense debate between the advocates of "free trade" and liberated entrepreneurial capitalism and those who for many different reasons favored retention—or, as in the case of "humanitarian" advocates of factory reform and "protection" of indigenous peoples, extension—of government regulation of the workings of the capitalist system. The balance was tilting more and more decisively in favor of the former. The shift of opinion in favor of leaving town development in Australia and New Zealand largely to private enterprise—or at least seeing it principally in the light of a service to capitalism —was one aspect of this trend. Among the most enthusiastic supporters of the capitalist system were the Benthamite Radicals with whom the Colonial Reformers were closely associated. Theirs has been called "the imperialism of free trade."[28] By 1840 the Colonial Office had moved part of the way toward adopting their position. Before the parliamentary committees of this period Edward Gibbon Wakefield was a tireless propagandist for leaving town creation to the private sector. In 1836 he reminded the Select Committee on the Disposal of Lands in the Colonies of the system that operated in the United States.

I think the Government does not interfere in the formation of towns at all. It allows individuals to purchase lands in large quantities; and, if they think fit to purchase land, to lay out streets, and form a town. There may be exceptions; but that is the general rule.[29]

Five years later Wakefield told the Select Committee on South Australia that, in his opinion, the establishment of towns and indeed of colonies, was "the business of individuals and companies, and not the business of the State." In the United States,

the government, the state, does not determine where people should live, they suppose that people will best determine that themselves, and the state sells land to companies or individuals who form towns in favourable spots, and obtain a very large profit by the resale of the lands.[30]

It was argued by the Wakefieldians that leaving town creation to private enterprise was one of the best ways of attracting the investment of capital in colonization and thus ensuring its success. Felix Wakefield, in *Colonial Surveying* (1849), urged observance of "the principle of free trade, or *laissez-faire*, by leaving to individual judgment and enterprise the business of establishing towns and dividing waste land into Town Lots, and Suburban and Rural Sections." The example to be followed was that of the United States government, which confined itself to selling waste land:

It merely performs a necessary and simple function of government, without undertaking the speculative and complicated business of laying out towns, and giving new values to different portions of land. This business it leaves wholly to individuals, whose freedom to engage in it, because the Government abstains from it, tends powerfully to bring capital into the work of colonization, and to accelerate the progress of settlement.[31]

In one major respect Wakefield's argument was un-Wakefieldian: in his work, which was subtitled "A Report to the New Zealand Company," he placed colonizing companies in the same position as governments, arguing that they too should do no more than sell land. The New Zealand Company should not undertake "a sort of business which private enterprise alone can perform in the manner most serviceable to the community." He wrote at a point very near the end of the era of Wakefieldian colonization. During most of that time Edward Gibbon Wakefield and his associates would have classified their activities as those of private enterprise and regarded as heresy the placing of a company on the same footing as a government.

Wakefieldian influence on colonial policy was at its peak in the late 1830s and early 1840s and helped to produce a major retreat from governmental involvement in town creation which had hitherto been so strong in all colonies—Australia and Canada in particular. In his *Lectures on Colonization* Herman Merivale quotes a letter written by Edward Gibbon Wakefield to the *Spectator* in December 1841, in which Wakefield questions

whether the government does wisely to encumber itself with the pursuit of a business so liable to miscalculation, so often ending in disappointment among the buyers and reproaches against the seller, and, above all, when undertaken by the government, so apt to stimulate merely speculative investment, as that of choosing the sites of intended towns, in a half-explored country, and selling suburban lots by auction.[32]

The reference to sale by auction excepted, the criticisms in this letter could have been applied very specifically to the operations in which Wakefield's New Zealand Company was then engaged. But obviously he did not intend them to be so applied. In 1840 the Colonial Office attempted to withdraw from town creation—although with two significant reservations—and leave the field open to capitalists by selling all land at a fixed price and letting capitalists decide what to do with it. The Land and Emigration Commissioners reported to the colonial secretary, Lord John Russell, on April 15, 1840, that in their opinion "the general rule should be to make no special reservation of sites for towns, and no distinctions of price or mode of sale." The only exceptions should be towns that were likely to become seats of local government, and sites on good harbors.

But we conceive that, in the case of ordinary secondary towns, the value of land depends altogether upon the spontaneous influx of labor and Capital; and this influx will be rapid or tardy in proportion as the Capitalists expect a high or low Return. If we charge the incoming Capitalist a high price for his town land, we diminish his returns, we render investments in town land and building speculations less advantageous than they otherwise would be, and thus check the influx of Capital, prevent the natural rise in the value of property, and retard the enlargement of the town.[33]

Russell's response was on the whole enthusiastic. He sent the report to the governor of New South Wales, Sir George Gipps, and instructed him to adopt the policy recommended in it. Russell accepted that, "in laying out entirely new Towns, the object must be to hold out the greatest encouragement to the resort of Capital" and that "the establishment of Villages, and their gradual extension into Towns, may there ['Inland'] be left best to the enterprize and judgment of Individuals." In reply Gipps acknowledged that leaving the formation of minor towns to private enterprise "is a return to the natural order of things, and to the way in which most Towns in the old World have been formed."[34]

But there were problems. One was the matter of government revenue, usually very dependent in colonial periods on the proceeds of land sales. By designating in advance some land as town land and then selling it at a higher price than that asked for rural land, government enhanced its revenues and therefore its ability to promote the general improvement of the colony—through roads and public works, for instance. But alternatively government could sacrifice that revenue by selling potential town land at a low price and hope for compensatory benefits both for the community and for its own revenues from the consequent influx of capitalists. One major argument for selling land cheaply was that it meant that the capitalist would have more money left over to invest in the colony and in the improvement of his property.

Enthusiasm for private enterprise in this sphere was intense in the United States, where its role was celebrated and equated with the operation of American freedom. One American writer saw the principle of freedom as operating at two critical stages of the development of towns:

Since the Revolution . . . cities have ceased to be founded in the United States by authority; the people have done it themselves, without supervision or interference from government. The sites have been selected by individuals or companies; the grounds staked off, and the lots offered for sale. This done, the balance rested with the people, and though the number of cities founded in this country west of the Allegheny Mountains is almost infinite, each of which was expected by its founders rapidly to become a great emporium, the people have built but few.[35]

There were those who regretted that Australia had not followed the American model. In 1860 C. J. Don told the Victorian Parliament that in Australia the government "in face of common sense" showed people where their towns were to grow. "In America no such nonsense was practised. . . . Lands had changed hands in some cases a dozen times before towns became built upon them; the Government never made themselves ridiculous by interfering."[36] But Lord John Russell's policy did stimulate some private enterprise whose manifestation took a distinctively Australian form. Before the authorities moved to reintroduce sale by auction in zones close to major Victorian cities, speculative suburban townships began to spring up. One such was Brighton, near Melbourne. After a game of cricket in December 1842 between the Melbourne and Brighton clubs, J. D. McArthur was quoted as saying:

Lord John Russell in one despatch had signified the wish that the formation of towns and villages in the interior should be left as much as possible to private enterprise, the wisdom of this policy could not be doubted when he called attention to the fact that the spot on which they had played one of the most ancient and noble of English games was two years ago merely the home of the aboriginal native. Within a short space a town had been erected the enterprising inhabitants of which had that day met and rivalled a town of much longer standing in a most manly sport . . . and no doubt Brighton would rival Melbourne in most matters before long.[37]

What happened in the 1830s and 1840s was an attempt to create a hybrid arrangement whereby government created the major towns and "capitals" and minor or "secondary" towns were left to private enterprise. By that stage it was rather too late for New South Wales and Victoria: many of the most significant sites had already been preempted by government, and Russell's policy attempted to ensure that this would continue to be the case. Since New Zealand was annexed as a colony, and organized European colonization began, in 1840, that country found itself right in the middle of this debate, and a very "mixed" system of town creation evolved in which governments founded many of the "capitals," national and regional, and considerable scope was allowed for private enterprise, in a country whose complex topography allowed for many small towns.

The 1840s saw a massive leapfrogging of western expansion in the United States with the growth of settlement in California and the Pacific Northwest. "Oregon fever" brought many settlers along the Oregon Trail, while others sailed from New England around Cape Horn to found towns that were very similar to those they had left behind. There was extensive and competitive promotion of towns along the Columbia and Willamette rivers. Portland and Oregon City date from the 1840s. The latter, on the site of a Hudson Bay Company post, seemed to have a strategic location at falls on the Willamette, but Portland, founded by two New Englanders, gained the edge as a port and had a population of 800 by the end of the decade. Other Oregon towns that were founded by New Englanders included Brownville, 1846, and Albany, 1849. Here location close to rivers was important. At the end of the decade came the California gold rush and the beginning of the spectacular growth of San Francisco.

Farther east the lake ports now grew very fast as migrants poured west. During the decade Detroit increased from 9,000 to 21,019, Toledo from 1,112 to 3,829, and Milwaukee from 1,700 to 20,061. These were examples of what were now commonly celebrated as "magic rises of cities in the wilderness." Passengers arriving by boat at Milwaukee were astonished.

Nothing there like the silence of the forest, or Indian scenery. The din of the thronged street, the bustle of the city, and the discordant concord of craftsmen fall upon the ear. Ringing bells, streaming flags, and fluttering canvass, and a full view of a city half a mile wide and a mile long, all force upon me the inquiry, "Is this in Wisconsin?" . . . This is the town,—Milwaukie, with its many churches, its fifty lawyers, and seven thousand souls.[38]

Iowa was opened up in this decade, with settlement spreading along the Des Moines River. Away from the ports, town development in Texas was slow. After a brief period at Washington-on-the-Brazos, a thriving cotton trade river port, the capital reverted to Austin, a site deliberately chosen in preference to Houston in the hope of encouraging interior settlement of Texas. Numerous towns in the region—New Braunfels, Fredericksburg, Comfort, Boehme—were founded as part of German colonization schemes. The railroad was becoming an important factor in the growth of towns. A town could now become significant even if it was not on a navigable river. An example is Indianapolis, which was linked to the Ohio River in 1847 by the Madison and Indianapolis Railroad and soon became a major railroad center. Town promoters and leaders began waking up to the need for their towns to devise and implement strategies for the acquisition and exploitation of this new phenomenon.

During the 1840s the rivalries of the great midwestern cities intensified, and there was a rich literature of speculation concerning which would turn out to be the metropolis of this region. Cincinnati was at the peak of its renown. By 1850 its population was 115,436, compared with 77,860 for St. Louis, 46,601 for Pittsburgh, 43,194 for Louisville—and only 29,963 for Chicago, whose *rate* of increase was, however, already attracting much notice. Steamboat traffic was the key to the prosperity of Cincinnati, the largest inland port in the United States. Not only was Cincinnati the nation's leading producer of pork, beer, and liquor; it was also a major industrial city (furniture, soap, candles, shoes, stoves, boats). As such it attracted large numbers of European immigrants, notably Germans. Cincinnati was also famous for its printing industry and as a center of cultural life.[39]

A new era in the relationships to one another of the towns of the Ohio and Mississippi river valleys seemed to be arriving. Many of the towns that had been founded earlier in the century were now stagnating or declining. Others had grown to the point where an irreversible momentum seemed to have set in. Two major factors were determining the "destiny" of towns: the rise of agriculture and commerce in the region consequent on the vast influx of immigrants, and the positioning of towns in relation to developing continental networks of trade and communications. There was already much debate as to the routing of transcontinental railroads.

The 1850s brought to the Midwest the full impact of the railroad, with many towns which had flourished in the steamboat era unable to devise a strategy of successful accommodation to the new technology. Competition among these towns intensified, and so did the quest for new capital and new bases for economic growth, such as manufacturing development. The result was a large outpouring of booster literature, as Chambers of Commerce and other agencies sought to publicize the advantages of their towns.

In addition to the river towns, there were many towns that emerged in the 1840s and 1850s and competed with one another for the business of the migrants who passed through on their way to the California gold rushes, to settle in Oregon, to escape religious persecution (as with the Mormons), and to settle the plains of Kansas and Nebraska as these opened up. Once the railroad came, these towns too had an uncertain future, one that depended very much on their capacity to attract resourceful entrepreneurs and to develop substantial and durable linkages with the major railroad networks that were evolving. The quality of boosting is stressed by historians who seek to explain why some towns were more successful than others in the struggle to acquire the assets on which the achievement of regional hegemony depended. Notable among these was

Kansas City, located by a town-site company in 1839 at a site on the Missouri River near the mouth of the Kansas River. It grew slowly at first, but prospered in the 1850s with the opening of Kansas to the west. Its population reached 4,500 by the outbreak of the Civil War. A small elite of real estate owners and boosters played a critical role in securing for Kansas City the railroad connections that enabled it to forge ahead of such rivals as Independence and St. Joseph after the war and become, with Omaha, one of the two principal gateways to the Far West. Its rapid growth as a cattle market and meat-packing center made it tenth largest among trans-Mississippi cities by 1890.

Town-site speculation reached new levels of intensity in Kansas and Nebraska in the antebellum decade. On the Kansas side of the Missouri River many towns were founded, but only a few survived to grow to permanence. The rivalries among these, e.g., Leavenworth, Topeka, Atchison, Lawrence, continued long after the war, and there was much speculation as to which would emerge as the "metropolis" of the region. None did. The dominance of Kansas City across the river in Missouri proved too strong. Many towns were also platted by speculative town-site companies along the eastern boundary of Nebraska when it was opened up in 1854 by the Kansas-Nebraska Act. The most successful town here and one which attracted much attention from travelers was Omaha, just across the river from Council Bluffs, Iowa, which had become a major migrants' outfitting center at the time of the Mormon migration and the California gold rush. Omaha underwent a brief boom in 1857. Many towns collapsed in the Panic of that year, but Omaha achieved dominance in its region as a result of being selected as the eastern terminus of the Union Pacific Railroad. However, when Nebraska achieved statehood in 1867, not Omaha but a site farther to the west— Lancaster, renamed Lincoln—was chosen to be the capital. By 1890 Omaha, with 140,000 people, was the second largest city west of the Mississippi.

Another "urban frontier" which attracted much attention in the 1850s was that which opened up with great rapidity in Minnesota. It has been estimated that no fewer than 700 towns were projected in the territory in 1855–57. At this point by far the most significant town was St. Paul, which was platted in 1847 near Fort Snelling and became an important terminus for steamboat traffic on the upper Mississippi. It became a popular place for travelers to visit and to use as a starting point for excursions into the wilderness country to the north and west. Visitors marveled at the startling juxtaposition in its streets of developing urban civilization and "savagery" as personified by Indians and fur traders. In 1849, when St. Paul had a population of 840, it was made the capital of the new territory of Minnesota. Across the river another 250 people inhabited the small village of St. Anthony. The town of Minneapolis was laid out by speculators during the 1850s but was overshadowed for some time by St. Paul. Its rapid development came in later decades, additional proof, it seemed, of the Americans' genius for fostering great cities in the wilderness. Here too, as in Wisconsin, a host of smaller towns was founded, mostly by speculators who made extravagant claims as to their prospects. Few of these were fulfilled.

Many tourists also visited and reported on Denver, another "mushroom" city of the West, which grew rapidly after gold was found nearby in 1858. Throughout the Rocky Mountain regions of Colorado innumerable gold discoveries over the next four decades produced a constantly fluctuating "urban frontier," with many towns "booming" briefly and then subsiding, perhaps even disappearing, once the tide of gold-seekers moved on. Denver remained constant as a supply point for this activity, and fine homes were built by the merchants who prospered as a result. In 1867 Denver became the territorial capital and in 1876 the capital of the new state of Colorado. By 1874 it had a population of nearly 15,000, which rose to 36,000 in 1885 and 106,000 in 1890. Its capacity for doubling its population every five years was spectacular even by American standards. A more durable basis for its growth than gold was provided by the connection to the Union Pacific Railroad which it secured in 1870.

However, the most exotic towns of the American West—certainly the towns which, apart perhaps from Denver in its early days, attracted most attention from the outside world—were Salt Lake City, final resting place of the Mormons after their great westward migration, and San Francisco because of its gold-rush origins and dramatic and sometimes violent early history. There were few more startling examples of rapid growth, of the almost overnight creation of an "instant city." In 1849 alone a population of 5,000 in July had reached 20,000 by the ensuing winter. By the end of 1852 San Francisco had some 42,000 inhabitants. By 1890 it ranked first among the trans-Mississippi cities. Its population of 298,997 was nearly six times as great as that of Los Angeles—which nevertheless was ranked fifth.

Until the 1890s, when the Superintendent of the Census reported that the "frontier" was no longer discernible in the American West and Frederick Jackson Turner made this development the central theme of his famous lecture, the urban frontier in the United States seemed a constantly recurring phenomenon. As new regions were opened up, for example Oklahoma at the end of the 1880s, pioneers rushed in to found and settle new towns. Railroad expansion produced a constant "mushrooming" of cities whose boosters proclaimed their destiny as the inevitable "metropolis" of their region.

Behind the frontier line the older established towns and cities developed hierarchical relationships with one another and became part of an increasingly urban nation. Their novelty quickly ceased to intrigue commentators, for in most important respects they closely resembled the cities of the East. Indeed, as we shall see, it was the desire of most of those who promoted them that this should be so, and that desire undoubtedly played its part in the rapid assimilation of the urban West to the urban norms of the rest of the country.

The process in Canada was not fundamentally different, except that there was a lengthy interval between the maturing of a Toronto-dominated urban system in Ontario in the 1840s and 1850s and the dramatic rise of large cities in the prairie provinces under the impact of the construction of the Canadian Pacific Railroad in the 1880s and 1890s. By the 1850s Toronto had emerged as the "metropolis" of Upper Canada, contesting with Montreal the commercial supremacy of eastern Canada as a whole. The major new urban development of this era was along the Ottawa River. At Bytown, where the Rideau Canal, completed in 1832, linked the St. Lawrence with the Ottawa River, a city emerged as a center of the lumber trade and sawmilling. Ottawa's population reached 8,000 by the mid-1850s. In 1859 it was selected as the capital of Canada.

In the 1880s a spectacular new urban frontier opened up in the prairie provinces. A succession of booms occurred, and visitors came to marvel at these new cities which had sprung so rapidly from the wilderness. Winnipeg grew from 25,000 in 1891 to 136,000 in 1911, while Calgary increased its population in the same era from 3,800 to nearly 50,000. Now the development of towns seemed much more "metropolitan," with

some towns, well located in relation to railroads and major mineral resources, growing very rapidly while few others were able to develop to
any significant size. This phenomenon was characteristic also of Australian and western American urban development at this period, and set
these regions apart from the Midwest and New Zealand where older,
more evenly distributed structures of urban population persisted.

By mid-century Australia already had several large towns. Sydney had
a population of about 54,000, while Hobart and Melbourne each had
23,000. Adelaide had reached 14,000. The pattern of Australian urban
development changed little from this point on. New "urban frontiers" did
develop from time to time, but these were mostly associated with gold
rushes. Most of the towns which "boomed" during the gold discoveries of
the 1850s in Victoria and later in Queensland and Western Australia
stagnated or even faded away once the rushes were over, and the only
permanent gainers were the metropolitan areas, notably Melbourne, which
acquired a reputation as a "marvelous" city in the 1850s. This reputation
reached new heights in the boom era of the 1880s but was somewhat
tarnished in the depression of the 1890s. Australia became notorious for
the weakness of town development at the intermediate levels. Country
towns mostly remained small, and each colony became dominated by its
metropolis—Sydney in New South Wales, Melbourne in Victoria, Adelaide in South Australia, and, to a lesser extent, Brisbane in Queensland.

A feature of Australian development which eventually attracted world-
wide attention and aroused increasing concern in Australia itself was the
concentration of population not just in urban areas but in a few large
cities. Writing at the end of the century, Adna Ferrin Weber compared
the Australia of 1890 with the United States at a roughly similar stage of
its development as a new society, in 1790, and discovered that, whereas
in America only 3.14 percent of the population had then been living in
cities of 10,000 or more, 35.20 percent of Australians lived in such
places.[40] Indeed, in 1890 approximately two-thirds of Australians lived
in areas classified as "urban" for census purposes. Such proportions were
to be reached by the United States only in 1920 and by Canada in
1950.[41] The trend in Australia was apparent much earlier in the century.
Even in the early 1840s Sydney had about 25 percent of the population
of New South Wales. The table below represents the percentage of the
colonial population in the respective capitals.[42]

	1871	*1881*	*1891*	*1901*
Sydney	27	30	34	36
Melbourne	28	33	43	41
Adelaide	23	37	42	45
Brisbane	13	15	24	24
Perth	21	20	17	20
Hobart	19	18	23	20

The most even and steady growth was that of Sydney, which rose from 54,000 in 1851 to 96,000 in 1861, 225,000 in 1881, and 383,000 in 1891. Melbourne made a spectacular rise in the gold rush era of the 1850s—from 23,000 to 140,000—and thereafter remained ahead of Sydney, reaching 491,000 by 1891. But by the turn of the century Sydney was close to overtaking Melbourne in population.

The Australian trends attracted publicity because they had set in so early. But by the last decade of the century they were trends that were characteristic of all "new countries." Indeed, they were not characteristic of "new countries" alone. Weber's thesis is that, in exhibiting this high degree of urban concentration, Australia in 1890, whatever one might have said about its condition earlier in the century, was not abnormal or deviant. "What is true of the Australia of 1891 is, in a greater or less degree, true of the other countries in the civilized world. The tendency towards concentration or agglomeration is all but universal in the Western world."[43] It was a tendency that became apparent in Canada and the United States as well. In *The Winning of the West,* Theodore Roosevelt, writing about western settlement in the late eighteenth and early nineteenth centuries, commented on the "comparative utter insignificance of town development"—"a very marked contrast to what goes on to-day, in the settlement of new countries."

In Washington great cities, like Tacoma, Seattle, and Spokane, have sprung up with a rapidity which was utterly unknown in the West a century ago. Nowadays when new States are formed the urban population in them tends to grow as rapidly as in the old. A hundred years ago there was practically no urban population at all in a new country. Colorado even during its first decade of statehood had a third of its population in its capital city. Kentucky during its first decade did not have much more than one percent of its population in its capital city. Kentucky grew as rapidly as Colorado grew, a hundred years later; but Denver grew thirty or forty times as fast as Lexington had ever grown.[44]

CHAPTER TWO

The Making of Images of
the Urban Frontier

MUCH of the work of forming images and shaping perceptions of New World towns was done by people who visited them and then set down their observations in books or articles—in particular, writers of travel books and of guidebooks for emigrants. The nineteenth century saw a great flood of literature of this kind, catering to a vast audience of potential migrants to, and investors in, the new countries as well as the many readers who were interested to learn about the creation overseas of new societies by people emigrating from their own "old world." Indeed, writing of this kind created the framework for a large part of the debate and discussion that took place concerning the character and destiny of these new societies. When one searches in bibliographies of contemporary publications on Canada, Australia, New Zealand, and the western United States, one finds that a high proportion of the material that contains comment on the evolution of these countries is of this type—works written by visitors or reporters from outside who wrote to satisfy or stimulate the interest of people not living in them. This is scarcely surprising if one considers what a major part in the shaping of the new societies was being played by the influx of migrants and external capital. Discussion about them was almost forced into this mold—which was in particular one of comparison with one another and with the Old World— by the sheer volume of publication of reportage and advice for external audiences. People interested in migrating to or investing in the new countries wanted guidance and information. The enormous number of agencies—including governments and colonization and shipping and railroad companies—involved in the business of persuading others to migrate or invest poured out material of this type.

It is impossible now to rediscover the thoughts, perceptions, and reactions of the great mass of the people who came to settle in the new countries. They left no records, or, if they did in the form of letters and diaries, these—not surprisingly—seldom contain any extended commentary on the character of urban society but mainly report on practical matters and day-by-day incidents. But we can at least get close to the people who tried to influence perceptions of the new countries, the main purveyors of information about them. To what extent the guidebooks were actually used is hard to determine.[1] Vast numbers were published and obviously satisfied a demand. Charlotte Erickson argues that the most influential source was letters written back home by migrants and not intended for publication.[2] A few such letters have subsequently been published, and many were published at the time, usually by land and colonization companies.[3] These have to be used with great caution. It is not always clear how or in response to what sort of inducement they came into the possession of the publisher. They always happen to promote the particular cause which the publisher is interested in and say little or nothing detrimental to it.[4]

Many books about the new countries were written by migrants or at least by people who had gone through the migration experience or a prolonged stay in the country concerned and then returned "home" to reflect on what had happened. A common title for such a book was something such as *Seven Years' Experience in New South Wales* or *Four Years in Illinois*. Even travelers, whether they liked it or not, could not help but become to some extent caught up in the migratory flow and experience. The traveler was a transient and so met other transients and in his or her reportage often captured something of the experience of other people who were moving about and, unlike in his or her case, searching for somewhere to settle. Indeed, many of the conversations which travelers recorded took place in trains, coaches, and hotels.

The experience of travelers was often very similar to that of people who, without intending to write a book about their journeys, traveled new countries in search of somewhere to invest their money or to settle and bring their family. This was particularly the case with the American West, which could be reached a good deal more easily than Australia and New Zealand by persons with this kind of exploratory purpose in mind. An example is Daniel R. Anthony, who visited Kansas in 1857 assessing towns and their potential for investment and for the opening of agencies of his father's insurance business. He listened to local people, calculated on a degree of exaggeration in their enthusiasm for local conditions, and walked around the towns, trying to arrive at an accurate assessment of them. Jefferson City "looks like a very slow town," he reported. Lawrence was "destined to become a large town" and so his father ought to secure the agency of the Aetna company there. Leavenworth was "very much like St. Paul Minnesota T[erritory]," full of "mostly young men— and fast men." He became "well satisfied" that it was "the most enterprising city in all Kansas," but added: "lots are high, high, high, wouldn't touch them at half what is asked for them."[5] A similar story is told in the letters of Charles Monroe Chase about a young New England man, Edward Russell, who traveled after leaving college and was given $30,000 by his father to invest. "He traversed the western states several times over; visited and studied all the border cities and towns," and finally decided that Elwood, Kansas, "bid the fairest for a large town." He invested most of his money in Elwood property "and was reaping handsome profits when the crash commenced." He lost $25,000.[6] Most people who were interested in settling in the West or investing there could not afford either the time or the money to undertake this kind of preliminary investigation or reconnaisance. Few indeed who were thinking of going to Australia or New Zealand could do so. What they needed were people who would undertake such a mission, in effect, on their behalf. This is a service that travel and guidebook writers sought to provide. The style in which some of their books were written was not dissimilar to that of Daniel R. Anthony's private letters.

Of course, not all visitors to the new countries wrote this kind of book. At one extreme, there were those who traveled extensively but did not intend to write travel books. Their aim was to collect impressions and information which would contribute to the making of generalizations about the new countries. Their books consist in large part of such generalizations, and there is no detailed account of their travels. Such writers include some of the most celebrated nineteenth-century commentators on the new societies such as Alexis de Tocqueville, James Bryce, and André Siegfried.[7] The diaries and other records which they kept of their travels sometimes remained unpublished for many years. Sidney and Beatrice Webb's journals of their visits to Australia, New Zealand, and the United States now make absorbing reading but were not written for publication and were intended to be the raw materials out of which books with broad, general themes would be composed.[8] Somewhere in between were writers such as Charles Dickens and Anthony Trollope, who maintained a basic travel-narrative structure but frequently interrupted it for extended reflections on general topics.[9] At the other extreme was the mass of "globe-trotters" who toured the world and wrote books that were usually very superficial or anecdotal to defray their expenses or relieve their boredom on the ship going home or to entertain family and friends. One feature which almost all writers of travel books and reports had in common was that they were well-to-do people: the expenses involved were usually considerable.

The most extreme example of the absorption of the travel experience by the generalizing impulse occurs in Alexis de Tocqueville's "Quinze Jours au Désert," his account of his journey to Michigan, which made its own contribution to the great generalizations of *Democracy in America* but itself remained unpublished. In it, as we shall see in a later chapter, he used the very experience of travel, in this case emerging from a forest to find a neat village and then plunging into it again, as a metaphor for the condition of American society.[10]

The travelers were mostly urban people, connoisseurs of improvements in urban amenities. They were excited by the new cities, which seemed to have in their development so many possibilities no longer available to the old cities of Europe.[11] Their travels tended to be town-oriented experiences.[12] Scenery had to be traveled to, often with great difficulty. It required a special effort to be able to study remote or scattered rural life. But journeys usually began and ended in, and were organized from, towns. Towns sustained and revived travelers in foreign parts. Towns were places with civilized amenities where one recovered from the rigors of coach or sea travel or expeditions into the wilderness. When train travel arrived, the country in between the cities tended to become a blur or not to be seen at all as the traveler slept or ate on his or her moving hotel. Travelers were bound, even if only subconsciously, to be biased in their reporting toward appreciativeness of the kind of urban amenity which made their journeying more comfortable and civilized—and to judge towns accordingly. It is no wonder that boosters made so much of hotels and that such efforts were made to erect grandiose hotels that were out of all proportion to the existing condition of towns.

Boosters knew well the truth of the complaint made by A. D. Jones in *Illinois and the West* (1838) that most travelers just passed through the West, staying only at hotels, "and know absolutely nothing of the internal structure of society, or the character of those who make it."[13] However, travelers often found themselves obliged for one reason or another—notably delays in transport—to spend longer than they had expected in a particular town, and this gave an opportunity for a fuller appraisal of the place, from which a historian can now derive much benefit. An example is the Englishman J. Richard Beste, who traveled through the Midwest with his large family in the early 1850s and subsequently published an account in *The Wabash*. A substantial part of the second volume is taken up with a detailed analysis of the Indiana town of Terre Haute. Upon arriving there, the family was smitten with illness. They were forced to stay at Terre Haute for a lengthy period. Here is Beste's comment on the experience:

The chances which befel my family brought us into familiar contact with American market-town citizenship. No English traveller would willingly remain weeks in a small town in the back settlements of the United States to study such; none have therefore described them. Terre Haute had become to us almost "our village." Let us describe it as we found it: we shall not see the social system of New York or Baltimore: but we shall see that which backs up those great cities.[14]

Thus the chance prolongation of the Beste family's stay in Terre Haute enabled them to appreciate that there was an American urban *system,* with a whole secondary layer of towns "backing up" the great cities.

Travelers' accounts did indeed, as Beste suggests, have a metropolitan bias in their reportage. The smaller towns were underreported. They were not regularly stopped at or easy to get to, whereas journeys tended to be from one larger center to another. This was particularly the case when the railroad replaced the coach as the principal means of travel. At the end of the century Michael Davitt, the Irish land reformer and nationalist politician, visited Australia and spent much of his time—and much of the space in his book *Life and Progress in Australasia* (1898)—examining Melbourne and Sydney, which fascinated him. But later in the book he recounted his experiences traveling overland from one to the other (rather than by sea). He expressed himself as "wishful to make these inland and prosperous towns better known to those who know little or nothing of even their existence." He urged other travelers to do likewise. Melbourne and Sydney were undoubtedly "great factors in the life of their respective colonies," but they were not everything. "Little or nothing is known about the towns, villages, and hamlets that are scattered in large numbers over the colonies, and in which reside the potential energies that are to make the future of this antipodean continent."[15]

Whereas the larger cities were the places where "civilization" and its amenities were most abundantly—and, for travelers who stayed at the great hotels, lavishly—available, the smaller towns tended to be dull and repetitive. Edward Dicey complained that American towns

have no sights. When you have taken your first half-hour's stroll about any town you happen to pass the night in, you know as much about it externally as if you had lived there for a month. Every town is built on the same system, has the same series of more or less lengthy rectangular streets, the same large spacious stores, the same snug, unpicturesque rows of villas, detached or semi-detached as the case may be, the same sombre churches, built in the architectural style of St. Clement Danes or St. Mary's, Bryanstone Square, and the same nomenclature of streets—the invariable Walnut, Chestnut, Front, and Main Streets—crossed by the same perpendicular streets, numbered First, Second, and so on to any number you like, according to the size of the town.

His conclusion was that "all western cities seem to have been turned out by a city-making machine, warranted to produce a city of any size, at the shortest notice."[16] This was a typical visitor's appraisal of the "external" character of a town, gained in half an hour's search for "the sights,"[17] although the acuteness of Dicey's delineation of the general type removes it from the realm of the superficial. The next stage would obviously have to be the type of prolonged immersion in the "internal" life of a town that Beste was forced to undergo. After a time the diaries and notes of many visitors degenerated into this type of comment: "There is little to say descriptive of Bismarck. Describe one of the new cities of the States, and you have described all."[18] After spending *Last Winter in the United States* (1868) F. Barham Zincke concluded that there was "not a particle of difference between one town and another, all having been cast in the same mould. . . . one city reproduced over and over again, wherever you go."[19]

The visits may have been brief and superficial, but the visitors still had to include some sort of description of a town in their books. This was especially the case with guidebook writers. As a result, they were prone to indulge in quick, shorthand summaries of a town's special character. They were fond of giving and perpetuating labels for towns, brief, snappy descriptions which provided some semblance of differentiation. The visitors were great purveyors of town "personalities." That was what their readers wanted, and it was one way of rendering more interesting books which might be required to describe fifty or sixty towns in a region.

However, one valuable feature of travel writing was that the travelers wrote comparatively. They compared the towns which they visited with one another or with other towns in the same country or with towns in the East or the Old World or other new countries. Their readers expected and needed such comparisons. They wanted to know what these places were like, and therefore the descriptions had to be couched in the form of comparisons with the towns that they were familiar with. Travelers devised a typology which was comparative in character and by their publication gave it very wide currency: the "Englishness" of Sydney or Christchurch, the distinctive features of an "American" or a "Yankee" town. Anselm Strauss has referred to the "subtle transmission" of urban imagery "across space and time—through 'travel talk' and travel literature."[20]

Many of the visitors' impressions of and generalizations about towns were influenced by their mode of travel, how they approached towns, how they moved through them. Many different perspectives were possible. Approach by train created a very different impression than that gained by arrival on a boat or by coach. Town promoters worried about the impact made on visitors by the part of the town through which their train happened to run—which could, unless great care was taken with landscaping, be a very blighted district because of railway construction and operations. C. P. Terry later wrote that he and others at Tacoma made a great mistake when they refused to sell the railroad company ten acres in what "would be the most central part of the town." The railroad bypassed that area. "For years the trains ran direct to the wharf and no one passing through saw anything of the town except the Chinese shanties and the wharf, and they were invariably informed at other points that they had seen all of Tacoma."[21] Here the interests of owners of prime real estate in Tacoma came into conflict with those of the boosting of the town as a whole.

Another example of conflict in the promotion of a town's image was the siting of the Northern Pacific railroad station at Helena, Montana. The location of the station some distance away in the valley was praised as the choice of "the point toward which the city must inevitably grow." This was not merely a matter of foresight on the part of the company. It also dramatized their confidence that the town *would* grow. Unfortunately, the traveler arriving at this station "gets rather an unfavorable first impression of the place. He sees big stretches of gravel beds and furrowed ground dug up in the eager search for gold." However, a booster publication assured visitors that this area was "soon to be covered with stores and warehouses and factories of the wholesale and manufacturing section of the city."[22]

Impressions gained from the window of a train really mattered, if the opinion expressed by Maurice O'Connor Morris, a visitor to Colorado in the 1860s from England, was representative. "In America," he wrote, unlike in England, "the sample seen from your cars may be considered a fair one." He explained why.

In America a tourist may draw conclusions from railway travelling, which in England would be very erroneous; for in the former the railway is the pioneer of all progress. Civilization and settlements follow it, and seem to cling close to it for protection. Towns and villages grow round it, and to show their gratitude, welcome it daily through their best streets, as they used to welcome the daily stage in the old country, in the merry days of the road. And, indeed, in most parts of the recently settled districts, civilization is bounded by the railway margin more or less wide; whereas in the older civilization of Europe, and England specially, railways had to skirt towns and villages, and to hide their heads in such neighbourhoods, either by tunnels or embankments, completely obscuring the view.[23]

It followed from this that whatever you saw of a town from the window of your carriage really was the very best that it had to show. Wilhelm Cohnstaedt, a German visitor to western Canada in 1909, certainly believed that businessmen were aware that travelers would react in this way to what they saw. "Most towns try to present their seven wonders right away—on a silver platter—to the traveller who gets to know them only through the train window." At one hamlet where he counted eight houses "a large sign had been erected which literally shouted to the traveller: 'Stay in X! Why go further? You can do better business here than anywhere else!—THE BOARD OF TRADE.' " Cohnstaedt went on to demonstrate in some detail how a traveler could interpret the economic condition of a town by what he could see from his train window. He arrived at the town of Rosthern from the south and, looking out his left window, saw "a clean and prosperous town." On observing this to a fellow passenger who was a member of the Municipal Council, the latter exclaimed with a shudder, " 'But what if he [the traveler] looks out the right coach window!' " Thus alerted, Cohnstaedt did look out the right window—and saw "a dozen straw-thatched roofs scarcely above ground." He discovered that "the affluent citizens fear that the traveller might draw the conclusion, from these sod huts, that there were also less well-to-do people in this town."[24]

Some visitors chose to alight from their trains or coaches and go exploring on foot. Anthony Trollope and George Augustus Sala found "walking tours" of Australian and American towns difficult and fatiguing to accomplish and asked why. The answer lay in the immensity of the scale on which they had been laid out. Sala wrote that to a European "a civilised city" was a place that you could walk about in, whereas "comfortable pedestrianism in the greater number of young American towns is next door to an impossibility."[25] A Russian visitor to America in 1857, Alexsandr Lakier, decided to walk to the city park at St. Louis and believed that he would be able to do so quite easily, a park being a place that "one imagines to be if not in the center of the city, then at least close to it." But he found that it was in fact at least five miles from the courthouse: "in walking to this place designated for strolling by city inhabitants, I had to pass by large empty lots next to huge buildings erected for schools or factories, lots on which corn was growing in its pristine beauty; beyond the field was an enormous building and again an empty lot."[26] Thus did Trollope, Sala, and Lakier all learn something about the ambitious scale on which American Western towns were laid out and the way in which visions of the future rather than the needs of present convenience dictated the location of important amenities.

Reactions to streets reflected the experience and perspective of travelers and contributed to the forming of generalizations about towns. There was a long-running debate between those who preferred straight streets, as in the grid plan, and those who yearned for the crooked irregularity of the streets of Old World cities. The straight streets struck some as convenient and aesthetically pleasing. Others found them boring. There was no mystery in such towns, no opportunity to get lost and explore narrow alleyways and have the kinds of adventures which sell books. The American travel writer Maturin M. Ballou wrote of Adelaide's broad, regular streets:

There are no mysterious labyrinths, dark lanes, or blind alleys in the city; all the avenues cross each other at right angles and are uniform in width. Somehow we missed the irregular ways of old European cities and those of the far East, where one can get delightfully lost and bewildered now and then.[27]

After visiting St. Louis in 1836, Friedrich von Wrede wrote that he could not see the point of having streets that always crossed at right angles.

I praise our German towns which also have their straight streets and carefully-laid-out quarters but which also have the crooked and winding passages that would make one forget the monotonous sameness of the former and remind one of a time which the carefully constructed buildings of this new era have never seen.[28]

Sydney became the great New World exception, the city whose narrow, winding streets appealed to many visitors. Anthony Trollope liked Sydney because it was

not parallelogramic and rectangular. One may walk about it and lose the direction in which one is going. Streets running side by side occasionally converge—and they bend and go in and out, and wind themselves about, and are intricate.[29]

In trying to make sense of a new city, to comprehend it as a whole, visitors liked to be able to stand back and view it from a distance. They appreciated towns which they could view as a whole.[30] Close up, towns tended to be too confusing and disorganized. Captain H. Butler Stoney wrote of Hobart's filthy streets and expressed the hope that one day "the interior of the city will correspond to the extreme beauty of the birds'-eye view."[31] The bird's-eye view was indeed a favorite way of depicting the nineteenth-century city. It was drawn—in the era before aircraft—from the imagined perspective of a bird flying over the town, and, because drawn, could depart from reality so as to emphasize and exaggerate order, progress, prospects for future unlimited growth, and other themes dear to the hearts of urban boosters.[32] In their written descriptions of young towns travelers and guidebook writers often strove to achieve a similar perspective.

Michael Davitt was a visitor who came to Melbourne—as Mrs. Trollope came to Cincinnati—with his head full of boosterish images and clichés, for example, the claim that Melbourne was "among her urban relatives at the antipodes what Niagara is among waterfalls." Unfortunately, however, the approach by boat up the Yarra River, lined with gasworks and tanneries, was so dismal that it punctured all such illusions. What was really needed to sustain them was, in Davitt's opinion, that one should

drop in upon the city in a balloon sailing down from the region of Mount Macedon. Coming upon it in this manner you would be inclined to forgive its professional beauty pretensions on finding a city of such combined magnitude and splendour in so new a country and so far away from Europe.[33]

There were a few towns which could actually be seen from a nearby mountain as if from a birds-eye view. Even here writers tried to compose their descriptions as much as possible in the bird's-eye view convention. One of the most frequently admired of such views was the one from Hamilton Mountain, Ontario. Here is David Kennedy on what he saw after climbing it:

From here we had a perfect bird's-eye view of the town. The prospect I have not seen surpassed from eminences of double the height. The town lay at our feet—the streets rigidly defined and squaring the houses into blocks, every block surrounded by a beautiful framework of yellow, red, or orange-coloured trees.[34]

In the 1840s A. W. H. Rose, the "emigrant churchman in Canada," made the same climb and generalized about the view in the same way as boosters hoped people would when they observed bird's-eye views. "I never saw or expect to see a place in which the principle of growth was so evidently and strikingly developed, in every stage, from the rough hut of the wilderness to the highly-finished public building."[35]

Visitors tried to frame and compose their literary views of towns and to invest the structure of their compositions and the relationships of the items within them with moral significance. They devised descriptions to bring out the inner life, the hidden moral and social structure of the town. An example of this is G. Butler Earp's interpretation of Sydney in *The Gold Colonies of Australia* (1853). Framing his picture, Earp draws the reader's attention to "the heights of Woollomolloo, rising above the city" and "crowned with the truly elegant villas of the *élite* of Sydney society." The effort of the mental eye in rising to observe these dwellings is then drawn on to make a point about the moral and economic structure of the town. The elite is "composed of men who have, for the most part, become so by their own efforts, aided, it is true, by the luck of circumstances, which, however, often casts them down, even from the Woollomolloo heights, only to find their way back in the course of a few years." The scene is thus made emblematic of the upward and downward social mobility of Sydney life and also of the desire to display one's wealth as conspicuously as possible while one possesses it. From the passion to do this "spring the elegant suburban edifices which crown the picture of Sydney, as seen from the harbour."[36]

Boosters and others who described towns liked to do so in ways which emphasized organic wholeness and harmonious relationship of the component parts. Here, for instance, is a description of the site of Olympia, Washington:

The sloping hillsides, occupied by homes, small orchard groves and garden patches, form an amphitheater; while the bay with its rising and falling tides, its commercial life, and pleasure seeking community, constitutes the arena. Thus situated, all parts of the city are brought into view from the other parts, and from the bay.[37]

As cities grew, it became increasingly difficult for writers to compose such views. One of the best commentaries on this change can be found in Charles Dudley Warner's *Studies in the South and West* (1889). Warner visited Cincinnati and compared his experience with that of Charles Dickens some forty years earlier. "When Dickens saw the place it was a compact, smiling little city, with a few country places on the hills." Here was a city that could be viewed and interpreted as a whole. But, however many of the traditional kinds of vantage point he tried, Warner could not recapture that impression.

The city is indeed difficult to see. When you are in it, by the river, you can see nothing; when you are outside of it you are in any one of half a dozen villages, in regions of parks and elegant residences, altogether charming and geographically confusing; and if from some commanding point you try to recover the city idea, you look down upon black roofs half hid in black smoke, through which the fires of factories gleam, and where the colored Ohio rolls majestically along under a dark canopy.

Cincinnati had become hopelessly fragmented into suburbs. Warner gave up in thankfulness "that there is no obligation on me to depict it."[38]

This trend is very similar to that which occurred in artists' depictions of towns. Most early paintings and sketches of new towns were composed from a distance and endeavored to show the whole. But gradually the focus narrowed and the depiction of streetscapes began to predominate.[39]

Another convention which literary and artistic depictions of new towns had in common was the framing of them in some sort of rural setting, either wilderness (often including aborigines or Indians) or pastoral, to emphasize progress and antithesis between urban society and primitive nature, existing in harmony or the one developing out of the other and gradually replacing it. Writers sometimes went to considerable trouble to construct such views. Sir Richard Bonnycastle took his readers up one of the "forested eminences" on the island of Montreal to compose a panorama of the progress from wild nature to the sophisticated modern city:

Here the grand rapids may be felt in all their magnificence and terrors; for you hear their tumultuous rage against the rocky barriers which oppose their incalculable force. Here you see the noble river again resuming its solemn course towards the ocean; and here, amid groves which give evidences of ages long gone by, you look through a clear atmosphere on a large city, irregularly grouped in lofty dwellings of dark limestone, wooden edifices painted of all colours, monasteries, churches, and public buildings, with tin roofs and spires shining as polished silver; and these are contrasted, immediately at your feet and around "The Mountain," by pretty country houses, gardens, orchards, and rich farms.[40]

To what extent were visitors to towns manipulated? How conscious were townspeople, especially boosters, civic officials, and businessmen, of the importance of impressing visitors, and what did they do to make the right impressions? Whenever a visitor was known to be writing a book, he was certain to be overwhelmed by the efforts of the local people to show their town and district to the best advantage. Many booster publications showed acute sensitivity to the impact that their town would make on visitors, and one purpose of the publications was to anticipate and influence reactions.

Buildings were regarded as especially important in this regard, and newspapers frequently urged townspeople to be aware of how the "architectural tone and style" of the buildings that they erected would be used to discover the character of the community. "Nothing," wrote one Iowa newspaper in 1852, "will more readily win the admiration of the stranger or visitor, and nothing more certainly decide the mind of him who is in search of a new and pleasant home."[41] A. D. Munson's *Minnesota Messenger* (1855) expressed the hope that in a few years the bluff above St. Paul would be "filled with the residences of our citizens." This prospect would then "meet the eye from the steamer, as she turned the point of land that hides the City from the view, and impress the stranger still more with the idea that the situation was well chosen." Munson, who appears to have been a not disinterested party in the matter, drew attention to the fact that two- to five-acre lots had already been laid out on this high ground and suggested that on these should be placed "the Cottage, *ornée* and Gothic, Byzantine or rural structure." He also praised a plan to put up a large mansion on this site: "the residents of, and visitors to Saint Paul, will at an early day have the pleasure of seeing, among the first objects that shall meet the eye upon one of our commanding bluffs, this splendid mansion."[42] Certain types of building should be made particularly impressive because of the significance which the visitor will attach to them: "on approaching many Western towns, the traveller beholds a large, elegant, brick edifice, attractive beyond all other structures in the place; and he soon learns to say: 'That is the schoolhouse.' "[43] Munson also advocated placing on the high bluffs above his city a College of St. Paul.

It would be a beautiful commentary upon the glorious institutions of our country, and upon the estimation placed upon them by the residents of the far North-West, if the stranger in coming among us, should from the deck of the noble steamer, miles below, recognize in the first building he saw, the towering walls of "The College of St. Paul," standing proudly upon some consecrated eminence, the resting place, as it were, of the spirit divine of wisdom come down for a brief season, to confer with man.[44]

Visitors could not be trusted to do all the work of publicizing a town to the outside world. Boosters knew this and showed an increasing sensitivity to the need to compensate for the defects of the reports of visitors. Charles Cist, who was one of the outstanding boosters of Cincinnati, saw one reason for his work as being that the real, vigorous economic life of that city was not seen by visitors because it was largely carried on in upper stories or the rear shops of ware-rooms and so was "to a great extent, out of sight." The visitor saw the smoking chimneys of Pittsburgh's factories and concluded that Pittsburgh was the more prosperous place. A book such as Cist's *Cincinnati in 1841* sought to redress the balance by drawing attention—through illustrations especially—to what went on in the rear shops and upper-floor premises of Cincinnati.[45]

The superficiality became worse as the "tourist" replaced the "traveler." The tourist was not as serious a visitor, more interested in pleasure and exotic scenery than in gathering impressions for informed reportage of social and economic conditions. The only towns and cities that appealed to tourists were the metropolises. A. Lillie complained of this metropolitan bias in most travel books:

having, it may be, entered [Canada] by way of Queenston, while his mind was dazzled with the glories of Philadelphia, New York, Boston, and the other cities south of the line ordinarily visited by tourists, it is a piece of condescension hardly to be looked for, that he [the tourist] should put himself to the trouble of noticing our smaller towns.[46]

Western cities began to lose their glamor and exotic character quite early. Isabella Bird visited Denver in 1873 and observed that it was "no longer the Denver of Hepworth Dixon. A shooting affray in the street is as rare as in Liverpool, and one no longer sees men dangling to the lamp-posts when one looks out in the morning." Denver had become an ordinary and therefore boring city—"a busy place, the *entrepôt* and distributing-point for an immense district, with good shops, some factories, fair hotels, and the usual deformities and refinements of civilization." Her eyes turned longingly to the wonders of nature. Denver "has a most glorious view of the Rocky Range. I should hate even to spend a week there. The sight of those glories so near and yet out of reach would make me nearly crazy."[47] In any event, methods of transportation and the routes commonly taken by travelers changed, and towns that had received a great deal of attention could suddenly find themselves consigned to oblivion, at least as far as description of them in travel books was concerned. This was particularly the case with river towns and coaching stations after the advent of the railroad. Bayrd Still has commented on how Milwaukee was pushed off the traveler's normal path and became a sideshow when travelers began to take the rail route west to Chicago and then on to the Pacific coast across the Mississippi and the Rockies.[48] It can be argued that the intensification of urban boosterism was in part a response to this state of affairs. There seemed to be an urgent need for many cities to get themselves noticed and publicized by means other than the publication of travelers' accounts.

The evidence certainly frequently suggests that visitors were influenced by boosters. Often, when visitors give samples of dialogue between themselves and the inhabitants of a new town which they are visiting, one notes a striking resemblance between what was said to them and the style and content of booster publications. It seems that no sooner had a stranger entered a town than its inhabitants would fall upon him and seek to boost it, to make sure that he did not leave without understanding that its attractions and prospects were superior to those of all other towns in the region, that it was the coming metropolis. Of course, visitors of the kind who wrote books were bound to receive special attention, especially if it became known that that was their purpose in visiting or they had some connection with newspapers."On entering a western city, as a first step you are pointed out all the advantages, which it has over every other place," reported a Boston newspaper in 1847.[49] John Gates Thurston reported to his brother from Galena in 1839:

To an eastern man who is unaccustomed to *stake cities,* as they were termed here, it is quite amusing to go on shore at the little villages that are daily springing up on the shores of the western rivers and which often consist of but two or three dwellings, and hear the proprietors expatiate on the astonishing advantages which their particular spot possesses over all other places for the rapid growth of a great city.[50]

In the 1870s the Atchison, Topeka and Sante Fe Railroad Company described the following as one of the experiences in store for the western traveler: "You stop at a city of 10,000, and upon every side you will hear it casually remarked that but a few years ago it was almost an unbroken wilderness."[51]

We shall be coming upon considerable evidence that booster clichés—or what we would regard as such—were the staple of conversation in western towns when their development and prospects were being considered.

An amusing account of the reception of a visitor appears in the fictional diary of John Parsons. Touring Indiana in 1840, Parsons arrived at Terre Haute and met the editor of the local newspaper, the *Wabash Enquirer*.

Mr. Chapman waxed most enthusiastic over the past and future of this city.

"Who," said he, "would have expected such rapid growth of a settlement in this situation? . . . Now in a location geographically on the direct line of travel from East to the far unexplored West, with the Wabash and Erie Canal on the way toward completion, and with citizens of intelligence and gentility, the town has grown beyond belief, and has a radiant future.

This editor talked just like one of his editorials, although whether Parsons was taking down his words verbatim or rephrased them later in what he considered the appropriate style is not clear. Certainly Parsons was taking down "facts" in a commonplace book while Chapman was speaking. On observing this, the editor was inspired to even greater flights of boosterish endeavor. He just happened to have in his pocket—no doubt ready for such an occasion—what any booster would have surely regarded as his trump card, a copy of a newspaper published in a rival town—the *Extra Equator* of Bloomington—which bestowed praise on Terre Haute. Chapman read out a selection of this praise.[52]

Australians—in particular, the people of Melbourne—gained a similar reputation for being extremely boosterish in the presence of strangers. As early as 1841 a visitor was complaining that the Melbournians had pestered him with their praises of the town "as if it were a second Rome or Babylon instead of being as it is a wen on the face of the earth."[53] Many years later Michael Davitt saw this as a trait that Americans and Australians had in common and that distinguished them from the British.

They take a pride in their cities and towns which does them credit. Visitors, as in the United States, are driven round to see the buildings, and to admire the general plan or situation or prospect of the place visited, and you find that all the citizens you meet with talk of their town or city in a spirit manifesting an honest pride in its progress, institutions, or plans for advancement.[54]

J. H. Roberts had a similar experience in Dunedin, New Zealand, in the 1880s—when Dunedin was sometimes described as a second Melbourne. Roberts was impressed by the way in which a local councillor was prepared to escort a stranger around his offices "and dilate to him of the wonders of his town." Like Davitt, Roberts observes that this sort of thing would not have happened back home in England. Furthermore, the councillor appears, like Parsons' editor, to have spoken in perfect boosterese: "The city you now see before you, all alive with the hum of active life and decorated with such buildings and bounded on one side by that forest of masts, was thirty-seven years ago but a hillside covered with ferns and moss."[55]

One thing which visitors found tiresome was being maneuvered into playing the boosters' game. Presumably it was obligatory at least to mutter polite words of agreement in response to the boosters' enthusiasm, but some were forced to go further than that. A peculiar Melbourne habit, complained about by many visitors, was to keep urging the newcomer to express his or her opinion about the city. David Kennedy tells of how the question, "How do you like Melbourne?," was "poured into our ears day and night." Here, according to Kennedy, is how a typical conversation went:

"You like Melbourne, do you?" "Yes." "Much?" "Very much." "But are you bearing very particularly in mind that the city is only thirty years old?" "Well, one is apt to forget that, but it's wonderful when you think of it." "Wonderful? Why, it's astonishing." "Undoubtedly."[56]

Nor would the conversation usually end there. The visitor would then be pressed to make a comparison between Melbourne and Sydney—which, needless to say, he was always expected to render very strongly in favor of the former.

The normal reaction of visitors was one of embarrassment. They often laughed—privately, or after they were safely away from the town—at the absurd aspirations of small western hamlets to become "the metropolis of the world."[57]

But it was the gravity that was intriguing. The people who uttered these apparent absurdities seemed to be very sincere and serious, to believe in what they were saying. They appeared incapable of seeing the humor, indeed the farce, in the situation—as did Charles Dickens, Mark Twain, and a host of other satirists who by their ridicule did so much to establish the modern image of boosterism. The question which one has to ask, without ever being able to arrive at a conclusive answer, is whether the people who talked in this style about their towns always did so, even among themselves, and instinctively fell into it when addressing strangers. Or did they reserve it for outsiders, calculatedly, and knowing the importance of the impression that they gained about a town and especially about the level of confidence felt by the local people in its prospects?

One of the key words in the travelers' reports is "pride." Given the contemporary assumptions about social evolution, it would be very surprising if there were not a large measure of genuineness in the pride expressed regarding the rapid emergence of towns out of the wilderness. People in the new societies of the nineteenth century seem to have been fascinated by the general phenomenon of town growth and to have liked to talk about it. The Russian Alexsandr Lakier traveled down the Mississippi in 1857 and found that,

if one meets up with a loquacious American . . . the latter can hardly avoid talking about every town and its advantages, and what kind of future it has in store. One town, he says, is flourishing, another is capable of improvement, a third will be a great commercial center; for every one of them he has a flattering hope.[58]

Many gazetteers and guidebooks were like this "loquacious American." They were ostensibly objective, but in their relentless accumulation of statistics of population, trade, numbers of churches, etc., became documents of exaltation of the urban West. Boosters in effect made a local application of this universal fascination and were in fact often torn between the desire to boost one town in particular and a wider enthusiasm for the general phenomenon of urban development on the frontier of which their town was but one manifestation.

In his study of the first decade of San Francisco Roger Lotchin concluded that boosterish language was infectious and that everyone used it.[59] Anselm Strauss has written:

The booster had an eager audience because the future concerned everyone. Perhaps most citizens of western cities had played this visionary game or listened in upon conversations and read the gazettes where such speculations were woven into the very reporting of daily events.[60]

Nor was the influence of boosting confined to the written word. Indeed, it could be argued that boosterism was so pervasive in the life of a young town that it became the dominant mode in which that life was perceived and interpreted.

For there were many manifestations of boosterism beyond the literary. It had an enormous impact on the physical form of a city and on how that form was understood. Buildings were used to convey messages about a town's character and destiny. Their purpose was defined not only in functional terms—which, had that been the sole purpose, would have often dictated smaller, cheaper, less grandiose premises[61]—but also in terms of what they "meant," what they conveyed about the inner life of the town. Arthur G. Guillemard visited Melbourne in the 1870s and observed that no expense had been spared "to make of Melbourne something whereof the nineteenth century might well feel proud; their sole aim to make it an object of wonder and admiration as the mightiest city of modern times." If this was indeed the case, the builders of Melbourne succeeded admirably as far as Guillemard was concerned. "One sees at a glance," he wrote, "the wonderful energy of the early settlers, which has enabled them in the short space of five-and-thirty years to plant a mighty city where before was a mere wilderness of scrub."[62] When a vast hotel opened in Tacoma in 1884, all the right responses were elicited. Rival cities were reported as marveling "at the daring of those who had poured their money into this beautiful hostelry, set down in the mud."[63] Indeed, if no "showy" buildings had been erected, boosters usually considered that some explanation was needed. For instance, the Oregon Immigration Board had to admit that Portland was not "a city of palaces."

While Portland has accumulated . . . a wealth which is greater in proportion to population than that of any other city in the United States, the very rapidity of their growth, has created a demand for additional capital to be used therein [in manufacturing and commerce], which has not only prevented the accumulation of a surplus which might be used in building for show alone, but has limited the use of capital in this channel to meeting, in part only, the pressing necessities of the hour.[64]

The tradition of seeing boosters as figures of farce, fit only for satirical treatment, owes much to Sinclair Lewis' *Babbitt* but can be traced back well before that into the nineteenth century when there was a persistent current of satire and debunking of the rhetorical extravagances in which many boosters indulged. In recent times there has been some rehabilitation of boosting. The popular image may remain intact, but some academic historians have been suggesting that boosting deserves to be taken a good deal more seriously as the predominant form in which discussion of the options available for the development of a community on the urban frontier took place. Furthermore, they have been providing examples of how boosting can be analyzed from this perspective. Carl Abbott has argued that boosterism was deeply serious because "urbanites took economic development as a moral imperative."

In Indianapolis and in other western cities, the antebellum boom triggered spirited public discussion about the character of the new commercial opportunities, about the economic needs of each city, and about the measures which might satisfy these wants. Newspapers, corporate reports, directories, pamphlets, and orations considered how each town could best exploit its new opportunities. Residents described current activities, advocated new projects, and detailed strategies for growth in a diverse and substantial body of literature which later historians frequently lumped under the term "boosterism." The resulting debate helped business and civic leaders to assess the situation they faced and to define a coherent economic program to be carried out by public and private action.[65]

But other historians, such as Don Harrison Doyle in his study of Jacksonville, Illinois, or Alan Artibise in his work on the Canadian prairie cities, especially Winnipeg, have placed less emphasis on the economic significance of boosting than on its role as community ideology, as a cement which held communities together or enabled them to form in circumstances in which the odds appeared to be strongly against the growth of community identity, cohesion, and sense of common purpose.[66] The more extravagant the optimism preached by the boosters, and the more determined they were to focus attention on the certainty of a great and glorious future for their city, the more likely it was that they were seeking to draw attention away from a present that was characterized by confusion, division, and doubt. Artibise has shown how boosters acted to foster the illusion that there was a unified community by creating an atmosphere in which dissent from growth goals or doubts about a town's prospects were treated not as objective and useful criticism but as a serious source of damage to those prospects and therefore deserving of censure and even suppression.

Both the seriousness and the extravagance have to be understood and explained. One expressed pride, optimism, determination to succeed; the other the need to counter forces and fears which often acted powerfully to undermine that determination and fragment a community's sense of purpose. Something of the background to boosting, and especially the extravagant kind that came to characterize cities such as Melbourne, may perhaps be understood by looking at the discussion which took place in Australia concerning the weakness of community in Australia's towns.

For at one stage Melbourne was criticized for deficiencies in the area of self-promotion. The famous American entrepreneur George Francis Train, when he was a merchant in Melbourne in the gold-rush era, 1853–55, condemned the elite of Melbourne for their lack of community-mindedness. The wealthy showed no interest in the improvement of the town. They preferred to make their money "and go home to England to buy a peerage and a name!"[67] Sir William Denison, who served a term as governor in the 1860s, also deplored the effects of people coming out to Australia just to earn enough money to be able to return to England and live in style. The result was a sacrifice of "duties to society." A man of this sort "has no general views; his thoughts centre upon himself; and he ceases, in fact, to be a member of a community."[68] One of the reasons why, in William Howitt's view, there was so little planning for the future in the Melbourne of the 1850s was "the fatal idea of going home."[69] Such remarks may help us to understand the effort that was put into fostering pride in the emergence of fine cities which were as good as those of the Old World.

Numerous studies have shown that one of the main functions of boosterism—and especially of the newspaper press, which in most young and growing towns was strongly oriented toward boosterish promotionalism—was to suppress information about, or divert attention from, the darker, grimmer, less hopeful aspects of urban life. This undoubtedly not only affects our perception of what actually happened—if, as we often have to, we rely on newspapers as our main source of information—but also affected the perceptions of contemporaries. The consequences of this will be examined in later chapters, for instance, in a discussion of the future-oriented atmosphere which characterized—or rather was commonly perceived as characterizing—many towns.

The purpose of most boosting was to preach, spread, and inculcate unqualified optimism. If problems or difficulties were referred to, they were usually referred to only in order to explain them away or to persuade people to believe that they were of little or no significance. The result was that eventually, in the twentieth century, boosters in the American Midwest in particular were accused of having damaged the development of the towns they had tried to boost by pretending that problems did not exist, diverting attention from them, discouraging criticism, and failing to get townspeople to face up to weaknesses in the town's economic condition while there was still time and opportunity to do something about them.[70] This problem was noted at the time in some towns, and not just in the United States. By the late 1850s it was evident that Geelong was falling behind in its rivalry with Melbourne. One writer attributed much of the blame for this to the way in which the town had been boosted:

Whatever the citizens assert the local press swear to, so that by the dint of energetic and exaggerated eulogies, Geelong has come to "assume a value though it has it not," and the Geelongese, from the effects of incessant repetition, are so familiarised with the deception, that they have become at length sincere believers in the mental mirage of their own creation, continuing incurable monomaniacs, buried in delusion.[71]

The negative, manipulative side of boosterism undoubtedly existed. But the other side was a strong vein of utopianism. Howard P. Segal has written: "The majority of boosters in late nineteenth and early twentieth century America were serious, practical, even reflective men who simply were convinced that American society was about to improve dramatically."[72] Even though they usually only boosted individual towns, what boosters were usually invoking was a broad utopian vision of what towns and cities should be and, in the case of their own town at least, certainly would be like. If one believed even a small part of their rhetoric, then one would be accepting that a type of community was in the process of realization in which most of the major social problems which confronted humankind would cease to exist and economic prosperity and social harmony would reign. Therefore, even though booster publications are mostly just about individual towns, collectively they amount to a celebration of the potential of urban development in new societies. This aspect is, indeed, seen at its most explicit in the work of writers on "the urban West" such as William Gilpin or Jesup W. Scott who, while seeking to confine their quest for the "great city" to one specific locality, kept being distracted from that enterprise by the instinct and desire to celebrate the rise of western urban society as a whole.[73]

There was a utopian aspect to interpretation of the "newness" of some towns. Here, for instance, is the mayor of Grand Rapids, Michigan, I. M. Weston, addressing a Burns Club banquet in 1889, and telling how he escorted an eastern gentleman around the city:

I drove him through our rich residence avenues on the hill, over the west side past our extensive factories and through the other interesting sections of the city, and asked if he desired to see more. He replied that he wanted to go away with a complete and correct idea of Grand Rapids, and he wished to be shown the poor part of the city. It required several minutes to think where I would take him, and it then occurred to me for the first time that we have no mean quarter in Grand Rapids. However, I took him to where I thought the poorest residences were, and there we found nothing but what was comfortable and even attractive. He asked with some surprise if this was the poorest part of Grand Rapids, and would hardly believe my statement when I told him it was. I assured him further that, besides having no crowded tenement district, no dilapidated quarters, every street and every block was absolutely safe for a respectable woman to walk unattended at any hour of the day or night.[74]

Mayor Weston would probably have claimed that his town was better in these respects than any other town in the region, but every other booster would have made the same claim about his own town. What unified their claims was that they were all made with reference to the same urban ideals. These ideals thus amounted collectively to a powerful vision of a new urban world in the process of being created free of the evils of the old. Indeed an 1890 booster publication of Helena, Montana, claimed that that town now had "a society in which even the cynic can find no fault—a society in its moral structure as pure as in any community on the face of the earth."[75] Cynicism and satire, not to mention our awareness of how things actually turned out, may have unduly distorted and damaged our perception of the genuine hopefulness which did suffuse such statements.

With the exception of the early decades of the nineteenth century in Canada and Australia, when colonial authorities endeavored to establish some control over urban creation and development, urbanization was almost always celebrated as an accomplishment of entrepreneurial capitalism. The rapid growth of fine-looking towns in the New World was seen as the achievement of capitalists far more than of any other section of the community. William M. Thayer's *Marvels of the New West* (1887) was quite unambiguous in its attribution of credit for what had been achieved. After describing the impressive buildings of the new towns of the northwest, it states that "there is a large class who give no attention to these matters, and doubtless undervalue them; but we speak of the ruling classes, who make the West what it is, and is to be."[76] When praise came to be assigned, there were few who expressed dissent from this type of proposition. Assigning blame for towns that did not look impressive was a different matter. Judging the Melbourne of the 1850s—"hurriedly put together," its buildings poorly constructed—to be "a most miserable failure" when compared with European cities, John Shaw noted that it was the creation of "the frequently uneducated gold-digger and uninstructed emigrant":

The town of Melbourne will remain, for some time to come, a memento of the old country; one, too, not of a very high and complimentary character. It represents, in a marked manner, and in dark and gloomy colours, the uneducated and tasteless classes which form so striking a feature in the great social fabric of the present community of Englishmen. It will remain a future indication to the rising generation of Englishmen and Melbournites, that their fathers and mothers belonged to a great and noble country, dispossessed, in a great measure, of good taste, and only partly educated.[77]

Workingmen were, however, not always inclined to remain silent when credit for what was "marvelous" about Melbourne was being given to others. That they could endeavor to appropriate the rhetoric for themselves is indicated by this extract from a speech by Charles Jardine Don, first workingman to be a member of the Victorian Parliament:

Look at yonder city, illuminated by its magic lamps, its windows glittering with wealth, a city with palaces worthy of kings, and temples worthy of gods, which labour has placed there in the short space of a quarter of a century. Twenty-five years ago where now the voices of the most accomplished vocalists resound, the wild howl of the savage corrobboree or the wind in the wilderness was alone heard, and by whom has this change been effected? By the rich, the wealthy, the kid-gloved, fine-handed gentry? No; by the horny-handed son of toil.[78]

However, the tone of most writing about the urbanization of new societies was one that equated it with the successful establishment of a capitalist system. Stewart Garvie Hilts has made an exhaustive analysis of editorials in the southwestern Ontario press between 1850 and 1900, and his conclusions would appear applicable more widely to the other new societies:

The efforts of entrepreneurial capitalists to promote urban growth were widely accepted in the communities of this era. There does appear to have been an "ethos" of progress and growth that represented much more than the individual booster or entrepreneur's position. . . . The pro-urban attitudes expressed in many community newspapers were boosting a capitalist economic system more than any individual urban centre.[79]

Poverty was seldom mentioned. If it was, the blame for it was usually attributed to personal weakness. Towns were usually judged by the impressiveness of their public buildings and by the fine commercial premises and homes of their leading citizens, the quality of which was given a moral interpretation as signifying what could be achieved in a particular town by hard work and enterprise. This bias in the assessment of towns was entrenched both by guidebook writers, whose aim was to encourage migration and investment, and by the accounts of travelers, whose visits were usually too brief and superficial to allow the gaining of impressions beyond those afforded by the most physically dominating homes and buildings. Rare indeed was the traveler such as James B. Brown who, after several pages of praise of the fine buildings of London, Ontario, "displaying variety of active industry, enterprise, comfort, and elegance," concluded with an account of the condition of blacks in the city.

Generally speaking, this coloured portion of the population, both in the country parts and in the towns and villages of Canada, live apart from the white inhabitants. They are very usually to be found collected together in the least valuable corners of the towns—their houses and style of living most frequently denoting a scale of civilization greatly inferior to the mass of the population surrounding them; among whom, it can scarcely be doubted, they too bitterly feel themselves to be merely "the hewers of wood and drawers of water."[80]

CHAPTER THREE

Old World and New World

THERE was much debate over what was distinctive about the new towns in the New World of the nineteenth century. Some commentators argued that there was no essential difference between them and the towns of the Old World and that urban development in the New World was best understood in relation to forces which were affecting the latter in very similar ways. This was one of the basic arguments of Adna Weber's *The Growth of Cities in the Nineteenth Century,* published in 1899. Weber showed that the urbanization of Australia in 1890 had a very different character from that of the United States in 1790, although at these respective dates they had basic similarities as countries of recent settlement. The answer was that "Australia is of the nineteenth, rather than the eighteenth century." "What is true of the Australia of 1891 is, in a greater or less degree, true of the other countries in the civilized world."[1] Boosters who wanted to present their towns as "normal," not "Western" or "colonial" and therefore freakish, liked to resort to this argument. "The city development, which is the characteristic feature of the West, is a necessary and natural result of the present aspect of civilization and its workings."[2]

In any event, were not the cities, like so much else in the New World, representative of, and made out of, the "invisible luggage" that migrants brought with them? This was the conclusion of Alexis de Tocqueville. In complete contrast to Frederick Jackson Turner sixty years later, he argued that the men who went out to people the American wilderness brought with them "the customs, the ideas, the needs of civilization" and implanted these in the wilderness.[3] There was not really a New World at all but a transplantation of the Old. A famous passage in a new Australian magazine published in 1849 argued against thinking at all in terms of the Old World–New World dichotomy. Worried that, if Australians thought that they were living in a "new country," they might think that they had to behave in a "new" way and social retrogression would follow, it urged its readers to understand that, "although the land we live in is a *new* country, its inhabitants are essentially an *old* people."[4]

Nevertheless, the notion of an antithesis between Old and New Worlds became well established, and most Old World visitors came to the New expecting to find great differences. They were amazed to find, in the urban sphere at least, great similarities.[5] One traveled a long way only to have the feeling that one might as well have stayed at home. F. Eldershaw wrote of new arrivals in Sydney that

> its being so like an English town seemed to strike them as positively absurd, that after having travelled sixteen thousand miles, to all appearance as much at home as if they had never left their own firesides, when by a trumpery journey of a few hundred miles in length they might have been in the midst of everything as charmingly foreign as the most fastidious admirer of change could desire.[6]

As for those who settled in the New World and played a part in the foundation of towns, there was surprisingly little consciousness that what they were doing was something special, historic, and never to be repeated, the founding of *new* towns for *new* societies.[7] Actual rituals associated with the reservation of a site or the laying out of a town were rare. We have seen that Governor Macquarie liked to perform them in New South Wales. A noted practitioner of this kind of ceremony, both in reality and in fiction, was John Galt, the Canada Company's principal agent in western Ontario in the 1820s. In his novel *Lawrie Todd* Galt included an account of "the ceremony of cutting down the first tree in the marketplace-to-be of Judiville." There was a procession through the woods, and seven cannon fired three times as the town's founders struck the first blow with their axes. A feast followed, and there was dancing.[8] There was also ritual associated with the founding of Stockwell in *Bogle Corbet*. But Galt was a real-life as well as novelistic founder of towns. In his *Autobiography* he described the founding of Guelph, a Canada Company town in Ontario. He elaborated a theory about the importance of ritual in the founding of towns. He planned to have work at Guelph begin on St. George's Day.

> This was not without design; I was well aware of the boding effect of a little solemnity on the minds of most men, and especially of the unlettered, such as the first class of settlers were likely to be, at eras which betokened destiny, like the launching of a vessel, or the birth of an enterprise, of which a horoscope might be cast. The founding of a town was certainly one of these, and accordingly I appointed a national holiday for the ceremony.

Here too there was the ritual of the striking of the first blow by an axe.[9] In another account Galt has his associate, Tiger Dunlop, dressed in blankets to suggest both kilt and toga and quaffing whiskey in a toast to "the unbuilt metropolis of the new World." An eyewitness also had Dunlop placing a lady's fan on the stump of the newly felled tree to suggest a layout for the streets.[10] Whether there were many other rituals of this kind is hard to say, but it is unlikely. Occasionally travelers record folk memories of a founding. When William Kingston visited Georgetown in Ontario, he was shown the spot "where, thirty-one years ago, George Taylor, who gave his name to the place, cut the first tree on that location." This inspired certain reflections by Kingston on the meaning of their telling him this. "Reminiscences such as those stood in the place of the historical records and legends of the Old World. George Taylor was the legitimate, the rightful conqueror of that once forest-wild."[11] But local histories were seldom clear as to whether a ritual was involved or not. Here, for instance, is an account of the founding of Granville in Licking County, Ohio, in 1805:

There was no work of human hands to greet their eyes except the little aboriginal mound of earth standing just in front of where the Town Hall now stands, and the surveyors marks upon the trees. They selected a very large beech tree, a little south of the center of the public square, and proceeded to cut it down. Mr. Coe, the surveyor, was present and assisted. All the men took turns in swinging the axes. While this was being done, Mr. Hiram Rose, either to have the prestige of cutting the first tree, or to prepare a support for the other, seized his axe and cut down a small, leaning hollow tree, and the other fell upon it. According to the letter, the hollow tree was the first one cut, but accordingly to the spirit the beech was the first.[12]

The normal state of affairs was probably that described in Edward Eggleston's novel *The Mystery of Metropolisville*. In the founding of that town there were no "mysterious rites or solemn ceremonies." "Neither Plausaby nor the silent partners interested with him cared for such classic customs."[13]

Some writers offered plans for new towns, for example, T. J. Maslen in *The Friend of Australia*.[14] In *The Happy Colony* (1854) Robert Pemberton included a large fold-out map of a model town for his colony which he proposed should be established in New Zealand. He was one of the few writers who actually argued that new towns should have new styles of design. He advocated using the circle, not the right angle, in town planning: "You must make up your minds to abandon the system of the old countries in everything relating to the bad formation of towns as well as the bad formation of minds; and discard, and for ever renounce, all crooked lanes, angles, narrow streets, filthy alleys, and nasty courts and *impasses.*"[15]

Few commentators showed as acute a sensitivity to the uniqueness of the opportunity as did the anonymous author of "Melbourne as It Is, and as It Ought To Be" in *The Australasian* in 1850.

Instead of inheriting the labours of fifty generations, *we* have to commence and carry out everything for ourselves. We have dispossessed the natives of their lands, but have taken possession of neither cities, nor vineyards, nor oliveyards. Whatever is done *now* in planning towns, laying down lines of road, selecting sites for townships, &c., receives augmented importance from the impress it must give to the future. The main streets and approaches of a new town are, so to speak, the skeleton to which every thing done subsequently must be referred and adapted. Collectively they form the *rough sketch* of the future city.[16]

There were those who, because of these opportunities, hoped that New World cities would be better than those of the Old.[17] Certainly there was, especially in Australia and New Zealand, a very adverse and disappointed reaction when Old World city evils began to appear in the New World.[18]

It is well known that Thomas Jefferson disliked cities and was fearful of the consequences of their development in the United States. However, what he had in mind were great industrial cities. He had little objection to such cities as had developed by the end of the eighteenth century. Nor did Crèvecoeur, another exponent of agrarianism. He admired New York and saw America as lucky in having been spared cities of the kind that he had known in Europe.[19]

But gradually, as the nineteenth century progressed, these attitudes began to change. There was a growth of concern about America's Eastern cities as they became too "European"—too large, congested, industrial, and slum-ridden. They attracted large numbers of immigrants, whereas the West was seen as being built up mainly by "Yankees," and so a West-East distinction began to replace or at least to supplement and complicate the old one that distinguished clearly between Europe and America. The hope was expressed that in the cities of the West the original hopes for a "New World" society could still be fulfilled. They would be different and better.[20] Charles N. Glaab has found Jeffersonianism alive and well in the writings of the enthusiasts for an urban West. They argued that the cities of the East had become corrupt, sinful, dangerous to republican virtues. But in the West cities would be different.[21] Probably the climax of the trend toward seeing the West as the area of hope for a better urban way of life was General Jackson Palmer's vision for Colorado Springs:

> It is more dangerous to live in the proximity of a great city such as New York than it would be amongst the Indians on the Plains. . . . We shall have a new and better civilization in the far West; only may the people never get to be as thick as on the Eastern seaboard. We will surrender that briny border as a sort of extensive Castle Garden to receive and filter the foreign swarms and prepare them by a gradual process for coming to the inner temple of Americanism out in Colorado, where Republican institutions will be maintained in pristine purity. Isn't that a logical as well as a unique notion?[22]

But the "frontier" phase of settlement was all too brief, and the fear of Eastern city life encroaching on and undermining Western society soon arose. In Daniel R. Curtiss' *Western Portraiture and Emigrant's Guide* (1852), a book designed to attract people to live in the West, J. P. Thompson wrote of how good life in a Western village would be for the mechanics and clerks "eking out a scanty subsistence in New York upon a precarious income." But then he added:

> If, however, *too* many should crowd at once into the same place, competition would ensue, and with it would come many of the evils of city life. Indeed I almost hesitate to let out the secret of this western paradise, and I surely dread to have its Arcadian repose disturbed by the puffing of the locomotive with an express train from New York.

This reminded Thompson of how the great railroads would "essentially modify the main features of western life." They would introduce "more of the city element into business," and in due time "these prairies will be attached to the suburbs of New York."[23]

In any discussion of the differences between Old and New World cities abundance of space and its implications featured prominently. New World cities were seen as having the means to escape congestion, to become all suburb. John Martineau reported in *Letters from Australia* (1869): "the space covered by Melbourne and its suburbs is, compared with an English or European town, out of all proportion large for the population."[24] This was the basis of the defence of the growth of large cities in Australia which was offered by H. H. Hayter, the Government Statistician of Victoria, in 1891.

It must be remembered that large towns of recent growth are spread out so as to cover a much larger surface in porportion to population than has ever been occupied by the older cities. The cheap and easy means of communication afforded by trams and suburban trains enables workmen and others, whose daily occupation requires their presence in town, to live in the suburbs; and, in consequence, slums, with their depraved and unwholesome concomitants, become proportionately reduced in number and extent.[25]

These new cities seemed to have no "heart" or focus of the traditional kind. "It all appeared to me as one great town," wrote C. R. Carter of Melbourne; "a stranger cannot of himself distinguish the difference; for the streets of the city are continued so as either to intersect, or nearly to communicate with, those of the nearest of the suburban boroughs."[26] The absence of the Old World type of city center was welcomed by those who disliked such areas, in part because of their reputation as a breeding-ground and shelter for crime and vice. Captain Willard Glazier praised the designers of America's western towns for having ensured that "no future increase of population, with its attendant demands for dwelling and business houses, can ever transform them into an aggregation of dense, stifling streets and lanes, such as are too often found in our first-class eastern cities."[27]

Another characteristic was rapidity of growth. This was an observation that was made by Old World visitors about almost every New World town founded in the nineteenth century. "Nothing earns our admiration as much as the rapid rise of towns in the domain of the American Union," wrote Count Adelbert Baudissin in 1854. After only a decade or so of growth a town will have become flourishing and populous and will "surpass by far our old, venerable, and expanded native town [in Germany] in prosperity and number of inhabitants." As a result, German visitors to such towns "fall into just astonishment at the wonder which unfolds itself to our sight."[28] This rapidity of growth came to be regarded as a characteristic of American towns in particular. In the other new countries, if a town was growing fast, it was said to be exhibiting "Yankee" rapidity.[29] The rate of Sydney's growth, wrote William Hughes "has no parallel, excepting in the newly-created cities of the United States."[30]

When it was asked why American towns grew so fast, one answer that was often given was that they were the products of "liberty," both political and economic. Timothy Flint compared Cincinnati in the 1820s with "imperial Petersburg," where a great and intelligent despot said, "Let there be a city," and a city arose upon a Golgotha, upon piles of human bones and skulls, that gave consistency to a morass. The awe of a numberless soldiery, the concentrated resources of thirty millions of slaves, the will of the sovereign, who made the same use of men that the mason does of bricks and mortar, must all conspire to form a city in that place. . . .

How different are the fostering efforts of liberty. . . . No troops are stationed, no public money lavished here. It is not even the state metropolis. The people build and multiply imperceptibly and in silence. Nothing is forced. This magnificent result is only the development of our free and noble institutions, upon a fertile soil. Nor is this place the solitary point, where the genius of our institutions is working this result. Numerous cities and towns, over an extent of two thousands of miles, are emulating the growth of this place. The banks of the Ohio are destined shortly to become almost a continued village.[31]

Some would, no doubt, have argued that all this high-flown talk about "liberty" concealed the fact that most new American towns were the product of rampant speculation and greed to maximize profit from the sale of town lots. That was what "liberty" permitted. "Gain! Gain! Gain! is the beginning, the middle and the end, the *alpha* and *omega* of the founders of American towns," wrote one critic, Morris Birkbeck.[32] But against this one could point to the vast number of American towns which failed after having been founded for speculative reasons. Something more than speculation was required to explain the great *growth* of towns in the United States. It was an open, competitive situation in which a vast number of locations was tried and only those survived where a town was "destined" by "nature" to be. By contrast, governments arbitrarily chose a few locations. These might prove to be unsuitable, but people had to live with the results of that choice. Timothy Flint responded to those who emphasized the speculative aspect of American town promotion:

speculation and wealth, without natural advantages, in the United States, cannot force a town. Every thing, with us, must be free, even to the advancement of a town. . . . If speculation, as is said, founded this flourishing town, it happened for once to select the place, where nature and the actual position of things called for one.[33]

The debate over the role—actual and desirable—of "liberty" in the making of new towns in the New World became focused in one set of contrasts which were constantly being made—between the towns of Canada and the towns of neighboring regions of the United States, especially upstate New York. To some it seemed that the American towns represented what all New World towns could be if their development were left unrestrained, and the Canadian towns were what they were because they had not been allowed to attain that potential.

The contrast, made so frequently because the towns were so close to one another across a major international border, was usually heavily in favor of the American towns. John Howison wrote in *Sketches of Upper Canada* (1821): "The villages on the American frontier indeed form a striking contrast with those on the Canadian side. There, bustle, improvement, and animation, fill every street; here, dulness, decay, and apathy, discourage enterprise and repress exertion."[34] The Durham Report of 1839 described the differences in strikingly similar terms. Like Howison, it drew particular attention to the fine city of Buffalo.[35]

The Durham Report used the contrast to advance a case for political and constitutional changes in Canada, particularly the union of the two Canadas, the United States being seen as proof of the advantages of having a central government capable of organizing "internal improvements" such as roads and canals. But some went further than this and attributed America's superiority to its possession of a free, democratic system of government. An example is Donald McLeod who participated in the 1838 Rebellion as Commander-in-Chief of the Western Division of the "Patriot" Army. From exile in Cleveland, Ohio, he published in 1841 a pamphlet on the settlement of Upper Canada in which he condemned British colonial rule over that region. British policy of frustrating the growth of colonial manufacturing was destructive of that "spirit of enterprise" which, among other things, "plants cities, towns and villages; paves the streets, rears the college dome and academy hall." The contrast between Upper Canada and western New York, with its "cities and well paved streets, populous towns, and flourishing villages," he attributed entirely to the fact that in America "THE PEOPLE GOVERN THEM-SELVES." He referred to the glaring contrast between, on the one hand, Rochester and Buffalo and, on the other, Toronto," a foul, loathsome, disgusting capital, abounding in filthy lanes and alleys; muddy and un-paved streets, [which] as a whole, presents a dreary and disagreeable aspect, both from its low situation, and the mean and contemptible ap-pearance of the buildings." His vision was of a self-governing Canada with "young cities rising up, as if by magic, among the stumps and trees," Canada's own "Oswegos, Buffalos[,] Clevelands and Detroits—very Liverpools in miniature."[36]

But such interpretations of the causes of town growth in the United States were not universally accepted. The debate over one city in particular—Buffalo—went to the very heart of the issue of the relationship between town-building and "liberty" in the New World. The alternative explanation for the more favorable impression that the American towns made was that it was the result of speculation, "liberty" in the economic sphere, and was therefore only superficial. Captain J. E. Alexander, an English visitor of the early 1830s, asked a Canadian farmer why the American towns were larger than the Canadian towns. The reply was:

"The American towns or villages are often larger than the Canadian ones opposite to them, because New-York speculators advance money to those who wish to build houses, and endeavour to turn them to account, by afterwards selling them; but most of those houses we see over the water are unfurnished, and have reverted to the speculators who advanced the sum to build them, the architects having been ruined." According to my informant's account, they were much in the same state as many houses in Moscow after it was ordered by his late Imperial Majesty to be rebuilt. Walls, roofs, doors, and windows, were all in order towards the street, but the inside was void.[37]

W. H. Smith in *Canada: Past, Present and Future* (1851) referred to contemporary opinion that "the *City* of Toronto will not bear mentioning in the same breath with either of the American *towns,* Rochester or Buffalo." But Smith argued that this appearance of greater prosperity was only superficial, to be explained by the fact that the Americans were "a trading, travelling, *smart,* speculating people" who "love fine houses, painted with fine colours (bright green, yellow, and red, being the predominating)." "Some American towns in good situations for business, certainly have sprung up like magic," he conceded; "but we have heard from pretty good authority that many of the establishments in these places are rather ephemeral." The American town tended to be "showy"; the English settlement, as in Upper Canada, was more solid and comfortable. Indeed, Smith broadened this into an argument that the same kind of contrast emerged wherever in the United States itself one found side by side an "American" or "Yankee" settlement—showy but with a high rate of business failures and other symptoms of commercial instability—and an "English" town, i.e., one founded by settlers from England. The latter might look "slow," but its business was usually much more solidly based.[38] Americans themselves frequently made comparisons between "progressive" "American" towns, and dull, stagnant villages founded by

Germans and other Europeans who did not have the "Yankee" genius for city-building.[39]

John Howison admitted that there were some who said "that not one-tenth part of the houses in Buffalo are paid for, and that the greater number of these are already mortgaged." But he responded with one of the most commonly argued defences of the American way of building towns: "of what importance are the embarrassments of a few individuals. if society in general derives advantage from the circumstances which occasioned them?"[40] Captain Frederick Marryat came to a similar conclusion. He was a great admirer of Buffalo, seeing it as "one of the wonders of America," "remarkably well built," a beautiful city risen like magic from the wilderness. However, unlike most other travelers, Marryat discovered the reality behind the "magic" explanation for the rise of a city such as Buffalo.

The person who was the cause of this unusual size was a Mr. Rathbun, who now lies incarcerated in a gaol of his own building. It was he who built all the hotels, churches, and other public offices; in fact, every structure worthy of observation in the whole town was projected, contracted for, and executed by Mr. Rathbun.

But Rathbun had now, as a result of the great crash, been found out in a massive operation of forging names of endorsers of two million dollars worth of bills and was awaiting trial. Thus the splendor of Buffalo was exposed as fraudulent, the product of massive dishonesty by a speculator. But Marryat warned against being too hasty in condemning the speculative character of American city-building.

If the parties who speculate are ruined, provided the money has been laid out, as it usually is in America, upon real property—such as wharfs, houses, &c.—a new country becomes a gainer, as the improvements are made and remain, although they fall into other hands. And it should be further pointed out, that the Americans are justified in their speculations from the fact, that property improved rises so fast in value, that they are soon able to meet all claims and realize a handsome profit. They speculate on the future; but the future with them is not distant as it is with us, ten years in America being, as I have before observed, equal to a century in Europe; they are therefore warranted in so speculating. The property in Buffalo is now worth one hundred times what it was when the first speculators commenced; for as the country and cities become peopled, and the communication becomes easy, so does the value of every thing increase.

Toronto was not like Buffalo, not because of any innate difference between "English" and "American" ways of city-building, but simply because "the Canadas cannot obtain the credit which is given to the United States, and of which Buffalo has her portion."[41]

It was not just in the economic sphere that the towns of the New World were seen as characterized by "liberty." It was defined also as a social phenomenon, and here too the adjective "American" was often used to describe the more extreme and unqualified manifestations. New World towns seemed to have a distinctive tone. Rupert Brooke thought that most of the towns that he saw in Ontario were "a little too vivacious or too pert to be European."[42] Captain Marryat had a theory that in a new country, because of the "constant change and transition," "go where you will you are sure to fall in with a certain portion of intelligent, educated people." Country towns in the Old World, "where every thing is settled, and generation succeeds generation," were usually very dull places.[43] Marryat's insight that all classes participated in migration and that in their early stages of development frontier towns reflected this in their social structure appeared also in Edward Dicey's *Six Months in the Federal States.* "This very mixture of all classes which you find throughout the West gives a freedom, and also an originality, to the society in small towns, which you would not find under similar circumstances in England."[44]

Charles Hursthouse referred to the effects of migration to explain why New Zealand's towns differed radically in social tone and structure from towns in England. They contained "multifarious populations," people brought together from many different places, and so there was "a social variety, a vigour, boldness, and orginality of character to these little antipodal communities, which we should find little trace of in the small town populations of the mother-country."[45] The exaltation of America's towns as the product of "liberty" received an antipodean echo in an English traveler's praise of the very young Melbourne of 1839: "In this town are already benefit societies and other institutions, which have rapidly sprung up, proving by their very creation, the firm and healthful bonds of society which already exist in a community progressing to maturity *through individual energy alone*."[46]

There was a negative aspect to the operation of this kind of "liberty." In gold-rush Melbourne, people's faces were observed to be marked by anxiety, bewilderment, indecision. In the streets they were separated by their intense busy-ness, hurrying to and fro, intent on making money.[47]

The non-relaxed, "busy" character of street crowds in young American cities was also often observed.

There was certainly plenty of effort to define what was distinctive about the new towns of the New World. But such definitions never really became firmly established, for constantly countering and undermining them was the force of an alternative standard of assessment. This was the Old World standard, used not only—and inevitably—by travelers and overseas commentators but also by the people of the new towns themselves. The questions that were customarily asked about a town were: how does it compare with an Old World city? How closely does it resemble one? And the scale that was used to interpret the responses was one of approval and disapproval. The more closely a town resembled an Old World urban community, the more likely it was to be praised. If distinctive "frontier" characteristics were detected, they were usually deplored. Promoters and boosters of New World towns drew attention to as many features of Old World urban civilization as they could with any degree of plausibility claim to exist in them.

The kind of description which, it seems, most town boosters yearned to have made of their towns is the following account of Denver by a visitor from the East in 1881: "Except that the town is *squared,* and not close knit, it might belong in Ohio, or even in New England. There are shops that would do credit to Broadway, and houses that would fit in our oldest towns."[48]

The tone was one of gratification that this was so. Of course, it was natural that writers from the East or the Old World would use towns there as their standard of comparison when describing the new towns. Migrants must have been constantly doing the same in the letters which they sent to friends and relatives whom they had left behind. It was commonplace for shops, buildings, houses, streets to be referred to as such as "would do credit to an English (or Eastern) city." "The first impression of Sydney was favourable," wrote Nat Gould in *Town and Bush* (1896). The reason was not that it was exotic or excitingly different and antipodean. "It reminded me of an English city transplanted in its entirety to the other side of the world. There is an Old-World look about Sydney that English visitors are, as a rule, surprised to see in Australia."[49] Perceptions of Sydney became dominated by the idea that it was a very "British" city. That Sydney was a thoroughly "English" or "British" city became a stereotype. Most Australian writers described Sydney and Melbourne with urban imagery that was derived directly from contemporary discussion of London. The same styles of urban writing were used, the same moral geography detected or imposed. Graeme Davison has shown how writers made Sydney over into an antipodean version or replica of London.[50] Melbourne was given similar treatment. In *Victoria in 1880* Garnet Walch traced a large number of apparent similarities between Melbourne and London and cited an article in which James Smith asked "why should many of the features—topographical and social —of London and its suburbs . . . repeat themselves in Melbourne and its precincts?" In trying to answer this question Smith referred to "certain natural tendencies and propensities operating unconsciously to ourselves, but with a constant and irresistible force." One of these tendencies, it appeared, was that "Englishmen reproduce England wherever they go."[51] Percy Clarke in *The "New Chum" in Australia* (1886) put it this way: "Melbourne appears in a great many points to be aping her mother metropolis of the other end of the globe."[52]

The "English," "Eastern," or "Old World" character of the towns was constantly described as causing surprise, even amazement. Assumptions as to what the towns were like were based on conventional ideas about social evolution (which will be discussed in the next chapter). Attached to the image of the "colonial" or "frontier" town were certain stereotypes. In a frontier town speculation raged, social status was determined by wealth, not by culture or intelligence. One expected that, if one went there, one would be constantly shocked by unconventionalities, by crude behavior in primitive surroundings. The conventional view and the effort made to combat it are both illustrated by Edward Brown Fitton's publication in *New Zealand* (1856) of a letter written back to England by a Canterbury settler:

I expect you would be surprised to see how very little the reality agrees with the notion formed at home of an early colonial life. There is all the refinement and civilization already of a country town in England. Our dress, manners, and habits, and every thing are the same; shops to supply you with every thing . . . Believe me, there is nothing wild or savage (hardly colonial), in our mode of life.[53]

Writers of guidebooks who described the towns of the new countries often referred to the combatting of ignorance and misconceptions as one of their principal objectives. One such writer, A. Lillie, wrote that most people who arrived in Canada imagined that, with the exception of a few large cities, the country was "covered with forests, in the midst of which there may present itself, here and there, an insignificant village, which may come, some time or other, to possess some size, and be of some importance."[54] William H. G. Kingston confessed in *Western Wanderings* (1856) to having supposed, when told that he should visit London, Paris, Woodstock, and Hamilton—all towns in Ontario—that these were "little villages with big names somewhere in the backwoods." From the writings of Susanna Moodie he had been led to expect to find everything "in the rough beyond the shores of the St. Lawrence." His image of Toronto was of "a primitive jumble of log-huts, brick-buildings, mud-cottages, and plank-houses and shanties." Then came the stock description of the response to the reality. "Our surprise, therefore, was very great, and very agreeable, to find ourselves in a large, handsome, admirably-laid-out city."[55] In another book Kingston wrote that many people in England did not imagine "that towns or houses existed in the colonies."[56]

If their heads were full of misconceptions of this type, it is no wonder that migrants and visitors were reported to react with amazement at what they found awaiting them in the New World—fine, modern cities that matched those of the Old World, indeed were extraordinarily similar to them. F. Eldershaw in *Australia as It Really Is* (1854) describes their astonishment at Sydney's magnitude and "the Old-English-like aspect of its houses, streets, and shops" as "often most ludicrously exhibited."[57] When the voice of the migrant is heard directly, it usually conforms to and confirms these generalizations made about migrants' reactions. When James Nichols arrived at Picton in New Zealand in 1874, he found it to be

a far superior place to whatever I had anticipated seeing in New Zealand, for having never read or noticed any account of the country before coming out, all I had got into my head was Mud Shantys. I soon learned however that this was but a poor town compared with others such as Christchurch, Nelson, or Dunedin, but this was quite enough to give me a more favourable idea of the country, for the buildings looked quite clean & homely.[58]

Nichols went out to New Zealand in spite of his belief that its towns consisted only of "Mud Shantys" and without having read any account of New Zealand. But promoters of and propagandists for emigration knew that they could not rely on this usually being the case. It was essential to try to remove such misconceptions from people's minds at the point of decision as to whether to emigrate. They had to be persuaded to "see" the new countries in the way that Nichols did upon his arrival. The descriptions of New World towns are a very important element in emigrant guidebooks and other works designed to boost the new countries, even if a substantial part of these books is devoted to the settlement of the land. Their condition was constantly used to combat stereotypes about colonial and frontier societies and to remove inhibitions about emigrating to or investing in them. The towns functioned as one of the most important indexes of the level of civilization attained in the New World.

In emigrant guidebooks descriptions of towns are one of the major sources of reassurance for prospective but frightened migrants. They are assured that the frontier or the colonies are not what many of them think they are, and the proof that is offered is the civilized state of the towns. The writers strive to show that the conventional view of frontier societies as crude, primitive places is not accurate.

The kind of reassurance that was needed can be illustrated by the case of the brother of Ludwig Leichhardt, a German who was one of the most famous explorers of Australia and who disappeared mysteriously in the desert. William refused to go to live in Australia because he "was especially scared by the thoughts of finding here a wilderness, cannibals, and coarse settlers." Ludwig wrote from Sydney: "Had he seen the growing city, supplied with everything that European luxury desires—even the needs of a scientist of some means—he would have come perhaps and shared my fate." It is ironic that that fate was ultimately to lead to Ludwig's perishing in the Australian wilderness which had so scared his brother. Ludwig was extremely enthusiastic about Sydney. "Abandon all ideas of a wilderness," he told his mother. "Wealthy people, and even paupers, enjoy greater comforts than do the inhabitants of Mark Brandenburg and yourself."[59]

Travel and guidebook authors, railway companies, and the other agencies engaged in promoting emigration constantly publicized and emphasized the "Eastern" or "Old World" characteristics of the cities of the New World.[60] W. H. G. Kingston provided the reassurance through the medium of a novel about a family whose decision to migrate was formed after a visit from a man who had emigrated some years earlier. He told them that Sydney was "a handsome city, well lighted and paved, with broad streets and shops, which may vie in magnificence with many in London." Kingston dwelt on the misconceptions that people in England had about colonial society and then, when his family arrived in Adelaide, he recorded their astonishment "when they found themselves driving between large houses and buildings of all descriptions, and shops full of merchandise."[61] Another novel with a similar purpose is *Life's Work As It Is* by "A Colonist," published in London in 1867. The author claims that his book is inspired by a real-life story of a young woman who, having emigrated to South Australia without knowing anything about Adelaide and thinking that she was going to "a land of uncivilization," described thus what she found there: "On every side I see fashion and elegance. Shops innumerable, and handsomely-appointed ladies in their carriages, and dresses nearly equal to Regent Street." The family in "A Colonist's" novel behave in a similar way to Kingston's. They arrive in Adelaide, are amazed at the shops and streets, and "could scarcely fancy themselves out of England."[62] Bernard Smith has argued that the purpose of many Australian paintings of this period was similar. "Evidence of the Britishness of colonial life is being provided for the information of friends and relatives back home."[63]

Enormous quantities of this kind of reassurance are to be found in the booster and travel literature of the American West. One example may stand for many. Here is the Board of Trade boosting Spokane Falls in Washington:

As all the citizens are from older portions of the Union, they have brought with them the social habits and observances of their former homes, and the stranger who takes up his abode in Spokane Falls will find as refined and cultivated a class of people as can be met with anywhere. . . . many of the private residences would attract attention in cities many times larger than Spokane Falls.[64]

Particular attention was drawn to the strength in a Western town of cultural features derived from New England or the East. Nathan H. Parker's *Kansas and Nebraska Handbook* in 1857 included the following passage on the population of Omaha:

They are generally from the cultivated and educated classes of the East. In the character of its society, as regards intelligence and culture, genteel, and even fashionable life, Omaha City rivals the best town of twice her population which can be named in New York or New England.

As an evidence of this, we refer to a course of ten lectures, delivered under the auspices of its library association, by citizens of the place, which, both in the character of the lectures delivered, and of the audiences assembled to listen to them, would do the highest credit to an eastern city.[65]

Proof of an Eastern influence was especially needed in view of the widespread impact of the 1847 lecture by the Connecticut divine Dr.

Horace Bushnell, on "Barbarism, the First Danger." In this Bushnell argued that in the West there was a tendency to "relapse into barbarism" which "grew out of the disruption of social, religious, and political ties in the case of those seeking homes in the West—the jarring and heterogeneous character of the social elements, drawn as they are from all quarters of the world—and the unbridled license resulting from the well known disregard, in new communities, of the various restraints by which men are moulded and held in check in the older States." A typical rebuttal of this appeared in Daniel R. Curtiss' *Western Portraiture, and Emigrants' Guide* (1852) in which is used what would now be called the "invisible luggage" argument: the migrants were intelligent Easterners, "many removes from 'barbarism', and we see no reason why a mere change of location should transform them from civilized to barbarous men."[66]

It was often claimed that migrants and travelers would—and did—feel that they were back in England or the East, that it was as if they had not left home.[67] James Ballantyne claimed that "many a one on coming to Melbourne has said that he felt as though *he had scarcely gone from home:* Everything seems to be *'just what he left behind him'* when he quitted the streets of Liverpool, Glasgow, or London, for this new shore. Melbourne is London reproduced; Victoria is another England."[68]

A Canadian example of the use of descriptions of towns to improve the image of a country or region in the eyes of potential investors and migrants appears in James B. Brown's *Views of Canada and the Colonists* (1851). Brown described London, Ontario, with its industries, its newspapers, its streets laid out "in perfectly straight lines," "the court-house, public square, market-house, mechanics' institute, stately churches, chapels, gay and spacious shops and streets, displaying variety of active industry, enterprise, comfort, and elegance." He commented on the town's appearance:

I have no doubt that many reading such particulars will have afterwards different views with regard to the condition of Canada as a prosperous field for emigration. I was myself very pleasingly disappointed upon visiting Canada; having had little idea that the country could show so large a share of solid comforts, with its numerous openings for enterprise, along with not only the enjoyments, but very many of the luxuries and elegancies of life.

Brown then quoted a statement made at a public meeting in London in 1843 by a traveler. This visitor referred to the quality of the town, its fine shops and buildings, and claimed that these facts, when publicized by persons such as himself, "will speak trumpet-tongued" and destroy the notion "that coming to Canada is coming to the back woods of a wilderness." As a result Canada will be recognized as "the natural and the fittest outlet for the superabundant capital, people, and enterprise of the mother country."[69] These were words that the business people and civic leaders of London must have enjoyed hearing, and they must surely have reinforced a determination to build their town along lines that the Old World would approve.

The negative image itself had a role to play in the boosting of the New World. The contrast between it and the reality was so striking that the sameness, the similarity between Old and New World cities, was transformed from something that might have been dull and disappointing into something special, even miraculous.

So far the reactions that have been quoted have almost all been ones of approval and gratification at the "Old World" character of New World towns. But there were some who were disappointed that these towns were so lacking in exotic features. Naturally, such feelings were associated in particular with tourists and writers in search of colorful copy for their books. They were often not at all happy about the absence of "frontier" characteristics. "After a long, wearisome voyage," wrote John Martineau of the arrival in Melbourne in *Letters From Australia* (1869), "the first impression is almost one of disappointment at having come so far only to see sights and hear sounds so familiar."[70] John Henderson in *Excursions and Adventures in New South Wales* (1854) expressed himself as disappointed with Sydney. "It was too like home; I had looked for something foreign and Oriental in its appearance; but I found that, excepting a few verandahs, and the lofty and stately Norfolk Island pine, it coincided much with a second or third-class town in England."[71] Nor does it seem that all migrants were excited and pleased by the similarity of the new towns to the old ones that they had left behind. They had, after all, made an effort to escape from the "Old World" environment, and the features of its cities would not have had happy associations for many of them. In *Colonial Experiences* (1877) W. J. Pratt thought that the negative reaction was quite common.

Recent arrivals are often surprised and disappointed at finding the provinces exhibiting the advanced civilization, and so many of the characteristics of the old established centres of population to which they have been accustomed, and which having so recently left, with perhaps too sanguine expectations, they can hardly realize the fact of being in a new country, and often wish it exhibited a little less of the old (which perhaps from a bitter experience they had hoped had been left far behind) and more of the new.[72]

On an "editorial tour" from Dayton, Ohio, in the late 1870s, William D. Bickham found in Denver "a general absence of frontier ruggedness" and "more of the repose of a settled city than I had anticipated." It was very good that "life in the City of the Plains compares so agreeably with our older civilization." But this conclusion bore a warning for migrants: "he who goes to Denver hoping to find something better than the home of his boyhood, will not realize his anticipations—a common mistake of people who go west to grow up with the country."[73]

William Westgarth, one of the most sensitive commentators on perceptions of the nineteenth-century Australian city, detected a variety of reactions among newly arrived settlers in Melbourne. He appears to have listened to what they had to say "as they stared about them with a visible interest and curiosity, on being landed at the wharf." The positive reaction which has been emphasized so far in this chapter—"surprise and admiration at the busy aspect and the indication of rapid progress they see around them"—is described by Westgarth as coming mainly from migrants with "educated and thinking minds," the sort of people most likely to leave a written record of how they felt.

But with a great proportion of the immigrants the expression is one of complete disappointment. They look around upon diminutive houses, many of them of wood, with a very tenth-rate appearance, and upon roads that are ever in the agonies of construction, and of course for the time making matters worse than before.

These were the roads that they would have to struggle along, the houses that they would have to seek accommodation in, often at exorbitant rent; ". . . at every step they are disturbed by experience of unwonted expense and inconvenience."[74] The present was too burdensome and worrying for these people to have any inclination to enthuse about progress and future prospects. It should be noted that Westgarth was writing about the Melbourne of the gold-rush era, a place of extreme confusion and rapid growth.

One of the most penetrating analyses of the migrant's state of mind on arrival in a new colonial city is probably that written by Charles John Baker in *Sydney and Melbourne* (1845). He too acknowledges that there is much initial disappointment at the sight of Melbourne. He tries to explain what there is in the scene that makes a newcomer so "depressed in spirit."

No snug quiet-looking residence is seen marking the abode of a man of leisure, or of a family voluntarily living there on their private fortune; the inhabitants, on the contrary, are an active people, immersed in the affairs of this world, and the busy aspect which the town thus acquires forcibly distinguishes it from any in England, where there is always some admixture of the idle, and the independent, and retired in life. Then again, at Melbourne, there are no old people, and not many even who are advanced enough to come within the denomination of middle aged; and the countenances of all have generally a keener and a more self-confident expression than those met with in an English town. Everything, in fact, unites in forcibly impressing a truth, painful to the indolent and timid mind, that to succeed, an emigrant must exert all the energy he can command, and rely, under Providence, on himself alone.

But Baker went on to argue that the migrant does not long remain in this state of mind. He begins to see Melbourne with different eyes and take "a far juster and more favourable view of it." No doubt Baker hoped that his own writing would help to effect this reinterpretation of Melbourne. The migrant begins to "ask himself what more could he have expected."

when he looks around and sees the very extraordinary progress which the capital has made in seven years, reckoning from 1837, and considers the difficulties attending every settlement unfostered by the Government, and more particularly one at such a remote distance from the Mother Country, he cannot fail to become imbued with a portion of that enterprising spirit which is so conspicuously the genius of the place.[75]

T. J. Maslen in *The Friend of Australia* (1830), a work offering guidance on the creation of new towns in new societies, warned against naming places in Australia after places in Great Britain.

I dare say, the Australian Liverpool presents not a single solitary feature that can be said to resemble the fine town of the same name in England, and it is anything but productive of cheerful thoughts. The exile, whether of compulsion or choice, cannot visit that straggling village without being reminded of the noble place he left in England; the name must create painful remembrances, the mind will be agitated with an association of melancholy ideas and comparisons, in no wise favourable to the newly adopted country; and it must be the same with the other English-named places, where the same comparisons and same feelings will be raked up by [e]very fresh-arrived settler.[76]

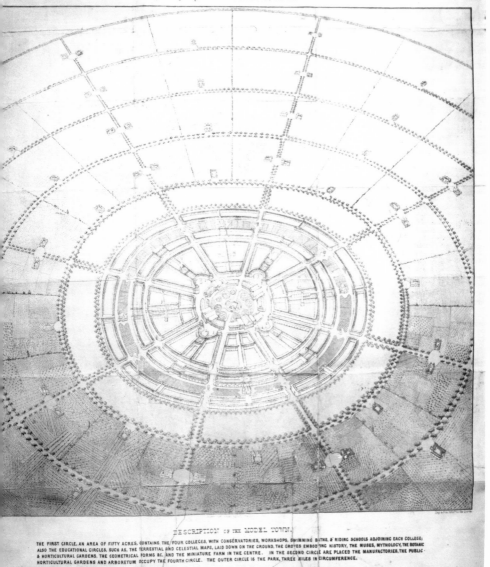

MODEL TOWN FOR THE HAPPY COLONY,

To be established in NEW ZEALAND by the Workmen of Great Britain.

Designed by ROBERT PEMBERTON, F.R.S.L.

DESCRIPTION OF THE MODEL TOWN.

THE FIRST CIRCLE, AN AREA OF FIFTY ACRES, CONTAINS THE FOUR COLLEGES, WITH CONSERVATORIES, WORKSHOPS, SWIMMING BATHS, & RIDING SCHOOLS ADJOINING EACH COLLEGE; ALSO THE EDUCATIONAL CIRCLES, SUCH AS, THE TERRESTIAL AND CELESTIAL MAPS, LAID DOWN ON THE GROUND, THE GROVES EMBODYING HISTORY, THE MUSES, MYTHOLOGY, THE BOTANIC & HORTICULTURAL GARDENS, THE GEOMETRICAL FORMS &C. AND THE MINIATURE FARM IN THE CENTRE. IN THE SECOND CIRCLE ARE PLACED THE MANUFACTORIES, THE PUBLIC HORTICULTURAL GARDENS AND ARBORETUM OCCUPY THE FOURTH CIRCLE. THE OUTER CIRCLE IS THE PARK, THREE MILES IN CIRCUMFERENCE.

This plan for a model town was published by Robert Pemberton in The Happy Colony *(London, 1854). (Courtesy of the Alexander Turnbull Library, Wellington, New Zealand)*

The proposal was to purchase 200,000 acres in New Zealand and establish ten separate societies on blocks of 20,000 acres each under a system of productive labor and perfect education. Nothing came of the idea.

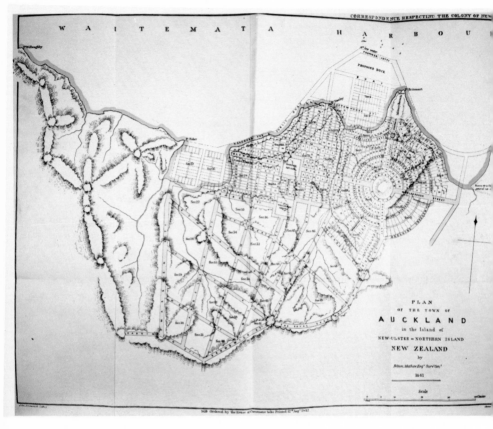

Plan of the Town of Auckland, New Zealand, 1841. (Courtesy of the Alexander Turnbull Library, Wellington, New Zealand)

This plan was ridiculed as "the great cobweb" and very little of the proposed "circus" was ever implemented. The terrain on which it is superimposed was very broken.

Graves Simcoe (1752–1806), founder of (Toronto). (Courtesy of the Royal Ontario um, Toronto)

oe was Lieutenant-Governor of Upper Can- rom 1791 to 1796.

Portrait of Governor Lachlan Macquarie. *Painting by Richard Read, 1822. (Courtesy of the Mitchell Library, State Library of New South Wales)*

As Governor of New South Wales, 1810–22, Macquarie did much to "improve" Sydney.

Portrait of Caroline Chisholm. *Painting by A. G. Hayter, 1852. (Courtesy of the Mitchell Library, State Library of New South Wales)*

Caroline Chisholm (1808–77) tried to help young female migrants to escape the Australian cities and find a new life in the bush.

BARBARISM.

CIVILIZATION.

These illustrations accompanied an article in the *Western Literary Magazine*, 1853, entitled "Barbarism and Civilization Contrasted." They were designed by D. C. Hitchcock of Cincinnati.

Across the Continent *by Fanny F. Palmer. Colored lithograph, 1868. (Courtesy of the Amon Carter Museum, Fort Worth, Texas)*

As the train arrives, towns spring up and the wilderness is cleared. Indian warriors stand detached on the "wrong side of the tracks." The smoke from the engine threatens to envelop them. It conceals the scene from their view.

The Pioneer *by Frederick McCubbin. Oil on canvas (triptych), 1904. (Courtesy of the National Gallery of Victoria, Melbourne; Felton Bequest, 1906)*

The triptych format not only conveys strong religious associations but also enables the artist to represent a sequence of social evolution, with the city appearing finally in the top right-hand corner of the third panel.

Helena, Montana. Business section looking southeast across Last Chance Gulch, 1890s. (Courtesy of the Montana Historical Society, Helena)

This photograph of Helena shows its jumble of incongruities—modern office buildings side by side with humble shacks.

Helena, Montana. Corner of Jackson Street and Sixth Avenue, 1898. Photograph by C. F. Pearis. (Courtesy of the Montana Historical Society, Helena)

This juxtaposition of log cabins and modern office buildings was often commented on by visitors to Helena.

Helena, Montana, 1890s. (Courtesy of the Montana Historical Society, Helena)

Guests at the Helena Hotel would have looked out onto this scene. The Paul Weidert cabin in the foreground was built in 1867 and demolished in 1898.

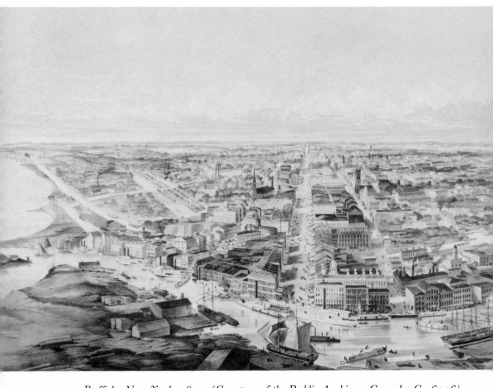

Buffalo, New York, 1853. (Courtesy of the Public Archives, Canada; C 46096)

Buffalo, especially when viewed from the Canadian side, was greatly admired as an example of American enterprise in town-building.

St. Paul, Minnesota. Pencil drawing by Seth Eastman, 1848. (Courtesy of the Minnesota Historical Society)

St. Paul had been platted one year earlier, in 1847. By 1849, when it became the seat of government of the new territory of Minnesota, its population was 840. In this drawing is depicted the bluff on which it was hoped fine homes and colleges would soon stand to impress visitors arriving by steamboat.

St. Paul *by S. Holmes Andrews. Oil on canvas, 1855. (Courtesy of the Minnesota Historical Society)*

In the painting can be seen the line of buildings, including spires and domes, that now presented itself to visitors. The painting typically depicts urban civilization in long view rising out of the wilderness. Note the Indian figures pointing at the scene but almost submerged in the rocks and bush at the lower edge of the painting.

Picton, New Zealand. From Illustrated Australian News, *August 13, 1872, p. 172. (Courtesy of the Alexander Turnbull Library, Wellington, New Zealand)*

Arriving here on January 12, 1875, James Nichols found it "a far superior place to whatever I had anticipated seeing in New Zealand, for having never read or noticed any account of the country before coming out, all I had got into my head was Mud Shantys. . . . The buildings looked quite clean & homely." Joyce Neill, ed., *Plum Duff and Cake: The Journal of James Nichols 1874–75* (Christchurch: Pegasus, 1975), p. 133.

The First House Built in Melbourne *by W. F. E. Liardet. Watercolor, 1863.*
(Courtesy of the National Library of Australia)

By 1863 Melbourne was a large city. Here is a recollection of its humble
origins.

Collins Street, Melbourne, c. 1862 [François Cogne]. A hand-colored lithograph from Charles Troedel, The Melbourne Album *(Melbourne, 1863–64). (Courtesy of the Alexander Turnbull Library, Wellington, New Zealand)*

Melbourne was founded in 1835. By the early 1860s its population was over 130,000, and its streets impressed visitors.

Colorado Springs, Colorado, January 1874. A color lithograph by E. S. Glover, c. 1874. (Courtesy of the Amon Carter Museum, Fort Worth, Texas)

Colorado Springs was a planned settlement from which saloons were banned. In the background is Colorado City, whose saloons gave it the "frontier" atmosphere that the founders of Colorado Springs sought to avoid.

Helena, Montana, 1890. (Courtesy of the Amon Carter Museum, Fort Worth, Texas)

The bird's-eye view was a common way of representing a town and its potential for growth. The fine buildings of a town were often depicted in insets. The population of Helena in 1890 was 13,834.

Woollomollo *by Conrad Martens. Pencil sketch, 1843. (Courtesy of the Mitchell Library, State Library of New South Wales)*

Along these heights above Sydney Harbour appeared the homes of the rich, symbolizing to some the heights to which the enterprising could aspire in a colonial city.

Hotel Tacoma (A View from the Sound). *From* Tacoma Illustrated, *an 1889 booster publication of the Tacoma Chamber of Commerce.*

Tacoma had been chosen in 1873 as the western terminal of the Northern Pacific Railroad. The hotel, designed by McKim, Mead, and White, was opened in 1884 when the completion of the line was anticipated.

1. J. R. WILSON'S BLOCK.   2. MASONIC TEMPLE.   3. INTERIOR MONTANA NATIONAL BANK.   4. GOLD B[...]

A page from Helena Illustrated, *Minneapolis, 1890.*

A typical booster publication uses Helena's fine buildings to impress the world with the progress of the capital city of Montana.

The Atheneum, Invercargill, New Zealand. Photograph by D. Ross. (Courtesy of the Alexander Turnbull Library, Wellington, New Zealand)

The Atheneum was built in 1871 and adorned with a large bronze statue of Minerva.

Lower Bytown (Ottawa), Canada. Painting by Philip John Bainbrigge, 1841. (Courtesy of the Public Archives, Canada; C 2163)

A town beginning to emerge among the stumps of trees. Note the dominance of the rocks in the foreground.

Ottawa. View of the Upper Town, looking up the Ottawa River from Government Hill. Painting by E. Whitefield. (Courtesy of the Public Archives, Canada; C 601)

An image of a city rising in the wilderness.

The City of Adelaide from the Torrens near the Reed Beds *by George French Angas. A hand-colored lithograph in* South Australia Illustrated *(London, 1847). (Courtesy of the National Library of Australia; Rex Nan Kivell Collection)*

Adelaide had been founded a decade earlier. It now had a population of over 9,000, but in Angas' lithograph the city is scarcely visible. It is viewed from a very low angle, and the scene is dominated—as in Whale's contemporary painting of Hamilton, Ontario—by natural forms, some of which are shattered or fallen. An intermediate area (Light's parkland) suggests a transitional zone of pastoralism.

View of Hamilton *[Ontario] by Robert Whale. Oil on canvas, 1853. (Courtesy of the National Gallery of Canada, Ottawa)*

The rising city (population about 15,000), with its rows of neat houses, churches, etc., is seen in the distance in a frame of natural forms. These appear to dominate the picture, but the emphasis in the depiction of them is on shattering and clearing. A small farm in the clearing symbolizes the beginning of the conquest of nature and of the process of social evolution. The irregularity and disorder of the wilderness contrast with the neatness of the town.

But others thought it valuable to emphasize and draw attention to Old World features in the New World scene. In *The Land of Promise* (1854) W. Shaw dwells on the London-like scenes in Sydney: a fashionable lady calling at a well-appointed shop, her footman, and so on. "These tokens of civilization gladden the heart of the emigrant by reminding him of home. Such spectacles are likewise an encouragement, as they indicate that wealth is attainable, and serve as beacons to light the wanderer on his weary way."[77]

As for the townspeople themselves, the resolve of those in a position to do something about it to bring their towns up to an Old World standard as quickly and fully as possible can be abundantly documented. For example, a settler newly arrived at Nelson in New Zealand wrote that he did not intend to live there in a "slovenly way." "If I reside in Nelson, I will do all in my power in conjunction with others to give a tone to the state of society that will as far as practicable be something in accordance with Towns in England."[78]

Town development in the New World was obviously affected by the strong pressure of disapproval of "frontier" or "colonial" town features wherever they manifested themselves. Typical of praise of Sydney, for instance, was the comment quoted by H. Mortimer Franklyn in *A Glance at Australia in 1880* (1881) that it was "uncolonial, and free from the dreadful newness and the garish rawness which characterise most Australian centres of population."[79] An example of an Eastern judgment on a Western town is the report made on Junction City, Kansas, by Josiah Copley to the *Pittsburgh Gazette* and subsequently published in *Kansas and the Country Beyond* (1867): "To have a superabundance of saloons, restaurants and billiard-tables, and not a single finished church edifice or a commodious school-room, is not the way to begin a city."[80]

Boosters of American Western towns did not want them to have or to acquire a "frontier town" image, and one of the main purposes of booster publications and other forms of boosterism was to ensure that that image was not associated with the town and was replaced by the perception of attributes characteristic of Eastern communities. There was a stereotype of the "frontier town" that became more and more pronounced and notorious as the nineteenth century progressed and the "mythic West" acquired its modern features.[81] One influence in the entrenchment of the stereotype was boosterism itself—the inclination of boosters to knock other Western towns, emphasize and exaggerate the extent to which they conformed to the stereotype, and then claim that their own town was the exception to this rule. For example, Joseph T. Holmes in *Quincy in 1857* (1857) not only stressed the high moral tone of that Illinois river town but also condemned its rivals, other "rising cities of the West" where "the rage for speculation and money-getting" had "vitiated the moral tone of the community to a very serious extent." Holmes had a theory to explain the difference. After Quincy had been founded, there was a quiet period before rapid growth began, and that quietness had enabled "an elevated moral tone" to become established. The people who came to settle in Quincy were "mainly from the better class of Eastern migrants, characterized by habits of industry, enterprise and business integrity, and by an orderly and peaceful disposition."[82]

This theme was important in the boosting of the West itself. In *Marvels of the New West* (1887) William M. Thayer set out to overturn the perception that the "New West" was "a rude, rough, half-civilized frontier, where men who escape the Indian scalping-knife may fall by the shot of the desperado." His method of doing this was to demonstrate that "New England is found throughout the New West; it is everywhere." Indeed, he virtually argued that "New England" had been transferred to the West. He referred to crime and vice in Eastern cities, claimed that "the most dangerous elements of humanity in Western cities, and even in mining cities," were not as bad, and listed the many features of urban civilization that had been reproduced from New England. The book is full of illustrations of fine public buildings in the cities of the West. Thayer explains his purpose in including these by quoting the editor of the magazine *New West,* which had a very similar style:

One of the deepest rooted and most erroneous impressions the East entertains of the West is that the towns and cities are all new, illy constructed, poorly provided with the conveniences for' health, comfort, and the transaction of business, socially and morally below par, of a mushroom growth, and possessing those peculiar characteristics which have always been associated with the "frontier."

"One purpose we have in presenting these views of public buildings," writes Thayer, "is to correct such incorrect and absurd ideas of the West."[83]

In a study of the early development of Burlington, Iowa, George Albert Boeck showed that people there hated to be identified with the Eastern stereotype of the Western town as crude, provincial, uncultured, and lawless. They found nothing quaint or romantic about whatever

"Western" characteristics the town continued to display.[84] Town boosters and editors sought to distance their towns from the stereotype as far as possible. Here, for example, is the *Calgary Herald* in 1884:

Calgary is a western town, but is not a western town in the ancient use of the word. It is peopled by native Canadians and Englishmen . . . citizens who own religion and respect law. The rough and festive cowboy of Texas . . . has no counterpart here.[85]

"Wild West" towns were very sensitive about their images. In the mid-1860s Hepworth Dixon published a book in which Denver was portrayed as a very rough and wild town. When an Englishman, John White, visited Denver a few years ater, he found the townspeople still upset about this and its persisting effects. One said to him: "Denver never at any time was half as bad as he describes it; and . . . while he was here, and for years before, Denver was a perfectly quiet and orderly town. You must remember, Denver only dates from '59; and all beginnings are a little rough. We claim for Denver that it ceased to be rough sooner than almost any other town in the West." He suggested that Dixon must have been told some tall stories. The problem was that "half the people of America have read the book, and I do believe it has scared men from coming here."[86]

Willard B. Robinson has analyzed the architecture of Helena, Montana, and discovered that the architects, many of whom had migrated from the East and Midwest, did their best to make Helena look like "a metropolitan city." Distinctive regional qualities were not wanted in the city's buildings. Businessmen, in order to "avoid any appearance of the provincial," "sought a derivative architecture that would create a metropolitan atmosphere."[87]

Lack or weakness or decline of Eastern influence over a Western town was often regarded as detrimental to its development. In 1870 James F. Watkins published an article on San Francisco in *The Overland Monthly* in which he reviewed the effect on that city of an isolation intensified by the absorption of the East in the Civil War. He saw San Francisco as having tried over the twenty years since the gold rush "to grow up to, or in the direction of, a certain standard—the only one she knows: that which prevailed at the East fifteen or twenty years ago." But that was becoming an out-of-date standard and so San Francisco was not "as great a success as she might be." Few of her businessmen had visited the East over the previous decade; a majority had never done so. The result was that the city was not up to "the modern standard." It had no park, baths, or drives, and only one theater. It was "unornamented." If only the city had been "within rail connection with the greater cities of the East," it is probable that "she would not have submitted to bear these things as they are. She would have had a park, a public library, and an art-gallery, and would long ago have learned that to do nothing but gather money was an offense against good taste."[88]

Where the development of a town was under the control of one individual or company, there was sometimes an attempt to create what might be called an "anti-frontier" town, a place from which what were perceived as the most notorious "frontier" characteristics had been eradicated or excluded. The worst of these was, by general consensus, the saloon. We have seen, for instance, Josiah Copley's criticism of Junction City's "superabundance of saloons." Some town founders sought to keep their towns free of liquor in order to prevent the development of a "frontier" type of community. An example is Stephen H. Taft, founder of Springvale, later Humboldt, in Iowa. He used the absence of saloons as a major point in boosting the town's attractions to Easterners.[89] At Greeley, Colorado, founded as a "Union Colony," there was a strong effort to keep liquor out and propagate an image of the place as everything that a typical frontier town was not.[90]

But the most systematic and determined attempt to create this type of "anti-frontier" town was at Colorado Springs, Colorado, founded by General William Jackson Palmer. In an article published in *Lippincott's Magazine* in 1883 George Rex Buckman summed up thus the significance of what was attempted at Colorado Springs:

The history of frontier towns is not usually a pleasant subject of contemplation for such as have any regard for social order. A period of turbulence, during which the baser elements of society are dominant, has been regarded as inevitable. Human life is held in light esteem. . . . Law is vindicated and order established only when, in the course of time, the turbulent element finds itself outweighed by better material and must either conform itself to the new conditions or remove to where restraining influences will not be felt. That intoxicating drink is one of the chiefest causes of this social chaos, is an assertion that needs no proof; and for illustrations we have but at the present writing to point to the border towns of New Mexico and Arizona. Hence it is that they who would found a frontier city designed from the start to attract to its citizenship people of high social and moral standing, and to offer no inducements to the drunken and dissolute, a city in which life and property shall be secure, and where churches and schools shall early afford all the advantages of an older community, must take high ground upon this vital question of temperance.[91]

What in fact happened to Colorado Springs, because of its ban on saloons, was that it became twinned with a "frontier" town, its old rival, Colorado City, just across the river. Irving Howbert, who was county clerk at Colorado Springs in the early 1870s, recalled in his *Memoirs of a Lifetime in the Pike's Peak Region* (1925) how fast Colorado City grew, attracting "many of the floating class, and others who did not approve of the liquor restrictions in the Colorado Springs deeds." It became as a result a town of many saloons and drunken brawls.[92] Other towns evolved within their own boundaries a compromise between the desire to appear "respectable" and the overwhelming pressures to be "Western." In 1877 the New York publication, *Frank Leslie's Illustrated Newspaper,* carried this report of a visit by the proprietors to Cheyenne:

For two or three blocks the main street of Cheyenne keeps up a character of solid respectability with neat brick buildings, a large hotel and an attractive show of shop-windows; but it soon drops such mimicry of the "effete East," and relapses into a bold disregard of architectural forms and proprieties.[93]

In other towns disreputable "frontier" activities were banished to officially approved or at least tolerated "red-light" districts, every effort being made to keep these hidden from the sight of visitors and others who might not wish to see them.[94]

Another way of eradicating the "frontier" from the image of a town was to blot it out, to assume that it did not exist. At Tacoma, Washington, the engineers employed to lay out the town were "instructed to lose all sight of the fact that it was as yet a wilderness; to forget the forest that bearded the hillsides; to forget that they were on the frontier." The result, according to the boosters, was a great success. "Those who come here . . . , expecting to encounter and suffer the crude associations of the wild frontier towns, will be very pleasantly disappointed."[95] In Australia writers describing the new towns did their best to enable their readers to "see" them minus their primitive "colonial" features. In *Three Years' Cruise in the Australasian Colonies* (1854) R. Edmond Malone, in telling migrants what to expect, had to eliminate a good deal in order to create this sort of illusion.

If you were this moment transplanted from your town at home into the streets of one of the towns of the Australasian colonies, out of sight of the plants, trees, and shrubs, the only way you would know you were not merely in another town of your own country would be by the beard and moustache of the many people around you.[96]

Godfrey Charles Mundy in *Our Antipodes* (1857), writing of a visit to Sydney in 1846, thought that all that needed to be removed in order to fancy oneself at Brighton or Plymouth was "an occasional orange-tree in full bloom or fruit in the back yard of some of the older cottages, or a flock of little green parrots whistling as they alight for a moment on a housetop."[97] The uniqueness and attractiveness of so many of the features that the reader was invited to remove from his "vision" make one wonder at the impulse which prompted the composition of these "scenes." Here is H. Mortimer Franklyn in *A Glance at Australia in 1880* (1881): "Divest an Australian city of its freshness, rawness, and newness of appearance, soften the brilliancy of the sky, draw a veil of filmy moisture over the surrounding landscape, and lessen the activity of the people who fill the streets, and there is nothing to remind the new arrival that he has quitted the shores of England."[98]

In the United States there was some reaction against the constant emphasis, with its strongly moral overtones, on the actual or desired similarities between Eastern and Western towns. At times local pride rebelled against the disparagement of "frontier characteristics."[99] As the great myths of the West gathered strength and popularity, towns which had divorced themselves from association with them were not always regarded with such admiration. The demands of "the East" and the expectations of tourists and other devotees of the cult of "the West" began to move in opposite directions and to come into conflict. This situation is well described in Harry C. Freeman's *A Brief History of Butte, Montana* (1900).

The West has developed so rapidly and transition from condition to condition has so speedily followed one another that today a new West is presented while the world is still wrestling with the traditions and the legends of the old. While the East is straining its eyes to catch a glimpse of some evidence of a higher degree of civilization, the unsatisfied traveler is wearing himself out in a vain search for lingering relics of primitive life.[100]

Towns and Social Evolution: Perceptions of the Relationship of Towns to the Evolution of New Societies

ALTHOUGH Frederick Jackson Turner's 1893 essay "The Significance of the Frontier in American History" has often been considered a major turning point in the interpretation of American history,[1] there was little that was novel in its basic thesis. This was essentially a restatement of the model of social evolution which was almost universally accepted in nineteenth-century discussions of the likely, indeed inevitable, course of development of new societies. That this was so is indicated by Turner's own use—not in the critical way one would expect of a historian or employing it as a piece of evidence of contemporary opinion, but as a "suggestive" interpretation of how things actually were—of a lengthy extract from an emigrant's guidebook written by J. M. Peck and published in 1837.[2] This passage is a striking anticipation of the "Turner thesis." It posits, in very simple terms, a progression of society from rural settlement to villages, then towns, and finally large cities. According to this model, towns develop in the later stages of the process of social evolution—which, according to Turner, begins all over again in each region of new settlement. Urban historians have been increasingly critical of Turner's thesis because of the paucity of references in it to towns.[3] There are some, but these are almost all couched in terms of the "evolutionary" model.[4] They give little or no indication of the abundant evidence of early growth of towns as revealed in such works as Richard Wade's *The Urban Frontier*.

Peck wrote during the Age of Jackson, an era with which, it seems, the Turner family felt a particular affinity. Turner was given "Jackson" as his middle name.[5] Ray Billington shows that much of Turner's reading consisted of works written in this era. In them Turner found ample evidence that expansion went on in well-defined stages. "Too many observers agreed that expansion duplicated the evolution of human society for the doctrine to be doubted."[6] It is clear that at this time, when there was a cult of such "frontier" figures as Daniel Boone and Davy Crockett, and William Henry Harrison won the presidency after a campaign one of the main features of which was his boast that he lived in a log cabin, there was widespread adherence to the evolutionary interpretation of the opening of the West as articulated by Peck. In her fictional diary of John Parsons' journey through Indiana, Kate Milner Rabb describes how he fell into conversation with a man named Cravens who told him that there were "three classes in the Western settlements." First came "the pioneer" with his "rude cabin in the primeval forest."

The next class comes in, purchases the land of the pioneer, who pushes on to more distant primeval forests, and adds field to field, builds roads, bridges, schoolhouses and leads a plain, frugal but civilized life.

The next class is composed of men of capital and enterprise, under whose leadership the small village rises to a spacious town or city, adorned with substantial edifices of brick.

This is a paraphrase of the passage in Peck. According to Cravens, this third wave—which we might call "the urban frontier—was now sweeping over "large districts of Indiana, Illinois and Missouri."[7] Most popular accounts of the process of westward expansion at this time and for a decade or so to come assumed that this was the form that it was taking and would continue to take. J. L. McConnel's *Western Characters,* published in 1853, has ten chapters that begin with "The Indian" and progress via "The Pioneer" to "The Schoolmistress" and "The Politician." The town itself is not explicitly described, but McConnel does draw an analogy between the flow of the Mississippi and the process of social evolution. "It flows from the country of the savage, toward that of civilization. ... Near its mouth, it has reached the culmination of refinement—its last ripe fruit, a crowded city."[8] The typical presentation of the process in popular literature about "the West" in mid-century can be seen in *Incidents and Sketches Connected with the Early History and Settlement of the West,* published in Cincinnati in 1854. This follows the progress of the emigrant out West and the establishment of his farm and log cabin. "In a few years, or even months, the retired cabin, once so solitary,

solitary, becomes the nucleus of a little settlement"; a schoolhouse and a church appear.[9]

The idea of a progression of society through stages, culminating in the emergence of cities, was not an American invention or used exclusively with reference to that country. It appears in discussions of the development of other new societies. For instance, Nathaniel Ogle in *The Colony of Western Australia* (1839) was relieved that, owing to the apparently cast-iron nature of the laws of social evolution, industry could not yet develop in Australia.

The new colonies are peopled by those who have left a kingdom the most advanced in human knowledge, but in the last of the progressive states, to *recommence their modes of life in the first state—the pastoral and agricultural,* which can only progress to the cultivation and preservation of all the productions of the earth: thus, a physical and moral barrier, in accordance with universal and unerring laws, is erected against that last state, which brings in manufacturing, and all its train of degradation and demoralisation.[10]

The Australia Felix Monthly Magazine argued in June 1849 that

the natural progress of nations may be traced from the prairie and the forest to the city and the town, the roaming flock gradually receding before the plough, the shepherd and stockman before the husbandman and artizan, the hut of the rural proprietor making way for the palace of the merchant-prince or the stores and buildings of the manufacturer.[11]

This theory of evolutionary progress can be traced back to the eighteenth-century Enlightenment, the writings on "progress" of Condorcet and others, and the ideas of the French Physiocrats.[12] As can be seen from Ogle's statement of it, the theory was that all societies progress through "stages" or "states." What these were was variously defined. A common formulation had four stages: primitive hunting and gathering, pastoralism, agriculture, and commerce. Cities were supposed to appear only in the last of these. The progress was also commonly seen as being towards "civilization" and away from a simple "primitive" form of social organization. Cities were thus identified with an advanced, sophisticated, complex form of society. The concept of "steps" or "stages" in the progress of mankind was especially prominent in the writings of the philosophers and economists of the Scottish Enlightenment such as Lord Monboddo, Lord Kames, and Adam Smith, and their ideas had much influence on thinking about the evolution of Britain's colonies. Similar theories continued to be propagated in the nineteenth century and to have an influence on thinking about new societies. Ray Billington, in tracing the ancestry of the Turner frontier thesis, has drawn attention to the influence of Friedrich List, whose *National System of Political Economy* (1856) distinguished five states: savage, pastoral, agricultural, agricultural-manufacturing, and manufacturing-commercial. Richard T. Ely, the eminent economist and mentor of Turner at Wisconsin, incorporated these classifications with slight variations into his lectures and his textbook, *An Introduction to Political Economy* (1889). Powerfully reinforced by the influence of Social Darwinism, such interpretations of the history of the frontier were commonplace in the United States at Turner's time. The concept of stages of progress, with city dwellers coming last, appears in the 1890 Census Bureau report which had such a strong effect on him.[13]

Connections between these interpretations of social evolution and early Australian art and literature have been traced in Robert Dixon's *The Course of Empire*. Dixon argues that depictions of Australian towns within the Australian landscape were consciously informed by the "four stages" theory. He instances the illustrations to James Wallis' *An Historical Account of the Colony of New South Wales* (1821). Wallis hoped that the illustrations would serve as a record of social evolution that would interest historians, philosophers, and others "who are fond of tracing the progress of countries." He saw them as depicting how "the primeval forests . . . may be converted into plains covered with bleating flocks, lowing herds, and waving corn; may become the smiling seats of industry and the social arts, and be changed, from a mournful and desolate wilderness, into the cheerful village, the busy town, and the crowded city."[14] It was common for artists in early nineteenth-century Australia to compose vistas of emerging urban communities within a frame of wilderness scenery or of aborigines looking on as passive and helpless spectators of an inexorable historical process. Distant vistas or visions of urban society emerging, as it were, from the bush were found quite frequently in nineteenth-century Australian art. The most celebrated example, which might be regarded as a culmination and summation of a century of exploitation of this theme, was Frederick McCubbin's triptych *The Pioneer* (1904). As Leigh Astbury observes, "juxtaposed images of the untamed bush, the first homestead and the resultant flourishing city had become a tired literary cliché in verse by early in the twentieth century," and McCubbin's painting "clearly reflects this literary convention in its pictorial organization."[15]

There are continuing echoes of it in Australian art, for instance, in the Ned Kelly paintings of Sidney Nolan which almost all depict bush scenes but culminate in a depiction of Kelly's trial in which the "flourishing city of Melbourne" is glimpsed in the background out a courtroom window rather in the style of McCubbins' third panel. In each painting a significant element in the "Australian legend"—the heroic pioneer of the bush, the bushranger—is shown succumbing to the inexorable advance of urban civilization.

The United States and Australia were often regarded as maps of the record of social evolution. This was an idea held very strongly by Jefferson and taken up later by Frederick Jackson Turner, who revived Jefferson's image of the procession of pioneers through Cumberland Gap[16] and distorted and downplayed the place of towns in the history of western expansion.

The image of "process" was sustained by the popularity of the story of Daniel Boone moving on whenever he saw the smoke of another settler's fire arising in the vicinity of his now log cabin. This was often used to dramatize how Westerners saw the evolution of their own regions.[17] In *Historical Sketch and Essay on the Resources of Montana* (1868) Henry Horr argued that the reason why the early pioneers came to that area was that the states they had been living in "were reaching a too high state of civilization."

Where once they roamed as free as the mountain air, in search of the precious ore, or in quest of the game of the West, and the spot where they were wont to lie, with no house or covering save their blankets, now would be found to be the center of a metropolis, "herding" its thousand and one votaries of fashion and Mammon, who usurp the former abiding place of the old pioneer.[18]

The orderliness and simplicity of the evolutionary model had an overwhelming attraction. Sydney Smith, reviewing David Collins' *An Account of the English Colony in New South Wales* in 1803, wrote: "There is a charm in thus seeing villages, and churches, and farms, rising from a wilderness, where civilized man has never set his foot since the creation of the world."[19] It provided an organizing principle that could be—and often was—used by those who sought to describe the development of new societies. Thus, in his preface to *Views of Canada and the Colonists* (1851), James B. Brown stated that he intended to survey "the various familiar aspects of the country in the stages of its progress, from the still uninhabited forest to the first openings of the pioneer settler, the half-cultivated clearances of older settlements, and the busy and more comfortable and home-like life presented by the rapidly-growing prosperous towns and villages."[20]

There were many references to a "natural" process of social evolution in which towns would arise at a late stage. "Towns should follow, and not precede general settlement in new countries," wrote J. C. Byrne in *Twelve Years' Wanderings in the British Colonies* (1848). The development of the country normally preceded the growth of towns: "cities follow civilization."[21] In *Ultima Thule* (1854) Thomas Cholmondeley gave the following prescription for urban development in New Zealand: "As the population increases, a village first and then a town will grow up, putting forth, first its cottages, and then its larger buildings, such as schools, churches, inns, and warehouses, just as a tree grows into leaves, flowers, and fruit." This was the "natural" process: "a settlement cannot be made any more than a tree or an animal, . . . it must develope itself according to laws of its own."[22]

Naturally, therefore, given the widespread acceptance of these notions, there was a good deal of surprise when towns developed so soon and so fast. In his *Autobiography* (1854) the Rev. James B. Finley wrote of the appearance in the West of "magnificent cities with streets extending for miles, all paved, and brilliantly illuminated with gas."

Such a change never entered the most fervent imagination of our backwoodsmen . . . All we hoped for or expected, was to have some rich farms in these luxuriant bottoms, and always plenty of deers and bear on our hills.[23]

If a town developed at an early stage in the settlement of a region, there were almost always plenty of critics to condemn such a development as "unhealthy," "unnatural," "forced," "premature." For instance, the disastrous condition of Adelaide in its early years was often used as proof of the correctness of such criticisms. According to J. F. Bennett in his *Historical and Descriptive Account of South Australia* (1843), "the South Australians began at first at the wrong end—they commenced by building a town, ere there was any country population or country produce to support it."[24] This offended against basic laws of "natural" social evolution, and the people of Adelaide paid the penalty. Towns should be allowed to develop naturally as needed.[25]

In our own times the validity of the "Turner thesis" as applied to towns has been challenged by many historians, notably Richard Wade and John W. Reps, who have developed the concept of an "urban frontier" which often preceded, and indeed facilitated, the development of farming and other forms of nonurban settlement.[26] Norman Harper has argued for the relevance of this idea to the Australian situation.[27] What needs to be asked is whether these authors have discovered truths about the evolution of new societies which were ignored by contemporaries or whether nineteenth-century people were aware of the existence of an "urban frontier" which paralleled or preceded more "primitive" types of settlement of the land and therefore complicated the application, and undermined the credibility, of conventional theories of social evolution.

In the United States the Peck model—or (anachronistically) the Turner model—certainly does seem to have held considerable sway in the 1830s and 1840s. Even then, however, it was becoming difficult to ignore the implications of the massive town-site speculative activity that swept the Middle West—and was satirized by Charles Dickens in *American Notes* and *Martin Chuzzlewit*. In the conversation in the "diary" of John Parsons, Cravens adhered to the Peck model but in his comments on what was then happening in Indiana and other Midwestern states came close to depicting the "stages" or "waves" as occurring simultaneously and not in orderly "natural" sequence. An 1836 work promoting Texas suggested the possibility of a speeded up process there. The early settlers of Texas had been scattered over "such an extent of country, as made it inimical to the growth of towns." But the prediction was that "it will soon be with the inhabitants of Texas, according to the western pioneer's proverb— 'Give me a rich country, and I will soon give you a large town!'" This suggests that the early advent of towns in the West was already proverbial.[28] However, the fraudulence associated with much of the speculation, the failure of so many towns to be translated from paper to reality, and the collapse of numerous others, lent continuing credence to the view that early development of towns was "unhealthy" and "unnatural."

By the 1850s perception of at least the midwestern situation seems to have changed significantly. One reason for this was the Kansas experience. The colonization of Kansas in the 1850s was not only heavily town-oriented but self-consciously so. Theories of the value of organizing settlement around an urban nucleus were applied to Kansas where the situation was dramatized by the slavery issue. Towns of Kansas became centers for the mobilization of pro-slavery and "Free Soil" forces. Commentaries on the Kansas settlement abounded in references to an urban frontier and to the emergence of a new type of frontiersman. There was a revised perception of frontier settlement processes. In her *Kansas; Its Interior and Exterior Life* (1856), Sara T. L. Robinson wrote of the flood of migrants to Kansas in 1854:

While they, for the most part, settle in the country, and will gather into their garners of the golden treasures of the rich and fertile soil, eastern capital will form a nucleus, around which the young, the adventurous, the enterprising, will gather, and new cities, new towns, will spring up with rapid growth, emulating in thrift and intelligence those of the old states.[29]

The second major change was the advent of the railroad which powerfully stimulated the creation of an urban frontier in the first stages of settlement, both through the colonization and town-site selling activities of railroad companies and through the intensive town-site speculation that so often attended and even preceded the establishment of railroad lines. In an account of his five years as an emigrant in the United States, William Hancock presented the advent of the railroad in Wisconsin in the 1850s as having greatly accelerated the "Boone exodus":

A new population, speculative, enterprising, and intelligent, enters on its [the land's] possession. Towns and villages rise in forest and on prairie with wonderful rapidity. The slow-going, plodding emigrant, either imbibes to some extent the prevailing spirit, or yields to others; and the sturdy frontier-man, whose enjoyment of life is in proportion to the number of miles he can traverse about his dwelling without a sight of human face or footstep. retires in disgust to wilder scenes as the scream of the locomotive sounds upon his ears, and its smoke rises among the forest trees.[30]

By 1867 Logan U. Reavis was proclaiming as gone forever the days in which the pioneer went first and built his log cabin in the wilderness.

The telegraph, steamboat, and railroad go before in rapid march; and, instead of the pioneer, with his ax and hoe and log cabin, the village is spread upon the prairie with the magic of the tinted field, and the plow takes the place of the hoe. Instead of the school-house, the church, and the printing office, being, as of old, the products of half a generation, they now take their places among the institutions of advancing civilization in a month and a year.[31]

In this description of the process is instantly recognizable the famous Currier and Ives lithograph of the advance of the railroad and of urban civilization across the prairie.

As early as 1849 the *Western Journal* was detecting a change in the character of "emigrants to new territories." The agriculturist was arriving in the company of the merchant and artisan, schoolmaster and minister:

the foundations of civilization are laid deep and strong in the begin[n]ing. The neat and comfortable dwelling, the farm, the garden and the orchard; the school house and the church; commerce, and the arts; all planted and established in a country of matchless fertility, grow up together.[32]

In 1851 it described the social and cultural institutions already created by the people of St. Paul. "Pioneers they are, but how unlike those of the last generation." ". . . much as we admire the character of the early pioneers, we rejoice that civilization has advanced beyond that state which required the existence and services of such a race of men. We know they no longer [sic] exist, as a distinctive class."[33]

By 1857 the urban pioneer was being defined and celebrated as a new type. The old sequential process of settlement seemed to have been utterly overthrown. James M. Woolworth wrote of *Nebraska in 1857:*

The history of the settlement of Nebraska is the reverse of that of all other Territories. It was not a gradual filling up; the ranks of civilization did not advance in succession: first the hunter, then the trader, then the farmer, then the merchant, and last the capitalist and speculator. All poured in together—sharers of the toils and exposure of the new settlements, and rivals in the one contest for wealth. Instead of the Boons [sic] and the Leatherstockings, who had broken the brush in the pathway of empire, came side by side the stout farmer and the keen-eyed speculator; the one as intent as the other upon town sites and choice farms —pioneers of the new civilization.[34]

There are many fascinating reflections of this confusion of frontier phases and types in the perspectives of the people who participated in the process in Nebraska. There was William Larimer, later founder of Denver, who acquired a large tract of Nebraska land in 1855 and did not know whether to farm it or turn it into La Platte City. "We have a situation for a city, large enough to build a Philadelphia, certainly. . . . I will go on with the farm and if the land is ever wanted for a town it is ready. Still we have abundance for a large town without touching what I intend farming."[35]

Edward Gibbon Wakefield's theories were in part based on the assumption that "dispersion" and primitive backwoods settlement were what happened "naturally" and that a mechanism such as the "sufficient price" was needed to counter this tendency. His critics challenged or at least sought to modify the assumption, and they used what was perceived as a change in the character of American frontiersmen to do so. *Sidney's Emigrant's Journal* declared in 1848: "The Backwoodsmen of the States *are rude for a generation,* or half a generation, but they are but pioneers; the next race are concentrated enough, and as like Europeans as climate and institutions of perpetual excitement and dollar worship will let them."[36]

Wilson Nicely, author of *The Great Southwest* (1867), a guidebook for migrants to Kansas and Missouri, was not sure that these urban frontiersmen deserved to be called "pioneers" at all.

Topeka, like Leavenworth, has been settled and built principally by Eastern men. With this class of pioneers, no town or village is planned or built in which the church and school house do not form leading features. The men of this class are not in reality pioneers of civilization, inasmuch as they carry their civilization with them. The true pioneers were men of a different type; men who hated cities and settlements, who loved solitude, who lived in huts and cabins, and fought single-handed against savage men and savage beasts. Boone and Kenton were examples of such. The modern pioneers are more gregarious in their habits. They love the hum of crowded streets, the excitement of trade; they take kindly to potent labor-saving machines, and delight in speculation.[37]

Another view was that, although the farming frontier may have come first, there was about *it* an element of the "forced" and "unnatural" since many of the migrants who entered it were urban people who knew nothing about farming. They soon reverted to their true urban selves, left the land, and helped to build the towns and cities of the American and Canadian wests.[38] This idea has surfaced in some modern accounts of the Canadian urban frontier.[39]

Eventually there was a reaction against what many saw as a premature development of towns. In 1871 Wayne Griswold in his book *Kansas,* in summing up the Kansas experience, showed that some aspects of it had revived and reinforced the view that early urban development could be undesirable.

There are some promising cities in Kansas even now, young as she is, and many thriving country towns, with good prospects for the future. There is one drawback to most of them for the present. They are far ahead of the country around, and many will have to wait in their growth the settlement and cultivation of the country. After all, there is a development and growth of the cities and towns in Kansas more rapid than in older States. The great influx of immigrants and speculators, and the rapid development of railroads by foreign capitalists, gives a far more rapid growth to Kansas, and especially to cities and towns, than you see in any other State, unless in a part of Missouri.[40]

The question of defying the "laws" of social evolution and forcing towns into an early and premature existence arose with particular acuteness in the case of organized colonization. Towns were commonly regarded as very important in settlement schemes. They had a vital role to playing in initiating, organizing, and cohering the settlement of the wilderness. Henry Sewell, one of the leading figures in the creation of the Canterbury settlement in New Zealand, argued that "one Town helps another and every new Township opens new lands; brings new Colonists, and however small contributes to general progress, in which all are interested alike."[41] If, for whatever reason, towns failed to develop or were not provided, settlement could go very wrong. This was the conclusion about Upper Canada in the Durham Report. Since so much of the land was in clergy reserves or in an unimproved condition after having been granted to officers and United Empire Loyalists, the settler "can hardly expect, during his lifetime, to see his neighbourhood contain a population sufficiently dense to support mills, schools, post-offices, places of worship, markets or shops; and without these, civilization retrogrades."[42]

Many nineteenth-century plans of colonization were town-based. Edward Gibbon Wakefield was a leading advocate of "concentration," and his theories included the attachment to land of a price "sufficient" to ensure only a gradual and orderly dispersal of settlement from the core or nucleus of the colony. Wakefield was obviously influenced by the ideas of classical political economy derived from Adam Smith's *The Wealth of Nations*. In Book 3 Smith places great emphasis on the value of towns for the development of agriculture. In his own day Wakefield was praised by John Stuart Mill, who saw the existence of a market in the form of a town as important for the raising of an agricultural surplus.[43] Countless promoters of emigration were to echo this argument when they drew the attention of prospective migrants to the existence of a town in the district which they were publicizing.[44]

One of the leading supporters of Wakefieldian colonization was William Hutt. In a speech delivered to the National Colonization Society and subsequently published as a pamphlet, he argued that one of the three great principles of "Systematic Emigration to the Colonies" was "a *concentration,* instead of a wide dispersion of the colonists." He reached back into antiquity to prove that this was the right way to develop a colony. The Greeks had not scattered themselves over large tracts of land but had erected fortresses, some of which turned into "great and splendid cities": "the quantity of land necessary for the support of a great city formed the whole territory of a great colony from the beginning to the end of its career." Wherever the people were free to disperse, degeneration ensued. He claimed South Africa and Canada as contemporary examples of this.

Reverse this system, and we may claim in those regions mightier states than Greece and fairer cities, where all the arts of refinement, where philosophy and poetry, and eloquence—yes, and physical science too—may find another and a congenial home; and where the European settler will not have reason to lament over the loss of any of the luxuries and elegancies which surrounded him on his native shore.[45]

Another practitioner of colonization who firmly believed in "concentration" and the importance of establishing a town first was John Galt, the Scottish novelist. Galt wrote two novels on settlement in North America —*Lawrie Todd* and *Bogle Corbet*. For three years in the 1820s he was principal agent in Canada for the Canada Company and, as such, played a role in the founding of two towns, Guelph and Goderich, in Ontario. In *Bogle Corbet* the hero is clearly stating Galt's own views when he says:

Reflection on the effect and situation of towns in the old country, as well as the best information to be obtained respecting the system adopted by the Americans in settling their wild lands, has persuaded me, that the first effectual step in colonization is to plant a village . . . the plan is so obviously judicious, that two opinions cannot be entertained on the subject; for we see it is from towns in all countries that cultivation proceeds; and history, in describing the colonies of antiquity, distinctly shows that the first object was ever the choice of a proper site for a fortress or a city.[46]

The reference to the United States is significant. It shows that there was a recognition of the role of an "urban frontier" in that country's settlement process. The great difference was that in the United States the development of towns seemed to happen spontaneously, without needing to be spread by government intervention. This lent support to the argument that the early appearance of towns was not necessarily an "artificial" phenomenon. Having referred to American practice, Bogle Corbet goes on to argue that, "by beginning with a town, you follow the course of Nature."[47] Of course, in the United States the most important frontier-settlement tradition of all—that of the Puritans of New England—was town-based.[48] It lived on in the nineteenth century in much colonization of the Midwest and in such organized settlements as the "free soil" companies in Kansas in the 1850s. Edward Gibbon Wakefield, who condemned the "slovenly and disgraceful methods" by which colonization was being carried on, would have been fully in accord with sentiments expressed by Charles Sumner when praising the New England Emigrant Aid Company in 1856:

The secret through which, with small means, it has been able to accomplish so much is that, *as an inducement to emigration, it has gone forward and planted capital in advance of population.* According to the old immethodical system, this rule is reversed; and population has been left to grope blindly, without the advantage of fixed centres, with mills, schools, and churches—all calculated to soften the hardships of pioneer life—such as have been established beforehand in Kansas.[49]

Schools and churches are usually provided in towns or villages, and Sumner's reference to "fixed centres" suggests that that is what he had in mind. Towns such as Lawrence were central features of "free soil" colonization. Nevertheless, there was some confusion as to what exactly Wakefield and others meant by "concentration" and whether it had to involve the development of large towns. How "concentrated" did settlement have to be in order to satisfy the criteria? When Wakefield used the term, he meant by it primarily the existence of a supply of "combinable labour," needed in order to give value to property and provide incentive for investment of capital in colonies.[50] He told the Select Committee on the Disposal of Lands in the Colonies that there were circumstances in which combinable labor could exist without towns. But, when he specified what these were—one was slavery—it became clear that "concentration" was certain normally to involve a high measure of collection of population into urban communities.[51] Other aspects of Wakefield's thinking on colonies, especially the instant re-creation of "civilized" society, tended in this direction. However, in a letter of 1830 the political economist T. R. Malthus, gave an interpretation of "concentration" which indicated the difficulties involved in implementing the principle and also the extreme and unbalanced nature of the "concentration" on one large center, which is what happened in most of the colonies founded under Wakefieldian influence.

It is quite impossible to say that any specific plan would secure the precise degree of artificial concentration which it is desirable to introduce into a new colony. . . . Anything like a persevering attempt at concentration round a single town would soon lower wages, and destroy the true principle of colonization. In colonizing a large country many centres of concentration are necessary, and villages in various situations must be established, which are to grow up into towns, and afford new markets for produce. Many of these will naturally be fixed at a considerable distance from the metropolis, determined by fertility of soil, vicinity of rivers, and other circumstances. . . . There is certainly danger of defeating the great object of colonization by prematurely forcing concentration.[52]

In evidence before a Select Committee of the New South Wales Legislative Council thirteen years later, Sir Thomas Mitchell, the surveyor-general, used very similar language in condemning the way in which the Wakefieldian principle of "concentration" seemed to have resulted in the premature growth of large cities.[53]

There was, however, fairly general agreement among colonizers that there should be at least an early provision of towns and villages. Governments, faced with having to entice migrants into what were regarded as wildernesses, usually had no option but to adopt some plan of this type. Mitchell may have been a strong critic of extreme urban concentration in a new country, but he actively pursued a policy of forming towns and villages in the interior. During his surveyor-generalship he caused no fewer than sixty-one towns and villages to be laid out. In 1843 he complained that, owing to inadequate spending on roads, he had not been as successful as he would have wished in implementing a policy which he defined as "to form the nucleus of towns and villages," "centres of location."[54]

A town was seen as representing community, "society," "civilization," and there was therefore usually an urban core in most utopian and communitarian settlements as well as in colonization schemes organized by companies which emphasized the benefits of cooperative effort in subduing the wilderness. A dilemma which often faced the migrant, especially in Canada, was whether to purchase land from a land company or accept a free grant or at least much cheaper land from the government. Handbooks for migrants quite often—and propaganda for the companies invariably —recommended the former, in spite of the higher cost, on the grounds that in company settlements one was guaranteed access to urban facilities —markets, schools, churches, post offices, civilized society.[55] John Galt, not surprisingly, thought along these lines. One of his hopes—and this was also very much the case with Wakefield—was, through the prominence of urban amenities, to give the colony the right sort of image to attract the "better class" of migrant, the "gentleman capitalist."[56] Humbler settlers needed villages for all sorts of more practical reasons, and there are instances of settlers petitioning for the laying out of a townsite in their vicinity—bad roads preventing access to more distant locations[57] —or, in America, where private enterprise was looked to for this kind of amenity, of farmers requesting one among them to subdivide a portion of his property, because of its convenient location, for a township.[58]

Towns featured prominently, indeed centrally, in any colonization scheme where one of the principal objectives was to transplant "a whole community" from the Old World or to reproduce instantly in the New World all the benefits of "an old society." Such an idea was of central significance in Wakefieldian colonization. One of the aims was to interest people in emigration, and capitalists in investing in the colony, by reassuring them that the colony would not be lacking any of the good aspects of Old World life, for example, "civilized" urban society. Only the undesirable aspects would be filtered out. The theme is also conspicuous in "free soil" colonization in the United States in the 1850s. The Reverend C. B. Boynton and T. B. Mason, forming a Committee of the Kansas League of Cincinnati, toured Kansas and Nebraska in 1854 and published a book in which they advocated town-based colonies.

It is not now an impracticable thing to transplant a whole community, with all its various members and occupations, so that nearly all the comforts and benefits of an old society may be at once enjoyed in the new position. Churches, schools, professional men, merchants and mechanics of all kinds, may locate themselves together, and commence the new life with all the operations and relations of the old.[59]

At the end of the next decade N. C. Meeker advanced similar arguments in support of his proposed colony at Greeley, Colorado. "Some of the advantages of settling in a village, will be: easy access to schools and public places, lectures and the like; and society can be had at once." He maintained that "schools, refined society, and all the advantages of an old country will be secured in a few years."[60]

Another reason why governments and private agencies alike were tempted to create towns at the start of the settlement process rather than let them "evolve" naturally was that they thereby could create prematurely an "unearned increment" and benefit from it both for profit and for purposes of promoting the general development of the colony.[61] The alternative was to allow the increase in the value of land which occurred when it was changed into the site of a town to go to those individuals who had initially bought it very cheaply before it was categorized as town land. The Wakefieldian companies created their towns and then in effect gave this increased value away, using the prospect of benefiting from it to entice people to buy land orders from them. Lord Howick asked Wakefield in 1841 whether doing this had not meant "a distinct loss to the society at large, to the whole body of adventurers" who settled South Australia. Wakefield's reply was that "it might not be, because there might have been no colony at all but for the temptation held out to the advance of capital and emigration by the prospect of obtaining that large premium for the most beneficially situated lands."[62]

The initial establishment of a town appealed also to organizers and administrators who desired a fixed center from which a settlement could be supervised most conveniently, efficiently, and cheaply. When Melbourne was founded, Governer Bourke argued that "a certain degree of concentration . . . enables Government to become at once efficient and economical."[63]

The strategy of building towns first in a scheme or program of colonization was often subject to criticism. To many critics it seemed "unnatural," doomed to fail because it defied the natural processes of social evolution with involved "country" being settled first and establishing the foundations, the "hinterland," for "healthy," durable urban development.[64] A characteristic clash of opinion on this issue was that between John Graves Simcoe and Lord Dorchester, the governor of Canada. Simcoe, in 1794, urged a policy of stationing troops in places in the interior which appeared "marked by natural advantages, the confluence of Rivers, the security of Harbours or the termination of Portages" for the development of towns.

It is . . . I conceive Wisdom to apply the means which Government must allow for the defence of this Colony in its Infancy to such purposes as may create a solid and permanent system, which would never spring up merely from Agriculture, and would be late indeed, if left to the culture of Mercantile Monopoly.[65]

This accepts that a natural process of social evolution involves only the very slow growth of towns and that government intervention to accelerate the growth is both wise and safe. Lord Dorchester took a very different point of view. When Simcoe unfolded his plans for this capital on the frontier, Dorchester wrote back anxiously:

I am also to desire you will inform me of the Progress of Population and Agriculture on the North side of those Lakes, and how near they approach Toronto; the settling and cultivating the Country round that Post must facilitate and bring forward every advantage its situation can afford, and well deserves encouragement: prior thereto every attempt must be attended with difficulty.[66]

The argument about the law of "nature" being a progression from "country" to increasingly sophisticated forms of urban community was met in two ways. Some, such as Simcoe, accepted it but argued for a "forced" acceleration of the process by government intervention in the general interest of the community. Meeker pointed out that in his method of colonizing urban amenities would be available within a few years, "while on the contrary, where settlements are made by the old methods, people are obliged to wait twenty, forty, or more years."[67] The result was the failure of settlement as people left the land, destroyed by loneliness and isolation. In *Bogle Corbet* Galt went further and claimed that it was unnatural to live scattered in the forest like "banished men." Human being were social by nature, and so, "by beginning with a town, you follow the course of Nature."[68]

The main problem of town-based colonization was seen as being that it could cause serious distortion and imbalance as the "town" element in a scheme became developed far in advance of the "country." The result could be disaster because no town could survive for long in a "healthy" condition if not supported by a prosperous agricultural hinterland. To some observers the condition of Guelph, the town that Galt founded, seemed to confirm the wisdom of respecting this "law." Adam Fergusson visited Guelph in 1831, five years after it had been founded, and reported that it

wears a stagnant appearance, and conveys somewhat the idea of the cart preceding the horse. When farms become numerous, and a mill is erected in a convenient situation, a town soon grows up; but here the town has been hurried forward, in the hope of settling the land. . . . At present, a very desolate complexion marks Guelph, as a city which may be very thankful to maintain its ground, and escape desertion.[69]

Indeed, in *Bogle Corbet* the initial instinct of the settlers was to react in much this way to Corbet's proposal that a village be planted first. They told him "that they did not think the beginning with a village was so good as the practice of the country, where every man worked for himself on his own farm." Eventually, they—or rather their wives—were persuaded otherwise when Corbet stressed the advantages of society and mutual aid that a village would bring.[70]

Another place where putting the village first as a deliberate strategy to promote the early maturing of "society" seemed to go disastrously wrong was Greeley. According to the historian of the Union colony, there was in the initial stages

too much of a tendency to push things in a magnificent style, and have a city spring as by magic from the bosom of the naked plains. The favorite figure of the "General" [N. C. Meeker] was to have the "desert blossom as the rose." It is true that, under the forcing process adopted, we had a sort of a town grow up in a hurry. But it was at first only a mushroom growth.[71]

When Horace Greeley, the man after whom the colony was named, visited it on October 12, 1870, "he found the settlement all town and no country—a state of affairs he very much disliked." In a speech he "found fault that so little had been done in the country compared with the town." He advised them to form a Farmers' Club.[72] Greeley in effect condemned the "town first" strategy which had been attempted in the colony.

He advised them [the people] to get out of town and build up the rural districts first, and the town would follow as a natural consequence. Our people were habitually gregarious and too fond [of] flocking to our cities and villages, where they help to swell the ranks of squalid misery and every manner of crime, and pestilence, and want, and all the evils that infest our densely populated places everywhere.[73]

Greeley clearly dreaded a repetition in the West of the processes that had built up his own city of New York.

What is particularly interesting here is a recurrence of the same theme that underlies the drama of the planting of "Stockwell" in *Bogle Corbet*. This is the conflict between human nature, which both Corbet and Greeley accept involves gregariousness and a desire for the company and aid of other human beings, and social "nature," which dictates that country must come before town or "unhealthy" consequences will ensue. If gregariousness and therefore city-building were American characteristics, so was the love of liberty, and that was what ultimately came to the rescue at Greeley and resolved the tension between the two forces of "nature." A majority of the people were opposed to the requirement to build in town, "holding that each individual had a right to build on any of his parcels of ground he might select."

So it happened that those who did not intend to make the town their permanent place of abode, just put up such shanties as would secure their deeds. Most of these inferior buildings were at length moved out into the country, but for a long time a part remained unoccupied, the glass in the windows nearly all broken out by the bad boys of the town.[74]

What happened in Greeley over the next decade was a complex process of readjustment of the balance which ended in some sort of reconciliation of the two aspirations. The value of town lots fell abruptly in 1871 and remained depressed throughout the seventies. The town's development was slow as it marked time waiting for agriculture to become established. Writing in 1890, David Boyd reported that many of the better-off farmers now lived in town.

All the farmers had originally lots in town, and many still held on to them when they moved out to the front, and then returned when they could afford it, while some never moved their families out. They preferred to give their wives and children the social and school advantages of the town, if they did make less material wealth.[75]

The "Sunday houses" in places such as Fredericksburg in Texas may have played a similar role in enabling farmers to continue to enjoy some of the advantages of town society; pastoralists in New South Wales maintained small houses in towns such as Yass;[76] while, on a much grander scale, wealthy squatters in Australia and New Zealand and cattle ranchers in Montana and Texas lived for much of the year in mansions in the cities and enjoyed a luxurious life-style.[77]

Settlements such as Greeley were the exception in the United States. For the most part, private enterprise, usually motivated by the desire to speculate, could be relied on to supply an urban component in frontier settlement, and, if there were an over-supply, then market forces would effect a remedy. But, in countries such as Australia and Canada, where the wilderness was so much more forbidding, the question was whether some sort of government intervention in natural processes was essential and could be carried out without risking an unhealthy and perhaps fatal imbalance between town and country. In a report to the Colonial Office on the state of the North American provinces in 1832, John Richards queried whether an uncontrolled, *laissez-faire* redemption of the Canadian wilderness would work:

With the Americans such a retail occupation of the wilderness is by no means objectionable, as it harmonizes with their habits of progressive advance; —First, settlement of any kind attracts attention to the district, then speculation creeps in, and various interests get engaged in it; enterprising young men of the professional classes soon follow; villages grow up; and if anything like commercial enterprise can take root, the bank completes the machinery of social life.

But nothing of this sort happened, or in his view could be expected to happen, in the Canadas. There the better-off migrants

take up lots for individual occupation, have no idea of speculating beyond their own farms, so that there are no means of concentrating energy for public purposes; and the district, however numerous its inhabitants, seems to be without any common principle of action. In the absence of such exciting causes, Government seems more called upon to set the machine in motion.[78]

The dilemma also became apparent in evidence given to a House of Lords Select Committee on Colonization from Ireland in 1847. The committee heard John Robert Godley, who was shortly to take a leading role in the settlement of Canterbury in New Zealand by a company, explain that one reason for the greater attractiveness of the United States to migrants was its "possession of towns and cities, securing the appliances of civilized life." They also heard from Earl Grey, the colonial secretary, of the "insuperable difficulties" which had frustrated a plan to establish villages in Canada for the reception of migrants.[79] What was the answer? To some witnesses and writers on colonization at this time it was that the government should organize a major scheme of railway construction in Canada: "the formation of a railway will involve the growth of flourishing peopled towns in the wilderness, with all the means, appliances, and accommodations of social life."[80]

In Australia too there was much concern to find a safe way of stimulating the formation of towns, one that would not offend against basic laws of social evolution and end in an absurdly unbalanced development of "town" in advance of "country." Several governors of New South Wales tried to plan regionally, to provide for an integrated relationship of town and country. The Waste Lands Act of 1842 set aside all land within five miles of a town for sale in small farms or suburban holdings. It was a common complaint by country townspeople in Australia and New Zealand that their towns stagnated because surrounded by what was from their point of view sterile country, owned either by speculators who made no use of their services or by large-scale pastoralists who did not make adequate use of them. Governor Gipps—like Meeker at Greeley—brought in a policy of concentric development in which lots available for farming became larger as the distance from the town increased. A very elaborate policy of this kind was adopted at Brisbane, while some of the Wakefieldian settlements, such as Nelson in New Zealand, had intermediate zones of "suburban" land, intended to keep small farmers close to the core urban community. All such policies, of course, required continuing regulation.[81]

All schemes of "systematic colonization" rested on the assumption that the development of "town" and "country" had to proceed simultaneously. Each needed the other. Laborers wanted land but also, for economic reasons, had to have access to urban employment opportunities. Farmers needed markets and the cultural, social, religious, and political facilities which only towns could provide.[82] To Wakefieldians the answer was the mechanism of the sufficient price which would prevent speculators from acquiring large tracts of land cheaply and mean that land near towns would be available in small quantities when laborers had saved enough to be able to buy it.

The critics of "concentration," even while admitting that it might be desirable for religious and social reasons, tended to feel that it was rendered nonviable by cast-iron "laws" of social evolution. Lord Glenelg, colonial secretary in 1836, maintained that the geography of southeastern Australia presented "a physical impediment to the close concentration of its inhabitants, with which it would be only futile to contend by human laws." In explaining this he appeared to be applying to New South Wales the classical four-stage model. "The age of manufacturing industry is of course remote, even tillage can scarcely be pursued advantageously to any great extent." But New South Wales appeared "marked out by nature for a Pastoral Country." That meant that its population would be very dispersed.[83] Critics of Wakefieldism saw it as forcing on a new and remote country a socio-economic system—close-knit agricultural villages—to which it was totally unsuited.

One of the most ambitious attempts to work out a theory of colonization that would allow a "natural" process of "concentration" to occur was that offered by J. C. Byrne in *Twelve Years' Wanderings in the British Colonies* (1848). Byrne was a firm believer in the principle that the development of the country must come first.

The townships founded by the Government, have never succeeded in inducing population thither, unless the surrounding country was already settled, and required the combined industry of trades and mechanism to supply their wants. Collective communities will always spontaneously form, if the population that require such are dispersed through the surrounding country. Towns should follow, and not precede general settlement in new countries, for they are only required to *supply,* and not *create,* the wants centralization administers to.

To bolster his argument Byrne cited approvingly an article in the *Sydney Herald* which claimed that experience in Australia proved that *"dispersion is the natural means to healthful concentration."* As population spread into the interior, new townships sprang up "spontaneously." Furthermore, there was then "an easy but vigorous system of action and re-action" by which people used these as a base from which to penetrate further inland and found new townships. The result was a process by which the wilderness would be transformed

into a series of domestic circles, and of large and flourishing communities. This seems to be the order in which it is designed by Providence that civilized men, in this new world of spontaneous pasturage, shall "be fruitful and multiply, and replenish the earth and subdue it."

At this point in his book Byrne's faith in the spontaneity of this process seemed absolute. But, as the book progressed, he placed more and more emphasis on the moral, religious, and economic necessity of towns in the wilderness. Eventually he moved halfway toward accepting that some sort of government intervention would be needed to ensure that towns were planted in the interior of Australia.[84] Sir Thomas Mitchell himself, while condemning the Wakefieldian principle of forcing "concentration," nevertheless did not leave the formation of towns and villages to the working of spontaneity and "Providence" but vigorously pursued a policy of establishing sites for them.

CHAPTER FIVE

Towns and Social Evolution: The Growth of Towns

A LTHOUGH—or rather, in some important respects, because—the evolutionary model assigned a small place to towns in the early stages of settlement, it provided ample scope for boosters of urbanism in the new societies. An evolutionary process of the kind commonly believed in meant that ultimately there would be great cities. Charles N. Glaab and other historians have abundantly documented the existence in the United States of numerous prophets of a "West of great cities," such as Logan U. Reavis, William Gilpin, and Jesup W. Scott.[1] Scott was in the evolutionary tradition. He accepted the thesis of the Physiocrats and of Adam Smith that agriculture comes before industry and trade. But he foresaw evolution of the West to the point where great cities would develop in the Mississippi Valley and eventually the majority of the people in that region would live in them.[2]

Similar prophecies were made about other new countries. For example, in *Our Own Country* (1889) W. H. Withrow reported a sermon given at Grace Church, Winnipeg, by Dr. Bowman Stephenson, who was traveling with him. Stephenson confessed to having had "his imagination greatly excited" by Winnipeg.

Let any man think what was going to happen between this place and the Rocky Mountains in the next fifty years; what great villages would rise, what homesteads would be planted all over these fertile plains, what great and powerful towns, what mighty cities would be built—who could say what was going to be in the next half century?[3]

One of the most celebrated and later oft-recalled Australian prophecies was Erasmus Darwin's poem, "The Visit of Hope to Sydney Cove," predicting the rise of a noble city at that location.[4]

The theme of "evolution" was also widely used in prediction and interpretation of the internal development of towns. The usual description of that development was in terms of "growth." Images of passing through phases of infancy and adolescence, of aging and maturing, were commonplace.[5] A German visitor to San Francisco in 1861 expressed a very common nineteenth-century perception of urban development. "Cities are like human beings; they have their period as suckling babes; their childhood; their gray old age."[6]

One of the most imaginative treatments of this theme and of how it affected townspeople's perceptions of their urban environment is Estelline Bennett's *Old Deadwood Days* (1928) in which there is a fascinating intertwining of processes of growing up and aging in people and in towns. The author, the daughter of Judge Granville Bennett, a leading personality in the early history of Deadwood, South Dakota, records no less a person than Buffalo Bill—William F. Cody—as using language of this kind and using it, furthermore, in a complex way which suggests how well established this rhetoric had become. Discussing the impact of the railroad on Deadwood, Buffalo Bill said that

railroads always aged a town. "A town is young", he said, "just as long as it stays off the railroad." "It's too bad the railroad came," I commented. "Oh, no," he said quietly but decidedly, "a town is like a baby. It either grows up or dies." And then he added with the ready optimism of the real Westerner, "But Deadwood, you know, was young so long it never will quite forget its youth."

This insight reverberates through and informs the rest of the book as the author strives to recall and relive the time when both she and the town were young. She remembers it as a place where there was no old age. "Only youth could make itself a part of the town that Deadwood was in the eighties."[7] A similar theme informs Edward D. Mansfield's 1855 biography of Dr. Daniel Drake, the famous early booster of Cincinnati. Mansfield shows us Drake coming to Cincinnati as a medical student in 1800. He was young, and Cincinnati was in its "infancy," "the *germ,* but the mere germ, the place only of a future city." Drake is seen as inspired by the "genius of the place," "a state in which a great future was to be produced, chiefly by the energy, will, and genius of the present actors."[8] Through the imagery of "growth" personal and civic destiny were intertwined.

There was recognition of an initial, very brief "pioneer" period.[9] This was the period which was characterized in later histories by a heavy emphasis on who was the first to do something or what was the first institution of a particular kind. This phase quickly passed, and a town "matured" and perhaps grew to "greatness." Stages of growth were also seen as marked by a town's architecture. There was much play on the concepts of a "wooden age" and a "stone age."[10] The immediate use of brick as a building material in Winnipeg was seen by one visitor as confounding conventional notions about the aging of a town.[11]

"Growth" was seen as the characteristic of New World and especially American towns. Old World towns, or towns in the New World that were still under some sort of Old World influence, for example, as the exclusive residences of particular ethnic or immigrant groups, were perceived as observing different rules. George Flower wrote of a French village in America: "As it was in the beginning so it is now. It is as old as Philadelphia. An American village would long ago [have] run to ruin, or grown into a town or city."[12]

Especially in the United States, names of towns were indicators of perceived stages of growth. In *Travels in Canada* (1861) J. G. Kohl has a theory to explain the frequency of name changes in North America.

The rapidly-growing American towns seem sometimes to be ashamed of their first European names which were given them while they were still mere embryos, and which are often associated with remembrances of which the city, when it has grown rich and grand, begins to be ashamed.

He instances the change from York to Toronto—there were too many contrasts of "Dirty Little York" with splendid New York—and from Bytown to Ottawa because the former suggested "Out-of-the-way Place."[13] "Denver City" was the first name of Denver, "City" being dropped once it became clear that Denver *was* going to be a city.[14] The word "city" became devalued by being peculiarly—and, to most foreign visitors, ludicrously—associated with small places that wished to signal their aspiration to become a city.[15] An early historian of Omaha—"Omaha City" until the late 1850s—explained that the word "city" was a "kite" attached to the names of Western cities in their infancy: "when they grow to some size and importance, when they can speak for themselves, they cut off the tail."[16]

Buffalo Bill's view that a town must either grow or die was widely held. It appeared in Australia too. "There is no state of standstill here," wrote Henry Cornish in *Under the Southern Cross* (1880). "A place either grows or declines. Rapid progress, or rapid decay, is the invariable order of things."[17] Similarly in America there had to be not merely growth but fast growth. In the usually intensely competitive relationship among towns doom was predicted for the slow developer. Such predictions had a habit of being self-fulfilling. When visiting Madison in Indiana in the early 1850s, Richard Beste gained the impression that it was "declining or stationary." After learning that its population had in fact advanced from 9,025 in 1840 to 10,031 in 1850, he wrote: "This is corroborative of my recollection of its state of decay: an increase of ten per cent in ten years is tantamount to a decrease in this country."[18] D. W. Meinig has written that, when in 1870 the population of The Dalles, Washington Territory, leveled off at 970, this was seen by many residents as "an oppressive stagnation."[19] However, there was a reaction against this notion whenever fast growth became identified with boom-and-bust conditions. Then slow growth came into fashion, being described as "healthy." This point was naturally resorted to by boosters of towns which were growing only slowly.[20]

Given that evolutionary models were generally accepted as relevant to urban development in the New World, there were several critical questions that had to be answered by those concerned to interpret and predict the course of that development. One was whether new societies had to start all over again at the first primitive stages of social evolution, as Turner suggested was the case. An alternative argument was that what happened was, or could be made to be, an extension and continuation of the processes of the Old World from the point which *they* had reached. The New World could take up evolution at that point and not need to repeat the entire sequence of evolutionary stages. In Darwinian terms the new towns would "evolve" because their builders were able to look at the cities of the Old World, observe what was wrong with them, and take care to avoid these defects in the making of their own towns. Anthony Trollope saw the founders of American cities as fortunate in having had "the experience of the world before them."[21] Fredrika Bremer observed in *The Homes of the New World* (1853): "First you see in the wilderness some log-houses, then neat frame and small stone houses, then elegant villas and cottages; and before many years are over, there stands, as if by magic, a town with its Capitol or State House, its handsome churches, splendid hotels, academies, and institutions of all kinds." This is a statement of the evolutionary theory in classic form. But to Fredrika Bremer the motor force driving this process was not the immutable laws of social evolution but the ability of "the West" to learn from "the East." "The West repeats the cities, the institutions, and the cultivation of the East, and their course is rapid and safe."[22]

Fredrika Bremer was far from being alone in believing that the New World reproduced Old World processes of social evolution in a vastly compressed, telescoped, and accelerated form. John Gates Thurston in *A Journal of a Trip to Illinois in 1836* commented that the rise of Cincinnati appeared to be "the work of ages" but had actually taken only a few years.[23] Condensations of the process tended to become ever briefer. San Francisco was described as having "accomplished in a day the growth of half a century."[24] One fascinating aspect of this to some observers was that one could actually witness and study an entire process which in the Old World had usually extended over centuries.[25] So rapid was the change that retaining any clear sense of process was often difficult. The whole thing could seem a blur with all the stages of growth mixed up together. Alfred Domett referred to York's "rapid rise and growth, a proverb of the sudden maturity of the towns in this young world, all of which are in a state of infancy and adolescence at one and the same period."[26]

All this was made to order for boosters who took up many of these themes and devised endless variations on them to suit the promotional requirements and strategies of their towns. For example, telescoping enabled large boasts to be made about small towns. In *The Present State of Australia* (1830) Robert Dawson predicted that Sydney would be superior to any other city of the world, adding the qualification "which was ever created in the same space of time."[27] Melbourne did become a very big city, but Rolf Boldrewood in *Old Melbourne Memories* (1896) tried to make it bigger still by referring to it as "the largest, the most highly civilised, the most prosperous city in the world, for the years of its existence."[28]

Boosters made a great drama out of the rapidity of the change. Their "histories" made the early days seem very primitive, and there was constant harping on the vast changes between "then" and "now."[29] Every city had its repertoire of extraordinarily similar stories and anecdotes of the early days to dramatize how far it had advanced in such a short time —grandmother's cow tethered to the tree where the town hall now stands; the colonist who declined, "because it was too far away in the bush," to take up a piece of land that later became prime city-center real estate;[30] the hat floating in a hole in the street which turned out to belong to a man sitting on a horse.

The character of change in cities was a favorite subject for contrast between Old World and New World. William Kelly in *Life in Victoria* (1859) described Melbourne's growth as "truly wonderful, not to be imagined or understood in the ordinary growth or progress of Old World cities."[31] "An English village," wrote William Westgarth in *Victoria and the Australian Gold Mines* (1857), "may be identified for an age together, without any material change of aspect; but in half that time a colonial village has become a city, and extinguished, perhaps, every feature of its pristine scattered and humble appearance."[32] In *Australian Sketches* (1861), Thomas McCombie commented on the great changes over the past ten years at St. Kilda, a Melbourne suburb: "Within that period but few changes have been effected in many towns in Europe, and in some considerable villages not a stone has been altered."[33] Not surprisingly, many comments of this kind were made about new cities in the United States. Count Adelbert Baudissin wrote in *Der Ansiedler im Missouri-Staate* (1854):

Nothing earns our admiration as much as the rapid rise of towns in the domain of the American Union. We Germans are accustomed to see a town as a place which doubtless stood hundreds of years ago and carried nearly the same features as today; we are amazed at the blossoming of a town if here and there some new houses are built, but we never see a new town in our fatherland arise as if through a stroke of magic.[34]

In his *Emigrant's Guide to the Western States of America* John Regan published letters sent back to the "Old Country" by immigrants. In one a Scottish farmer wrote: "The difference between towns here and with you is, that with you they are finished, but here it is not uncommon to have large cities spring up in a few years."[35]

The two perspectives on time came into amusing confrontation during a train journey which the English poet Rupert Brooke took from Edmonton to Calgary. Two fellow passengers swapped statistics about their cities:

Edmonton had grown from thirty persons to forty thousand in twenty years; but Calgary from twenty to thirty thousand in twelve. . . . "Where"—as a respite— "did I come from?" I had to tell them, not without shame, that my own town of Grantchester, having numbered three hundred at the time of Julius Caesar's landing, had risen rapidly to nearly four by Doomsday Book, but was now declined to three-fifty. They seemed perplexed and angry.[36]

Most of the comparisons were couched in extreme terms, as the foregoing examples indicate. Boosting reinforced this tendency. Only occasionally was there any acknowledgment that rapid urban growth was also now occurring in the Old World. W. E. Adams did refer to Middlesbrough, Barrow, and Jarrow in England as examples of "the sudden and rapid rise of populous communities," but added: "these instances of rapidity of development are so exceptional in England, as indeed in all old countries, that it would be difficult to recall any others of an equally striking character."[37] R. Therry in *Reminiscences of Thirty Years' Residence in New South Wales and Victoria* (1863) was almost the only writer to place statements about Melbourne's rapid growth in the perspective of an admission that changes of equal magnitude had been in progress in society in England.[38] Most writers ignored such qualifications and complications and assumed that the New World was very distinct and special.

Why did change occur so fast in the towns of the New World? James S. Ritchie in *Wisconsin and Its Resources* (1857), while describing the classic log cabin-to-village-to-city pattern of frontier evolution, commented on the psychological force behind the rapidity of the process. Urban growth happened so fast because it was wanted by the log-cabin dwellers from the very start. It was a product of pioneers' dreams and anxiety to escape from the grim initial phases of settlement. At the outset the pioneer sees not just a farm but, "perhaps, an Addition to the future city." Eventually his cabin is in the midst of a village.

One of his dreams is accomplished—his *"claim"* is now included in the town; where he once toiled from morn till night to clear a few acres, is now selling at so much per lot; he sees himself growing richer every day with the growth of the town; the railroad bill is passed, and the road commenced a short distance from him. He cannot realize his good fortune; his children now are well dressed, and you meet their smiling faces on their way to the little log school-house. One would think that they had never known the hardships of a "pioneer life."[39]

This emphasizes enthusiasm for rapid change. There were few observers who ventured to suggest that all this rapid and "unnatural" change might be having an adverse effect on the people who were caught up in it. Most boosters and visitors preferred to highlight the positive—"wonder," "marvel," "magic." William Westgarth did refer to "an agony of turmoil that does not suit every temperament": "The levellings of new streets and roads, encroaching on the primeval sod where we had rambled in fresh country air but a year or two before; the everlasting uproar of bricks and mortar at every turn."[40] Indeed, boosting should be seen as in part an attempt to help people cope with this state of affairs by placing emphasis on the positive aspects and drawing attention away to the glorious future that this noisy, painful present was preparing.

Indeed, there was a darker, less optimistic side to the evolutionary theme which was used most of the time to celebrate marvelous rapidity of growth. There was a widespread contemporary belief in a cyclical pattern of history, that societies both rose and fell and that it was an inexorable law of social evolution that "decline and fall" must eventually happen to every society. This idea has had a powerful influence on western interpretations of world history, from Edward Gibbon's *Decline and Fall of the Roman Empire* in the eighteenth century to Arnold Toynbee's *A Study of History* and Paul Kennedy's *Rise and Fall of the Great Powers* in the twentieth. The downfall of the British Empire and the decline of Britain's status as a world power have extended the life of the rise-and-fall thesis into our own times—when there are even those who look for signs of the decline of the "American empire." A major nineteenth-century writer on America who believed in rise-and-fall cycles was Alexis de Tocqueville.[41] Numerous foreigners who visited the United States incorporated a vision or prophecy of decline into their reactions to the spectacular rise of American Western cities. Here, for instance, is what a Scottish clergyman, John Kirkwood, was thinking as he journeyed by train across Iowa on *An Autumn Holiday in the United States and Canada* (1887):

My thoughts, perhaps my dreams, were of these attempts to found new cities on this unpeopled wilderness. I imagined them as, in many respects, a repetition, after fully four thousand years, of the work of a Nimrod, or an Ashur, making a beginning of Babylon and Nineveh, with a few mud or wooden huts, on the plains of Shinar and Assyria; while other foundations, equally hopeful at the time, faded like Jonah's gourd, and have left only names behind. May not history repeat itself still further, so that some promising new Indianapolis or Minnieapolis [sic] will end, even with the present generation, only in a Necropolis; and long before the next four thousand years, the most successful cities of the West will have passed away, and their very sites be long lost, as were those of the East? And may not some future Layard be found making diligent search among deserted mounds, and vast heaps of rubbish, for traces of Capitols and Custom-Houses, Churches and Colleges, Exchanges and Elevators, remains of the proud cities of the prairies of Iowa? The picture is just as probable of realization and as pleasing as that of Macaulay's New Zealander on the ruined arches of London Bridge.[42]

This last reference leads us back to Old World thinking on the rise and fall of urban civilizations.[43]

In Britain such ideas strongly influenced early nineteenth-century reactions to the growth of industrial cities. The most notorious pessimist was the Reverend Thomas Malthus, who saw the pressure of population on resources as a likely mechanism for triggering the "decline" part of the cycle. The relieving of this pressure was one of the motives behind advocacy of the promotion of emigration by the State in the 1820s and 1830s. It was not until the 1840s, under the influence of the great public health reformer Edwin Chadwick, that "optimists," those who believed that the ills of the cities could be controlled by human action and cities made habitable for large populations, gained the upper hand and it began to seem that "decline" was not inevitable.[44]

As for the United States, Stow Persons and David Lowenthal have shown how widespread was belief there in the cyclical interpretation of history, at least in the eighteenth and early nineteenth centuries.[45] John Quincy Adams warned Americans to "remember that we shall fall . . . into the decline and infirmities of old age."[46] But in America such reminders seem to have had little power to frighten, largely because the country was seen as being still at an early stage of the life cycle. The cyclical view was present, but "decline" was a long way off. In 1836 Ralph Waldo Emerson exulted in the founding of great cities. "We see the camp pitched, & the fire lighted which shall never be extinguished until great natural revolutions set a limit to human empire."[47]

But lurking not too far below the surface of much discussion of urban development in America was fear that the downward side of the cyclical process would all too soon be putting in its appearance. Some observers betrayed their sensitivity to what might be interpreted as early signs of this happening. Here was a major source of deep underlying insecurity. A visitor to Canada in the early 1880s was very impressed by the substantial brick buildings that had been erected at Winnipeg. He commented: "No one looking at them can feel here, as is so commonly felt in other places of rapid growth on this continent, that the citizens apprehend their city will decay as rapidly as it has sprung up."[48] Occasional apocalyptic visions of catastrophic "fall" disturbed the boosterish optimism of American Western urban promotionalism. Some retained their optimism as far as the West was concerned by prophesying that that region would be the beneficiary of such a development. In 1830 a writer in Timothy Flint's

Western Monthly Review couched in the following form his prediction of the rise of great cities within the Ohio Valley in the next twenty years.

Who shall say, that when decay shall have laid his finger on the pride of Atlantic greatness,—when luxury and corruption shall have defiled the cities and over-spread the shores of the great *Salt Lake;* when their science shall have degenerated into sophistry, and their liberties have become the prey of tyranny, when the splendour of their early history shall have ceased to kindle emotions of patriotism —who shall say, that the glories of the American name may not beam with unabated lustre over the waters of these inland seas?[49]

As this extract indicates, there was a widespread belief that the cyclical process was essentially a *moral* phenomenon and that decline and decay were produced by a deterioration in moral standards, seen as peculiarly a result of the rise of large cities. In other words, the pessimistic interpretation of cities was that, splendid as they might be in their "rising," their "greatness" contained the seeds of their decline because of the moral degeneration inevitably associated with city life. Even Daniel Drake, optimist and booster although he normally was, sometimes lapsed into this species of pessimism. In 1834 Drake lectured on "the Philosophy of Family, School, and College Discipline." He spoke of the advance of the West and referred to "the *vice and anarchy,* which may overwhelm it, as the angry snows of the mountain dissolve and swell with troubled waters the peaceful Ohio, till they deluge our pleasant places, and rush in deso-lation along our streets." Indeed, Drake said that cities "are justly said to be the grand sources from which vice and immorality flow upon the country; the *foci* whence the principles of wickedness and crime are radiated far and wide."[50] Disease was one of the most dominant issues in perceptions of the early nineteenth-century city,[51] and few cities were more prone to repeated and devastating epidemics than those that lay along the interior rivers. This was a major reason for the perceived vulnerability of towns, and interpretations of the causes of disease were often strongly moral in character.[52] Carl E. Kramer has written that there was "a deeply ingrained fear that cities were inherently dangerous and a belief that constant vigilance was necessary to keep them from becoming breeding places for disease and death."[53]

John Kirkwood's "thoughts," quoted above, capture very well the style of much of the discourse about the destiny of American cities. There were constant references to Tyre, Nineveh, Athens, and other great cities of antiquity. "Modern" though he may seem to be in, for instance, his use of statistics, Jesup W. Scott filled his essays with analogies between the history of those cities and the course that Western urban development was taking and was likely to take in America. The frequent use of classical names for new American towns was often commented on by visitors and often laughed at and satirized. Newspaper editors and boosters were very fond of developing classical analogies. In 1820 the editor of a Cincinnati newspaper conceded that "Cincinnati may be the Tyre, but Lexington is unquestionably the Athens of the West." Another Cincinnatian, however, argued that mounting an ambitious lecture program might "convince those persons at a distance who pronounced us a *Commercial* people alone, that we have here, both the *Tyre* and the *Athens* of the West."[54]

But there was, of course, a darker side to all this rhetoric about the cities of antiquity. For where were they now? If American cities were the new Tyres and Sidons and Palmyras, were they not therefore destined to suffer the same fate?

But Americans had no need to look so far afield in order to derive from "antiquity" thoughts and clues concerning the prospects of urban civilization in the American West. For throughout the West were many mysterious mounds and other earthworks, the relics of an "Indian" civilization long since vanished. These looked remarkably and, to those addicted to cyclical theories, depressingly like the remains of *cities*. In 1838 the *Western Messenger* published an article on "Western Antiquities" in which the author pointed out that the earthworks

are evidently the productions of a people of settled habits, who lived in cities, and congregated together for mutual support and defence. The immense cemeteries which have been discovered at Grave Creek, near Wheeling, at the "Big Bone Bank" on the Wabash, and other places, indicate that this people lived in cities, or in large communities, and that the population of the valley of the Ohio, was once as dense, if not more so, than it is at present.

The contemplation of these monuments

involuntarily excite[s] in the mind a train of melancholy reflections upon the uncertain tenure by which even nations hold their existence. The mightiest empires have been dissolved; the proudest cities have crumbled into ruins. In this favored land, where the energies of a free people are now exerted in building up a system of things which they hope will be perpetual, a mighty nation once existed, who little thought their fame would be lost in the revolutions of ages.[55]

Daniel Drake was himself an amateur archaeologist who liked to investigate the mounds at Cincinnati. His first book on Cincinnati, *Natural or*

Statistical View (1815), included an account of what had been found there. He devised cyclical interpretations of the history of man in the Ohio Valley. Migrants had arrived and developed cities. But then "to the unwilling view is presented the gloomy spectacle of exterminating wars, and decline in civilization; with his ultimate degradation into the present savage, his exile to some distant country, or entire annihilation."[56] One striking feature was that, as Mansfield pointed out, the ruins were "uniformly found on the best sites for towns, and the modern cities of the Ohio valley almost invariably replace and represent those of antiquity."[57] Some found in this an auspicious omen of a great destiny for a new town. David Thomas, who traveled through Indiana in 1816, referred to Vincennes, near which rose two enormous mounds, as "this ancient capital of *the West*." "These remains of antiquity show that this plain has been the seat of wealth and power; and though it is now only the frontier town of a new race, it will probably long retain a superiority over the towns and cities of this country."[58] Others, however, found contemplation of the mounds less encouraging. Citizens of many of these new towns had every day to confront evidence of the ephemeral character of urban civilization in their region. Perhaps this is one reason why they were often so anxious to obliterate the mounds or at least took so little care to ensure their preservation.

To some observers it did seem that similar processes were already beginning to occur in the American West. Perhaps no refuge could be taken even in the thought that, as America was still in its infancy as a nation, the "decline" part of the cycle would not begin for a very long time to come. For, if, as everyone acknowledged, American towns rose with unprecedented rapidity, might not their fall be equally rapid? In 1834 Carl David Arfwedson wrote of towns disappearing with the same speed as others rose: "what in Europe is formed or undone in the lapse of ages is here effected in as many months."[59] A major cause of this high mortality rate among new Western towns was speculation. In most newly opened Western regions rampant town-site speculation set in almost immediately, and a high proportion of the towns thus given initial life failed and "died." Count Adelbert Baudissin noted how towns would acquire characteristics of age and decay within a short time of their foundation:

The Americans, as a preference, seek out the newly founded towns; but if the new town does not thrive in a hurry, they vacate house and yard and take themselves on to another place which promises more advantage. For this reason one finds in nearly all towns half and wholly fallen-down houses, the owners of which are often completely unknown.[60]

These houses thus instantly joined the ancient "mounds" whose owners were also "completely unknown." Travelers would come across and comment on towns that it seemed were well on their way to becoming just as mysterious as those mounds. Thomas Ashe discovered in 1806 that Chilicothe was soon to cease being the Ohio capital. It would then be abandoned and "the traveller who follows me will hardly find an inhabitant in it to tell him when it rose and how it fell: when it flourished, and by what means it so soon decayed."[61] E. D. Mansfield saw the many towns that had been founded in the Ohio Valley and had subsequently disappeared as having "performed the circuit of Tyre or Nineveh, in rising to splendor and falling to decay."[62]

Later in the century there were the innumerable mining towns which rose and then declined to "ghost town" status with incredible rapidity.[63] The fall as well as the rise of towns fascinated American writers such as Mark Twain, whose *Life on the Mississippi* contains many accounts of his discovery of the disappearance of river towns which he had known in his youth. Here the implications of personal aging are intertwined with reflections on the life and death of these places.

Mining towns were dramatic reminders of the possibility of urban mortality. They were the specter at the feast. It is not surprising that town boosters, who emphasized the "magic" of the rapid rise of their towns, found them an embarrassment and often demonstrated much anxiety to prevent the making of analogies between the two types of town.[64]

But there remained the problem of how to deal with a process of "growth" and "maturing" without also being obliged to acknowledge that one day a town—perhaps even an entire urban civilization—would "age" and "die." J. L. McConnel, who likened the progress of civilization in the West to the course of the Mississippi, had the river reaching "its last ripe fruit, a crowded city," and then observed that, "beyond this, there lies nothing but a brief journey, and a plunge into the gulf of Eternity."[65] Towns were so often personalized that it seemed impossible to prevent extension of the analogy to the entire range of human life. "Cities are like human beings," said I. J. Benjamin, a German visitor to San Francisco in 1861. "Yes, many even die . . . Nineveh, Pompeii, Palenque had their beginnings, matured, flourished, aged, fell, and were forgotten in their graves until [Layard], Stephens, and others gathered their dust and preserved it in their classical urns."[66] The progress of a town from "infancy" to "old age" was often described, and it seemed like a frighteningly brief transition. Samuel Bowles, writing in *Across the Continent* (1866) of a visit to California, records how astonished he was to "see towns that were not in 1850, now wearing an old and almost decaying air."[67] The "ghost town" phenomenon developed very rapidly. In Colorado nostalgia for the already vanished but in fact very recent past with which they had been associated was evident by the late 1860s.[68] Several decades earlier Tocqueville had referred to a town in America as becoming "very old when it counts thirty years of existence."[69]

The "oldness" often seemed absurd and unnatural. Trollope found Sydney's appearance of antiquity hard to take, almost a pseudo-oldness.[70] A visitor to Peterborough, Ontario, in the early 1860s found it "a most eccentric-looking place." "Though quite in its infancy, it appears to have grown prematurely aged—a sort of young child with an old man's face."[71] Nathaniel Hawthorne was struck by the extraordinary appearance of Rochester in New York State. It seemed to challenge all conventional conceptions of age, decay, and growth.

Its edifices are of a dusky brick, and of stone that will not be grayer in a hundred years than now; its churches are Gothic; it is impossible to look at its worn pavements and conceive how lately the forest leaves have been swept away. The most ancient town in Massachusetts appears quite like an affair of yesterday, compared with Rochester. Its attributes of youth are the activity and eager life with which it is redundant.[72]

New towns soon acquired cemeteries, and the sight of these sometimes touched off reflections on the connections between youth and mortality in the life of a new town. In *The Great Southwest* (1867) Wilson Nicely devotes a paragraph to meditations on the cemetery at Leavenworth, Kansas. "There are comparatively few dwellers in this silent city. As yet, Leavenworth is in its youth and prime, and is, *par excellence,* a city of the living."[73] A visitor to Melbourne's cemetery found it both sad and fitting that in a young town the only people buried there were people who had died young.[74] An early booster of Prairie du Chien, Wisconsin, claimed that visitors to that town "who were looking for a future home," that is, a place to *live,* sought evidence in the town's cemeteries: "finding so few new graves in a population of some 3000 [they] have come to the sage conclusion that comparatively but few die among us."[75]

How could a town escape the laws of nature, especially when in so many other respects these were invoked and the personalizing tendency so often indulged in? Boosters liked to refer to the injection of "new life, and new blood." Analogies with the body were used to justify on these grounds the seeking out of new sources of capital for investment in a city.[76]

The most important development, however, came in the 1840s and 1850s when the cyclical interpretation of the course of human progress was challenged and to a large extent abandoned or at least replaced by a confidence that "decline and fall" were not inevitable. The rethinking of the prospects of urban civilization in the New World—and indeed in the Old as well—had two main thrusts. There was a questioning of the assumption that the growth of large cities must inevitably result in the erosion of the moral foundations of a civilization. Second, there were more and more commentators who expressed doubt about the relevance of the Tyre-Nineveh precedents as a predictor of the destiny of cities in the American West of the nineteenth century.

Many critics who deplored the "barbarian tendencies of the West" assigned a major role in the countering of this to the cities of the West. In doing so, it began to seem that they were offering these cities a chance to escape from the seemingly inexorable cycle of rise and decline that had affected all urban-based civilizations in the past. In the same speech in which he described cities as "the grand sources" of "vice and immorality," Daniel Drake went on to offer an alternative vision.

If we have sent forth, from the fountains of wickedness and pollution, with which our city [Cincinnati] abounds, the streams of moral death and desolation, let us now send out streams of moral life, peace, and happiness, from the pure springs of benevolence and intelligence, with which our city also abounds—*intelligence* elevated and sanctified by the holy principles of divine revelation.[77]

This was the era in which, inspired by the writings of Horace Bushnell and Lyman Beecher, whose *Plea for the West,* published in 1836, sought New England aid for educational institutions in the West and called for a Protestant crusade against Catholicism in that region, young New Englanders migrated to Cincinnati and devoted themselves to making it into a center of religious and cultural influence. They have been seen as instilling into perceptions of the West and of the place of the city within it a strong current of optimism that marked a decisive break with the pessimism of the believers in the cyclical model of social evolution.[78] Daniel Drake, one of the earliest mid-western civic boosters, was just the man to respond to this new idealism. By 1855 his biographer, E. D. Mansfield, a long-time collaborator with Drake in works of Cincinnati boosterism, was able to hold out to the city a vision of escape from the prospect of decline and fall. Cincinnati, he wrote, was

ready to receive the fine arts, the polish, and the refinement, which added fame and splendour to the grandeur of Rome. If, in a Christian country, it shall escape the vices which brought Rome to decay, then it may expect to endure through future ages, a noble testimony to Christian civilization.[79]

In the 1840s and 1850s many writers—notably clergymen—exalted the potential of great cities for the exercising of moral influence over society. Of particular importance was Robert Vaughan, a Congregational minister and professor of history in London. His book *The Age of Great Cities: or, Modern Civilization Viewed in Its Relation to Intelligence, Morals, and Religion* (1843) sees great cities as the major source of moral, political, and social progress.[80] There were several publications of this kind in America which challenged the thesis of the inevitable decline of great cities.

Great cities have a vitality stronger than that of great nations. The governments within whose jurisdiction they are included from time to time may change; but, unmoved by the rise and fall of empires, great cities often survive a long succession of sovereignties exercising dominion over them. As it was with Babylon, Rome, Byzantium, Vienna and Paris, so it may be with London and New York.[81]

The most important of the writers who sought to reject the relevance of the cyclical theory to the cities of the West was Jesup W. Scott. In his articles, published from the late 1830s to the mid-1860s, Scott argued that the great cities which were growing up in the interior regions of the United States were fundamentally different from the cities of the past whose decline allegedly foreshadowed the fate in store for these modern American metropolises. The difference was that the cities of antiquity were all either capitals, founded by states and therefore vulnerable to changes in political fortunes and the disintegration of empires, or ports dependent on foreign trade. American Western cities grew, not because governments willed them into being, but because of the growth of their vast hinterlands. They were based on *internal* commerce, and that, in Scott's opinion, rendered them secure from the causes which had ruined seaports. Indeed, he went so far as to prophesy the ultimate decline of London and New York and their *permanent* replacement as the great "world cities" by St. Louis or Chicago or Toledo.[82]

The influence of these ideas is obvious in an article in the *Western Journal* in 1849 in which the editor, M. Tarver of St. Louis, proclaims the overthrow of the cyclical thesis as far as the American West is concerned. He predicts that great cities will develop in the Mississippi Valley and that

the causes which have compelled the abandonment of ancient commercial cities, will no longer exist; and we have good reason to hope that this continent will never be marked by the ruins of an extinct commerce, like those that indicate its route through other countries. Many ages have elapsed since Babylon, Palmyra, Tyre and Cartharge [sic] were left in ruins; and even the cites [sic] of some of these are becoming doubtful. Alexandria and Venice, though not fallen so low, have long been in a state of delapidation. Bruges and Antwerp, though not so renowned as the more ancient commercial stations, have also declined; and we predict that the time is not far distant when the scepter of commerce will depart from London, its present imperial seat. But whether this great commercial emporium is destined to share the fate of the ancient commercial cities, can only be revealed by time. All these great cities were built by foreign commerce, aided, in some instances perhaps, by political power; and when the power which brought them into existence failed, they fell into a state of decay; for the resources of the surrounding countries were insufficient to sustain what foreign commerce had created. But such is not likely to be the case in respect of the great commercial cities that may rise up in this valley; for the immediate resources of this country, will of themselves be sufficient to sustain cities, in all respects as important perhaps, as were those of Asia and of Europe.[83]

If ever a city seemed to offer a case by which to test the validity of the "decline and fall" thesis, at least in its moral aspects, that city was Chicago. Its moral deficiencies, as diagnosed in an article in *Putnam's Monthly* in 1856, bore a close resemblance to those often claimed to have been the cause of the downfall of ancient cities such as Carthage.

Speculation, too great eagerness to get rich on the part of men who have nothing to lose, and a lack of those healthful restraints which exist in an older community, have, undoubtedly, combined to weaken and lower the moral sense of the people, in regard to business transactions. There is a leniency exhibited towards sharp bargains, over-reaching, undue coloring, and actual misrepresentation . . . which, if allowed to go unchecked, will, by degrees, destroy that vital morality which is indispensable to the prosperity of a commercial state.[84]

The turning-point was the Great Fire of 1871, which reminded many of the catastrophes which had overwhelmed some of the great cities of antiquity. A newspaper in New Orleans predicted: "Chicago will be like the Carthage of old! Its glory will be of the past, not of the present."[85] Chicago's boosters were themselves happy to invoke the great fires of the past and to portray the city as "great in its ruins."[86] Nor were there missing those who, especially in Chicago's rival cities, revived an old tradition in seeing moral causes for such a catastrophic setback to Chicago's rise. "It is retributive judgment on a city that has shown such devotion in its worship of the Golden Calf," declared the Rev. Granville Moody of Cincinnati.[87] But Chicago was not ruined. The city's rapid recovery and continued advancement to new prosperity and commercial dominance were marveled at all over the world.[88] This seemed conclusive proof that here at least in the greatest city of the American West the old assumptions about the decline and fall of great cities had no validity. In a paper on *Chicago and the Sources of Her Past and Future Growth,* read to the Chicago Historical Society in 1880, William Bross pronounced Chicago's valedictory for the cyclical theory:

Her site was not selected by some great conqueror, like that of Constantinople, Palmyra, and Alexandria, with reference to the channels of commerce then existing, and which the capricious changes of the currents of trade have reduced to comparative insignificance. . . . Nature, it is believed, or, to speak more reverently, He who is the Author of Nature, selected the site of this great city, not till next May forty-three years old, and hence her future will not be subject to those causes which have paralyzed or destroyed many of the cities of past ages.[89]

As for the moral weaknesses which in the past had been alleged to be such a source of danger to Chicago's long-term prospects, boosters quickly and effectively promoted the themes of heroism, self-reliance, and energy in community reconstruction as proof of the strong moral qualities of the people of Chicago.

Once the cyclical model of social evolution has been laid to rest, interpretations of the destiny of American's Western cities became firmly linear. But now the question arose: if city growth was not going to lead to eventual decline and fall, where would it lead to instead? Some remarkable new predictions of urban evolution began to take shape. There were those who dreamed of their city growing into a "world city" or some such phrase: "The Apocalyptic City" was another of the more fantastic notions.[90] This type of fantasy has become linked in particular to Logan U. Reavis, the promoter of St. Louis. He was sure that somewhere in the world what he called "the final great city" would emerge, and believed it would be an American city. He expounded the case for considering St. Louis to be this city. His vision was a city which

> will result in the final organization of human society in one complete whole, and the perfect development and systematization of the commerce of the world; will grow to such magnificent proportions, and be so perfectly organized and controlled in its municipal governmental character, as to constitute the most perfect and greatest city of the world—the all-directing head and heart of the great family of man. The new world is to be its home, and nature and civilization will fix its residence in the central plain of the continent, and in the center of the productive power of this great valley, and upon the Mississippi river, and where the city of St. Louis now stands. All arguments point to this one great fact of the future, and, with its perfect realization, will be attained the highest possibility in the material triumph of mankind.[91]

Such a fantastic prophecy was not new. In the 1850s Count Adelbert Baudissin picked up the label of "the future world-city" for St. Louis when visiting Missouri.[92] Even earlier James Silk Buckingham in *The Eastern and Western States of America* linked the grandiose names given to tiny backwoods "cities" to the belief that "before a very short period, half a century at most, America would sway the entire destiny of the globe."[93]

Some saw New World towns as distinctive in having escaped altogether the evolutionary process. They were "cities" from the start—in intention at least—and because they were regarded and treated as such by their inhabitants did not go through "the chrysalis stage of village or town."[94] In *Six Months in the Federal States* (1863) Edward Dicey developed the insight that American towns began "as the fragment of a city," instancing a hotel in a small Illinois settlement that was appropriate to a much larger town. This place had not had "to develop from a village into a town."[95] A common description of a Western town was "a metropolis in miniature."[96] Boosters sought to make their cities seem exceptionally "marvelous" by employing this concept. In *Wichita* (1886) Andrew A. Hensley wrote: "Cities, systems and business are usually growths. Wichita seems to have been an exception, and to have sprung full-armed into the arena at the bidding of American will."[97]

If the old laws of evolution of towns did not explain the way in which

New World cities developed, then perhaps new ones should be sought. In America many town developers and boosters seemed to feel that there was a need for new theories to explain and (the most important point) to predict "the rise and progress of western cities."[98] William Gilpin, Jesup W. Scott, and others saw themselves as meeting this need. They sought to devise theories of evolution that were distinctive to America and at the same time capable of including and explaining the rise of great cities in the West. The form which their evolutionary theories took was usually that of geographical determinism, for example, Gilpin's Isothermal Zodiacs and Zones of Intensity.[99] His purpose and that of S. H. Goodin at Cincinnati were to find geographical "laws" that would enable one to predict where great cities were "destined" to grow. Goodin devised a principle of evolution in "circles" which reads extraordinarily like modern "central place" theory. "I pretend not to say, that this is the process of development always in a new country," he wrote; "I simply declare it to be the law, always more or less affected by neutralizing or counteracting forces."[100]

All this was a reaction against the most common alternative to evolutionary laws as explanation for city growth: the reference to "magic." "Magic" was the most frequently employed *popular* interpretation of the rise of cities in the New World. It is the one usually to be found, for instance, in private letters. In a letter to his father in 1839, James Graham, a pioneer merchant in Melbourne, first of all refers to the language used about the new town by "the Auctioneers in their advertisements": "The beauteous capital of Australia Felix—the rapidity of whose growth stamps with a semblance of truth the enchanted tales of yore." But, instead of laughing at such extravagant language, Graham goes on: "Indeed such is the case for it is most marvellous how quickly it has risen and more particularly so when the infancy of this Colony is considered."[101] In a diary which he kept on a visit to Australia an Englishman, W. J. Douglas, simply reproduces the clichés, still in their inverted commas, as his own reaction.

Reviewing the history of Melbourne, its growth and development is simply "marvellous" . . . I should wish to be able to convey to you something like a graphic yet true description of this "marvel" "The Queen City of the South." The Metropolis of the Colony of Victoria.[102]

Some visitors became impatient with the reiteration of the cliché. Touring the West in 1857, the Russian Alexsandr Borisovich Lakier observed the rapid growth of cities but complained: "If you ask how it happened, you are told all about the same western miracles, which have become absolutely commonplace as a result of frequent repetition."[103]

Boosters kept resorting to the cliché and then checking themselves as they remembered the dangers associated with relying on it as the sole explanation of their town's rise. A booster publication of 1890 called Helena, Montana, "a city sprung up as if by magic," but added, "yet no magician had anything to do with it; pluck and perseverance have accomplished all."[104] For references to a town's growth as "magic" made it appear to have happened automatically, without any need for human effort. The *Early & Authentic History of Omaha 1857–1870* (1870) declared that, "as the magic wand of enterprise is lifted, with giant step civilization strides on, and cities, towns and villages dot the wild prairie soil. Our young city is a noble specimen of this enterprise."[105] This attempts to have it both ways, the "magic" and the "enterprise." The danger was that over-emphasizing "magic" could breed complacency and damage a town's development by encouraging the belief that that development would occur without any need for human exertion. The town might as a result attract the wrong kind of people, those who sought reward without effort. The *Chicago Tribune's* correspondent on Rufus Hatch's Northwest Pacific Railroad promotional trip of 1882 was very critical of the attitude that he found prevailing in Duluth. "The people are enterprising, but they are over-confident, and seem to believe that a permanent town can spring into existence, like Jonah's gourd, in a single night."[106] Writing also in 1890 David Boyd in his history of the Union Colony at Greeley, Colorado, argued that that town had not grown because there was too much of an expectation that a city would "spring as by magic from the bosom of the naked plains".[107]

It certainly was the case, that unanchored to any "laws" that could explain what was going on, thinking about the development of new towns in America could tip over into unrestrained, extravagant fantasy. In Independence, Missouri, in the mid-1840s Alfred S. Waugh, the artist, met Major Robert A. Rickman "a dreamer [who] lives in a world of his own creation": "so firmly convinced is he that Independence is the center of the continent of North America, that he believes it will ultimately become the greatest and most important city, not only in the Union but,—the world."[108]

The desire not to have to rely on "magic" as an explanation was the driving force behind much of the search for new "laws" of urban growth. John S. Wright, who had many prophetic visions of the future of Chicago —and finally went insane—offered his book *Chicago: Past, Present, Future* (1868) as "a philosophic inquiry into the general causes of past progress, and of their future continuance." The problem, he wrote, was that "our growth is a marvel even to ourselves, until operating causes are examined." His book was, he claimed, a service to local newspaper editors who "want the philosophy of a subject elsewhere studied out, which their readers can be supposed to be familiar with, the truths of which they apply practically."

is it not quite time that Chicago ceased to be a baby-wonder of precocity, and rested upon her natural endowments and her acquired improvements as not being at all extraordinary, but entirely legitimate? a result to have been naturally expected with reasonable forecast? Until we are able to take and maintain that position, we shall continue as hitherto to be looked upon as of mushroom growth.[109]

The Commerce of Kansas City in 1886 (1886), a booster publication, similarly warned that it was "a grievous mistake, which leaves an altogether wrong impression, to speak of the development of this city in language that is only applicable to speculative, mushroom towns that have their origin in the brain of some interested land agent." It too tried to develop general theories, exploring, for instance, the role of "natural advantages" and a city's relationship to broad general national trends.[110]

In the United States theories about space became intertwined with theories about time in the attempts that were made to establish new laws to explain and predict social evolution and the growth of cities. Indeed, from Thomas Jefferson to Frederick Jackson Turner there was a very strong tradition of seeing American westward expansion, that is movement in space, as being also a journey through time as the record of social evolution moved backward and then forward again as the districts of the West became settled.

There were innumerable theories as to the appropriate or the inevitable spacing of towns. These theories were of great importance to persons involved in town development and speculation as they strove to obtain the most accurate and reliable prediction as to where cities were "destined" to develop. An example is the attempt by James M. Woolworth in *Nebraska in 1857* to persuade prospective settlers and investors that somewhere in Nebraska a great city was certain to emerge.

It is conceded by all that near the mouth of the Platte is to be, at no very future day, a great commercial emporium. If we look on the map we shall find that either by accident or a law of nature and of trade, large towns have grown up in a line running from east to west at distances of from two to four hundred miles. Commencing with New York, we have perhaps, first Albany, then Buffalo, then Detroit, then Chicago, then Davenport, and then—some place on the Missouri. To each of these places nature has given commercial advantages which she has withheld from other towns. The fact of the regularity and the disposition of the provisions of nature, can not fail to strike the mind of any person who regards the peculiar position, relation, and distance from each other of this line of towns. Similar lines might be run from other points on the Atlantic coast, to the west.

Some point which we can not now name, on the Missouri, possesses like distinction of advantage with the great cities named above.[111]

In their various ways William Gilpin, Jesup W. Scott, and Logan U. Reavis all sought to place American Western urban development in a spatial as well as a temporal perspective. Gilpin, for example, derived from the German geographer Alexander von Humboldt the concept of the Isothermal Zodiac, a belt of land that encircled the globe across the Northern Hemisphere. Through this zone ran an Axis of Intensity where, Gilpin claimed, all the great cities of the world had arisen and would continue to arise. It passed right through the center of the United States. Along it America's great cities of the future were destined to grow.[112]

Boosters seized on such theories or concocted new ones of their own to promote their towns. Wayne Griswold, promoting Kansas in 1871, drew his readers' attention to Baxter Springs:

Nature had made the site of this place for a city. No human effort can prevent Baxter from becoming a large place, or from doing a most extensive business. It is just the right distance from St. Louis for another large city. Commerce, on land, must stop to rest every three or four hundred miles, and there it naturally builds a city.[113]

Julian Ralph, visiting Denver in the early 1890s, discovered that the people of that city had

adopted what they call their "thousand-mile theory," which is that Chicago is 1000 miles from New York, and Denver is 1000 miles from Chicago, and San Francisco is 1000 miles from Denver, so that, as any one can see, if great cities are put at that distance apart, as it seems, then these are to be the four great ones of America.[114]

Complicating all these theories was the constant and powerful tug of the "westering" impulse. A strong magnetic force from the West unstabilized neat spatial relationships. A migrant to Michigan in 1838 experienced this when he reported that "I supposed I had got to the far west when I came here but now they talk of cities rising up 1000 milles [sic] west of me."[115] In 1857 the Russian visitor Alexsandr Lakier was uncertain whether even Chicago would prove to be "the metropolis of the west."

> The restless Americans are constantly moving west, from the old to the new, and are delighted when at last they stumble upon a place with so favorable a location. But they do not stay long here either, and move even farther west in search of a rival to the lucky spot. One cannot guarantee they will not find it somewhere. Then in some ten or twenty years people will begin talking about another city.[116]

One writer even tried to make a precise calculation of the rate of this process. Charles Richard Weld noted that Canadian towns grew westward, "thus following the course of the great human wave, which, breaking on the eastern shores of North America, advances across the western wilderness at the rate of seventeen miles yearly."[117] Allied to this is the theory, which appears frequently in writings on Western towns, that successful towns always grew on the west banks of rivers.[118]

All "laws" about the spatial relationships of towns in the American West seemed to be rendered invalid and obsolete by the advent of the railroad, which seemed to be capable of creating relationships that were completely independent of the dictates of "nature." But, as several studies of Western towns have shown, many town builders were slow to recognize this and struggled to present even railroads as controlled by the requirements of geography. New visions of railroad-determined spacing of towns did begin to emerge. The Parsons "diary" has people in Indiana talking of the "crazy idea" of former governor James Brown Ray that railroads should "radiate like a spider's web" from Indianapolis "with villages at intervals of five miles, towns at ten miles, and cities at twenty miles."[119] The most ambitious attempt to devise new theories of spatial development of towns to accommodate the railroad was S. H. Goodin's contribution to Charles Cist's *Sketches and Statistics of Cincinnati in 1851*. He saw the railroad as having brought about "the almost entire annihilation of space" (and the telegraph of time). But he constructed a new theory of circles to show that eventually even with the railroad a new structure of spatial ordering of cities would develop.[120] However, later in the century the introduction of differential freight rates, discriminating in favor of larger centers, seemed to destabilize the situation all over again. One writer in 1890 observed of the railroads:

They assumed greater powers than those of Deity; they abrogated time and space; they changed the geography of the country. If rates were a guide, Omaha was situated between Chicago and Iowa, Denver was on the Mississippi, and San Francisco on the Missouri, while the interior towns of Iowa and Nebraska were located on Behring Strait.[121]

The predominant image which townspeople, and especially boosters, used to define the relationship of their particular town to the space surrounding it was that of a center radiating out influence and control. This image was obviously important in creating a counter-balance to the extreme transience that characterized the populations of young Western towns and also to the magnetic pull of "the West." Wilson Nicely commented on this phenomenon:

The traveler cannot but notice in western towns and villages a peculiarity that may be termed *hub-ism*. Every considerable place is certain to be located in a central position. The Bostonians do not more pertinaciously believe in their city as the hub of the universe than do these western city builders in their own favored town sites.[122]

There was an obsession with appearing to be the center of something. Innumerable towns claimed to be at or near "the geographical center" of the country. There were many different ways of calculating where that place actually was and many variations on the theme.[123] Atlases to this day abound with "Central Cities" and "Centervilles." In practical terms, a central location mattered with regard to becoming the county seat.[124] Sometimes that centrality was measured with close precision.[125] New counties were created to enable a town to become the county seat.

Promoters of Western towns specialized in circle maps by which a town appeared as the center of a series of circles radiating out from it. Usually the circles were based on nothing more significant than actual distance from the town, but somehow they conveyed the impression of a vast magnetic field and an enormous region subject to the dominating influence of this town at the center of it all.[126] A favorite image was that of the hub with the spokes radiating out to all points of the compass.[127] Nothing lent itself better to the production of this kind of image than the railroad.[128] A map with railroads as the spokes gave a particularly reassuring impression of a town's position. In 1850 Alphonso Taft said of the coming of the railroad to Cincinnati: "When . . . the main trunks are laid toward the cardinal points, *then* will her position be secure. East,—West, —North,—and South,—her prosperity will be firmly anchored." [129] By 1858 Indianapolis businessmen were expressing their great satisfaction that "Indianapolis and our railroads present upon the map, an appearance not unlike the hub and spokes of the wheel of a wagon—the roads, like the spokes, running from the center to the circumference in every direction." [130]

CHAPTER SIX

Antipodean Patterns of Urban Development

For most of the nineteenth century the westward expansion of the United States and the "opening up of the frontier" were seen as ongoing processes. Indeed the image of a procession was commonly used, as in Jefferson's vision of the Cumberland Gap or paintings of Boone leading the settlers into Kentucky or Currier and Ives representations of "Westward the Star of Empire." The U.S. Census Bureau and Frederick Jackson Turner both recognized a process of this kind as having taken place and come to some sort of end in 1890. At every stage cities rapidly "rising out of the wilderness" were celebrated as part of the process, as indeed a principal agency in facilitating its continuation. Each decade saw major new cities rise farther and farther west. The overwhelming impression was of a constantly changing and unfolding pattern shaped by the forces of westward expansion and "manifest destiny."

An Australian historian, Robert Dixon, has recently argued in a book entitled *The Course of Empire* that there was at one stage in the early nineteenth century, when the Blue Mountains were crossed and settlement began on the interior plains of New South Wales, a perception of Australian expansion that resembled Jefferson's vision of American expansion.[1] But the Australian process was to turn out to be very different from that in America. Throughout the nineteenth century attempts to expand settlement significantly into the interior of the Australian continent met with repeated frustration and often disaster. In Australia there was no ongoing process, spread over a century, in which new cities kept rising as new regions were opened up for settlement. The dominant position of a few metropolitan areas was established at an early stage, and the pattern of Australian urbanization has varied little since. The result was a very different kind of debate about the place of towns and cities in this new country, one which focused much more on the implications of the early and persisting dominance of large cities and of the high and growing proportions of the population which lived in them.

The founding of a city, intended to be a "capital," was the way in which European settlement was initiated in most of the colonies of Australia—New South Wales, South Australia, Western Australia, "Australia Felix" (later the colony of Victoria). At first the dominance of one large town within a region did not cause major anxiety. One historian who has looked at the role of Sydney in New South Wales in the 1840s has found that citizens of the "Middle District" usually did not resent the centralization on Sydney. They tended to think of their region as a unit with Sydney as the inlet and outlet for migrants and trade.[2] However, opinions on the healthiness and desirability of the dominance of one "metropolis" and the concentration of population within it began to change and become more adverse at about this time. There was controversy surrounding the foundation of Adelaide as chief city of the new colony of South Australia. The disastrous state of the South Australian economy in the early years seemed to many to prove the wrongness of starting this way round in the foundation of a colony, with a large city laid out and inviting a preoccupation with speculation in town lots rather than a concentration on the development of farming.

When Melbourne also developed very rapidly, and speculation, encouraged by a government that needed revenue from the sale of town lots, was seen as one of the major causes, criticism of what was being allowed to happen began to mount. In *The Present State and Prospects of the Port Phillip District of New South Wales* (1845) Charles Griffith pointed out that of an estimated 20,000 people now living in the Port Phillip district 9,000 were said to be in Melbourne and its suburbs. "This is far too large a proportion; in fact, the town of Melbourne is large enough to supply the wants of a rural population of 60,000 souls." He was confident that "this will in time cure itself." The problem was that it would not do so "without considerable individual distress," as people were forced to leave Melbourne as a result of unemployment and poverty.[3]

A marked *Australian* phenomenon began to be perceived. In his 1859 *Rambles at the Antipodes* Edward Wilson discovered that the Moreton Bay district (in Queensland) had a population of about 22,000, "of which, according to the usual badly adjusted proportion incident to Australian settlements, about a third are located in the towns."[4] Severe unemployment and distress among the working people of Sydney led in 1859 to the setting up by the New South Wales Legislative Assembly of a Select Committee on the Condition of the Working Classes of the Metropolis. An important part of the background to this, as revealed by the evidence given before the committee, was deep concern that Sydney's population had grown far too large in proportion to that of the rest of the colony. Indeed, Dr. J. D. Lang asked one witness: "Are you aware of any instance in any other country, either in ancient or modern times, where the population of a country bore so small a proportion to that of its capital?" The witness being unable to "remember an instance just now," Lang went on to get him to agree that "such a state of things is of itself a fruitful cause of privation and suffering among the working classes." Nathanael Pigeon, a city missionary, gave his opinion that "there is too much centralization,—that there are too many people in the city for the wants of the country, in proportion to the country."[5]

By the later part of the century the criticism had reached a crescendo. Nor was it confined to Australia itself. British journals of opinion published numerous articles commenting adversely on what was seen as excessive and unhealthy metropolitan development in Australia. For example, here is Matthew Macfie—a former resident of Melbourne—writing on "Aids to Australasian Development" in the *Proceedings of the Royal Colonial Institute:* "How striking is this abnormal and unproductive concentration of an excessive proportion of the inhabitants of Australia in a few towns, compared with the wholesome distribution of population in the most prosperous countries of Europe and America, where land culture is properly held to be the chief industry."[6] Such criticisms mattered greatly, because they affected decisions about investment. British investors might well withhold their capital from situations judged to be "unhealthy," "abnormal," and therefore in danger of collapse. Such lessons were indeed drawn from the dramatic end of the great Melbourne boom in 1893.

Numerous commentators compared the trends in Australia with those in other countries, especially in the New World, and came to the same conclusion as Dr. Lang, namely that it was indeed an extreme case. Writing in the 1880s, the eminent Australian statistician T. A. Coghlan found the proportion of city people in the population much higher than in the United States. In the Old World itself there was no parallel to the progress of Sydney and Melbourne.[7] One of the most widely read explanations of the Australia of this time to an English readership was Francis

Adams' *The Australians.* He described the aggregations of people in the main cities as astonishing and referred to "the extraordinary system of centralisation which has made this enormous Australia the appanage of four or five cities."[8]

In 1882 the *Bulletin,* Australia's best known literary journal of this period, made a comparison between New South Wales and Canada. "With a nation of five millions, it chief city, Montreal is little more than half the size of Sydney, while the whole of the town population of the Dominion seems to be little more than New South Wales shows with only one seventh of the number of inhabitants." Yet in most crucial respects Canada and New South Wales appeared to be very similar as new societies. "Both colonies are engaged in reclaiming the wilderness; both derive their wealth from the soil; both are creating great public works, and both are reputed to be equally prosperous." Why then the difference in the distribution of their populations?[9]

It is certainly true that down to this point opinion in Canada appears to have been a good deal more relaxed about the rise of large cities. There are few alarmed statements of the kind which became so common in Australia. The remark made about York (Toronto) in 1834 by Henry Tudor, that it was not as big as he had expected, "the emigrants believing it better to scatter themselves over the face of the country, than to crowd themselves into large towns,"[10] strikes a note which even by that stage would have been unfamiliar in Australia. Of course, Toronto did grow greatly in the ensuing decades, but in an article published in 1874 John Costley, Secretary of Statistics at Halifax, could still sum up the Canadian situation thus: "In a comparatively newly settled country like our own, the great bulk of the population is necessarily rural." In Canada there were as yet only five cities with a population exceeding 20,000, and only twenty that came up to even 5,000. In these twenty cities lived a mere 12.3 percent of the Canadian population. By contrast, in the United States 15 percent of the population lived in fifty towns or cities whose inhabitants numbered over 25,000, while in England and Scotland the proportions were, not surprisingly, far higher. "As commerce and manufactures extend, similar results will occur here, though many generations will probably pass away before we can boast of a dozen cities with each a population of 100,000 or upwards."[11] Such complacency—or modesty —would still have been justified in the early 1880s when the *Bulletin* made its comparison with Australia. But then began the dramatic growth of the prairie cities which soon dominated the population structure of their provinces in much the same way as Melbourne dominated Victoria or Adelaide South Australia.

There were some distinctive aspects to debate in a new society about the rise of large cities and the trend toward the concentration of population in those cities. Were these developments in a new country healthy and desirable? Why were they taking place? What, if anything, could or should be done about them? Could they be reversed or at least slowed down?

There were some influential commentators on the development of Australia who approved of these trends—and, indeed, may be said by their approval to have helped to strengthen them. Perhaps the most authoritative pronouncement in favor of concentration of population was a report issued in 1891 by H. H. Hayter, the government statistician of Victoria. In this he referred to "the evil arising from there being several small or medium-sized centres of population instead of one large centre," notably the wasteful duplication of facilities and public works.

It would [he wrote] no doubt be desirable, especially in newly settled states, that more persons should live in the country, where they are generally producers of wealth, than in either small or large towns, where a much larger proportion of them are merely distributors or dependents; but, since this cannot be the case, the balance of advantage is, I think, as I have already said, in favour of cities being large and few instead of small and numerous.[12]

In taking this view Hayter had some important predecessors, notably Dr. John Dunmore Lang and William Westgarth. In his long and intensely controversial career Dr. Lang, a Presbyterian clergyman, wrote many books about Australia.[13] They were usually compiled in haste and while traveling, for Lang was notably restless and peripatetic. Indeed, some of his writing was done on board ship during his many voyages between Britain and Australia. This aspect of his life is in some respects advantageous for the historian. Lang traveled extensively around Australia, often in arduous conditions, saw more of it than most of his contemporaries, observed its social development at close range, and commented on it shrewdly and perceptively. Of course, as a result of his constant mobility and the circumstances in which his books were written, they are highly miscellaneous in structure and lack organization and cohesion. Lang never organized his thoughts about urban development, for instance, into a coherent whole. His observations on the subject appear intermittently throughout his books and are characterized by much confusion and numerous contradictions and changes of attitude. But this too makes them of value, for they appear for this reason to reflect well the ambivalence of many Australians toward the dominance that large cities were acquiring within their new society.

In general, Lang disapproved of the concentration of population in the cities. But in the course of his writings he found himself conceding certain points in favor of concentration in large towns. For example, in *An Historical and Statistical Account of New South Wales,* which went through several editions and was a combination of history and guidebook, he spent much time deploring concentration. But near the end of the book a different note is struck when he tells of visiting the small town of Albury on race day and witnessing the gambling and drinking that went on.

I am strongly of opinion, with the able and Reverend Dr. Vaughan of Manchester, that large towns or cities are, after all, the most fruitful sources of moral influence, as well as of civil and religious liberty, in the world. For example, bad as we are reputed to be at Sydney, by Archbishop Whateley and others, a scene such as this at Albury could not have taken place within a hundred miles of that city.[14]

Lang condemned the moral effects of dispersion and argued in favor of having only one school, one church, and one unit of other forms of social and moral control (e.g., police) instead of the many which result from settlement in numerous small towns and villages. Lang became convinced that only in large towns was a strong, concentrated, effective public opinion capable of cohering and manifesting itself.[15] His reference to Dr. Vaughan, author of *The Age of Great Cities* (1843), shows that he was aware of a similar growth of enthusiasm for large cities in England.

William Westgarth was a merchant who was present in Melbourne in the early years of its development.[16] Although he later lived in England, he retained substantial business links with Australia and was an indefatigable publicist of the country, publishing books at regular four- or five-year intervals reviewing its progress. These books are an invaluable record of changing opinions on many aspects of Australia's—and especially Victoria's—development. They contain numerous descriptions of Melbourne and commentaries on its place within the wider Victorian social and economic context. Westgarth was a great booster of Melbourne. One of his reasons for adopting this position was that he was a strong believer in the benefits for a community, especially a new society such as Victoria, of being dominated by a single large urban center, a metropolis. In his *Personal Recollections* (1888) he discussed the state of a country with many small towns and argued that "the ultimate creation of a surpassingly great city, with all its powerful concentration of resource, seems on the whole the more promising for a country's advance in all the interests of human life."[17] In the 1850s Westgarth expressed great unease about the rise of a second large city in Victoria, Geelong. He was worried that the resulting rivalry between it and Melbourne would waste energies and delay projects that would benefit the people of Victoria. To him a metropolis meant concentrated and effective developmental energy. He deplored the likelihood that

there will always exist a considerable and rival capital in Geelong, dividing those operations which, under a happier selection, might almost all have been carried out with more effect in one central spot, where there would most likely have stood at the present day an Australian city, even already of European magnitude, and more elegant, rich, and populous, than those two conjoined, which at present divide between them the commercial and general intercourse of Victoria.[18]

Westgarth was the eager prophet and celebrant of centralization, which he believed was essential for the progress of his own colony of Victoria and indeed of the country as a whole. Westgarth justified the rise of large cities and a concentration of population into them in terms of the character of new societies. His view was that in a new country, with population and settlement in such a state of flux, there was no natural source of cohesion and unity. There was a strong fissiparous tendency, manifested in both New South Wales and Victoria (the latter itself a product of this tendency), as well as in New Zealand, by the constant clamor of outlying districts to be allowed to secede and form new colonies or provinces. To counter this natural tendency, destructive of national or colonial progress, it was essential to foster the development of a controlling center, a large city, preferably a seaport, so that it had some major economic justification for existing. Here is how in *The Colony of Victoria* (1864) Westgarth explained the benefits that the growth of Melbourne was bestowing on Victoria. "The colony has poured wealth into Melbourne, and Melbourne has reciprocally projected roads, railways, and telegraphs into and across the colony, in order to group its territory the more securely around herself."[19]

If Westgarth's emphasis was mainly economic, other proponents of centralization followed Lang in stressing the moral advantages of having a colonial population concentrated in a few centers of population.[20] Walter

Windeyer, a member of the New South Wales legislature's 1859 Committee on the Condition of the Working Classes of the Metropolis, did not agree that the concentration of so many people in one city was bad for their moral condition: "I think the influence for good, that is the education of the rising folks—the young ones, must be pressed upon the people from without, and that pressure may be brought to bear in the town better than in the bush."[21]

In much the same way as the contrast between towns north and south of the Canadian-American frontier was frequently used to illustrate arguments about North American urban development, an important role was played by New Zealand in the debates about "concentration" in Australia. New Zealand was presented as an example of either the good or the undesirable consequences of a lack of concentration and a decentralized urban structure. The absence of dominance by one large city was often observed to be a striking feature of New Zealand's development. William Westgarth attributed this feature to New Zealand's complicated, mountain-strewn topography which created many barriers to ease of communication between one district and another, leading to a multiplicity of small towns servicing small but self-contained regions. In his view, this would ultimately prove to be to New Zealand's disadvantage as a nation.[22] In *The Colony of Victoria* (1864) he compared Australia and New Zealand thus:

Australia, with the vast interior of its unindented sea-coast, is peculiarly favorable to this great grouping system, and therefore to the rise of one great central city in each colony—an advantage which in the end perhaps much more than repays the defects and disadvantages of such a country otherwise. New Zealand is an instance of the opposite kind. The interior is nowhere remote from the sea, and the colony is consequently distinguished by many small ports, around which are clustered a continually increasing number of subcolonies or provinces. New Zealand possesses no Sydney or Melbourne, nor ever will acquire such proportionately large capitals, saving always as to possible realizations from gold-mining, and such like noncalculable accidents of the future. Such colonies certainly enjoy some early advantages in physical facilities, but such facilities seem unimportant compared with the ultimate superiority of the other kind of colony in all the powers of wealth, enterprise, and intellect that arise from great and busy centres of population.[23]

There were a few who preferred the New Zealand model of evolution, regarding it as healthier than Australia's.[24] But criticism of it reached a peak in the 1880s when some commentators, notably J. A. Froude in his

very influential *Oceana,* blamed New Zealand's very high level of indebt-
edness on the capacity of that country's many ports and regional centers
to exploit the political system to obtain wasteful spending of borrowed
money on the duplication of public works such as railways.[25] A notorious
instance of this, remarked on by numerous visitors, was the development,
because of local pressures, of extensive port facilities at both Timaru and
Oamaru, close to each other on the east coast of the South Island.[26] New
Zealand commentators of the time acknowledged the damaging effects of
excessive rivalry among New Zealand's small towns.[27] James Coutts
Crawford, a New Zealand landowner and geologist who came to New
Zealand first in 1839, summarized thus his views on New Zealand and
Australia's development in *Recollections of Travel in New Zealand and
Australia* (1880):

In some respects the Australian capitals have a great advantage over New Zealand
in the centralising of their institutions. While all the roads and railways of Victoria
converge to Melbourne, and those of New South Wales to Sydney, New Zealand
has numerous centres in the capitals of the provincial districts. The consequence
is, that instead of one large town in that colony, there are Auckland, Napier,
Wellington, New Plymouth, Nelson, Christchurch, Dunedin, and Invercargill.
Put all these towns into one, we should find a city of some 90,000 or 100,000
inhabitants, making a great show, and with institutions on a large scale; but as
the matter stands, colleges, schools, hospitals, lunatic asylums, libraries, and so
on, are on a comparatively small scale in each place. Possibly the division of force
in New Zealand has its advantages in giving a greater variety of life and manners,
but in the way of institutions there is a drawback.[28]

The criticism of New Zealand reached a climax in H. H. Hayter's 1891
report when he referred to it as an example of "the evil arising from there
being several small or medium-sized centres of population instead of one
large centre." Every center wanted its own railway, port facility, and so
on.[29] Thereafter the criticism was less commonly heard as the reaction
against "concentration" set in in Australia.

In North America similar arguments for and against concentration of
population in large cities were expressed from time to time. For instance,
in the Durham Report appeared the suggestion that in such concentration
lay the solution to some of Canada's most serious deficiencies as a colony.
It was the same argument as Westgarth used in Victoria concerning the
binding, cohering impact of a large center. The Report pointed out that
the inhabitants of Upper Canada were scattered along an extensive frontier and "have, apparently no unity of interest or opinion."

The Province has no great centre from which all the separate parts are connected, and which they are accustomed to follow in sentiment and action. . . . Instead of this, there are many petty local centres, the sentiments and the interests (or at least what are fancied to be so) of which, are distinct, and perhaps opposed.

It is intriguing to find the New Zealand example being used also in this context. In his 1912 edition of the Durham Report C. P. Lucas appended a footnote to these passages:

It is not always an advantage for a colony or province to have one great centre overweighting all the rest of the territory in wealth and population. New Zealand has probably gained by having three or four different centres, none of them overshadowing the others, and the same may be said of the Canadian Dominion at the present day.[30]

In the American Midwest satisfaction with that region's large number of medium-sized towns mingled with pride at the "metropolises" which did emerge. Here too, as in Canada, concern about concentration of population in cities remained at a low level compared with Australia. In 1827 Timothy Flint's *Western Monthly Review,* while noting that "Ohio has, palpably, more of the northern propensity to form villages, and condense population, than any other of the western states," expressed pleasure that most of the people living in the Ohio Valley were cultivators of the soil. "The inhabitants of crowded towns and villages, the numerous artizans and laborers in manufactories, can neither be, as a mass, so healthy, so virtuous, or happy, as free cultivators of the soil."[31] The German visitor Charles Sealsfield also approved of the state of Ohio at this time:

There is . . . not any city in the state of Ohio to be compared with New York, Philadelphia, or Boston, nor is it probable there will be. At the same time this want is largely compensated by the absence of immorality and luxury—evils necessarily attached to large and opulent cities—which may be said to attract the heart's blood of the country, and send forth the very dregs of it in return. In Ohio, wealth is not accumulated in one place, or in a few hands; it is visibly diffused over the whole community.[32]

However, over the ensuing two decades there was a growing body of "Western" opinion which argued that large cities were "destined" to develop in the Midwest and that their growth ought to be encouraged and welcomed because they were essential for the prosperity of the region and the nation. In an article in 1851 in the *Western Journal,* the editor,

Hamilton, Ontario, 1854. Lithograph from a drawing by E. Whitefield. (Courtesy of the Hamilton Public Library)

This is a closer-up view than that depicted by Whale. It diminishes and tames nature and emphasizes order and regularity. This view from Hamilton Mountain was much admired by visitors.

Hamilton from the Mountain, 1875. (Courtesy of the Hamilton Public Library)

The framing of the scene has some similarities to that employed by Whale, but "nature" is now thoroughly suburbanized and domesticated.

York (Toronto) from Gibraltar Point. *Drawing by J. Gray, 1828 (Courtesy of the Royal Ontario Museum, Toronto)*

The young city is distant, almost invisible, and the picture is dominated by trees and Indian figures. But civilization is intruding very prominently, and the smoke being emitted from the steamer asserts itself above the "dying embers" of the Indians' fire.

Toronto *by Augustus Kollner, 1851. (Courtesy of the Royal Ontario Museum, Toronto)*

Again the view of the city is a distant one. The foreground emphasizes the taming and civilizing of nature which has been converted to park land. The strollers are still in the scene; the Indians have gone. Toronto's population in 1851 was 30, 775.

Toronto, Canada West *by E. Whitefield, 1854. (Courtesy of the Royal Ontario Museum, Toronto)*

This is the scene that so impressed visitors to Toronto in the 1850s. The perspective is the reverse of that in Kollner's 1851 picture: nature has almost vanished, and even the strollers are being crowded out by the commerce that is tai.ing over the shore.

Montreal, 1851, by Augustus Kollner. (Courtesy of the Public Archives, Canada; C 13448)

A popular view from the elevated ground of Mount Royal. The fringes of civilization in the foreground are denoted by decaying trunks and the pioneer figure setting forth with his axe to chop down more trees.

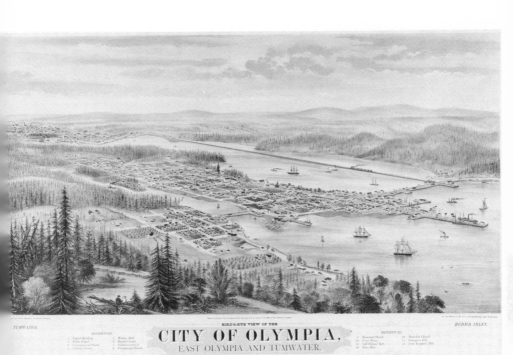

Olympia, Washington, c. 1879. Lithograph by E. S. Glover. (Courtesy of the Amon Carter Museum, Fort Worth, Texas)

This is the panoramic scene that so impressed visitors. Note the artist sitting on a fallen tree, symbol of the transformation of the landscape.

Title page of Victoria in 1880. *(Courtesy of the Alexander Turnbull Library, Wellington, New Zealand)*

This title page exemplifies pride in the evolution of Melbourne out of the Australian bush. Note the disappearance of the aboriginal figures and the taming of "nature," with a fence neatly separating city from country.

View of Melbourne, Port Phillip, *c. 1846, engraved by J. W. Lowry from a painting by W. F. E. Liardet. (Courtesy of the National Library of Australia; Rex Nan Kivell Collection)*

This view of Melbourne about ten years after its foundation is arranged in two bands—the higher one the young town, and the lower, nature well on the way to being tamed.

Sydney from the Parramatta Road *by Joseph Lycett. Watercolor, 1819. (Courtesy of the Mitchell Library, State Library of New South Wales)*

The young town conforms to the natural contours of the landscape, but the conquest of nature is evidenced by the fences, the stumps and broken tree trunks, and the line of houses creeping out along the road.

Sydney and Botany Bay from the North Shore, 1840 *by Conrad Martens. Oil on canvas. (Courtesy of the Dixson Galleries, State Library of New South Wales)*

The city is distant and hard to discern in a painting dominated by trees, rocks, and sky.

Sydney from the North Shore. *Painting by George Edward Peacock, 1845.*
(Courtesy of the Dixson Galleries, State Library of New South Wales)

The city is embowered in a pastoral landscape. The North Shore was a favorite
vantage point for artists because of the contrast it afforded between primitive
nature and the rising city.

Sydney Cove, 1861 *by Oswald Rose Campbell. Oil on canvas. (Courtesy of the Mitchell Library, State Library of New South Wales)*

Rocks and trees frame the vision of the growing city.

A View of Sydney Cove, New South Wales, *engraved by Francis Jukes from a drawing by Edward Dayes (after Thomas Watling). Colored aquatint, 1804. (Courtesy of the National Library of Australia; Rex Nan Kivell Collection)*

Aborigines camp heedlessly, as they have long been accustomed to, on The Rocks at Sydney. But the growing urban-commercial civilization threatens to engulf them and their way of life.

Oregon City on the Willamette River *by John Mix Stanley. Oil on canvas, c. 1848. (Courtesy of the Amon Carter Museum, Fort Worth, Texas)*

Oregon City was laid out in 1842–43 by John McLoughlin, Chief Factor for the Hudson's Bay Company. It was the capital of Oregon Territory, 1848–51. The Indian figures are literally marginalized, on the fringes of the settlement. They are turning their backs on the scene and are semi-submerged in the gloomy rock area. The neatness and order of the town are emphasized. Note how the light plays on the houses and the falls, source of the town's economic well-being.

Sydney from Bell Mount *by S. Taylor. Oil on canvas, 1813. (Courtesy of the Dixson Galleries, State Library of New South Wales).*

The young city is a very distant vision in a painting dominated by natural forms. The aboriginal figures already have a transitory, ghost-like appearance.

Sydney. *Painting by Joseph Lycett, 1827. (Courtesy of the Dixson Galleries, State Library of New South Wales)*

Nature—and the aborigines—retreat before the advancing tide of urban development.

General View of Sydney from the North Shore. *Painting by Samuel Thomas Gill, 1861. (Courtesy of the Dixson Galleries, State Library of New South Wales)*

The trees and aborigines have now disappeared, and suburban development is just beginning.

Sydney. Harbour *by George William Evans. Oil on canvas, date unknown. (Courtesy of the Dixson Galleries, Public Library of New South Wales)*

Somewhere in this scene is the young city of Sydney. It is dominated by massive, contoured natural forms and by the figures of the two aborigines, but the viewer's gaze is drawn from their frozen and resigned stance to the town just appearing on the horizon.

Adelaide in Embryo *[W. H. Longway]. Watercolor, 1838. (Courtesy of the Alexander Turnbull Library, Wellington, New Zealand)*

Adelaide had been surveyed in 1837. The title conveys the artist's sense of a "future city" just starting to grow amid the trees. Note the aborigines at ease among the huts of the newly arrived European settlers.

Red River ox carts on 3rd Street, St. Paul, Minnesota, 1859. (Courtesy of the Minnesota Historical Society)

We glimpse here the intermingling of "savagery" and "civilization" which so fascinated visitors to St. Paul in the 1850s.

The Strater Hotel and Navajo Indian Camp, Durango, Colorado. (Courtesy of the Amon Carter Museum, Fort Worth, Texas; Mazzulla Collection)

The corner of 7th and Main Streets was reserved for Indian camping. This photograph from the early 1890s shows the Strater Hotel, opened in August 1888.

Camp of Sarcee Indians, Calgary, 1890s. (Courtesy of the Glenbow Archives, Calgary)

The angle at which this photograph is composed is similar to that of many paintings: the town is distant, low on the horizon, and "rising," while the foreground is dominated by rough nature and "primitive" Indians.

Blood Indians at Lethbridge, Alberta, c. 1908. (Courtesy of the Glenbow Archives, Calgary)

Photographers liked to have their groups of indigenous people posed against a Main Street backdrop in order to highlight the contrast of cultures.

Sarcee Indian tea dance, Calgary, c. 1887. (Courtesy of the Glenbow Archives, Calgary)

Indigenous peoples became objects of curiosity and entertainment for the people of the new towns.

The Newly Arrived. *Sketch by Samuel Thomas Gill (undated). (Courtesy of the Dixson Galleries, State Library of New South Wales)*

To the migrants newly arrived in the Australian town the aborigines are mere figures of fun.

M. Tarver, pointed out that "it is the policy of every country to encourage the growth of its own towns and cities" and went on to deplore the fact that this policy "has not been sufficiently appreciated by the people of the Southern and Western States of the Union until recently." "The growth of our western cities," he argued, "is especially necessary to the full and speedy development of the wealth of this region. It is the surest means of diversifying labor; of introducing new pursuits; and building up a home market." While it was true that "large cities are nurseries of vice, and, that, there, human nature sinks to the lowest degree in the moral scale," it was also true that they were "the homes of learning; the nurseries of science, and, of the arts that promote the advancement of civilization."[33]

Over the next three decades many midwestern cities did grow very rapidly, and occasional expressions of concern over this were made. For example, in June 1880 in an address at Franklin College Daniel Pratt Baldwin argued that Indiana and the Midwest did not want a "single great city like Chicago or St. Louis" but "hundreds of neat, tidy little villages—each self-sustaining, independent." He found the intense urban competitiveness of the Midwest, with each town trying to "break down the growth of all competing villages," "as suicidal to State growth as the great, plantation system of slavery was to Southern prosperity." He deplored the tendency to dominance of each county by its county seat. "The two most prosperous rural counties in our State are Henry and Wayne, both of which boast of ten or more considerable towns. Our future prosperity consists in fostering every one of these villages, and making each one of them centers of wealth, intelligence and power."[34] There are echoes of this attitude to the small towns of the Midwest in Harry Truman's remark that "a thousand county seat towns of 7,000 people each are a thousand times more important to this republic than one city of 7 million people."[35] On the whole, however, spokesmen for smaller towns in the American West very seldom expressed resentment concerning the growth of the larger cities and metropolises. Most boosters expressed unqualified admiration for the successful cities. The reason was quite simple. They wanted their towns also to become "metropolises." This attitude of small town boosters to the larger cities was satirized by Sinclair Lewis in *Babbitt*.[36]

To Westgarth and others the rivalries of smaller centers fragmented, and checked the progress of, the general community. The metropolis transcended this struggle. It offered alliance to particular centers in their struggle with others. They accepted, only to find that they had gained "victory" in that level of urban competition at the price of absorption into the urban system that was dominated by the metropolis. Westgarth analyzed how this happened in the relationship between Melbourne and Ballarat, which then formed a system that gravitated against the potentially secessionist ambitions of Portland in the west of the colony.[37]

Large cities had a negative image in some respects because of what many of them were like in Britain and Europe and the East of the United States. H. H. Hayter admitted that large cities in the Old World had their undesirable aspects but argued that these were much less likely to develop in New World cities because of their great extent. The abundance of space, made usable by modern developments in transportation, meant that the new cities were mostly made up of suburbs. It was far less likely that slums would develop in them.[38] Frederick Law Olmsted advanced similar arguments in regard to the United States.[39]

To numerous commentators all such debates were pointless. Adna F. Weber was but one among many to see New World countries as inescapably caught up in a world-wide trend to the concentration of population in large cities.[40] The mid-nineteenth century was defined in England by Dr. Vaughan as *The Age of Great Cities*. His book was read and its message assimilated by Dr. Lang in Australia. In San Francisco in June 1854 yet another clergyman, Dr. Scott, gave a lecture on "the Influence of Great Cities" in which he advanced the same theme: *"Our age is preeminently the age of great cities. . . .* the tendency of modern society is towards building large towns and cities. . . . Everywhere, in Europe and America, there is a prevailing disposition to converge upon great points. Large towns are increasing in number, and absorbing all the smaller within their vicinity."[41] According to this point of view there was nothing abnormal about the rapid growth of large cities in the new countries. It was a reflection of world-wide trends.

Nevertheless, the new countries contained numerous boosters, not just of individual cities, but of the trend to what in America was called "a west of great cities." Logan U. Reavis, while doing his utmost to boost St. Louis as "the final great city," also devoted space to celebrating great cities in general as "the mightiest works of man."[42] Foremost among these enthusiasts were the statisticians such as Weber and, in Australia, Hayter and T. A. Coghlan. They liked what their statistics told them was happening and became very excited over the projections that they could make on the basis of present trends. As early as 1841 Ralph Mansfield of the *Sydney Herald* discovered that the rate of increase of Sydney's population was over 10 percent per annum. At that rate, he argued, Sydney would overtake Boston in eight and a half years, Liverpool in twenty-one, and New York in twenty-three.[43]

Some argued that the trend to concentration in large cities was "unhealthy" and "unnatural," a perversion of the order of nature. Analogies with the body were frequent.[44] In 1852 Dr. Lang described the ratio of urban to rural population in New South Wales as unheard of, "unnatural," and an "enormous disproportion."[45] When in 1882 the New South Wales census revealed that 30 percent of the population lived in Sydney and its suburbs, 28 percent in other towns and villages, and only 42 percent in the country districts, the *Bulletin* referred to this as "an overwhelming disproportion in the numbers supported otherwise than by the soil."[46] That so young a country should so quickly have developed this concentration of population in large cities was an increasing theme of adverse comment by overseas visitors and analysts.[47]

The changing attitudes of Australians to their large cities, and the persisting ambiguities in these, can be illustrated by reference to the successive editions of T. A. Coghlan's *The Wealth and Progress of New South Wales,* a statistical publication that was later to become the New South Wales official yearbook. In the 1886–87 edition no trace of concern appears. Indeed, there is more than a hint of pride in the phenomenon. Coghlan traces the trends in the statistics. Between 1861 and 1886 Sydney's share of the population of New South Wales has risen from 26.70 to 33.20 percent and Melbourne's share of the population of Victoria from 25.89 to 37.05 percent. Coghlan comments as follows:

The progress of these cities has been extraordinary, and has no parallel amongst the cities of the Old World. Even in America the rise of the great cities has been accompanied by a somewhat corresponding increase in the rural population. In these colonies, perhaps for the first time in the history of the world, is seen the spectacle of magnificent cities growing with wonderful rapidity, and embracing within their limits one-third of the population of the territory on which they depend.

He also remarked about America, but without making any comparison with Australia, that "there seems no reason to suppose that, large as the proportion of urban population has become, it has reached an unhealthy stage."[48] But two years later, in the edition of 1889–90, a sentence was added at this point. "In Australasia, however, the case is different, and it is impossible to believe that healthy progress is consistent with the wonderful growth of the metropolis at the expense of the country." The adjectives "unhealthy" and "wonderful" were now coexisting.[49] In the 1894 edition another change was made, intensifying the ambiguity: in the passage quoted above from the 1886–87 edition the word "disquieting" was inserted before the words "spectacle of magnificent cities growing with wonderful rapidity."[50] In 1898 Coghlan published a book of more general scope entitled *A Statistical Account of the Seven Colonies of Australasia, 1897–8*. In this he again used the passage which he had first used eleven years earlier, but instead of adding qualifying adjectives he inserted a new sentence: "The abnormal aggregation of the population into their capital cities is a most unfortunate element in the progress of the colonies, and one which seems to become every year more marked." But he did not try to integrate this perception into the earlier portion of the paragraph with the result that the two descriptions of the same phenomenon—"magnificent cities" growing with "wonderful rapidity," and an "abnormal aggregation" that is "most unfortunate"—were allowed to stand side by side.

By this stage even New Zealand was beginning to receive more favorable comment. Coghlan noted that the population of Auckland, New Zealand's largest city, was only 8.18 percent of the population of the country as a whole, whereas 33.86 percent of New South Wales's people lived in Sydney and 41.59 percent of South Australia's in Adelaide.[51] Of course, by this stage also the reaction against concentration in large cities was becoming an important element in the making of the "Australian legend," which will be discussed in a later chapter. Henry Lawson, the famous poet of the "bush," wrote an essay in which he described the social evils of Sydney and came to conclusions which were diametrically opposed to those expressed by William Westgarth thirty years before.

The rivalry existing between the several towns of a colony is conducive in its effects to the general welfare of the colony, because such emulation is favorable to the formation of more equally balanced centres in different parts of the country, and thus leads to the general decentralisation of the population.

Centralisation is admitted to be a blunder in any country, but in a new colony, which it is necessary to populate, centralisation is directly opposed to the principles of colonisation.

The congregation of the bulk of a country's population in one or two large towns is about as sensible in idea, and as injurious in its effects, both physically and morally, as the crowding together of a family in one room of a large house, when all the other rooms are empty and available. A country with but one city deserving of the name is about as natural as a horse with one leg.[52]

Because of the slums and "hells" and dreadful poverty in Sydney which Lawson described so graphically, he was able to disembarrass himself entirely of the pride in "magnificent cities" to which Coghlan continued to cling.

Coghlan repeatedly suggested that in the United States the situation was less "disquieting" than in Australia. One reason was the size of the country which made the rise of great cities seem less traumatic: "in America there exist many large cities; in this Colony we have practically only one." He also noted that, owing in large part to the fact that their growth was attributable to foreign immigration, the rise of America's cities did not appear to have been at the expense of the rural population.[53] When rural depopulation did occur in the Midwest in the late nineteenth century, there were indications of an ambiguous anxiety similar to that which developed in Australia at this time. Bayrd Still has brought this out in his study of the attitudes of Wisconsin people to the growth of Milwaukee. In 1886 one newspaper regretted the shift of population to the big city but acknowledged that living there was cheaper: "there is good in the great cities and also a vast deal of evil in them."[54]

However, Australians seem to have developed a conviction that there was in respect of concentration of population something distinctive about their country. In a perverse way, however deep their anxiety, this became a source of one sort of national pride. It was something that made Australian society different, even unique.

Australians argued endlessly as to why this had happened. Some saw the "original sin" as being the policies of those who had established the first settlements. They had, for a variety of reasons, forced "capitals" into a premature existence and built in to Australian development a metropolitan bias. The metropolitan areas became enormous vested interests which were able to perpetuate and entrench their dominance once self-government and adult male suffrage were established. This was seen notably in the growth of protectionist tariff policies which were regarded as artificially fostering urban employment.[55] One problem with that argument was that New South Wales pursued a free trade policy and yet Sydney developed a position in that colony approximating to Melbourne's in Victoria. In New South Wales blame tended to focus on high government expenditure which intensified "centralization."[56]

Much comment emphasized the behavior and preferences of migrants. T. A. Coghlan did not believe that Australia was unique in this regard. He wrote of "a common tendency operating in all new countries for immigrants to locate themselves in and near the large cities. This Colony has been no exception to the rule." His statistics revealed the percentage of persons born outside Australia to be higher in Sydney than for New South Wales as a whole.[57] It was often observed that migrants tended to stay in the port at which they arrived. "Immigrants to Australia linger long in their port of debarkation, and experience shows that they seldom care to leave it while employment is procurable."[58] Of course, the same thing also happened in the United States. But that country, unlike Australia, already had a large interior population. In Australia the behavior of migrants worsened a state of already considerable imbalance.

It was often observed, notably in evidence to the 1859–60 Select Committee of the New South Wales Legislative Assembly, that migrants from British towns did not want to go into the interior and take up farm laboring and sheepherding. If they were men with artisan backgrounds and skills, they naturally preferred to work at their trades in the cities where they could be much more sure of finding regular, well-paid employment. There were many reasons why migrants from British cities should have wanted to stay in cities such as Sydney. Often they had been sent for by friends and relatives already living there and did not want to leave them for the loneliness of life in the Australian bush.[59] In 1836 a British M.P., George Poulett Scrope, argued that Edward Gibbon Wakefield's "sufficient price" theory, which assumed that by some such mechanism migrants had to be restrained from a natural tendency to disperse and relapse into "barbarism," was founded on a totally erroneous view of human behavior.

I think the theory on which that principle is founded a very doubtful one, namely, that man has a strong though unaccountable desire to settle on a tract of land of his own, even though he may be thereby obliged to forego the advantages of civilization and society, nay, even to risk starvation and absolute want of the necessaries of life, in preference to labouring for hire in the way in which he has been accustomed to do in another country, and on wages which will supply him with all the necessaries and many of the comforts of civilized life, the enjoyment of society, and the exercise of his religious worship. I have always been in the habit of believing man to be by nature a gregarious animal, to be disposed to harbour together, to co-operate and combine their labour, and not to isolate themselves in the way Mr. Wakefield's theory seems to suppose.[60]

It was argued that the fault lay in the selection of migrants.[61] The people brought out should be farm laborers, not townspeople. Others maintained—on the basis of experience—that English farm workers were of little use in the very different Australian conditions. Indeed, it was said that urban migrants, if only they could be induced to go into the bush, were more adaptable and flexible. Or perhaps the answer was to have the migrants landed at ports other than Sydney and Melbourne and dispatched immediately into the interior before they could be subjected to the allurements of the big cities. There was much talk about the need to do this but little action followed. Similar concerns were expressed in Canada.[62]

There was a dilemma for propagandists for emigration who wanted to use the civilized state of Australian cities to induce people to emigrate. In his novel *How to Emigrate* (1855) W. H. G. Kingston has a character returning to England after a spell in Australia and talking to people about what a handsome city Sydney was and how its shops "may vie in magnificence with many in London." But Kingston also has this character admit to one problem: "The difficulty we have is to induce people accustomed to live in towns to go up the country, where the true means of acquiring wealth is to be discovered." Kingston solves this problem by having his own emigrant family arrive in Adelaide and spend only one hour there, just time enough to allow him to quote their exclamations at the splendor of that city's shops and houses. Then they proceed on their way "up country."[63]

Promoters of emigration often assumed that the major reason for migrating was to escape from the evils of big city life, not to rediscover or recreate them in the New World. If nevertheless the latter turned out to be what happened, there must be some obstacle to passage into the country that had to be removed. Land policy, and in particular the concentration of the ownership of land in the hands of a few and the failure of governments to do anything effective to deal with this state of affairs, were often blamed for the excessive confinement of population within the cities. It was assumed that the cities would shrink if only more land were made available for settlement. To make it available was one of the principal objectives of agitation in both Australia and New Zealand for land reform. A common explanation of the over-crowded condition of antipodean cities was "land monopoly."[64]

Much of this debate was controlled by what has been called the Arcadian vision.[65] Many of the people who were living in the cities were not there, it was assumed, because they wanted to be but because "land monopoly" or the failure of the government to make land accessible prevented them from leaving. A favorite twentieth-century explanation, that large city populations developed in Australia because of the predominance for economic reasons of pastoralism, which required few workers on the land, was slow to develop.[66]

An important part in the Australian debate on land reform was played by such questions as whether the workers and the unemployed in the cities really did want to go on the land, whether they would take advantage of opportunities to do so, and whether policies of promoting closer settlement and ending "land monopoly" would be able to reduce, or at least stem the increase in the rate of growth of, the large cities. The assumption behind much land reform may be illustrated by the claim made by one member in debates in the Victorian Legislature in 1862 on a Land Sales Bill that "a large number of mechanics in Melbourne hoped that the day was not far distant when they would cease from their present labour, and retire upon a piece of land of their own; and the object of the Legislature should be to assist them in that object as much as possible."[67]

The subject was much discussed at the meetings of the Select Committee of the New South Wales Legislative Assembly on the Condition of the Working Classes of the Metropolis, 1859–60. The general consensus was that social distress and unemployment in Sydney—which had caused the committee to be set up—were the consequence of a surplus of population, especially of immigrants, in Sydney. There was also a widespread feeling that these problems would be alleviated if these surplus people could be persuaded to leave the city and go to work on the land. "It has been my impression for many years," said N. Pigeon, a city missionary, "that the city will not be in a healthy state till the people have turned their attention to agriculture . . . there is an overplus of hands in the city."[68] Many reasons were advanced as to why working people in the city did not go on to the land, the assumption being that if the obstacles to their doing so could be removed they would pour out of the city. But there were some skeptics who argued that the preference for city life was rooted in a liking of it and a fear of life in the bush. Others felt that the idea of frustrated land hunger was a myth, convenient for politicians who sought a scapegoat for urban problems that they were not prepared to seek a solution for within the city itself. One country town newspaper declared in 1862: "The hundreds of people in Melbourne, who were to flock into the country on the advent of the liberal land law, existed nowhere but in the imagination of those who made the cant of a liberal land law their political stock in trade."[69]

The perceived imbalance in favor of the large cities in Australia was not just in the relationship between city and country (the "bush") but also between city and town. There was—and still is—considerable argument as to whether the country towns should be counted within the "urban" or the "country" part of the equation.[70] As for the country townspeople themselves, they could almost be described as schizophrenic in their perception of their situation. On the one hand, there was a strong tendency in both Australia and New Zealand for them to blame their problems, especially slow growth, on "land monopoly," the control of surrounding land by a few "squatters" and pastoralists. In New Zealand a major political issue of the late nineteenth century was the demand for the subdivision of estates, if necessary by compulsory expropriation. Much of the pressure for this came from country towns. People in these referred to the towns being "suffocated" by land monopoly.[71] But, when they turned to face in the opposite direction, they uttered similar complaints about the metropolitan areas. When David Kennedy, a Scottish entertainer who visited many small towns in Australia and New Zealand with his theatrical party and is an excellent source of insights into their predicaments, visited Geelong in the 1870s, he was told by one local person: "I never expected Geelong to have the come-down it has had. It's been regularly sat upon and smothered by Melbourne—sat upon and smothered, I say."[72]

A common perception of the Australian situation was of the weakness of the small towns. This state of affairs was seen as being both cause and consequence of the ascendancy of the metropolitan areas.[73] Many towns came into existence for reasons that guaranteed but a brief life. The vast number of "ghost towns" that can now be traced in all four countries is testimony to this. Commentators traced a connection between this phenomenon and the growth of large metropolitan centers. Charles Lindsey, in *The Prairies of the Western States* (1860), described the vast number of speculative "cities" founded in Minnesota, Wisconsin, and other prairie regions in the 1850s. Most were in a collapsed state, utterly lifeless, and "retrograding." And he had the impression of worse to come. In Illinois "an enormous proportion of the population is crowded into villages, of which the existence only serves as a monument of the folly of extravagant speculation." One did not have to look far to see where the people were going. St Louis "presented a remarkable contrast to every other place that I visited in the West." Everything, he concluded, "showed a tendency to converge towards a few great centres; of which St. Louis may be accounted one. The effects of the crisis of 1857 were not visible at St. Louis."[74]

Gold rushes and many other exploitative industries brought a large number of towns into existence. Some flourished impressively, most disappeared after a short time, and only the "metropolises"—Melbourne, San Francisco, Dunedin, Denver—were able to achieve permanence. Mining towns were recognized as places where most people would stay for only a short period. If they became wealthy, they would naturally prefer to go to spend or invest their wealth in the metropolis. Apart from anything else, mining itself made the environments of the towns where it took place very unattractive. If people did not make money, there was no reason why they should remain in such a town. In *Australia Revisited* (1891) Josiah Hughes tells of a visit to Sandhurst, near Bendigo. He found the immediate surroundings very "barren and desert-like" and heard the tradesmen—stranded from the gold rush era—"complain that their wealthy people do not continue to live at Sandhurst; after making fortunes at mining they leave for Melbourne, or the old country, to spend it." "There is no doubt that this will always continue," wrote Hughes. "The fault is not in the people, but in the locality."[75] In *Wealth and Progress of New South Wales 1895–6* (1897) T. A. Coghlan gave the following as one of the reasons for the predominance of the large cities in Australia:

Gold-digging, to which the colonies owe so much, is not an industry likely to promote permanent settlement in the interior. The miner of the past was in every respect a nomad: if successful in his quest after the precious metal, he became an emigrant to the old world or a sojourner in an Australian capital.[76]

The extent to which both townspeople and outsiders perceived vitality in a town and had confidence in its prospects was very dependent on the quality and intensity of the boosting undertaken on its behalf. Here there is a major difference between the United States and Australia. Probably because metropolitan cities were so clearly established and defined as such from the very outset of settlement and were given the full weight of government support in sustaining and extending this dominant position, and also because economic realities pointed so strongly to a perpetuation of metropolitan ascendancy, the boosting of Australia's secondary towns —as distinct from the metropolises such as Melbourne—was very low-key and feeble by American standards. Ambition was kept at low levels and only occasionally had enough momentum to sustain a vigorous American-style boosting campaign. Melbourne-based writers such as William Westgarth advocated strategies to bind provincial centers to Melbourne and to play them off against one another. The country towns were weakened vis-à-vis the metropolis by their own lack of unity and inability to form a common front of resistance to encroaching metropolitan influence. They functioned mainly as regional centers and behaved toward other towns as rivals of those towns or of their regions. Rivalry was expressed particularly in competition for railroad connections with the metropolis —which, of course, further enhanced the latter's dominant position.[77]

From the very outset government policy seemed biased in favor of the metropolitan areas. The future of medium-sized regional centers never became a major issue and motivation for government programs to redress the balance and promote decentralization.[78] One who deplored the lack of concentration in Australia's population outside the metropolitan areas and urged action to remedy this was John Dunmore Lang.[79]

But, in the view of many commentators, the imbalance between the metropolitan areas and the rest of the community in each colony only became worse as the century progressed. In his book *The Government of Victoria (Australia)* (1897) the English constitutional lawyer Edward Jenks analyzed the situation. He traced the imbalance back to the origins of the colony at a time when, in the 1830s, central government in England was abnormally strong and local government unusually weak. In the early history of Victoria the emphasis was on the reproduction of parliamentary institutions. "Municipal institutions awaken no enthusiasm." Furthermore, Victoria was topographically not the type of country in which strong, independent, self-reliant local government was likely to develop. "A country which contains many mountains and impassable rivers, dense forests and wide lakes, which is also infested with physical dangers, is the country of local government. The scattered settlements are cut off from one another by substantial boundaries, and their members do not lightly risk the dangers of travel. They find their interests at home, and devote their attention to the regulation of them." Victoria was not like this. There was also the character of migration. Migrants "came as individuals, not as groups." The "villages" that they settled in therefore lacked cohesion and any source of group identity. Transience into and out of them was very high. "It is not wonderful, therefore, that the spirit of local cohesion should have been singularly absent all through the history of Victoria, and that no local organisation should have grown up at all able to balance the central organisation at Melbourne."[80]

In Australia the vast flat expanses between the big cities held few attractions for visitors who usually wanted to pass over them as rapidly as possible. By the late nineteenth century it was becoming quite common for writers to describe the big cities and assure their readers that these descriptions held all that they needed to know about the colonies of which the cities were the capitals. In 1871 the Rev. James Ballantyne wrote that

in one sense at least it may be said that Melbourne is Victoria. Its numerous rising townships, in so far as their institutions and social habits and advantages are concerned, are simply other Melbournes in miniature. A sketch of the metropolis will virtually, and in some of its most important aspects, be a sketch of the colony.[81]

The effects of writings which emphasized the "marvelous" rise of Melbourne to reassure migrants about the level of civilization attained in the country to which they were thinking of going can be illustrated by remarks made by the London agent of the *Sydney Morning Herald* to a New South Wales Legislative Assembly Select Committee in 1880: "In many places in England, if you speak of Victoria, very little of it is known by name, but almost every one has heard of Melbourne—indeed Melbourne seems to be considered Australia."[82]

What could the smaller towns offer to counter the fascinations of the metropolis? It seemed to many that an irresistible momentum set in. The larger the metropolitan areas grew, the greater was the range of employment opportunities and social, charitable, recreational, and educational facilities that they offered.[83] In *Another England* (1869) E. Carton Booth acknowledged that "Melbourne itself is perhaps the most wonderful thing in connection with Victoria. It is as handsome and well-to-do a city as any of its size in Europe. All the appointments and appliances of a high civilisation and luxury are to be found within its bounds."[84] Before the development of "Marvellous Melbourne" Catherine Spence foresaw what might happen. In her novel *Clara Morison* she has a character write concerning Melbourne in 1852: "I heard a gentleman say it was no bad thing for the colony that Melbourne was not a desirable place of residence; for that in a new state comfortable and luxurious cities impede the spread of the people and the subjugation of the soil."[85] Much of the evidence to the 1859–60 New South Wales Select Committee suggested —often just as anxiously and regretfully—that this was already happening in the case of Sydney. Positive attractions as well as negative aspects such as fear of the bush were acknowledged. One witness told the committee that working people "feel happier" in the city. There they could get "more comforts" and amusements.[86]

Australia's small towns acquired and could never shake off a negative image. They turned out in most cases to be a long way from the villages of the Arcadian myth that, according to Coral Lansbury, played such a prominent role in the publicizing of Australia in England.[87] The belief grew that the smaller a town was, the more faction-ridden and given over to "abusing and slandering their neighbours" its people were likely to be.[88] In 1876 a newspaper in one small Queensland town described "cliquism" as "in all small towns the detestable bugbear."[89] By contrast, large cities appealed on account of their assumed tolerance.

Similar trends have been detected in the United States. The negative view of small towns probably set in there a good deal later, perhaps because the vigor of boosterism sustained morale and confidence in the future longer than in many cases they deserved to be sustained. It has been argued that boosterism obscured, and diverted attention from, the weak economic foundations of many smaller American towns and, by suppressing "bad news," helped some to maintain undeservedly favorable images. D. N. Jeans—an Australian geographer—has studied the place of the small town in American fiction and concluded that the "storm of literary abuse" against it which culminated in Sinclair Lewis's *Main Street* began in the early 1880s. He instances E. W. Howe's *The Story of a Country Town* (1883) in which appears the earlier Australian perception of townspeople as mean-minded and fond of gossip and slander. The theme of escape to the big city from the small town grew in popularity and, Jeans argues, reflected the experience of the writers themselves.[90] This theme reached its culmination in Sherwood Anderson's *Winesburg,*

Ohio, as well as in Carol Kennicott's flight to Washington, D.C., at the end of *Main Street.* A parallel trend is the growing fascination of the metropolis for writers. An example is Theodore Dreiser, whose excitement mounted as he first compared Evansville, Indiana, with smaller towns ("Those poor scum back in Sullivan, I thought! What could they know of a place like this? A city! And such a city!"), and then reacted with still greater enthusiasm to Chicago.[91]

CHAPTER SEVEN

Time and Space
on the Urban Frontier

VISITORS to the new towns of the New World often remarked on what they called their "future city" atmosphere. Everybody's thoughts seemed to be focused on the future—to such an extent that the present was scarcely noticed. "Thought and speech about cities are replete with temporal imagery," Anselm L. Strauss has argued. In the case of the United States the "vocabulary of urbanism" has always had a particular orientation toward the future, "since the nation at large is committed to notions of progress."[1] If this is true about the "nation at large," how much likelier was it to be the case with the cities of the westward expansion of the nineteenth century! One of the most celebrated labels for these towns was George Augustus Sala's "Cities of the Future," which, he wrote in *America Revisited* (1882), referred to "the resolve character-istic of the Americans to make their towns, even in the inception thereof, big things."[2]

In *Land, Labour and Gold* (1855) William Howitt wrote that in gold-rush Melbourne "the future is so palpable and positive that none can miss seeing it."[3] There are many references to the way in which people who visited the new towns or arrived to settle in them soon fell into a "future" frame of mind. They were described, or described themselves, as having been "infected" by an "atmosphere." Even when they were initially skep-tical, visitors usually seemed to undergo this kind of transformation. They were moved to reflect on what the city would be like in the future, and such thoughts could blot out all perceptions of what it was like in the present. "Who knows where the city limits will be in about ten years, perhaps on a mountain that one can only imagine," mused Alexsandr Lakier as he looked at the Cincinnati of 1857.[4] Or here is the Rev. Frederick J. Jobson, sailing down the Mississippi: "Each forest-clearing and embryo giant city lead you to ask, amidst the exhaustless resources of the vast country, 'What will this America and its people be in the Future?' "[5] Australian towns induced similar reveries. John Askew in *A Voyage to Australia & New Zealand* (1857), records walking to the outskirts of Melbourne early one Sunday morning when the town was "silent as a deserted city" and not a single inhabitant was to be seen.

Both time and place were peculiarly favourable for evoking a day-dream and speculative musings about the destinies of the future Melbourne, whose germ lay before me, with its inhabitants wrapped in slumber only agitated by golden visions. . . . Temples devoted to religion and science may then have risen along the shores of Hobson's Bay. Institutions which the Western and Old Worlds never conceived of, may have sprung into a flourishing condition.[6]

Askew's striking image of the people of Melbourne existing not in the present but in dreams of a golden future reflects the atmosphere into which visitors often felt themselves absorbed almost mesmerically. An *Atlantic Monthly* article in 1858 referred to the effect on the visitor of the "resolute and occupied air" of Chicago's crowds. "Hardly any one stays long among them without feeling a desire to share their excitement, and do something towards the splendid future which is evidently beckoning them on."[7] In his *Recollections of a Pioneer Lawyer* Othman A. Abbott recalled coming to Grand Island, Nebraska, in 1867 and finding the place at first "very small and inconspicuous." But

the few men who were there, those early Hall County pioneers, believed in its future. I soon found myself adopting the same point of view. I acquired almost by instinct a firm belief in the future of the great plains. There must be a metropolis somewhere in the great prairie wilderness of central Nebraska,—why not here? . . . From whatever or wherever it came, I know that I did not try to analyze or explain my early feeling that Nebraska would be a great state and this small settlement a thriving city.[8]

The speculative atmosphere of the early days of a town could be particularly infectious. J. Max Clark was one of the early settlers at Greeley, Colorado. He came out intending to farm. In his *Colonial Days* (1902) he told of how ridiculous he found, on his first day there, the spectacle of "men running hither and thither, up and down the ridiculous little furrows that at the time marked off the magnificent imaginary streets, all seemingly laboring under great excitement, and all of them engaged in looking up desirable lots for location." Clark and his companion were "disgusted with the enterprise into which we had been foolishly duped." The next day they returned to the town, and somehow it did not look quite as absurd. Their spirits rose, "and then the first thing we knew, we were running frantically about looking for lots for ourselves, and quite disgusted, too, to think we had wasted so much time. We got some and that settled the business; we settled."[9]

There were those writers who were convinced that all the rhetoric about great cities of the future was just a confidence trick designed to lure and deceive migrants and investors.[10] But others were convinced that it was genuine, that in a sense the townspeople mesmerized themselves.[11]

One of the most remarkable accounts of a city's obsession with its fantasies of a great and glorious future and of how one man felt himself drawn irresistibly into this is Denton J. Snider's *The St. Louis Movement in Philosophy, Literature, Education, Psychology with Chapters of Autobiography* (1920). Snider was in St. Louis just after the Civil War and found that its "city-soul"

was getting to have one all-dominating psychical trait when I first breathed of its atmosphere, which trait I soon caught, and then it caught me. I quickly found the one faith universal, that St. Louis could not help becoming the largest, richest, most influential city in the land, with all the gain and glory and dominion resulting from such pre-eminence. In religion, politics, and love its multiracial polyglottic people might differ, but in one creed they were united, or rather fused to a kind of fanaticism: the doctrine of the future supremacy of St. Louis.

This "divine belief" became "a kind of St. Louis religion, and entered deeply into the character of the city, of the individual citizens" who failed for fifteen years (until the census of 1880, which showed Chicago to have moved far ahead in terms of population) to appreciate that it was really no more than a "huge mendacity," "a huge mirage floating before the vision of a great population across the empty desert of the future."[12]

In 1861 an article in the *Atlantic Monthly* referred to "this rage for cities in America" as "prophetic."[13] Prophecy was, indeed, a standard mode of discourse about the future of towns. As Wilson Nicely put it in *The Great Southwest* (1867), Western towns were called "cities" in "a prophetic spirit, the name being a prophecy of future importance."[14] Prophecies were no doubt expected to be self-fulfilling through the way in which they instilled confidence in the future. Also much favored were what might be called retrospective prophecies, prophecies that, if made, would have been proved accurate but were not made because they would have seemed beyond the range of credible prediction.[15]

Some Americans took to an extreme their obsession with the future.

"No people build wisely who do not build for the future," wrote Logan U. Reavis, the hunch-backed prophet of "St. Louis the Future Great City of the World," whom Snider described as "the living body of its own Great Illusion in its visible deformity." "It is the sensuous, the slothful, and the ignorant who live in the ever-present time." [16] John Howison saw Americans as so obsessed with the future that they sacrificed the present for it. "The Americans build houses and make improvements entirely for the benefit of posterity, as they generally engage in speculations so disproportioned to their means, that ruin and insolvency overtake them before they can realize what they have projected, or enjoy what they have accomplished." In Canada, by contrast, people had no such anticipation of the future, and their towns showed this. [17] The same point was made—very approvingly—by Mary O'Brien when she commented in her diary in 1830 on the improvements "surely but quietly going on in York. The style of these bespeak them to be the effect of increasing prosperity rather than speculation. This makes a very marked distinction between it and the recent towns of the United States, where everything bespeaks hurry and anticipation." [18]

Trying to locate the stage of a town's development on a temporal continuum could be a difficult exercise, involving a complex structure of tenses and an intertwining of perceptions of "past, present, and future"— the title of Wright's book on Chicago. Here, for example, is the *Chicago Tribune* correspondent's perception of Duluth in 1882:

The inhabitants of the "future great" have an abiding faith in their city. They believe that what Chicago was Duluth is, and what Chicago is Duluth will be. A visitor who suddenly drops into the place is sure to be impressed with the idea that Duluth is emphatically a city of the future, and not of the present. It has no past. [19]

Gustaf Unonius had a similarly tangled perception of Green Bay, Wisconsin, a town where at one time "large, magnificent buildings arose as if by magic." Now he found it "a phenomenon rarely met with in America: a city that is not looking ahead to future magnificence and progress, but rather permits its mind to dwell on the past." [20]

Perception of an orderly temporal pattern in a town's development was also confused by something that was often observed in the appearance of growing towns, the presence of incongruities among the buildings, the juxtaposition of old, primitive pioneer shacks alongside millionaire's mansions and modern commercial premises. "Besides the four-story brick house one finds the modest log house of the first settler," Count Baudissin observed of Missouri towns in the 1850s.[21] Whether intentional or not, such appearances were valued by boosters, and taken by many visitors, as proof that the town was growing and changing, that there was a process of evolution under way, that the town was not stuck at one point, present or past.[22] The appearance of "palaces and shanties side by side" in Chicago led Charles Dudley Warner to write of that city as "forming—full of contrasts and of promise." "Its forces are gathered and accumulating, but not assimilated."[23] Some visitors liked the evidence of energy and growth which the incongruities revealed,[24] others were repelled by the untidiness and confusion and absence of overall control and planning.[25] Some discovered economic reasons for the diversity. Arthur G. Guillemard in *Over Land and Sea* (1875) discovered that the reason why some of the small, badly built houses of early settlers lingered in the streets of Melbourne was that the owners were holding out for a high price. "When this is reached down comes the pig-sty, and a very few weeks suffice for the erection of a palace in its place."[26] When the process of evolution was over, the incongruities would have disappeared. In 1831 James Hall's *Illinois Monthly Magazine* published a prophecy of what the scene from the bluff overlooking the Mississippi at Alton would be like in three hundred years' time. There would be a magnificent city one circumstance in particular about which was "remarkably dissimilar" to all that the writer had ever before seen.

There, elegant mansions and mean huts might be seen alternately. A splendid street of fashionable houses, would have a dirty lane of wretched habitations in its neighborhood. Not so here: the buildings were elegant, but not gorgeous in ornament. Many were large, even magnificent, but all plain. A quaker neatness, simplicity, and beauty, pervaded the whole scene. Little of poverty, and nothing of meanness or wretchedness, was to be found.[27]

To grasp and define the process was not easy. Those who reported on the new towns, for example, travellers and writers of guidebooks, found that their reports became out of date with incredible swiftness. In the preface to *The Wabash* (1855) Richard Beste demonstrates sensitivity to the criticism that his book is likely to encounter on these grounds. "I am aware that the lapse of thirty or forty *months* since they took place, could make a description of the cities of the United States as much out of date as would the same number of *years* intervening after a visit to the towns of the Old World." But he seeks to offer his descriptions as generally illustrative of a recurring American process. "Although the villages and the towns and the countries which I most visited, may be now more filled up and 'fenced in,' yet will my description of them and of their inhabitants apply to localities, similarly placed in regard to the onward march of civilisation across that mighty continent."[28] People in Denver were very annoyed when William H. Dixon in *New America* described the Denver of 1866 as if it were still the crude settlement of 1860 and 1861.[29] The out-of-dateness of guidebooks became a matter for local pride. In Chicago in 1857 Alexsandr Lakier went into a bookshop to buy one. "In giving it to me, the bookseller added, as if showing off the city where he lived and worked, that he was afraid the guide might prove unsatisfactory, although it had been published only two or three months before." Lakier records that this did indeed prove to be the case: there were numerous new streets with a large population living on them.[30]

Their "future" orientation was seen as a key feature distinguishing New World towns from Old World towns. Trollope described Old World towns as being "built as they have been wanted" with no thoughts as to the future, whereas an American city "at its commencement is laid out with an intention that it shall be populous."[31] A commonly used description of a New World town was that it looked "unfinished."[32] In *The Englishman in Kansas* (1857) T.H. Gladstone insisted that "Western cities must not be judged by European rules. They are always more remarkable on paper than in reality; and, whatever they can show in existence, they have much more in prospect."[33]

But what rules should be used instead? We have a rare glimpse of a Western city-builder wrestling with this problem in an address by the mayor of Keokuk in 1856, published in Orion Clemens' *City of Keokuk in 1856*. This shows how complicated—both exciting and bewildering— was felt to be the task of devising policy for a new town's development.

Those who participate in the municipal government of old, staid, and well organized states and cities, have only a particular, well defined class of duties to perform, and a beaten path to pursue; but those who engage in the management of young and prosperous communities of the West, have a changing, increasing, uncertain accumulation of duties to perform, and their plans and policy must not only contemplate present infantile existence, but probable future growth and wide expansion. The application of steam to commercial and agricultural purposes has suddenly augmented the value of Western lands, brought the rich prairies of the West in contact with the markets of the East, causing a flood of emigration to the rich delta formed by the Mississippi and Missouri, where cities rise suddenly into being and beauty, with prospects of future wealth and grandeur that may hereafter rival many of the great cities of ancient and modern times. Those who establish their lines, and guide their destiny, exercise a fearful responsibility, since their labors must affect the interests and attract the scrutiny of future generations and indefinite masses. The past five years of progress in Keokuk, is sufficient to awaken reflections of a foreshadowing future which dazzles and bewilders the imagination, and baffles the most sagacious attempt at solution. To make rules that are neither too narrow nor too wide, too stringent nor too lenient, that will apply to-day, and in future, defies human intelligence, and only admits of approximate success.[34]

The dominance of thinking about "the future" was reflected in attitudes to the past. The towns of the New World were seen as towns without a past, defined in Old World terms. They had no relics or ancient monuments, no remnants of a "feudal" past.[35] Melbourne was often likened to Rome: both were built on "seven hills." "There the likeness to Ancient Rome ceases," wrote William Fairfax in *Handbook to Australasia* (1859); "for it is but the growth of a single generation, and therefore possesses no monuments of antiquity, or works of ancient art of which it can boast."[36] James Ballantyne in *Homes and Homesteads in the Land of Plenty* (1871) put the contrast thus: "Rome is rich in the past—Melbourne in the future."[37]

Treatment of the continuing presence of the past in a New World city could be quite ruthless. There was no sentiment about it in and for itself. If any relic of the past was in the way of the town's progress, few qualms were felt about removing or obliterating it. J. S. Buckingham in *The Eastern and Western States of America* commented on the fate of the ancient mound which gave Circleville, Ohio, its name, original shape, and distinctiveness as a town:

So little veneration . . . have the Americans for ancient remains, and so entirely destitute do they appear to be, as a nation, of any antiquarian taste, that this interesting spot of Circleville, is soon likely to lose all trace of its original peculiarities. The centre of the town contained, at its first building, an octagonal edifice used as a Town Hall, with an open space all around it; and the streets beyond this were laid out in a circular shape, corresponding with the ancient walls, from whence its name of Circleville was derived. But though the octagonal building still remains, the circular streets are fast giving way, to make room for straight ones; and the central edifice itself is already destined to be removed, to give place to stores and dwellings; so that in half a century, or less, there will be no vestige left of that peculiarity which gave the place its name, and which constituted the most perfect and therefore the most interesting work of antiquity of its class in the country.[38]

Retention would only be considered if the relic could be utilized in some way to point up the extent of the town's progress. This treatment of the past survives today in the conservation of historic buildings. For example, in Houston, Texas, a dozen or so are grouped in a Heritage Park in dramatic and well publicized juxtaposition to that city's modern skyscrapers.[39]

In *Our Great West* (1893) Julian Ralph commented on the extreme, blatant "newness" of Denver. "How the people lived five years ago, or what they have done with the houses of that period, does not appear, but at present everything—business blocks, churches, clubs, dwellings, street cars, the park—all look brand-new, like the young trees." "Five years" seems to have been an eternity in the life of Denver: it was the same lapse of time as had rendered Dixon's *New America* hopelessly out of date. Even the people in Denver were "new." Ralph was told by a citizen: "You notice there are no old people on the streets here. There aren't any in the city. We have no use for old folks here."[40] The attitude to old people seemed to be just as ruthless as the attitude to old things. Ironically, Denver was the place to which many people came in the nineteenth century in search of a renewal of health, an elixir of youth—although Lyle W. Dorsett tells us that many, once they had arrived, suffered greatly, were neglected by a callous community, and may well have died sooner than they would have had they stayed at home with friends and relatives.[41]

Attitudes to old age and death—the view that they did not belong in a frontier town, that, as Estelline Bennett put it about Deadwood (ironically named in these circumstances!), "only youth could make itself a part" of such a town[42]—came out in the observations on cemeteries referred to earlier in this book. Many graveyards were initially planted in central parts of the town and later became an embarrassment because of the amount of valuable space that they occupied. Of course, as we have seen, even they were initially inhabited only by the young. There was no place for old folk even in the cemetery of a new town. Cemeteries were removed if they became an obstruction to progress. A booster publication, *Chicago in 1860,* reflected on what happened to them in Chicago. "We are emphatically a utilitarian people, and do not regard it as a virtue to prolong the existence of anything from motives of simple veneration. The dust of our forefathers even, we hold it not religious to preserve undisturbed, if by removal we can add to our many living conveniences or

better our condition."[43] Much was made of the unexpectedly rapid encroachment of a city on its original burial grounds. Life conquered and
replaced death. A Chicagoan asked about Graceland and other cemeteries: "How long will it be before the cemeteries mentioned . . . will have to
give way to the living, their necessities and improvements? Nothing will
be able to withstand the growth of this still young giant [Chicago]—not
even death."[44] On the other hand, if a town failed, its spirit seemed to
pass into and inhabit the only part of it which had grown, this "city of the
dead." Here is a Nebraska pioneer reflecting on the fate of Fontenelle,
which once aspired to be the state capital:

A short distance south of the village on a high bluff overlooking the river valley,
and covered with oaks and evergreens, these early pioneers started a city which
has grown for many years, and which will continue to grow for years to come. In
this city of the dead we find many of the people who did much for the little village
which failed, but who have taken up their abode in this beautiful spot, there to
remain until the end of time.[45]

Many townspeople would have found their attitudes to life and death
in their new towns well summed up in Jefferson's declaration that "the
dead have no rights. They are nothing, and nothing cannot own something. . . . Our Creator made the earth for the use of the living and not of
the dead. . . . One generation of men cannot foreclose or burden its use to
another."[46]

Fires, which were numerous and often devastating in the early history
of most frontier towns, were more often than not welcomed because they
destroyed the past and provided the opportunity for a fresh start. When
Augustus F. Harvey decided to write a history of the "early days" of
Nebraska City, he gave thought as to what date to fix on as the close of
that era in its development and chose May 12, 1860, "the date of the
Great Fire." "With a will of iron the people rallied and commenced life
anew. The calamity of the fire closed, however, the youthful days of the
city, and became the foundation of the strength of its manhood."[47] Attitudes to fire exemplify that desire for "periodic purification," for public
edifices that would "crumble to ruin" once every twenty years, that David
Lowenthal has found in the minds of many post-Revolutionary Americans.[48]

A frequent response to a fire was to adopt the phoenix image to
symbolize recovery and achievement of new life. Fires were, of course,
often very good for business because of the sums spent on rebuilding and

improvement of the town. The town of Oshkosh in Wisconsin suffered a series of very bad fires, one of which, in 1875, destroyed almost the entire business district and many private residences as well. One reporter wrote about this situation: "If there is anything that fills the hearts of true Oshkoshites with entire satisfaction, it is the fact that they have had a fire which cleaned out their principal streets, and that the same is now built up with substantial and beautiful lines of buildings, of uniform appearance, such as are not usually seen."[49] In similar vein Ben Casseday wrote in *The History of Louisville* (1852) that a great fire at that city "proved in the end rather a gain than a loss to the city in general, as the site of the fire was speedily rebuilt in a much better style than before."[50] The most celebrated use of the phoenix theme was, of course, in connection with Chicago's recovery after the great fire of 1871.[51] There was little publicized mourning over loss in fires, only rejoicing at the opportunities which they offered to become young and new all over again.

Sentiment was only about progress. One or two old buildings might be left, but only as symbols of the dead past to show how far the city had progressed since then. There was minimal interest in the "history" of a town in and for itself. Although it was usually quite recent, it somehow seemed unreal and impossibly remote. Henry Sienkiewicz wrote of Chicago:

There are no stones or marble ruins, no churches or museums to conjure up memories of a historic past. Everything is new and contemporary. Everywhere people look to "tomorrow." "Yesterday" to them means only deserts, primeval forests, and the vast silence of the prairies.[52]

If anything old did survive, then the sooner it was removed the better. In 1890 a booster publication praised what the Board of Trade had done for the advancement of Kansas City, Kansas. "It has done much . . . to encourage the dropping of old names and the obliteration of old landmarks."[53] When George E. Loyau published in 1880 *The Gawler Handbook,* which he subtitled *A Record of the Rise and Progress of that Important Town* (in South Australia), he took the reader for a stroll down Murray Street, apologized for occasionally encountering "a few dilapidated structures," and gave an assurance that these "merely stand as landmarks of the past" and would soon be swept away by "the daily marked progress of Modern Athens" (a booster nickname for Gawler) to be replaced by "new edifices worthy the town."[54]

Every new town soon acquired a past, but it seemed that nobody wanted to know about it. In 1876 Charles Gavan Duffy wrote that people did not yet clothe Melbourne's past

with poetry and romance. Young Australians are, indeed, apt to glance at the early history of their country with the eye of the scorner; to find pleasant subjects for banter and burlesque in the legend of the twin Founders, reared at the dugs of the same she-wolf of convictism, struggling over the site of the future metropolis. . . .[55]

In 1849 the editor of the *Western Journal,* M. Tarver, wrote an article on "St Louis—Its Early History." At its conclusion he announced his intention to make "a few observations in reference to the future" and admitted that this was "the department of history that the people of this country most delight in—the privations, the self-reliance and daring adventure of the pioneers no longer excite emotions of admiration; and even the glorious deeds of our revolutionary ancestors fade before the bright visions of future greatness which present themselves to the imagination of the Americans of the Anglo-Saxon race."[56]

There were some who began to give thought to the writing of a history of their city, but they had much difficulty in devising an appropriate philosophy of history to guide their work, and many such so-called "histories" ended up as thinly disguised booster publications. The spirit in which most nineteenth-century histories of new towns were written is probably best summed up in Logan U. Reavis' dictum: "The Past often interprets the Future, and is always interesting in connection with it."[57] When in 1885 the Butte Chamber of Commerce issued a booklet on *Resources of Butte,* it included a review of the city's history. "From the past," it explained, "we can sometimes tell of the future, and thus a retrospective view of the conditions existing in Butte fifteen years ago may be of interest." The extent of progress was then highlighted by descriptions of how primitive those conditions were and how hopeless seemed the town's prospects.[58] In his *History of Louisville* (1852) Ben Casseday discussed "the utility and profit of the local history of cities." It clearly could not be the traditional type of local history. It was impossible to "relate any of those local traditions that make many of the cities of the Old World so famous in story and song." But what it could do was to direct "the attention of those abroad to the rise, progress and present standing of places which may fairly claim, in the future, what has made others great in the past." In other words, "history" should be fundamentally future-oriented and serve boosting purposes.

It is a matter of more than ordinary interest and value to all, to note the practical advancement, and so to calculate upon the basis of the past, the probable results of the future of those cities in the New World, which seem to present advantages, either social or pecuniary, to that large class of foreigners and others, who are constantly seeking for homes or means of occupation among us. Nor is it to these alone, that such local history is of value. The country is beginning already to possess much unemployed capital seeking for investment; while many, having already procured the means of living well, are seeking for homes more congenial to their tastes than the places where they have lived but for pecuniary profit. In both of these, the history of individual cities is an invaluable aid in helping the one to discover a means of advantageously employing his surplus money, and in aiding the other to find a home possessing those social advantages which will render him comfortable and happy.[59]

There were some writers, such as Charles Cist at Cincinnati and William Westgarth in Victoria, Australia, who assiduously chronicled the progress of their cities and published numerous, statistic-laden reviews of their history. But their aims were very similar to Casseday's. For example, in 1864 Westgarth published a book about *The Colony of Victoria* which included "History" in its title. But he informed his readers that he would not write in detail about historical episodes except insofar as they "furnish pleasant or instructive comparison, as we go along, with the later condition and attainments of the colony."[60]

Many people, not surprisingly, attributed the future-oriented atmosphere of frontier towns to the prevalence of speculation in town lots and the general rage to make money. But some saw that there was more to it than that. J. S. Buckingham, in *The Eastern and Western States of America,* found in the St. Louis of the 1840s "an absence of the merely sordid spirit of amassing wealth as the only end and aim of existence—and an enthusiastic delight in anticipating the future, and drawing glowing pictures of what this country, and especially their own particular City, is to become." There was a spirit of "personal adventure" as well as a desire for financial gain.[61] The total faith in a great future for one's city had its psychological as well as its speculative, money-making aspects. One of the most important of these was seen as being its role in ensuring the survival of the townspeople in the grim conditions that so often characterized a frontier town's early years. Town builders and boosters saw encouragement of this preoccupation with a glorious future and a city's "inevitable destiny" as essential for a town's survival.

In *A Lecture on Cincinnati and her Rail-Roads,* given in Cincinnati in 1850, Alphonso Taft explained the psychology behind this. He argued that "the golden hopes of our people" formed "no inconsiderable part of their happiness." "They dwell more on the great hereafter, than on the past, and present, both. They rejoice in anticipated triumphs, to be won by them, and their children." It was vital that people be distracted from the present. "If the present were *all* of Cincinnati, she would be dull and insipid, to the taste of her citizens."[62] The muddy—or dusty—streets, the minimal state of public services, and many other aspects of the early urban environment on the frontier did not make for comfortable living. After the travels recorded in *Minnesota and the Far West* (1855), Lawrence Oliphant concluded that "it would require a good deal of faith in the future prosperity of an embryo town in the Far West, to induce one to live in it through the first stages of its existence."[63]

The intense focusing on "the future" seems to have been a product both of manipulative strategies by town boosters and builders and of the need and desire felt by many townspeople for this form of relief from the miseries and confusion of the present. The basis for the manipulation of their perceptions of their urban situation was there already, of course, in the hopes and expectations which many had when they emigrated to this New World. When John Gates Thurston visited Alton, Illinois, in 1836, he judged it "the rudest and most uninteresting spot that I ever saw." But he found that the people there did not have the same perception of it. They were "determined that nothing shall prevent them from having a flourishing and business like place."[64]

Townspeople seemed not to notice the present and to be so preoccupied with "the future" that they were prepared to put up with all sorts of present inconveniences. The *Chicago Tribune* correspondent found, when he visited Duluth in 1882, that "the town of the present is anything but a cheerful place," but that the inhabitants were sustained by an extravagant faith in the town's future.[65] It seemed as if the most desirable state of affairs was the total obliteration of the present from people's perceptions. Sometimes this could be achieved, quite literally, through the onset of darkness. When Charles H. Allen visited Rockhampton on *A Visit to Queensland and Her Goldfields* (1870), he noticed how sparsely settled were the squares or "blocks" of the embryonic city. "Little by little, however, these are filling up; and when, at night, the bright kerosene lamps are lit, the town has an appearance of great size; for the eye, wandering from lamp to lamp, is unable in the darkness to see whether the intervening spaces are filled in with houses or not."[66] The image of the traveler needing to be a "blind man" to "see" the infant towns in terms of the grand classical names which they were given occurs in Henry Tudor's *Narrative of a Tour in North America* (1834).[67] The intensity of the preoccupation with the future played strange tricks with people's perceptions of the present. Caroline Matilda Kirkland recorded her impressions on arriving at the site of a new town in Michigan in the company of a guide who had "showed in the course of the day six different points, each of which, the owners were fully satisfied, would one day echo the busy tread of thousands, and see reflected in the now glossy wave the towers and masts of a great commercial town":

The dead silence, the utter loneliness, the impenetrable shade, which covered the site of the future city, might well call to mind the desolation which has settled on Tadmor and Palmyra; the anticipation of future life and splendor contrasting no less forcibly with the actual scene than would the retrospect of departed grandeur.[68]

A complex story of the overlaying of different types of perception of a new town is told in the autobiography of John A. Nash, who was assigned to Des Moines, Iowa, in 1850 by the American Baptist Home Mission Society. To prepare him for his assignment the secretary of the society sent Nash a report of a visit to Des Moines written by the society's exploring agent. This referred to the city in "the most glowing language," to its population of 1,500, whereas it was only 500, and to "the din of rolling machinery," which in reality consisted only of "two old saw-mills, which probably by no amount of urging could each count up a month of work during a year, and one grist mill, which semi-occasionally could be made to run long enough to grind a few bushels of corn." Here was a case of actual blindness obscuring present reality and leaving the "viewer" wide open to the insertion into his "vision" of future fantasies. "The agent was very imperfect of sight, and his report was less based on what he *saw* than what he *heard,* which were emphatically *Western yarns, spun to snare gulls.*" Nash saw the town all too clearly: its dead appearance, its scattered houses and many vacant lots. But he soon fell into a "future" frame of mind which blotted all this out.

I did not particularly care how small and new the town then was, but what were its prospects and possibilities. And in our entire trip from Davenport to Des Moines, there seemed among the people but one conviction, and that was that Des Moines had a great future before it. If this should prove true, I was not here a month too early, not a day too soon.[69]

One might define three stages in the evolution of the perception of a frontier town. The first was when one could see only the dirt and squalor and miserable, scattered shanties of the present. It was at this point that most people felt depressed and disgusted. The second was when, as well as seeing that reality, one heard the local people express their visions of the future. Much depended on whether one could move on from this stage to the third where only the future was "seen." Many visitors became stuck at the second stage. Hence a predominant literary reaction to frontier towns, especially the boosted variety of the American West, was ridicule and satire. The most famous example of this is Charles Dickens' *Martin Chuzzlewit*, with its satirical contrast between Eden on paper and the real Eden on the muddy, mosquito-infested banks of the Mississippi. There is a similar satire on the city of Babylon in fantasy and fact in Albert D. Richardson's *Beyond the Mississippi* (1867). Or there is Lawrence Oliphant's first sight of Superior, as recorded in *Minnesota and the Far West* (1855): "that celebrated city now burst upon us in all its magnificence, and one lofty barn-like shed, surrounded by an acre of stumps, represented the future emporium of the resources of the fertile and prolific country of which it is destined to be the metropolis."[70] If one "saw" only the present, the "future" of the townspeople's dreams could seem quite ludicrous. Francis Jameson Rowbotham, in *A Trip to Prairie-Land* (1885), laughed when he found "Ninth Avenue West" a long way out of the tiny Dakota prairie town of Jamestown.[71] Part of Mrs. Trollope's offence in presenting Cincinnati in *Domestic Manners of the Americans* (1832) was that, having heard all the boasting about its "future greatness" before she went there, she could see only the present reality and found the contrast ludicrous rather than finding what had actually been achieved impressive. Her head was stuffed full of clichés—"this 'wonder of the west,' this 'prophet's gourd of magic growth,'—this 'infant Hercules.' " She then complained of "the flatness of reality after the imagination has been busy." She had not expected that that reality would be merely "a little town, about the size of Salisbury, without even an attempt at beauty in any of its edifices, and with only just enough of the air of a city to make it noisy and bustling."[72]

However, if a visitor "saw" or could be persuaded to "see" the future and to take it seriously, then it could all start to make sense. Some visitors began by finding boasts of "future greatness" ludicrous and then discovering behind them a psychological truth which was an important aspect of the inner life of the town. "When a settler at Odin [in southern Illinois] boasted to me of the future greatness of the city," wrote Edward Dicey in *Six Months in the Federal States* (1836), "the boast struck me at first as ridiculous, but I reflected afterwards that it was this pride and this belief in future greatness which had settled and civilized the New World whereon I trod."[73]

Seeing the future rather than the present was not just left to chance. Town promoters and speculators liked to christen their infants with grandiose names that both reflected their ambitions and directed attention to the future. But most important of all in forming perceptions were the plans—usually vast grids—that were usually given to new towns. In many ways these plans manipulated perceptions because, being future-oriented and making little sense in the present, they forced people to "see" and indeed to live in the future. That plats should be far larger than was necessary for the town in the early stages of its development was a commonplace of frontier town planning. In his basic plan for a new town in a "newly discovered country," T. J. Maslen envisaged planning streets on the assumption that what began as a village would grow into a city.[74] "In planning the city," wrote John Galt, founder of Guelph, Ontario, in his *Autobiography* (1834), "I had, like the lawyers in establishing their fees, an eye to futurity in the magnitude of the parts."[75] Plats were essentially maps of the future.[76] Bird's-eye views used the plans for this purpose, to create a vision of the future in which all the space designed for expansion is clearly delineated and progress toward filling it in could be followed through the publication of revised bird's-eye views at regular intervals.

The use of space often seemed wrong or extravagant in the present. People saw the present reality, noticed how odd it was or what inconveniences it created, asked why this state of affairs existed and was tolerated, and so were gradually manipulated into thinking about the town as it would be when the arrangements of the plan finally did make sense.

In *The Englishman in Kansas* (1857) T. H. Gladstone wrote that to make sense of Leavenworth one had to carry a plan of the city "in mental vision."[77] In his Indiana "diary" of 1840, John Parsons expressed the view that Indianapolis had "a ridiculously large plat . . . even to so thriving a population." But he was answered by prophecies from local people that the city "will eventually fill the entire space included in these encircling streets.[78] Emily Pfeiffer wrote of Denver in *Flying Leaves from East and West* (1885):

> It is curious to note how its future vast proportions seem to exist already in the minds of its projectors. Instead of its new streets and buildings being huddled together as with us in our urban beginnings, they are placed here and there at suitable points, with a confidence that the connecting links will soon be established.[79]

The wide streets that were usually part of the grid plan were read as indicative of ambition and expectation of a great future. Frank Bullen in *Advance Australasia* (1907) noted how spacious Palmerston North in New Zealand was. This, he wrote, "fills one with the idea that it must some day be a great city." He added, however, that "the railway running along through the main street for its whole length bordered by grassy breadths upon which may be seen feeding the casual horse or cow, does not inspire much hope that it ever will be."[80] George Augustus Sala found that "every town in the West is laid out on a plan as vast as though it were destined, at no distant date, to contain a million of inhabitants."[81] The result was a lavish use of space that appeared to many to be absurd and inconvenient. William Archer, visiting Australia in the mid-1870s, wrote that Australian towns all looked "flattened down." "At home twenty or thirty thousand people would be accommodated comfortably in the same space which here supports seven thousand."[82] The resulting large spaces between buildings were seen as having much "future" significance. Alexander Begg in his *Practical Hand-Book and Guide to Manitoba and the North-West* (1877) drew attention to the way in which buildings at Emerson were not "huddled together as observable in some new western towns, but placed as if inviting the erection of other and more imposing buildings in their midst."[83]

Few plans aroused more controversy and provoked more criticism than that which Colonel Light gave to Adelaide. Light was severely criticized on account of the six miles that separated the site from the coast and the harbor. Migrants and carters toiling along the road had ample time and occasion to curse the man who had inflicted this ordeal on them. But there were reasons. Light saw the site as ideal for a city that would start large and would be expected to expand. B. T. Finniss, his assistant, explained that "as wealth and population increased Adelaide would soon approach nearer the harbour than six miles. Those miles would then become a vast suburb studded with shops and warehouses."[84]

But settlers were bewildered by Adelaide's size. Few could develop a "mental vision" of future "connecting links." Mary Ann Beasley wrote in her diary in 1839:

Adelaide is a very large straggling place so that it is impossible to see all over it at any time. In many places the houses stand at 50 yards one from the other, and in some places as many as 100 yards. It would puzzle a newcomer to understand how all these straggling houses could possibly come together at a future period so as to form a regular street.[85]

E. Lloyd wrote in *A Visit to the Antipodes* (1846) that his first impression of Adelaide was of "the perfection of desolation and wretchedness." Then he remembered "the magnificent and extensive city upon paper, which figured in England as the representation of this colonial capital," and his response to what he saw before him changed:

I was impressed with the Liliputian grandeur of the whole affair, that seemed to say in the spirit of its projectors, "Were my means only as gigantic as my desires." It seemed like something mighty begun and left unfinished, a promising young sapling nipped in the bud, an intention without a realization, a beginning without an end, and the end of a beginning. It is a town large enough for the metropolis of a great nation, with about three good streets properly built upon. It is so large as to be quite unwieldy; so large as, with its present population, to preclude public improvement, and to render any co-operation for the purpose impracticable.[86]

T. Horton James found the plan an odd creation by people who professed to believe in the principle of "concentration." He relates stories —very common in the reminiscences of life on the urban frontier—of people getting lost, especially at night, in the midst of what was supposed to be a city.[87] The problem was that, if there was not progress fairly soon toward Dutton's future noble city, the whole thing could start to look very wrong. When Robert Harrison, author of *Colonial Sketches* (1862), reported on Adelaide after twenty-four years, he could only refer to "a scattered population of some eighteen thousand" "dispersed over a space that could contain the inhabitants of any large European city." Only three streets were used for commerce, and the back streets were in a melancholy state.[88] The vast plan could inspire thoughts that moved from "future" to present instead of the other way around. In *What We Saw in Australia* (1875) Rosamond and Florence Hill recalled having "the impression, afterwards renewed whenever we drove into Adelaide, that we were approaching an important city which we never reached.[89]

In such cities it often seemed as if the present was being sacrificed for the future. George Augustus Sala noticed that in "at least fifty promising American cities that I have seen within the last four months" the roadway was "three times too broad." "Its excessive breadth renders the task of paving it one of extreme difficulty; and in the majority of cases the municipal authorities tide over the difficulty by not paving the roadway at all." The "monstrous breadth of the streets" also, in his opinion, gave a town" an aspect of unsightliness and untidiness. In summer time the road is a dusty desert; in the rainy season it is a Slough of Despond."[90] Indeed, as early as 1838 T. Horton James was predicting problems when the municipal authorities had to light and pave, cleanse and provide sewers for, the extravagantly large streets of Adelaide's vast plan.[91] Nearly thirty years later Anthony Forster in *South Australia* (1866) confirmed the accuracy of this prediction. "The great space which the site of Adelaide covers necessarily gives it a somewhat straggling and vacant appearance, and it has the effect of limiting those municipal improvements which can with greater facility be brought to bear upon a more compact and restricted area."[92] It seemed to some that the extreme emphasis on "the future" did much harm to a town's development. For instance, settlement within a town often became prematurely dispersed because owners of centrally located lots believed the prophecies of future greatness for the town and asked "future great" prices for them. T. H. Gladstone observed that "the high price which is put by anticipation upon the land is a sufficient reason why, in Leavenworth, as elsewhere, the settlers have preferred to get cheaper sites by spreading to a distance from the centre of business."[93] In 1848 the English publication, *Sidney's Emigrant's Journal,* referring specifically to Otago in New Zealand but more generally also to New World towns, attacked the deconcentrating effects of vast plans. They gave an artificial value to too much land, tempting people to speculate in it rather than to cultivate and improve it.[94]

One of the New World's most notoriously straggling towns was Toronto. Governor Simcoe had hoped to "condense" the population through setting aside land as Crown reserve, but this did not prove effective.[95] In his *Travels in Canada* (1861) J. G. Kohl tried to analyze why Toronto was so spread out. It was "built on a much larger scale than is required for a city of 50,000 persons." The result was an extraordinary sacrifice of present convenience and urban sociability. Indeed it subverted the basic idea of a town as a community, preventing it from working as such. One often had to drive miles to pay a visit.

The inhabitants are scattered over a vast space, and their dwellings are often separated by great town deserts; and since this is excessively inconvenient and of course often expensive, and since the very idea of a town involves that of the proximity of the inhabitants, and of the members of the community being mutually within reach, one cannot see why these American towns should not be allowed to grow naturally, the second house being built near to the first, the third to the second, and so on, instead of running off into endless streets that will not be paved perhaps for fifty years, and where the school is to be found in the far west and the schoolmaster in the remote east, and you have to go a mile to your shoemaker's, and two miles to your tailor's, and it takes an hour's drive or run to get to a little *soirée*.

There had to be an explanation for so universal a phenomenon. It appeared to stem from the way in which every town was founded "with the idea that it is certain to grow rapidly." Open spaces were left for public buildings, streets were made very broad, and owners of land near the center asked such high prices for it that schools and other institutions needing considerable space and the poor needing cheap land sought locations some distance out of town.[96]

Finally, to complicate still further this analysis of the perception of urban development along a temporal continuum of past, present, and future, one has to consider the case of those towns which were oriented toward "the future" but for whom that "future" never arrived and so in effect became their past. Observers found that they were a melancholy spectacle and a uniquely New World phenomenon. They were the exceptions to the rule. Frederick Law Olmsted tells in *A Journey Through Texas* (1857) how depressing he found the towns along the Ohio River.

Each had its hopes, not yet quite abandoned, of becoming the great mart of the valley, and has built in accordant style its one or two tall brick city blocks, standing shabby-sided alone on the mud-slope to the bank, supported by a tavern, an old storehouse, and a few shanties. These mushroom cities mark only a night's camping-place of civilization.[97]

In the early 1870s Tauranga on the east coast of the North Island of New Zealand was reported by some of its residents to be destined to become the "hub of the Antipodes." Twenty-five years later a visitor who found it "the embodiment of decay" commented: "That Tauranga was originally planned to fill an important part in the fortunes of the colony may be noted from the proportions of its broad, boulevard-like streets."[98] In *Our Antipodes* (1846) Godfrey Charles Mundy tells of a visit to Port Macquarie whose economy had collapsed following the closure of the convict settlement there. Now there was

Something about the place which denotes decay rather than growth. It looks like a little man dressed in the clothes of a large one. The streets are very wide, and cut out to be very long, like a certain street of Toronto, in Canada, whose name I forget [Yonge Street], and which maintains its title for upwards of twenty miles into the unpeopled bush,—but the houses are so few and far between that, in the oppidan sense of the word, there can be no such thing as a next door neighbour among the citizens.[99]

The citizens of such places sometimes gave the impression of being stuck in "the future," unable or unwilling to contemplate the present. Gustaf Unonius went to dinner at the luxurious home of one of the families of Green Bay, Wisconsin, a failed "future" town. "The host was the owner of a great tract of unsold city lots; he still harbored sanguine hopes for the future greatness of the city, and rated his vacant land at a value that made him worth well over a million."[100]

CHAPTER EIGHT

The Town in the Garden

O NE of the most dramatic features of the town on the frontier was its setting, the contrast between it as a would-be outpost of civilization and its primitive wilderness surroundings. Many towns were created by the clearing of the site, the removal of trees. But the stumps often remained in the ground for some time to come, impeding movement in the streets. Meanwhile, the forest or other manifestations of wilderness continued to surround the infant towns, evoking a variety of responses in witnesses and considerable use of the situation as a simile or metaphor to describe the advance of civilization. The contrast between "civilization" and "wilderness" was often very striking. A traveler on the Mississippi in 1849 saw Davenport and Rock Island, "two towns opposite each other—two bright eyes looking out from the wilderness."[1] To some commentators this was a special point in the history of the frontier, soon to pass.

The most striking characteristic of the environs of St. Paul ... is the utter wildness of the surrounding country. In whatever direction you ascend the hills which encircle the town, with the exception of the busy, gay-looking city, all is gloomy forest or solitary prairie; and there can be no stronger testimony to the rapid growth of the place, than the fact that the country in the immediate vicinity is still in a state of savage nature. No doubt a few years will work a marvellous change here too; but the most interesting element of the scenery will be destroyed when this wonderful combination of civilization and barbarism has disappeared.[2]

In Australia there seemed to be two very distinct ways of life, that of the "bush" and that of the "town." Overlap between them was minimal. In the phrase "the city and the bush" was to be encapsulated a widespread perception of the basic division in Australian development. The heroine of the novel *Life's Work As It Is* (1867) by "A Colonist" found that "bush life and Adelaide life lay as widely different as London and some little village in the South Seas!" In England" the broad word Australia encompasses everything in a heap—blacks, whites; civilization, unciviliza-

184

tion; log huts, and splendid stone edifices; bullock waggons, and the equipages of the rich and great."[3]

The contrasts made a particularly strong impression on travelers and migrants who often describe coming into a town after a long journey passing through forests and wilderness. They come suddenly upon all the luxuries and comforts of Old World civilization—something that is very welcome and also very unexpected. In *Six Months in the Federal States* (1863) Edward Dicey describes his arrival at Cincinnati. "It is strange, after travelling for hundreds of miles through the half-settled country, to come in the Far West upon a great city, filled with every luxury and comfort of old-world civilization."[4] A Hungarian visitor of 1831 wrote: "Traveling in the American inner states is similar to those fairy tales where through some magic force you tumble in the midst of deserted forests on bright cities, or else you wander in the region of great waters and find hotels similar to splendid castles."[5]

Alexis de Tocqueville during his "fifteen days in the wilderness" had a very similar experience and used it, characteristically, to start a train of thought about American society in general.

> From time to time . . . the aspect of the country suddenly changes. On turning a wood one sights the elegant spire of a steeple, some houses shining white and neat, some shops. Two paces further on, the forest, primitive and apparently impenetrable, resumes its sway and once more reflects its foliage in the waters of the lake.
>
> Those who have travelled through the United States will find in this tableau a striking emblem of American society. Everything is in violent contrast, unforeseen. Everywhere extreme civilization and nature abandoned to herself find themselves together and as it were face to face. This is not imagined in France. . . .
>
> Without transition you pass from a wilderness into the streets of a city, from the wildest scenes to the most smiling pictures of civilized life. If, night coming on you unawares, you are not forced to take shelter at the foot of a tree, you have every prospect of arriving in a village where you will find everything, even to French fashions, the almanac of modes, and the caricatures of the boulevards. The merchant of Buffalo and of Detroit is as well stocked with them as he of New-York.

In reflecting on why this is so de Tocqueville arrived at conclusions which were precisely the opposite of those reached by Frederick Jackson Turner nearly seventy years later. "Those who inhabit these isolated places have arrived there since yesterday; they have come with the customs, the ideas, the needs of civilization."[6]

In *Eight Months in Illinois* (1843) William Oliver has a similar account of the experience of a traveler from "the old country."

He may have toiled all day, through the tracts of the primeval forest, without seeing a live thing, except, perhaps, a deer or a squirrel, and come upon a town, stuck down among the woods, with the undecayed stumps in its streets, and there, where he might suppose it hopeless to expect anything beyond the bare necessities of life, he will find stores containing many of the luxuries of cities long settled in civilization. I saw at Pittsburg a large wareroom full of upholstery and cabinet work, consisting of elegant mahogany tables and chairs, sofas, chests of drawers, bureaus, work-tables, pianofortes, etc. At every step one encounters the anomaly of semi-barbarism joined with civilized existence.[7]

The image of towns as points of light amid darkness was used by George Henry in his *Emigrant's Guide* when he wrote about the Canadian situation: 'A person traveling through the bush, feels much about the same sensation as he would, were he to be traveling through any part of the United Kingdom, with a bandage over his eyes, and only having it released upon his coming to any town or village.'[8]

Some observers found the contrast attractive and saw a harmonious relationship between the elements in it. In an article in *The Overland Monthly* (April 1872) Joaquin Miller painted most agreeable word pictures of Portland, Oregon, in its forest setting. "Here," he wrote, "is a sort of blended savage and civilized life, that is encountered nowhere else."[9] But far more writers found the juxtapositions disturbing, jarring, the reverse of picturesque. To some they were even absurd. No one loved to compose and describe a "romantic," "picturesque" picture of a frontier town within its natural setting more than Edmund Flagg, author of *The Far West* (1838). But his sense of the picturesque was severely offended by some of the sights that he saw. For instance, he thus describes his arrival at Vandalia when that town was the capital of Illinois:

Its unusually large and isolated buildings, few in number as they are, stationed here and there upon the eminences of the broken surface, give the place a singularly novel aspect viewed from the adjacent heights. . . . Such huge structures as are here beheld, in a town so inconsiderable in extent, present an unnatural and forced aspect to one who has just emerged from the wild waste of the neighbouring prairies, sprinkled with their humble tenements of logs. The scene is not in keeping; it is not picturesque. Such, at all events, were my "first impressions" on entering the village.[10]

Few towns aroused more adverse comment of this kind than Alton, Illinois. This was on account of the huge state penitentiary that was erected there in a very conspicuous position. Flagg himself refers to the domination of Alton by its "gloomy, castellated walls."[11] Another who was repelled by the discordance between towns and their river setting was Frederick Law Olmsted who, in *A Journey Through Texas* (1857), described the towns along the Ohio as, almost without exception, "repulsively ugly and out of keeping with the tone of mind inspired by the river."[12]

Observers came to appreciate that, in order to understand the existence of a town in the wilderness, it was often necessary to abandon conventional ideas of "picturesqueness." Wilderness and towns could also be organically connected. C. R. Carter in *Victoria, The British "El Dorado"* (1870) found Sandhurst "a smart, compact town" surrounded by desolation. But it was mining country, the mining had caused that desolation, and it was therefore "to the surrounding desolation that this town owes its existence, otherwise it would have been merely a village. The picturesque and the useful seldom go hand in hand; utility and beauty are rarely combined."[13]

In the early years of a town's development there could be some strange and unexpected connections between wilderness and town. Gustaf Unonius later recalled the excursions that he made with his gun in Milwaukee in the 1840s. "To be armed with guns to take an excursion within a city sounds perhaps a little strange, but we must remember that Milwaukee, like most American cities, had been laid out on a rather large scale and that most of it was still nothing but an uninhabited wilderness."[14] Or there could be an absence of connection where you would have most expected to find it. When J. G. Kohl, authors of *Travels in Canada* (1861), visited Toronto, he found it extraordinary and ironic that wood was scarce and expensive "though immediately behind the town begins the endless forest of the North." There was an explanation: "the high wages of labor. Wood is in boundless abundance indeed, but not so axes, saws, and hands."[15]

Strange too, and sometimes grotesque, were the ways in which the towns tried to differentiate themselves from the wilderness. John Dunmore Lang, like many travelers, found ridiculous the grand names given to insignificant villages on the frontier. Although such names were often intended to make the visitor or resident dream of future greatness, Lang thought that "the place actually looks much worse than it really is, simply from its unfortunate name."[16] A French visitor to America in the late nineteenth century, Paul de Rousiers, was struck by the use made of the new electric light by the boomers of prairie towns.

> They often begin with the electric-light, because that most vividly impresses the visitor. At Guthrie I saw the sparkling globes throw their brilliant light on plank barracks, built a year before; while sometimes in a quiet street they illuminated the prairie flowers still growing in the natural turf. Such contrasts please the Westerner, by telling how rapidly transformations are taking place in regions till now untouched. His principal effort is to give an air of prosperity to the town, rather than to benefit any of its inhabitants who may happen to be out at night, as is easily seen at Guthrie. The town is built on the side of a little hill, and is crossed by a series of sloping streets. A huge wooden scaffold, narrow and high, is built on the very top of the hill, at the end of the most important street, and bears four or five electric lamps which are carefully lit every evening. There is no need for them whatever, but the settler, far away in his homestead, sees the brilliant point across the immensity of the prairie, and becomes confident of the future of Oklahoma.[17]

To some, indeed, the presence of the towns in the wilderness where they clearly did not "belong" seemed almost like play-acting.[18] The towns were "unreal," an observation reinforced by the discovery of the "shamness" of the buildings, the false fronts and fine facades that concealed primitive squalor. Travelers became well aware of this. Almon Gunnison in *Rambles Overland* (1884) visited Helena, Montana, and stayed in a hotel which was "pretentious in outward appearance, but having behind this, where the lodgings are, the rudeness of the pioneer days." Of Helena generally Gunnison wrote that, "while the business streets have showy solidity, one has but to go to the rear to see that behind these ambitious fronts there is a conglomeration of shacks and shanties, the architecture being, as some one has said, 'Queen Anne in front and Crazy Jane behind.'"[19] In *The Newer Northwest* (1894) John M. White describes the red sandstone buildings of Hot Springs, South Dakota, which then— as now—impress and also surprise the visitor. There are the blocks of business houses with their fine facades, "as if always dressed for visitors,'" while the courthouse tries to "look sedate."[20]

There were remarkable juxtapositions of civilization and primitive nature, as in the shops filled with luxuries and standing along streets in which still remained the stumps of trees.[21] The same contrasts thrust themselves upon the observer's attention in the area of life-styles. "Luxury and rudeness jostle each other," wrote Gunnison of Helena; "frontier barbarisms mingle with the latest fashions from 'the States.'"[22] Anna

Brownell Jameson, in *Winter Studies and Summer Rambles in Canada* (1838), described the social situation in Toronto as absurd and "false": "With the interminable forests within half a mile of us—the haunt of the red man, the wolf, the bear—with an absolute want of the means of the most ordinary mental and moral development, we have here conventionalism in its most oppressive and ridiculous forms."[23]

Yet these remarks were but snapshots of a very rapidly changing situation. The reality was usually one of constant encroachment of "civilization" on the "wilderness." An anecdote told by G. H. Haydon in *Five Years Experience in Australia Felix* (1846) is typical of what was seen and recounted when the snapshot became a moving picture.

Having been absent in the bush for eight months, I wished to pay some friends at Brighton a visit, and was taking the shortest way across the country without any guide, except the stars, and when about as I imagined, three miles from the town, and expecting nothing but a wilderness, I suddenly came on several well-built brick houses, and I was surprised to find myself in the midst of substantial villa residences.[24]

Increasingly between "nature" and "civilization" lay a depressing transition zone. E. Lloyd in *A Visit to the Antipodes* (1846) wrote of approaching Adelaide from its port. "With just sufficient amount of civilization to spoil the verdure of the country, but not enough to form an apology for the invasion on the beauty of nature, the view here is most dismal and disheartening."[25]

Early travel writers and artists of the frontier liked to depict the young towns in "romantic" and "picturesque" settings. It was very common for towns to be judged according to their ability to provide "a pleasing effect." Indeed, their ability to do this seemed to be regarded as an indicator of a moral harmony and beauty within. Here is a word picture of Galena in 1843. It can be paralleled by many depictions of towns by artists.

Galena is the most picturesque romantic place I ever beheld, it is situated on fever river, between or on two hills, the buildings which are generally good, are scattered here & there without any regard to order, rising so romantically and playfully, here on a precipice a beautiful dwelling with scarcely room for a rosebush before it, there a neat little cottage with a fine flowergarden in front, on one side the houses appear to touch the sky, on the other the city and river are far below our feet, and when I take into the view the scenery on the opposite side of the river I scarcely convince myself that I am not looking at some romantic picture.[26]

A yearning to "see" the "picturesque" led some to compose these scenes in styles very different from others who described them more "realistically."[27]

There was also a craving on the part of many to discover "villages" in the landscapes of the New World, even although it was obvious that economics and social structure and the emphasis on individualism usually did not permit the formation and maintenance of communities that were in any meaningful way comparable to the "villages" of the Old World.[28] This did not stop numerous observers from strenuous and often strained efforts to detect villages in the landscape. It was admitted that one purpose in doing this was to satisfy "perceptions of picturesque beauty." Migrants were enticed from the Old World with descriptions of New World settlements which bestowed upon them the idyllic features of the idealized "village."[29] The "return to Arcady" was a prominent theme in Australian emigration literature.[30]

Nothing satisfied the devotees of the village ideal more than the appearance of the spires of churches in a rural landscape. Innumerable travelers admired the scenery along the St. Lawrence River between Montreal and Quebec City for this reason. "Both sides [of the river] from Quebec to Montreal," wrote Francis Fairplay in *The Canadas as They Now Are* (1833), "are enlivened by villages, whose churches are never long absent from the view, and, by the glittering of their bright tin-covered spires, constitute a singular and pleasing feature in the landscape."[31] It was a feature less frequently come across in the landscapes of Anglo-Saxon settlement. Very different was the Brisbane River in Australia when John Dunmore Lang sailed up it and "could not help thinking how much the fine scenery around would be improved, if a smiling village with its tall spire pointing to heaven were ever and anon appearing among the trees, with rows of white cottages embowered in semi-tropical foliage, and groups of happy children playing on the river banks."[32] In *Canada in 1864* (1864) Henry T. Newton Chesshyre, admitting that an English migrant "will yearn for the sight of that far-away spire among the trees in the old country village," finds a novel way of devising a replacement for that missing feature in the New World landscape. One day his log cabin will probably become the center of a thriving town or even city and "temples will be reared," but in the meantime "he will be encompassed by the grand old temple of God's own making, the pathless, illimitable woods, such woods as in the eastern hemisphere suggested to his Teutonic ancestors the idea of their Gothic piles, and invested their architecture with its distinctive character of vast and noble simplicity."[33]

But the New World consistently disappointed those who hoped or promised that it would give rise to Old World style villages.[34] Town and country failed either socially or aesthetically to blend or overlap in this way. When Alexis de Tocqueville visited Pontiac in Michigan, he recalled

what Mr. Gallatin had said in New York a month before: "There are no villages in America, at least in the sense you give this word." Here the houses of the farmers are all scattered through their fields. One assembles in a place only to establish a market for the use of the surrounding population. You see in these so-called villages only men of law, printers, and merchants.[35]

The church spires were frustratingly slow in appearing. James Fenimore Cooper, comparing American and European scenery, complained that, whereas in European towns the church occupied a central place, in America "half a dozen ill-shaped, and yet pretending cupolas, and other ambitious objects, half the time in painted wood, just peer above the village, while the most aspiring roof is almost invariably that of the tavern."[36] When New England-style villages did appear in the Midwest, there seemed to be something unreal and artificial about them. To J. P. Thompson Jacksonville, Illinois, looked just too neat, too exactly like the village ideal, "like a model New England village made to order, with such improvements as old villages that have grown up gradually do not admit of, and transported hither by some magic machinery and set down in the midst of the prairie, for picturesque effect, or as a wholesale speculation in city lots."[37]

What some hoped could be achieved and sustained was what has been called a "middle landscape," with towns belonging harmoniously within "the garden."[38] This was Fenimore Cooper's ideal landscape, complete with church spires. In *A Tour From the City of New-York, to Detroit* (1810) William Darby defined the ideal as a place where "enough remains of rude nature to recal[l] the mind to the ages of primitive simplicity, whilst enough is created by art to gratify the wants of civilized man."[39] James L. Machor has shown the emphasis that was placed in descriptions of midwestern urbanization on a harmonious, balanced, integrated relationship of town and country. Descriptions highlighted the beautiful natural surroundings of western cities, suggesting that the latter grew out of, were an organic product of, "nature." This myth of an urban-pastoral West was exploited by boosters who sought to project an image

191

of their towns as having a "destiny" that was determined by "nature" and not dependent on "artificial" factors such as speculation in urban real estate.[40]

As cities grew in size, and as they industrialized, it was less and less easy to see them as belonging to this "middle landscape." There were two principal ways in which the realization of at least a substitute for the ideal was pursued. One was the creation of city parks and gardens. These often enabled artists once again to discover angles from which a city could be depicted in an unexpected pastoral setting—New York from Central Park, and so on. In *Australia: Historical, Descriptive, and Statistic* (1845) Richard Howitt described how delightful Melbourne was in its early years, standing "open on every side: your ingress and egress unobstructed by any kind of fences." "All the country so smooth, tree-studded, and park-like: with a deal of its old primaeval freedom and gracefulness about it." He expressed the hope that, as this disappeared, ample provision would be made for parks and squares.[41] Second, both the Arcadian ideal and the "middle landscape" began to find a home in the residential suburbs and especially in the literature of real estate agents and promoters of suburban subdivisions.[42]

But, even when the village did seem to emerge in this kind of New World setting, one had to be careful not to allow one's perception of it to be distorted by Arcadian fantasies. When Caroline Chisholm, the famous advocate of immigration to Australia, saw working-people's cottages in Melbourne, she was delighted. "Cottages in hundreds at every turn forced themselves on my sight . . . all was so clean, brilliant and gay; gardens with towering hedges of roses and geraniums—cottages with their walls and roofs buried in splendid creepers, intermingled with vines, roses, passion-flowers, ivy and sweet-briar." Her joy was doubled when she learned that the cottages were owned freehold. And then she noticed something odd. There were no men about. The cottages were almost all occupied only by women. Their husbands were away at the diggings. What had happened was that the building societies had persuaded them to invest their small accumulations of capital in these properties. When the gold rush was over, what would support the financing of the loans? She began to think again about what had first seemed to her a simple, Arcadian beauty. "If I had seen a little Birmingham smoke, I should have had some relief to my thoughts, but there seemed a treacherous beauty that I must watch and unravel before . . . writing home." Here were lonely women, broken families. Here were cottages "but no children, no chickens."[43]

The "middle landscape" ideal implied balance between "town" and "country." But in a new country the balance was much more likely to be perceived as one between "civilization" and "wilderness." The image of "wilderness" aroused many fears and undermined the premises on which the "middle landscape" ideal was based. Many town dwellers saw themselves as confronting not "nature" as a benevolent force but "wilderness" as a threat which must be overcome and suppressed. In his vivid description of "By Town," Ontario (soon to become Ottawa and Canada's capital), J. G. Kohl probably captures well the way in which people who lived in towns newly hacked out of the forest saw their situation:

> The old rough boulders and masses of rock are lying about still among the groups of houses, and firs and other forest trees are springing up again out of the stumps. Here and there amongst elegant colleges and churches are to be seen fragments of the primeval forest, lofty pines and firs, and thick underwood that occasionally may give shelter to a bear. . . . As yet the unbroken mass of the primeval forest fences in the town on all sides, up to its very streets, and if you get a view of it from a high point you see for miles and miles nothing but a sea of woods, in which the town lies like the nest of a heathcock.[44]

"Nature" is a strong, resilient foe, as is seen in the new growth already sprouting from the stumps of felled trees. John Robert Godley in *Letters From America* (1844) has a similar description of Bytown and claims that there were points in the middle of the town "where you would almost lose sight of buildings altogether, and might fancy yourself in the primeval forest."[45] Stories of getting lost within or on the fringes of frontier towns appear frequently in pioneers' recollections.[46] "Nature" was often seen as pressing in on a young town and threatening to overwhelm it unless great effort is exerted to make sure that it does not. In his travels through forest regions in Canada, Australia, and the American West, Anthony Trollope came across two types of town. In one the pioneers have clearly "got the better of the forest." But there are other towns "in which it is too clearly evident that man's endeavour in regard to that enterprise is destined to failure. The wildness of the woods is too strong for the amount of energy which the limited advantages of the place can produce."[47] In Echuca in northern Victoria David Kennedy noted how each end of its main street terminated in "rough wild bush—which bush lurks in back-yards and gardens, and creeps in at all corners."[48] From an early stage old mining towns and other failed towns served as a reminder of how rapidly the "wilderness" and the "bush" could reclaim the locations so ephemerally occupied by urban civilization. Riding through Ohio in 1825, Chester A. Loomis came across a town deserted because of disease. It was

the melancholy spectacle . . . of a village beautifully situated; laid out with taste— and embellished with art, but no longer the abode of man . . . The site of this village will soon be lost in the rising growth of the forest; and such I am afraid is the history of many of the projected villages in this section of country.[49]

In part no doubt because of the fears and sense of vulnerability that this sort of situation gave rise to early urban development on the frontier was often seen as a contest against "nature." Towns developed through the ignoring or the eliminating of "wilderness." It has often been observed that in all new countries the terrain and topography were to a large extent ignored in the planning of new towns and in the implementation of the plans.[50] Dull gridirons were imposed again and again, even when the terrain can be seen by us as having offered superb opportunities for the devising of imaginative cityscapes and street patterns fitted to natural contours. Indeed, there were some people at the time who regretted what was being done.[51] But they seldom had much influence. William Howitt in *Land, Labour and Gold* (1855) could find in the Melbourne of the 1850s no open spaces that were being preserved for any other purpose except speculation. A unique opportunity was being lost. He feared that greed, lack of aesthetic taste, and "the fatal idea of 'going home' "—that is, the lack of long-term commitment to the city on the part of those who made their fortunes there—would "effectually nullify or annihilate all the advantages which nature has offered as if they did not exist."[52]

Surveyors frequently ran lines for roads straight up and over hills, which then often had to be excavated for convenient passage, rather than following contours around the hills.[53] It seemed extraordinary that this should be done when one considered the great expense that was almost invariably required later to make the terrain conform to the plan. The case against laying out streets at right angles over any site other than a perfectly level plain was put thus by Captain H. Butler Stoney in *A Residence in Tasmania* (1856):

They are, in consequence of the hills over which they run, so steep in some places as to cause great drawbacks to speedy traffic—a matter of essential service in a trading town: if they had been laid out in terraces and crescents, it would have greatly added to the beauty of the city, and would have been of infinite advantage to trade, tending also to equalize the value of sites, now so exorbitant in one locality and moderate in another.[54]

One of the few surveyors who tried to adopt a more flexible and imaginative approach was Felton Mathew, New Zealand's first surveyor-general, who laid out the new capital of Auckland in 1840. He claimed that

in the disposition of the Streets &c, I have consulted the peculiar character and formation of the ground, a practice which I conceive to be indispensable in the arrangement of New Towns, as a means not only of promoting the immediate convenience of the early inhabitants, but of avoiding also the enormous expense entailed on the community, by the necessity which subsequently arises for cutting down hills and filling up hollows, where the streets are laid out in parallel lines, and at right angles, without any reference to the form of the ground. Guided by this principle, I have in several instances, adopted the Crescent form, as one to which the ground is peculiarly adapted: indeed it could not be made available in any other shape.[55]

Unfortunately, Mathew's grand scheme of crescents, which was ridiculed as the Cobweb, was just about as abstract as the gridiron itself, and it was only very partially imposed on the complex, gully-scoured terrain of Auckland. One problem about most of the fancy plans that were offered as an alternative to the grid was that, while aesthetically more appealing on paper, they really suffered from just the same defects. The shapes of nature are always complex and infinitely varied. Frederick Law Olmsted's notorious—and rejected—plan for Tacoma, in which there was not a single straight line but many curves in which some people detected the shapes of bananas and other fruit, was more an anti-grid conceit than a plan realistically derived from Tacoma's topography.[56]

The same problem arises in connection with a widely read article on "Melbourne As It Is, and As It Ought To Be," published in *The Australasian* in 1850.[57] This condemns the grid plan and the adoption of the principles that the natural features of the site need not be taken account of and that the site must be made to suit the plan, not the plan the site. But the article then defines "the true principles on which a town should be planned" and advocates the application of these to Melbourne. It is clear that these features—an open square in the center, arcades or colonnades surrounding it, fountains and statues, broad arterial streets, a noble river lined with boulevards—have a good deal more to do with what is referred to as "the ideal of a great city" than with sensitive appraisal of the precise and unique characteristics of Melbourne's site and topography. Certainly surveyors of the time wished their towns to be ornamental features of the landscape and not mere reflections of the untidy confusion of natural forms. In New South Wales Thomas Mitchell wrote that "I consider it important to supply by art the natural defects of the country even with respect to the ornamental."[58]

There was also much criticism of planners and surveyors for neglecting to use prominent natural features as points of departure for novel and exciting town plans. Failure to exploit the curves of river frontages and coastal beaches was deplored. For example, in *Phillipsland* (1847) John Dunmore Lang commented on what had happened at Portland, Victoria:

Now, common sense would surely have dictated, that in such a situation, the principal street should have formed a semicircle along the beach, having cross streets diverging from it like the spokes of a wheel. But Common Sense is unfortunately very rarely consulted about the formation of colonial towns, and therefore a surveyor's parallelogram, adapted for the ground-plan of a town where there is no remarkable feature in the natural scenery to serve as a general point of departure for the entire locality, had to be wrought out, as far as practicable, in the town of Portland; the streets forming tangents to the curve of which the otherwise striking and beautiful effect is thus neutralized and lost.[59]

Nearby Port Fairy had a beautiful river setting which was ignored and largely ruined as a result in the establishment of the town. William Earle, the town's first historian, described the natural beauties of the site before settlement began. "The laying out of the town necessitated the clearing away of natural beauties of outline; and the inevitable angular highways were substituted for pretty undulating park-like spots."[60] In the United States there were many notorious cases of insensitivity in planning to features which, had they been incorporated into a plan, would have necessitated an exciting departure from the boring uniformity of the grid. J. S. Buckingham in *The Eastern and Western States of America* described what happened to the ancient Indian mound that was at first made the central feature in Circleville, Ohio, complete with an octagonal building on top that was used as the Town Hall: ". . . the streets beyond this were laid out in a circular shape, corresponding with the ancient walls, from whence its name of Circleville was derived." But gradually all these features were being removed. Soon, Buckingham lamented, "there will be no vestige left of that peculiarity which gave the place its name."[61]

Yet in spite of the objections and criticisms the destruction went on. The weight of opinion, or at least of the influence that counted in these matters, seemed overwhelmingly in favor of right-angled streets and the systematic obliteration of "nature" in the creation of the urban environment. By no means all published opinion on the subject was in favor of what were sometimes derisively called "fancy plans." William Westgarth's writings exemplify well the ambivalent attitudes of many toward grid plans. In *Victoria* (1853) he expressed regret that Melbourne had originally been laid out on "the rectangular principle" and explained the recourse to "this poverty-stricken design" with its "summary simplicity" as a reflection of a lack of expectation that the city would achieve "greatness." He wished that, once "the obvious destinies of the place" had begun to become apparent, "a more varied and graceful selection from the ample list of mathematical forms" had been made.[62] A decade passed, and few could doubt that Melbourne was amply satisfying nineteenth-century criteria of urban "greatness." Westgarth returned to the subject of its layout in *The Colony of Victoria* (1864). Melbourne's "seven hills" pleased him less now. They were fine for a town where the main object was "scenic effect," but a level—or levelled—site was far more convenient for a thriving "metropolis." Hills were a nuisance and a great complication in city life. Their eminences might be picturesque and healthy, but one could not have heights without gullies and valleys, and "the hollows are sickly." As the city grew, its "straight lines and precise rectangles" appealed to him more and more because they created—rather than, as had been originally thought, frustrated—the appearance of noble and impressive cityscapes.

The *Coup d'oeil* of a great and busy street is a noble and striking object of its kind, and there can be no such enjoyable vista, at least from ordinary stand-points, if we do not condescend to the straight lines. Melbourne furnishes a dozen or more of such urban effects from as many of the principal streets, the length of view being generally about one mile.[63]

There was a growing appreciation of the contribution made by long, straight streets to cityscapes. But undoubtedly also underlying the widespread adoption of grid plans and the imposition of these straight lines on the terrain was a variety of negative attitudes toward nature and the wilderness. The approach adopted by many town planners and promoters to the sites on which they decided to establish towns is typified by the instructions given to the engineers who laid out the city of Tacoma: "to lose all sight of the fact that it was as yet a wilderness; to forget the forest that bearded the hillsides; to forget that they were on the frontier, and to anticipate the coming of a city of hundreds of thousands; to anticipate every demand in broad avenues and noble streets, having due regard for accessibility."[64] Indeed, it was said that Americans could not "see" natural landscape. They could only "see" what was to supersede it, the towns and the civilization that were to come and without which the landscape seemed deficient.[65] For some frontier towns "looked" best when "seen" in the dark because then one could literally "lose all sight of the fact that it was as yet a wilderness."

There was a powerful urge to develop order in the landscape. Straight streets did not occur in nature, and a town's grid, when so prominently displayed, for example, in bird's-eye views, was the ultimate symbol of the imposition of human order on the wilderness.

Initially there was no escaping the fact that wilderness and city-to-be were not merely juxtaposed but indeed intermingled. "Nature" seemed to mock the early efforts to subdue and replace her "wildness." F. Lancelott in *Australia As It Is* (1852) noticed how the parklands at Adelaide, eventually to be a splendid ornament to the city, "at present add to the wild, straggling appearance of the city. Indeed, the aspect of the park lands is most un-English and wilderness-like."[66] But it seemed often that even parks were not to be allowed because of the settlers' extreme hostility to the wilderness. Charles Richard Weld wrote in *A Vacation Tour in the United States and Canada* (1855):

It is much to be regretted, that in Canada, as well as in the United States, so little consideration has been shown for the preservation of open places for recreation within the towns. It seems as if the desire were to shut out the free wilderness by every means. In the infancy of a settlement, when a few log-huts contained the population, this was natural; but when these swelled into large and flourishing communities, the importance of securing parks unfortunately remained unheeded. War to extermination against the forest is the settler's rule; and thus the instances are very rare of groves of the primeval woods amid the rising town.[67]

One town founder who has, on account of his fame as a novelist, received more attention than most is John Galt, responsible during the 1820s for the establishment of the Canada Company towns at Guelph and Goderich, Ontario. Elizabeth Waterston has traced Galt's extreme discomfort in the presence of elemental forces of nature, such as Niagara Falls and the sea.[68] She suggests that a reaction against "the powerful romantic mystique of nature" was a significant influence over his town-creation activity. Galt had the sort of North American dread of the forest to which Weld referred. To him a town was a form of protection against nature. In his descriptions of town founding, both actual and fictional, one finds a very heightened sense of urban life replacing nature and wilderness forever. Indeed, this interpretation of the significance of what was happening was even transmuted into ritual. In his *Autobiography* (1834) Galt described the founding of Guelph. As he struck the first axe blow at a tree, "the silence of the woods, that echoed to the sound, was as to the sigh of the solemn genius of the wilderness departing for ever."[69] In his novel *Lawrie Todd* (1832) there is a procession through the woods, seven cannon fire three times as the founder of the town strikes the first blow, and the tree falls "with a sound like thunder, banishing the loneliness and silence of the woods for ever."[70] Many visitors and emigrants to Canada were oppressed by the extreme gloom and stillness of its forests. But once the primeval forest was hacked down and a town created in its place, nature itself seemed to undergo a blessed transformation. "In the young woods near the towns, the case is different," observed W. Henry. "Animated life and abundance of wild flowers will here be met with, and the sportsman will find woodcocks and partridges in respectable numbers."[71]

The assault on nature might look ugly at first and offend the romantic sensitivities to which the site had originally made so powerful an appeal. But contemporaries consoled themselves with the reminder that a higher social and moral beauty would eventually evolve and effect a healing. Thus we find in an 1870 directory of Grand Rapids, Michigan:

The east side bluffs, once an ornament to the town, are now marred with deep cuts and unsightly excavations, which may be likened to constantly open sores on the face of nature. But the sores are likely, we must add, to be soon healed, and covered by a crown of comfortable homes, with church spires shooting up from their midst to point the way to the home above.[72]

Sometimes it was not easy to free oneself from the grip of romantic attraction to nature. In 1858 George B. Sargent, mayor of Davenport, Iowa, went to Boston to deliver a lecture on "the West." This took the conventional form of a celebration of the progress of civilization and so opened with an evocation of what the site of Davenport was like twenty years earlier when it began to be settled. Here Sargent's words are so eloquent as to betray what he later admits to, a strong nostalgia for the pleasure of early "primitive" frontier conditions. The railroad brought progress and prosperity, but on the day that the line between Rock Island and Chicago was completed "a thousand hammers filled the air with the din of labor, and the hoarse panting and the shrill whistle were heard of the metallic giants who had not only disturbed the quiet of the wilderness, but were covering the earth and filling the air with the soot and smoke of civilization."[73]

Where conservationist attitudes appeared in the early years of a town's growth, they usually took the form of the notion of preserving a small vestige of the original wilderness as a contrast with what had happened since, a reminder of the extent of the town's progress. When Robert Gourlay proposed a scheme of 1841 for the improvement of Kingston, Ontario, he included in it the preservation of a few "ancient pines" as "sacred memorials of the primeval forest."[74]

A frequently used image was of the new city as not merely carved out of "the primeval forest" but actually made out of it and therefore literally replacing it. Several writers dwelt on the ideas which arose out of this conceit.[75]

Fear of "the bush" among migrants was especially strong in Australia and Canada and was widely regarded as an important influence on the growth of towns there. Migrants to Australia were notoriously reluctant to leave their ports of arrival. In 1843, when there was severe unemployment in Sydney, some of the unemployed organized a petition asking for relief and pleading with the authorities not to compel them to go into the interior. They did not want, they said, to be "thus deprived of the comforts of civilized life."[76] Joseph Pickering, author of *Inquiries of an Emigrant* (1832), a handbook for migrants to Canada, wrote: "The disadvantages of all new countries (particularly away from towns), are the want of conveniences, comforts, and society—these have to be made."[77] The Durham Report dealt with the problem of the many migrants who could not cope with life in "the bush" and abandoned their holdings to go to live in the large towns.[78] Life in "the bush" could be desperately lonely, and it was scarcely surprising that so many settlers fled to where they could find social amenities. One of the most influential writers on conditions in mid-nineteenth-century Ontario was Susanna Moodie. Her first book, *Roughing it in the Bush* (1850), described life in the backwoods of Canada and emphasized the loneliness and the hardships. The last paragraph read:

If these sketches should prove the means of deterring one family from sinking their property, and shipwrecking all their hopes, by going to reside in the backwoods of Canada, I shall consider myself amply repaid for revealing the secrets of the prison-house, and feel that I have not toiled and suffered in the wilderness in vain.[79]

Her second book, *Life in the Clearings Versus the Bush* (1853), posed the alternatives in its title. The book is mainly about life in Belleville, to which the Moodies moved. She leaves no doubt about her strong preference for that life. The book is in large part a celebration of social existence in a small town.[80] Frances Stewart, who settled in the same area as the Moodies—near Peterborough—also described how lonely the settlers were and how they welcomed the growth of the town.[81]

In *New South Wales and Victoria in 1885* (1886) Douglas M. Gane noted "a strange peculiarity" in most migrants to Australia.

They will not leave the town—whether Melbourne, Sydney, Adelaide, or Brisbane—in which they land. Whether they view the bush as a kind of trap from which there is no receding, it is difficult to say; but certain it is that, in a vast number of cases, they cannot be induced to stray beyond the confines of the capital town.[82]

There is abundant evidence that the bush was indeed viewed in the way Gane describes. The Rev. H. Berkeley Jones in *Adventures in Australia* (1853) tells of traveling to Queensland with a shipload of migrants.

They all have a great aversion to going up the country into the bush, and this they often individually expressed during the voyage. One poor girl, who appeared to belong to a more respectable class than the emigrants ordinarily come from, wept bitterly at the idea of having engaged to go into the interior.[83]

In Charles Dickens' *Household Words* (1850) a resident of Sydney is quoted as describing the "weak and fantastic minds" of migrants who "conjure up a thousand Hobgoblins in the shape of Blacks, Snakes, flying foxes, Squirls and other dreaded Animals."[84]

Committees of the legislature of New South Wales repeatedly tried to find out why Sydney kept growing in spite of frequent unemployment, and one of the main answers that witnesses gave them was terror of "the bush," both as a physical environment and as a way of life. The aversion of women from life in "the bush" was often referred to. In 1843 Richard Windeyer told a committee that "it is generally the women who want to be in Sydney, they do not like the solitude of the bush." The Commissioner of Police, W. A. Miles, said that the Sydney working class had "a dread of the seclusion of the bush" and were accustomed to "the sociability, the luxuries, or dissipations of the town."[85] In 1849 John Badcock, secretary to the Colonisation Society in England, reported an experience similar to that of the Rev. H. Berkeley Jones:

> From what I heard on my passage to this country from people on board the vessel there was a great dread of going into the country; the men used to ask questions about the blacks and dogs and they evidently did not know what Australia was, and it appeared to be the wish of every one as they said, to try their luck in Sydney before they went into the country at all.[86]

"The bush" seemed to start very close to Sydney indeed. "A new arrival looks upon going to Ashfield as going into the bush," said one witness in 1859. The keeper of a registry office for female servants said that single women invariably preferred remaining in Sydney: "they consider Waverley, Balmain, the North Shore, as the country." Fear that "the bush" would be "a trap" from which they would be unable to return was often described. Edward Wise, the Attorney-General, believed that the unwillingness to go into the interior was "partly attributable to the notion that to go into the country is to relapse into a state of barbarism." The Irish were described as "frightened that they will be entirely out of society, and be unable to go to mass or anything of that kind." They were worried by reports that in the bush one did not see a clergyman "for months together."[87] As late as 1880 it was being alleged that, when migrants landed in Sydney, they listened to stories about the interior and "were led to believe that if they went into the interior they would be eaten by blacks."[88]

The advice of most writers of emigrants' guidebooks was that new arrivals should try to get out of the cities as soon as possible before they succumbed to the temptations that life in them offered. As for loneliness in the bush, James Dixon's advice in *Narrative of a Voyage to New South Wales* (1822) was that the migrant "ought to consider *well* before he leaves England, whether he can retire into the woods, and hardly see a face or social being perhaps for months."[89] Someone who took a less defeatist approach than this and became famous for doing so was Caroline

Chisholm. She organized a large-scale operation to help migrants, especially young women who were taking up employment, to go up country.

But not all the advice flowed in the same direction. Caroline Chisholm found that there were many people who were all too ready to warn her—and the migrants—of the perils of life in the bush. She wrote to police magistrates asking for information "to meet the prejudices of some amiable and pious persons, who tell me the town afford[s] more protection to young women than the country, where they consider the danger greater, and the protection less." She told of one "old colonist" who called on her and, waving in her face extracts from Sydney newspapers describing up-country crimes and outrages, stormed, "You are doing wrong, ma'am—you are sending souls to perdition! to send girls to the country is monstrous. . . . you don't know the country—they are worse than barbarians, they are monsters."[90] The advice given in some publications for migrants was scarcely calculated to make them want to venture far outside the city limits. In December 1841 the *Sydney Herald* reprinted an article in the *Colonial Magazine* in which appeared the following passage: "The number of snakes that infest the long grass, and some of which are extremely poisonous, make it impossible for ladies to walk five miles beyond Sydney; where also it would be unsafe for them to venture on account of the bushrangers or escaped convicts, who lie about concealed."[91] It is no wonder that many women were reported as believing that "the bush" began on Sydney's North Shore! Charles Dilke found that a governmental report, which migrants were recommended to read, contained a listing by the curator of the museum in Sydney of all the snakes, including poisonous ones, to be found within twelve miles of that city.[92]

CHAPTER NINE

Towns and the
Evolution of "Civilization"

T HE process of social evolution in new countries was commonly perceived and described as the "conquest of the wilderness." A key role
in the replacement of "primitive" nature by "civilization" was played by
towns. They were the most conspicuous sign of the advance of "civilization," and travelers and pioneers alike constantly expressed amazement at
the rapidity with which urban communities evolved on sites which only a
short time before had been covered with forest, "barren wildernesses." To
judge from the frequency with which such observations were made, this
was one of the most remarkable features of the new societies. Much was
made of the rural pioneers, the backwoodsmen, the first settlers on the
prairies. But Laurence Oliphant in *Minnesota and the Far West* (1855)
maintained that "amongst the most novel and characteristic experiences
of a traveller in the Far West" were witnessing what had been achieved
by urban pioneers.[1]

In travelers' accounts and in booster literature there are countless
references to towns that are "fresh risen from the woods." Towns "sprang
up in the midst of wildernesses."[2] The forest and wilderness which they
replaced were usually described in the most pejorative terms possible—
as "dismal," "interminable," "desolate." The howlings of wild beasts and
"savages" were frequently mentioned. All this was done to establish the
most vivid contrast with what had so rapidly developed on these sites.
Here, for example, is a description of Adelaide from the novel *Life's Work
As It Is* by "A Colonist" (1867):

> Little more than twenty years ago that plain was covered with trees, that city
> was one vast forest. . . . So different then to what it is now. The noble gum, the
> beautiful blackwood, and the wattle, all flourished in Hindley and Rundle Street.
> Where now there are pavements and macadamized streets, the tall grass waved so
> high that the cattle could not be seen when lying down at a distance, and the

cockatoos shrieked and built their nests where gentlemen now walk the Exchange; while the rosella and the beautiful blue mountain-parrots flitted from tree to tree; and the curlew uttered its mournful cry at midnight in those very spots where at the same hour carriages are rumbling home from the theatre, and cabs and Hansoms are returning from White's Rooms, where a concert very different to that of birds has just ended.

Hard it is for the mind's eye thus to wander back, and picture noble forest trees standing in the same spot where now looks forth a milliner's shop that would not disgrace Bond Street. . . . Such is life, and such was life, as thousands of colonists can testify.[3]

If this kind of perception of the evolution of towns in new countries is captured in a thousand literary accounts, it is also the commonplace of artists' depictions of the new towns. Almost invariably they are drawn or painted from a distance with a framing that represents the wilderness out of which the city has so miraculously emerged.

Attention was drawn not only to the primeval forest and wilderness but also to the very primitive character of the original buildings of the settlement. Horace Earle in *Ups and Downs* (1861) wrote of a typical Australian town: "Where a log-hut did duty for a post-office, is now a large and elegant structure of solid masonry. Theatres, concert-rooms, hotels, and churches, spring up with magical rapidity. . . ."[4] Such "primitive" features as survived were used to highlight the extent of progress. Here is James B. Brown in *Views of Canada and the Colonists* (1851) endeavoring to compose a word picture of Toronto from the viewpoint of the arriving traveler:

A close mass of houses, with several spires, warehouses, market-houses, and public works, meet the eye; and towards the upper part of the city, fronting the lake, are the fort, houses of legislature, and several excellent private residences and public hotels. The line of wooden wharfs along the shore, with their ragged and temporary appearance, serve only to remind one of the comparatively recent forest origin of this extent of progress and civilization now presented along the northern shore of Lake Ontario.[5]

If such primitive buildings no longer existed, then artistic representations were made available to help people make the same points. "In the lobby of the National Gallery," wrote C. Gavan Duffy in 1876 when starting to compose a sketch of Victorian history, "there hangs a rude pencil sketch of a weatherboard hut on the slopes of the Yarra, overshaded by sombre masses of the primeval forest, which less than forty years ago was the sole seat of state and authority in Melbourne."[6]

Of course, all these phrases—"fresh risen from the woods," and so on
—became clichés, the stock in trade of writers who wanted to describe
the new towns but had no insights of their own to offer or perhaps had
not even been there. The clichés often became embedded in the pioneers'
perceptions of their experiences and make regular appearances in collections of reminiscences.[7] But there was also obviously much pride felt by
the settlers themselves as they watched urban society evolve around them.
Edward Gibbon Wakefield described seeing this happen as one of the
great pleasures of colonizing activity.[8] There was excitement and anticipation in watching a new town take shape where once there had been
"only wilderness."

Settlers used in their private letters what now seem clichés to us. A
prominent lawyer in early York (Toronto) wrote in 1829 of the life of
high society there, the many balls and dinner parties:

What think you of this for a place in wc. 20 or 30 years ago the Lady of the then
Chief Justice lost herself in attempting to explore her way along a path which is
now the main street of a populous Town? . . . What think you of a Town of nearly
4000 inhabs. occupying the ground where 30 years ago the sound of an axe in
felling the Forest with wc. it was covered was as rarely to be heard as at this day
when not a Tree remains to bear record to the astonishing rapidity of its Dissolu-
tion . . .[?][9]

Towns caused delight and satisfaction because they represented the
creation of order and tidiness. Here is how Caroline Chisholm argued her
case for group- and family-based settlement of the interior of Australia:
"towns and hamlets would spring up; the spires of churches would guide
the traveller on his way; civilization would advance hand-in-hand with
religion, and this, Gentlemen, is what I consider colonization to be."[10]
When the founder of Portland, Oregon, returned to inspect what he had
started, he exclaimed: "It fills my heart with joy to see this great city
where I once saw dense woods."[11] Observers commented in particular on
the neatness of towns. They would mention fences and regular streets and
tidy gardens.[12] Although the reality was usually mud and mess and
disorder, the perceived reality was often something else.[13] Early artistic
depictions of frontier towns were obviously highly sanitized and betray
an obsession with fences and neatness and order, with houses carefully
labeled. Bernard Smith has written that the earliest drawings and paintings of Australian towns were made "to provide evidence of civil progress

and good government." Lycett's townscapes are "clean and precise; tokens of British order in a southern wilderness."[14]

To most the progress from "wilderness" to order and "civilization" seemed an uncomplicated process, wholly and unambiguously satisfying. Only occasionally do darker perceptions—of the kind typified by the modern phrase "the urban wilderness"—surface. Perhaps a new kind of "wilderness" would rise in place of the old. In November 1830 the *Illinois Monthly Magazine* published an article entitled "Three Hundred Years Hence" in which the author describes a dream about St. Louis when it has become a great world city. "The sun was now setting over this wilderness of houses. His parting beams flamed on the gilded spires of this metropolis; and reminded me of the years when I had beheld him sinking behind an unbroken line of forest." The author then dreamed of going into St. Louis, which was now an enormous industrial city, and witnessing an insurrection by its working people, many of whom were starving.[15] So disturbing was this vision that ten months later the editor published *another* dream, the author of which prophesied a far happier outcome for St. Louis—because of "the general spread of the gospel, and its principles, among men."[16]

Reinforcing the idea of towns as the chief agency for the spread of "civilization" was the image of them as cultural centers in the wilderness. We have seen how widespread was the belief that life on the frontier or in the bush or backwoods brought with it demoralization, a relapse into "primitivism" or "barbarism." The presence of towns was essential to counter this.[17] That towns and the "civilization" that their social and cultural amenities represented already existed became an important aspect of the promotion of emigration to frontier regions. In *Readings in Melbourne* (1879), a book which, as its subtitle indicates, he wrote for "the Emigrant and Uneasy Classes," Archibald Michie combined an alleviation of the "uneasiness" of prospective migrants to Victoria with some knocking of a major alternative migrant destination:

In no part does he [the migrant] leave civilization behind him, as the settler seems to do who plunges into the back woods of America. In every little town and village and agricultural and mining settlement the newspaper is found, the Mechanics' Institute or the reading-room soon makes its appearance; the sound of the piano and of pleasant female voices falls on the ear of the passer-by everywhere.[18]

Yet only three years earlier, in a pamphlet called *How and Where to Get a Living: A Sketch of "The Garden of the West,"* the Atchison, Topeka and

Santa Fé Railroad reassured migrants to its lands in southwestern Kansas that that region already had "prosperous towns, churches, schools, mills, and the conveniences of a well-settled community."[19]

Many advocates and promoters of colonization schemes attached great importance to the fostering of towns so that "civilization" might be injected into the frontier situation, even if the "laws" of social evolution suggested that the growth of towns ought not to come at so early a stage of frontier history. In *Twelve Years' Wanderings in the British Colonies* (1848) J. C. Byrne urged the authorities to have the land beyond the settlement boundaries of New South Wales, where only "squatters" so far lived, surveyed and offered for sale, not so that more farmers would come into these regions—which were suited only to extensive pastoralism— but so that inland towns might be started. These, he argued, were needed as "stations, where pastors of religion can assemble flocks to teach them that morality and religion which is so little understood or practised in the interior of Australia." "Education," he added, "also finds a focus in an inland town. . . ."

The establishment, in various places beyond the frontiers, of small towns would undoubtedly act as a check on the progress of vice; for, in these towns, clergymen and teachers could be established, as within the colony, who, by degrees, would gather a congregation, and even induce the less depraved to attend their services and instructions.

Indeed, Byrne had a vision of scores of small towns "acting as points from whence civilisation and education could be extended around."[20]

As we have seen, it was an important aspect of Wakefieldian colonization to get towns established at the inauguration of the colony, and one reason for this was to facilitate the transference of "civilization" and its implantation in the new society. This would mean, in Wakefield's words, that colonists would go "to a new, but not to a barbarous country."[21] This aspect of settlement schemes such as Wakefield's has been described as "cultural imperialism."[22]

The sort of remedy which Byrne prescribed for the "barbarism" of outbacks and "interior" life in Australia was a constantly recurring theme in planning for the settlement of these regions. In the late 1860s the government of South Australia decided to embark on a systematic program of settling the vast interior of that colony, occupation of which had so far been mainly confined to the coastal areas. The chief architect of this policy, G. W. Goyder—who devised a famous "line" beyond which rainfall was inadequate to permit wheat farming—went to Victoria to study how their land settlement policies were working and returned convinced that urban centers were "a necessary and civilising part of frontier life" and should not be organized merely as "a belated after-thought." Accordingly, a major feature of the government's program over the period 1869–1880 for opening up the hinterland to occupation for wheat production was the systematic surveying of towns. The pathetic fate of these towns, most of which never came to anything, and the disasters that befell the attempt to establish wheat farming up to the "Goyder line," have been very well described in books by D. W. Meinig and M. Williams.[23]

In 1865 the New South Wales Legislative Assembly set up a Select Committee to report on "the Present State of the Colony." One of its concerns was the policy of "free selection," whereby "small" settlers could "select" holdings on land occupied by "squatters." Comments by some witnesses anticipated the criticisms that Goyder would make when he examined how "free selection" worked in Victoria. The Rev. J. West, for instance, argued that "settlement, instead of permitting the wide disper-sion of the people, and endangering all the advantages of civilization, should have been confined within limits which would have afforded facilities for the operations of the clergyman and schoolmaster." The chairman, Henry Parkes, then asked West a question which embodied the classic model of social evolution in a new country. "Must it not be the case, in any system of pioneering in a new country, that the pioneer must advance without these accompanying conditions of civilisation?" West's response was: "If these people are scattered at a distance of five or six, ten or fifteen miles from a school or place of worship, you will have a very doubtful race of people by and by. I have always looked upon that as the most serious aspect of free selection." He believed that the government had to incorporate the establishment of towns in its planning. The idea of "a nice village of Auburn, with a schoolmaster whose small head carries wonders," just forming among free selectors, was "all utopian." H. R. Francis, a District Court Judge, thought it wrong that the one area from which free selection was banned was the neighborhood of existing towns. "I consider that the moral question is paramount to all others; I consider that the system as it works at present, away from towns or considerable villages, is one calculated to make savages; I cannot put it more strongly."[24] In fact, in Victoria within each of the 127 "Agricultural Areas" declared open in 1862 one square mile was reserved "in order that churches, schools, savings banks, mechanics' institutes, courts, post offices, public gardens, baths, markets and other agencies of civilisation might in good time follow."[25] Experience both here and in South Australia was to show that it was not enough to rely on "good time" for the evolution of towns with so extensive a range of urban amenities.

Towns in new countries were often defined as centers from which radiated—or ought to radiate—moral, intellectual, and religious influence.[26] This idea can be seen underlying the "free soil" colonization of Kansas in the 1850s, a basic feature of which was the establishment of towns. One anti-slavery writer, clearly drawing on the New England tradition of settlement of the wilderness, referred to American towns as "the central points from which knowledge, enterprise, and civilization stream out upon the surrounding country."[27] Many New Englanders saw the towns of the American West as of critical importance in the fulfillment of their missionary goals.[28] When a Baptist conference was held in Chicago in 1867 to consider establishing a theological seminary in that city, Dr. Hague of Boston declared: "God has made Chicago to be a great centre of trade. It is destined also to be the great Baptist head-quarters, a foundation of life and influence to the West. This it must be, in spite of everything."[29] Similar significance had been attached to Cincinnati several decades earlier.[30] As America expanded westward, so did this idea. Theodore Gerrish in *Life in the World's Wonderland* (1887), written for a New England readership and full of references to the powerful civilizing influence of New Englanders in the West, wrote: "The Christian churches of America should sustain these frontier outposts of our Zion until that mass of developing wealth is redeemed from the power of Satan and becomes consecrated to the use of our glorious Saviour." To Gerrish, Helena, Montana, was "a dispenser of civilization to the plains and mountains—a true capital."[31]

In America, as in Australia, this aspect of town development on the frontier was often emphasized. *The New States* (1889), another publication directed at Eastern readers, warned them not to scorn and dismiss North Dakota's cities just because they were so small and seemed by Eastern standards cities "only in name." There were now cities with populations of 2,500 to 10,000 all over North Dakota and "they exercise an influence on the life of the rural population and furnish an outlook toward a broader civilization which is most helpful and salutary."[32] Many years earlier James Fenimore Cooper had had a similar vision of fifty to one hundred "centres of exertion" spreading their civilizing influence over the frontier of the Mohawk Valley.[33]

It was an idea that also appealed to colonial governors. When Governor Bourke founded Melbourne, he said that he wanted to establish townships and ports and so "provide, though but imperfectly, centres of civilization and Government, and thus gradually to extend the power of order and social union to the most distant parts of the wilderness."[34] When John Graves Simcoe formulated his grandiose plans for the inauguration of settlement of Upper Canada in the 1790s, he attached the highest priority to the establishment of a capital "to give power & energy to civilization." This city would become the principal agency by which British civilization would be transferred to the wilderness: "a great Body of Emigrants should be collected in its Vicinity so as to become the very transcript & Image of the British People & to transfuse their manners, principles, & attachments thro' the whole Colony."[35]

But Simcoe intended to go further than just creating a town and expecting its influence to operate automatically in this way. He wanted to take steps to make it a center of culture on the frontier. In January 1791 he expounded his plans for the capital that "I mean to call Georgina" in a letter to Sir Joseph Banks, the leading patron of science and the arts in England. He sought Banks' help in the founding of a public library, a college, and other such cultural amenities. He wanted the city to have "every Embellishment that hereafter may Decorate and attract Notice." His particular aim was to impress the people of "the Neighboring States" with the superiority of the British form of government over their newly adopted republicanism.[36]

In the United States the aspiration to convert a town into a cultural center is a recurring theme of Western urban boosterism.[37] Image-making along these lines was a striking feature of urban life in the Ohio Valley in the first half of the nineteenth century when there was great competition among towns to be accepted as "the Athens of the West."[38] This phrase frequently appears in booster literature throughout the history of American westward expansion—and indeed in Australia as well. Gawler in South Australia, for instance, liked to call itself "the Colonial Athens."[39] The goddess Minerva adorned innumerable mechanics' institute buildings. Mechanics' institutes, libraries, opera houses, schools of art, and a wide range of other cultural institutions usually occupied some of the finest premises in town and were greatly valued as conspicuous embodiments of the roles of towns as centers and sources of "civilization" on the frontier.[40] To judge from the number of favorable comments in the writings of travelers, the effort put into erecting such buildings usually paid off in terms of creating the desired image. In *Views of Canada and the Colonists* (1851) James B. Brown quotes a visitor to London, Ontario, in 1843 as congratulating the people on their new mechanics' institute, which gave "a stamp of respectability, intelligence, and a taste for the fine arts, of which you may be justly proud."[41]

Satirical accounts of the young frontier towns often focused on the absurdity and hollowness of much of this cultural boosterism. Cincinnati people, who had been taught to regard their city as "the Athens of the West," were very upset when Mrs. Trollope preferred to emphasize the pigs running around the streets. There are echoes of this controversy in John Parsons' fictional experiences at Terre Haute in 1840. After receiving a strong dose of conventional booster rhetoric from the editor of the local newspaper, Parsons walked down a street in the company of a young lawyer and encountered a drove of pigs.

"Behold, Mr. Parsons," said Mr. Griswold, in tones of mock solemnity, "behold a vision of Porkopolis. Mayhap you have not heard that in spite of our culture, our schools, our professions, the real source of our prosperity lies in our pork-packing establishments, of which we have so many. Can it be that none has as yet vouchsafed you a view of those elegant edifices, those slaughter houses, our pride, that cluster on the river's brink? Mayhap it has been whispered to you, young sir, that our great fear, at least the fear of those of us who own no porkers, and no packing house, but who breathe the refined air of the heights of culture, that our adopted city may yet receive the name of Porkopolis! Perish the thought! Rather may our boasted prosperity vanish!"[42]

The problems of making a town work culturally in the manner intended quite often turned out to be formidable. The idea of having scores of centers of religious influence sounded fine in theory, but, as John Dunmore Lang was at pains to point out, dispersing religious and other forms of "civilizing" effort over large numbers of small towns and villages meant a fragmentation of energy and loss of efficiency. Where were so many able clergymen to come from? Towns rose and declined so rapidly, especially in mining areas, that there was much reluctance to erect permanent and substantial church buildings. It was sometimes claimed that clergy who located in a village became too involved in its affairs and paid inadequate attention to the spreading of religion through the surrounding districts.[43]

Another word that was often used to describe what towns were regarded as replacing and expelling was "savagery." The primitive state that was giving way before the advance of "civilization" with its urban spearhead was identified not just with nature and wild beasts but also with "savages," the indigenous peoples of the land. As settlement expanded, towns replaced one another in this spearhead role. For example, William Darby in *A Tour From the City of New York, to Detroit* (1810) perceived Detroit as occupying "the point of contact, between the aboriginal inhabitants of the wilderness, and the civilized people, who are pressing these natives of North America backwards, by the double force of physical and moral weight." The result was that in its streets could be seen "at one glance the extremes of human improvement, costume, and manners. You behold the inhabitants in habiliments that would suit the walks of New-York, Philadelphia, London or Paris, and you also behold the bushy, bare-headed savage, almost in primaeval nudity."[44] Soon the "savage" was gone, and books describing the new cities almost invariably contained passages such as the following from *Maclehose's Picture of Sydney* (1839): "The short space of fifty years has converted the horrid and tractless wilderness—the transient resting place of some migratory tribe of naked and unideaed savages—into the busy mart of civilised and enlightened intercourse. . . ."[45] The title page of Garnet Walch's *Victoria in 1880* (1881) juxtaposes two scenes, "1830," with a river, some aborigines, and two kangaroos, and "1880," with a city of spires and tall buildings and, in the foreground, sheep grazing in a fenced paddock.[46]

For some the passing of the "red man" or the aborigine was matter for unqualified rejoicing. In J. C. Myers' *Sketches on a Tour* (1849) appear the following reflections on the landscape of upstate New York:

When we reflect on these highly cultivated regions, bespangled with the most flourishing cities, towns and villages, whose foundations were laid by persons still living, and which region already numbers a population greater than the whole of the aboriginal hunting tribes, who possessed the forest for hundreds of miles around, we soon cease to repine at the extraordinary revolution in the history of those tribes, however much we may commiserate the unhappy fate of the disinherited race.—Because here now the noble enterprise of the white men has so changed the aspect of this region, that upon every hand attractive beauty meets the eye; and here now far and wide the aboriginal forest has lost its charms of savage wildness, by the beauties of cities, towns and villages, and the intrusion of railroads and canals.[47]

Some did "repine" but only to the extent of indulging in a little romantic nostalgia for what had to "pass." Books on the frontier contained numerous elegaic passages on this theme. "Where is now the mighty Iroquois?" asked Sir Richard R. Bonnycastle in *The Canadas in 1841* (1841).

A century has not passed, the sun has not made his annual revolution one hundred times, and yet the Iroquois, his wars, and his people, have alike been forgotten and lost. His very memory at Toronto is involved in utter obscurity; and those forests in which the white man has erected a stately city from the bosom of a howling desert, no longer give even the protection of their shade to his red brother.[48]

In 1865 A. D. Munson's *Minnesota Messenger* wrote of St. Paul:

Where but a short time since the wigwam of the Indian stood amid the native foilage [sic], now may be seen the Church, the School House, or the Store House. . . . The red men have departed, and their huts are now placed miles away from the scenes of civilization and their existence is now almost forgotten.[49]

In most accounts of the changes on the frontier the main purpose in bringing in the Indian is to point up the progress that has occurred since he left.[50] Don H. Doyle has described the symbolic uses to which the Indian was put in the centennial celebrations of Nashville, Tennessee, in 1880. His account is familiar to the reader of local histories. The Indian was seen and presented as "the antithesis of the civilization Nashville had achieved by 1880." The keynote speaker sounded a note typical of such "celebrations": "The shriek of the locomotive and the hum of industry is heard instead of the howl of the wolf and the whoop of the red man." It was suggested that a group of Indians be exhibited "in their native costumes" in order to "show to the children and rising generation the great contrast between then and now." One way in which the centennial was commemorated was by the placing of fourteen printed placards indicating where and when pioneers were ambushed and scalped by Indians.[51]

A familiar feature of early drawings and paintings of towns is the figure of the Indian or the aborigine standing to the side and in the foreground and pointing at the newly risen town which is the focus of the scene. His gesture is usually somewhat indeterminate in significance, conveying a mixture of awe, regret, and submission. The image of the Indian warrior astride his horse on a bluff overlooking a town was a commonplace of American Western art. A favorite image to describe the change was one which adapted the phoenix theme, used so often to boost the recovery of towns after conflagrations. Ignatius Donnelly, who hoped that in his speculative Minnesota promotion, Nininger City, he had founded the Chicago of the Northwest, employed the phoenix image when he told the Minnesota Historical Society in 1856: "The embers of the Indian's fire will scarcely have disappeared from the heath where his wigwam stood, before the halls and palaces of the most elaborate social life will rise upon their site."[52] Similarly, William Kelly in *Life in Victoria* (1859) referred to Melbourne's "stately dwellings and magnificent terraces, arising, as it were, out of the ashes of the aboriginal corrobborees."[53] The image is one of destruction of one way of life to make way for another, and this certainly illustrates very well the way in which, for all their bouts of nostalgia, most city builders approached the question of what should be done about surviving relics of the pre-European past of the site such as the Indian mounds.

Towns were often located on sites which had been used by indigenous peoples and were still being used by them when Europeans arrived and by a variety of means "acquired" the land for use in this distinctively European form. Indeed, it seems that in America it was often regarded as a good omen that Indians had selected a site for a purpose of their own.[54] Indians were considered by some as good judges of what constituted a superior location for a settlement. For example, they would not have lingered at a place which was subject to periodic inundation. A Minnesota booster publication of 1856 pointed out that Red Wing, the Goodhue county seat, "is located upon the well known village site of the Red Wing band of Dakotas; and its situation illustrates the unerring judgement shown by Indians, in selecting places for permanent abode."[55]

For this among other reasons, notably trade, indigenous peoples were usually to be seen in large numbers in towns in the early stages of their history. Visitors commented on this. "To a casual visitor of Moreton Bay," wrote Edward Wilson in *Rambles at the Antipodes* (1859), "nothing is more striking than the very large number of aborigines who still flock into the towns and present themselves to observation in all directions."[56]

Richard Howitt in *Australia* (1845) wrote that in 1840, only three years after Melbourne's foundation, there were aborigines everywhere in the town.[57] A history of Tacoma, Washington, recalled how in its early years Indians "hovered about the settlement in considerable numbers. They were very friendly and not infrequently entered the houses without invitation and squatted around the fires."[58]

The town was a European form of settlement, and indigenous peoples seldom manifested any desire to "live" in it in the European sense. But for some time they continued trying to use the land as *they* had traditionally used it, and the two forms of land use overlapped and intersected in complex ways. Indians who had camped on locations long before the Europeans came did not cease to do so just because those locations had been surveyed for incorporation in a town. They might have "sold" the land but in their "selling" had no idea that what was involved was permanent loss of all right to use the land in traditional ways. The same was true of aborigines in Australia and the Maori in New Zealand. Use of land by aborigines and Indians tended to be intermittent rather than the permanent possession and occupation to which Europeans were accustomed. Townspeople were therefore sometimes surprised when they would suddenly turn up and commence some sort of activity on land within the town's boundaries. The purpose of such visits was usually understood only dimly, if at all. Thus in 1865 the newspaper of a town in Victoria, Inglewood, reported a visit by aborigines from the Murray River "to see their white bretheren [sic] inhabiting this town. It is some time since they paid us a visit and their appearance in the street, with their long spears, opposum cloaks, etc. form quite a novel feature." The aborigines camped at a gully "right upon the spot where, six years ago a lubra was buried."[59] In the winter of 1873–74, churches, schools, hotels, and shops having sprung up on the site of the new town of Colorado Springs, 300 Ute Indians arrived at their old "stamping ground" and made it known that they intended to stay "for many moons." The governor persuaded them to move on.[60]

There were also misunderstandings as the indigenous peoples converted to their own purposes land that was designed to serve very different European urban needs. An example is the parkland that surrounded Adelaide and was planned as an adornment to the city of the future. In the present it looked very rough and un-"park"-like, and the local aborigines took to camping on it.[61] At Fairbury, Nebraska, the public square initially had a very indistinct "European" appearance. "There were not enough buildings around the public square to mark it." While it was in this condition, the Otoe Indians camped on it when going out on their annual buffalo hunts.[62] The local Maori people, forced into Palmerston North to attend hearings of the Native Land Court in order to defend their claims to ownership of their land, found that town's capacious square very convenient for camping and holding of feasts. Ironically, they were among the principal defenders of the square when local European businessmen desired to subdivide it for occupation by commercial premises.[63]

But, given that indigenous peoples were perceived as "primitive," indeed part of the "wilderness," and that "wild beasts" and "savages" were almost indistinguishable in descriptions of the denizens of the backwoods and forests, it is not surprising that their presence soon came to be felt to be wrong, incongruous, and intolerable in towns which were, after all, usually described as the chief centers and agencies for the spread of "civilization" on the frontier. More and more Europeans began to say that towns were not appropriate places for them to live in. Their reasons for arguing along these lines were many and various, but one often resorted to was the corrupting and demoralizing effect on indigenous peoples of a civilization with which, as people at a more "primitive" level of social development, they were not fitted to cope.[64] A town was a European form of community. Aborigines, Indians, and Maori did not "belong" there.[65]

As to how the indigenous peoples themselves saw towns, we have only fragmentary evidence to guide us, but such as there is suggests that they too came to feel that they did not "belong," being helped greatly to arrive at this perception by the increasingly unfriendly treatment which they received in them. Probably exceptional was the case of Salisbury, Indiana, which, according to John Parsons, had declined almost to the vanishing point since two curses had been put on it, one by an Indian "that it should not live, but should disappear from the face of the earth."[66] The Maori did have some ideas about town planning. As the Palmerston North experience revealed, they appreciated large public squares. When some Maori land was sold in a region near that town, and a new town was proposed, they inserted into the treaty of sale requirements for this town which included a square. The European developers of the town, Levin, subsequently ignored this provision and instead gave it a very wide Main

Street.[67] Occasionally one comes across a statement by an Indian or Maori rejecting European urban civilization or remarking on the alienness to his way of life of this kind of community.[68]

European colonists and indigenous peoples seldom lived harmoniously side by side on the same urban site for very long. Soon complaints against the latter began to appear and to be voiced with mounting intensity and urgency. In Adelaide the aborigines caused offence by cutting down trees on the parklands and by the noise of their corroborees. Citizens began writing letters to the local newspapers expressing the wish that they would remove their "discordant orgies" to the bush.[69] Visitors' reports on Adelaide carried similarly disapproving remarks on the situation. In *Australia As It Is* (1852) F. Lancelott told his English readers about the aborigines of Adelaide: "Their noisy carobbories [sic] at night, and occasional exhibition by day, are . . . somewhat annoying. They possess no sense of shame, wear few garments, and, but for the law, would walk the streets uncovered."[70] Aborigines did not convey the desired image of the new settlement to arriving migrants. Sarah Brunskill wrote after disembarking at Adelaide in 1839: "On our way up from the Port to the City, I felt very low and uncomfortable, the ground appeared burnt up, and as we reached the town, saw a gang of natives, my heart sank and I wished myself dead."[71] At Hamilton in western Victoria aborigines frequently camped on a hill behind the Market Square. The *Hamilton Spectator* complained about the "Black Nuisance" and the noise from their corroborees.[72]

It was very common for townspeople, as well as farmers, to object to the offences committed by indigenous peoples against European notions of privacy and private property. "The squaws, often with a papoose on their back, peered into the windows of the homes, sometimes frightening the children within," recalled an early settler at Dillon, Montana.[73] Travelers were not impressed by the sight of Indians in towns. John Mortimer Murphy, in *Rambles in North-Western America* (1879), described the two most disagreeable objects relating to Port Townsend, Washington, as the mosquitoes and "the constant presence of a colony of Indians, who are anything but models of virtue."[74]

Almost every European who described the "presence" of indigenous peoples in towns seemed to start from the premise that they did not "belong" there. This clearly shaped their perceptions which emphasized incongruity, ugliness, lack of accord with the setting. Charles Dilke found the Indians who were "swarming" around Denver buying arms very "unprepossessing."[75] Indians in streets were described as "lounging about."[76] There were complaints that the Maori obstructed the pavements of New Zealand cities and generally did not respect European conventions regarding the use of streets.[77]

Before long in almost every town where there was initially a large population of indigenous people there arose a European demand for them to be expelled or to be prevented from coming into the town if they did so intermittently. The excuse often given was that the European city or town was a bad place for them and that forcing them to leave was for their own good. At Maitland, New South Wales, in December 1841 the *Hunter River Gazette* complained that aborigines wandered about the streets "in a state of perfect nudity" and called for measures to keep them out of the town "where they can meet with nothing to their advantage, considering the white society which they frequent."[78] In Melbourne in the early years many blacks were to be encountered in the streets. E. M. Curr, in *Recollections of Squatting in Victoria* (1883), recalled seeing large numbers wandering around "making strange noises" and doing odd jobs.[79] Several historians have pointed to the attraction of European food supplies as an incentive to come into the town and beg or do work. According to Richard Broome, this food enabled them to have larger and longer intertribal gatherings than ever before. These large-scale gatherings of course only intensified European indignation at their presence.[80] A Protector of Aborigines was appointed with the task of deterring them from visiting Melbourne. But they did not want to go, taking the view that they were prior occupants of the site and insisting that for their part they were quite happy to share it with the white settlers. In 1839 the Protector summed up their feelings thus: "I fear their removal by force will be attended with much prejudice—they have this morning distinctly told me that Plenty White Man set down, Black fellows no sulky, Plenty Black fellow set down & White men Sulky. No good that—Long time ago before White man came Goldborn Black fellow sit down here, Why Gago now." Beverley Nance has argued that there was in fact a conscious effort on the part of the aborigines at Melbourne to alter their behavior so that they might continue to co-exist harmoniously with the whites.[81] But during the 1840s European observers almost all found the aborigines whom they saw on the streets repulsive and degenerate and argued that the town environment had caused a marked deterioration in their physique and style of living. Their removal was demanded by the local press. Much the same happened in Sydney. There were constant complaints about seminudity and drunkenness.[82]

Robin Fisher has documented similar pressure for removal of Indians from the vicinity of towns in British Columbia. He shows that much of the justification for this was couched in terms of a desire to prevent the Indians from harming the morals of the European population but that a less publicly expressed reason was to get access to Indian lands in or adjacent to towns such as Victoria.[83] The same motivation appears at times in the American West, for example, the demand at Durango, Colorado, for the Indians to be shifted from a nearby reservation: "we fear that the close proximity of the reservation to Durango has heretofore kept away capital, and we know that the appropriation of this land by white settlers will make Durango another Denver." The Durango Board of Trade then added hastily in case anyone should take the wrong message from this admission: "But Durango has grown and waxed great in spite of the Indian incubus."[84]

When Mrs. Simcoe, wife of the first lieutenant-governor of Upper Canada, saw Indians in the streets of the new town of Kingston in 1792, she instantly contrasted them with London urbanity of which she judged them to be a grotesque parody:

They are an unwarlike, idle, drunken, dirty tribe. I observe how extremes meet. These uncivilized People saunter up & down the Town all day, with the apparent Nonchalance, want of occupation & indifference that seems to possess Bond street Beaux.[85]

Frederick Jackson Turner's concept of the frontier as a place where one phase of settlement yielded to inexorable pressure from the next may have been influenced by observation of what happened in his own home town of Portage, Wisconsin, where his father was joint owner and publisher of the *Wisconsin State Register*. Indians in the 1870s were still in the habit of wandering into Portage to beg, to trade, and to drink. The newspaper demanded that the government expel these "worthless savages" from "a community where they are utterly despised, disgusting everyone with their filthiness and alarming timid women by their frightful appearance as they go begging from door to door." Soon the authorities did act to remove the Indians.[86]

It was not long before indigenous peoples, under the weight of many pressures, of which disease and alcoholism were especially significant, began to disappear from towns or to become marginal presences, confined to the outskirts both of the towns and of the minds of the townspeople. By the time that Godfrey Charles Mundy visited Sydney, in 1846, the colonial town was so lacking in an aboriginal population that he complained that it

wants the foreign and exotic interest of others of our colonial capitals. Neither the aborigines themselves, nor any object belonging to them, nor the natives of any other country, mix with the nearly exclusively British population and products of the place.

Only on the outskirts did he come across "a chattering, half-besotted group of the wretched natives of New Holland itself," begging money at the doors of pot-houses. Sydney, he concluded, had become "more exclusively English in its population than either Liverpool or London."[87] John Askew, in *A Voyage to Australia & New Zealand* (1857), found that only a few aborigines remained in Adelaide. Five or six years ago there had been about 400–500. Now only 150 were left, and they led the most marginal and ghostly of existences, sleeping under trees or "behind whurlies in the domain," sitting under verandas during the day, and were occasionally glimpsed waving spears or dancing on the banks of the Torrens.[88] In *What We Saw in Australia* (1875) Rosamond and Florence Hill report not seeing any aborigines in Melbourne and only two in Sydney, "one a drunken woman in the street, the other a poor imbecile in the Receiving-house for lunatics."[89]

There were those who wanted the obliteration even of non-English place names. However, John Dunmore Lang preferred aboriginal names. He criticized the widespread use of grand-sounding names derived from English towns for new frontier settlements:

When one goes to "Liverpool," or "Windsor," or "Richmond," forsooth, and finds it a small insignificant village, he cannot help saying to himself—
O what a falling off *is there!*
and the place actually looks much worse than it really is, simply from its unfortunate name.

With aboriginal names one would never be disappointed.[90]

Local histories contained many references to episodes connected with the disappearance of the indigenous inhabitants of the locality—the last black left alive, the last corroboree, and so on. These seem to be regarded as landmarks in the history of the town and district. In his *Personal Recollections* (1888) William Westgarth remembered an aboriginal encampment on the outskirts of Melbourne and the grand corroboree of 1844. Many Europeans went out from the town to witness what proved to have been the last such demonstration in or near Melbourne.[91]

Authors of books of advice for emigrants were quick to mark and welcome the disappearance and to use it to reassure them. The extremes to which such writers could go are illustrated by Alfred Simmons' *Old England and New Zealand* (1879). Simmons was determined to dispel "a stupidly foundationless idea abroad among Englishmen at home that New Zealand is essentially a foreign country—foreign in appearance, in habits, and customs—and, as we have remarked elsewhere, overrun with blacks." Wellington, for instance, had 25,000 inhabitants, and "we doubt if anything approaching 500 of that number are foreigners." And who were these "foreigners"? Just "a few friendly natives and a few Chinese," "both . . . as respectful and harmless among Europeans as they well could be." Thus the Maori became reclassified as a "foreigner" in the new towns of his own land. On the other hand, Simmons rejoiced that "troops of chirping English sparrows flutter about the streets of most of the towns."[92]

Certainly, it became true that when indigenous people returned to or visited the towns they were treated as oddities, essentially as "foreigners" who did not belong and whose stay was expected to be only temporary. They were expected to don disguise, in effect to look like Europeans. Sir Richard S. Bonnycastle in *The Canadas in 1841* (1841) noted that the "red man" was seldom seen in Toronto, "and when there, as he is usually clothed as the Europeans are, and wears their garb, he excites no attention or surprise."[93] In *Capper's South Australia* (1839) Henry Capper assured prospective migrants to Adelaide that, "appreciating our notions of modesty, they [the local aborigines] never think of approaching the settlement without being sufficiently clad."[94] Towns were regarded as European territory on which the "natives" were intruders.

If they entered towns and refused to conform to European norms of dress and behavior, indigenous peoples were either scorned as "miserable vagabonds" or else tolerated for a time and even welcomed as freaks, sources of entertainment. Indeed, many townspeople saw Indians only either when they came in to collect food, blankets, etc. from the government or when they participated in a parade or circus or were exhibited at sideshows in fairs.[95] Towns often had their "local black" or Indian, a character whose outlandish and eccentric behavior offered a sort of jester-like counterpoint to the prevailing European norms of respectability. The "Duke of York," for instance, was found by one visitor to be "the great aboriginal personage in Port Townsend, and he affords much amusement to visitors and citizens."[96]

In his *Six Letters From the Colonies* (1886) R. C. Seaton described what happened when aborigines came in to Adelaide to receive their government blankets. "On these occasions they are accustomed to exhibit themselves in their native antics and dances for a little gain." While Seaton was in Adelaide, he went to witness a corroboree which the Adelaide Cricket Club had induced them to hold on the cricket ground. Fifteen thousand spectators turned up, and a pitiable scene ensued, extraordinarily anticipatory of one-day cricket spectacles in our own time. Spectators invaded the "pitch." As this happened, Seaton overheard one of the aborigines saying, "Me tink dis white fellows' corrobboree."[97]

CHAPTER TEN

The Urban Frontier and the Development of Myths of National Identity

THERE were close connections between the rise of towns and the consolidation of territorial consciousness, identity, and "pride." This occurred at many levels ranging from local districts to states, provinces, regions, and ultimately, nations. Towns became the foci of rivalry, and their state of advancement was usually a major criterion for demonstrating how impressive was the progress of the territorial unit as a whole in which they were located.

John S. Wright, in *Chicago: Past, Present, Future* (1868), gave the division of the country into states as a major reason why America would have a West of great cities. This division "will have strong influence to build important cities, each State having becoming pride in its own offspring." Some people expressed concern about the fragmenting effect on state development of intercity rivalries and competition for facilities better concentrated in one place. It was true, Wright conceded, that towns "will bark and snarl at the city that attains superiority." But, he added, "as against other States and the world outside, they will be a unit to do whatever their own chief emporium requires for its advancement." It was also true that railways were now to be "the chief motive power" for city development in the West. But legislatures had great influence over railway construction, and this was another reason why there would be many large cities. Wright extolled both *"State Sovereignty,"* which would "insure the erection of many important cities throughout the West," and *"National Union,"* which would prevent the imposition by the states of "improper restrictions" on trade.[1]

The city-building consequences of state rivalry were seen in, for example, the Wyandotte convention which met in December 1858 to devise a railroad strategy for Kansas, a new state. One aim of this strategy was seen as the supporting of the ambitions of one city in Kansas so as to ensure that the metropolis of the region would not develop in Missouri, as seemed all too likely.

Our internal improvement system, draining as it will, the richest section of our vast Union, should meet the Missouri river upon Kansas soil, and build up within our limits one of the most wealthy cities of the nation, upon whose coffers we could not call in vain, to develop all our natural resources, to assist in paying our taxes and to make other sections tributary to us, rather than we should be tributary to others[2]

Pride in the rapid rise of great cities was, as we have seen, a major element in the boosting of new countries in the nineteenth century. In Canada and Australia this seems to have reached a peak in the 1880s. It was not just individual cities that were praised but also urbanism in general, the rise of an urbanized society.[3]

But underlying this pride there was always a certain ambivalence. What did people feel proud about? Often it was that they had built towns which were comparable to those of the Old World or the East or the "mother country," were acceptable replicas of an urban civilization developed elsewhere. We have seen earlier in this study how much effort went into investing towns and cities with this kind of image—to encourage migration and the investment of capital.

What some regarded as the "colonial" framework within which appreciation of the new cities was often formed is well illustrated by William Westgarth's account of what he said to a German visitor at the 1888 Centennial Exhibition in Melbourne:

I gave him my impression that the large and varied foreign element, assembled for the Exhibition, would do more justice to Melbourne's position and prospects in the world, than was done by her own parent country. The memories of the latter were mingled with the babyhood of the place, which seemed as only but yesterday, and rather hindered the full realisation of what Melbourne now was. The Mother would begin to do so all the more now when she found her child presenting so objective a form to other nations.[4]

Much of the early celebration of cities in Australia, New Zealand, and Canada was a celebration of British enterprise. They were manifestations of the power of British imperialism. This was the regular theme of books by visitors from Britain who were writing for British audiences. In *A History of New South Wales* (1846) Thomas Henry Braim described walking along George Street, Sydney, and feeling "peculiar admiration for Old England, whose enterprise had extended so far from her own little sea-girt Isle, formed a flourishing colony almost at the antipodes, and there completely stamped her own impress." Sydney was the product of "well directed British influence and energy."[5] In *Sydney and Melbourne* (1845) Charles John Baker relates how his visit to Melbourne filled him with "patriotic pride, at the practical enterprise and energy which so remarkably distinguish our countrymen."[6] In *Twenty Years' Experience in Australia* (1840) J. Marshall referred to Melbourne as proof of "the enterprising, determined, obstacle-surmounting character of our countrymen."[7] The theme persisted into the 1880s. W. J. Woods in *A Visit to Victoria* (1886) reported on Melbourne as "a great emporium of British wealth and commerce, built and occupied by British people," essentially a "reproduction of a British metropolis."[8]

But there were also signs of an effort at synthesis of "imperial" and "colonial" contributions to the making of Australia's cities. In *Australia Visited and Revisited* (1853) Samuel Mossman and Thomas Banister described Sydney as presenting "a complete panorama of English customs and institutions, established and perpetuated by colonial enterprise."[9]

However, the weight of emphasis on the "English" and "Old World" characteristics of Australian cities crushed these tentative quests for Australian distinctiveness and left the cities exposed and vulnerable when the time came, as it did in the last decade of the nineteenth and first decade of the twentieth centuries, for the formulation of symbols of Australian national identity. It was very difficult to incorporate into the emerging national myths, "the Australian legend," cities which had so often been celebrated and publicized as being so "Old World" in character.

Furthermore, "reproductions of a British metropolis" were all very well if what were being reproduced were the attractive, "splendid" features. But, unfortunately, selective transplantation of only the desirable aspects of Old World urban civilization proved impossible. Soon the less pleasant aspects, such as poverty and slums, also began to put in an appearance. The "Old World" image, an object of so much celebration, grew increasingly tarnished. In *Victoria, The British "El Dorado"* (1870) C. R. Carter made the conventional reference to Melbourne as "wonderfully like a great and prosperous commercial city in England" but then went on to acknowledge that

Melbourne, indeed, like the older cities of Europe, to some extent affords contrasts between plenty on the one hand, and poverty on the other; proving, by the "logic of facts," that poverty in one shape or another, is a permanent evil—inseparable from the social system—always to be battled with and relieved, but never to be wholly extinguished.[10]

These negative attitudes to "Old World" cities reached a climax in the 1890s when the boom economy of Melbourne collapsed and "marvelous" city growth became equated with speculation, fraud, and human misery. There was a marked trend from pride to shame in Australians' perceptions of their cities.[11] The façades of the magnificent banks, hotels, and commercial buildings on which had been based much of the evaluation of Melbourne as a "marvelous" city by Old World standards were shown to be hollow, as false as the "fronts" of the early colonial days, concealing the fraudulent speculation that alone had enabled them to be built so splendidly and then to play their part in the deception of investors. In *Lights and Shadows of Melbourne Life* (1888) John Freeman translated to Australia a style of analysis of big city life well known and long practiced in Britain—although it reached its peak there too in the 1880s. He described the hidden life behind the magnificent buildings and the symbiotic relationship between wealth and squalor.[12]

When Henry George visited Melbourne in 1890, he began his first public lecture by using conventional booster rhetoric about the city: "The citizens here were building up the metropolis of the Southern Seas (applause)—a great—in all possibility the greatest—city of that new nation of English-speaking people that was to arise in this hemisphere." But then he drew attention to "a dark side to the picture." Was it possible that Melbourne would remain exempt from the appalling evils to be seen in other great cities of the modern world? "Already Melbourne had charitable institutions, and if he was correctly informed they were crowded nightly."[13] In a perverse sort of way such observations fueled pride because vice and slums seemed part and parcel of what it meant to be "a great city."

But there was also a widespread reaction against big cities in the quest for distinctive "Australian" attributes that could be used to define the identity and purpose of this new society—which became a nation when the colonies federated into the Australian commonwealth in 1901. In 1907 a writer in the *Herald* put the reaction in its most extreme form:

"The civilisation in the Australian cities is not new, but an old, hoary-headed, decrepit European civilisation . . . The civilisation of Australian cities is already decadent."[14] The form of the reaction which is best known today is the romanticization and idealization of the "bush" and its denizens—the "Australian legend."[15] By the 1880s writers of books about Australia—not just Australians, but also English visitors—were suggesting that the "true Australian" was a type that was developing elsewhere than in the cities. Douglas M. Gane wrote in *New South Wales and Victoria in 1885* (1886):

The Australian proper is not much seen in the large cities, for in such places congregate a body of people, either purely British or foreign, or people who would illustrate our idea of the term "colonials." . . . Examples of the Australian race are better seen in the inland parts of the colony, on the sheep-farms and in the minor townships scattered plentifully over the Australian bush.[16]

But writers of fiction, at least, needed little prompting. As Edward Kinglake noted in *The Australians at Home* (1892), most novels so far set in Australia dealt with bush and station life or "the lurid days and doings of the convicts and bushrangers," even though only a small minority of Australians actually lived in the bush.[17] Many historians have pointed out the city origins and readership of most of the literature which made "the Australian legend."[18] There was a romanticization which took little account of the grim realities of life in the Australian outback—realities of which most of the writers were unaware or on which, like Henry Lawson, they had gladly turned their backs.[19] In fact, as a literary phenomenon the "Australian legend" was a manifestation of the maturing of an urban literary culture in Australia. Yet most of the writers and artists drew their inspiration from an idealized "bush" rather than from the cities in which they and their readers lived. According to Judith M. Woodward, "in the face of the financial crash and depression of the 'nineties many writers considered that Australian cities were poor second-hand reproductions of undesirable overseas urban developments, especially those of England." The "undiscriminating adoption of overseas traditions and customs by the cities was felt to be conservative and inhibiting to Australia's future as a nation."[20] "In our overgrown cities health and strength are sapped," wrote A. J. Stephens in 1900; "the habit of productive labour is lost; and the character of the people sensibly deteriorates." "If our cancers are not extirpated, they may yet destroy the nation."[21] Some writers were later to argue that the nationalizing impulse itself derived from "the bush." Thus Vance Palmer in *The Legend of the Nineties* (1963):

There was less temptation than in the cities to regard Australia as merely an offshoot of the old world, a world whose habits and institutions must be copied with rigid fidelity. This country, with its periodic declines and dazzling recoveries, made a fool of those who came to it with fixed minds and refused to adjust themselves.[22]

The difficulty with this is to reconcile it with the urban origins of the "bush" legend. Bushmen may have had these liberated perspectives, but it was not they who wrote the poems and painted the pictures.

A revival of agrarianism and a reaction against cities appeared throughout the western world at this time. It is not surprising to find them especially marked in new societies where there had always been a rather uneasy emphasis on the "magic" character of rapid city growth and there was abundance of scope for believing that the processes of social evolution had become unhealthily distorted or accelerated. In Canada there was never quite the same emphasis on city-building as a characteristic of the people as in the United States or Australia. Indeed, it became rather notorious for its deficencies in this regard through publicizing of the comparisons with the United States in the Durham Report. When the western prairies opened up, the aim was to fill them with farmers, and, when large cities began to appear, writers displayed a rather ambivalent attitude toward them. Cities such as Winnipeg were regarded with pride, and their rise was publicized to dramatize the rapid progress of their regions. But there was also unease, fueled by the speculative booms and collapses which marked the history of prairie cities. George Grant warned that, "interesting, and after a fashion, phenomenal as Winnipeg is, it must not be supposed that we can find the true North West in its towns and cities."[23] When cities and their share of the Canadian population grew so rapidly after 1890, there was an alarmed response similar to that in Australia. People in towns and cities were described as "degenerating," and there was a cult of "nature" and the outdoor life. In Canada, as in Australia, New Zealand, and the United States, the virtues of rural life and the evils of large cities were preached aggressively by farmers' movements and newspapers and politicians claiming to represent farmers' interests and viewpoints. Concern was strengthened by the widespread intensification of rural depopulation. Cities were denounced as sucking the life blood out of the country by exercising a fatal attraction over young people.[24]

The history and force of the agrarian myth in American westward expansion have been abundantly documented.[25] The assumption that most migrants were going to settle on the land and that that is where they should go underlay the advice given in most emigrant guidebooks, gazetteers, and other works about the Midwest. The characteristic preference for country over town is well summed up in this extract from an article published in the *Western Monthly Review* in 1827. Its title is "Present Population and Future Prospects of the Western Country."

The inhabitants of crowded towns and villages, the numerous artizans and laborers in manufactories, can neither be, as a mass, so healthy, so virtuous, or happy, as free cultivators of the soil. The man, whose daily range of prospect is dusty streets, or smoky and dead brick walls, and whose views become limited by habit to the enclosure of those walls, who depends for his subsistence on the daily supplies of the market, and whose motives to action are elicited by constant and hourly struggle and competition with his fellows, will have the advantage in some points over the secluded tenant of a cabin, or a farm house. But still, taking every thing into the calculation, we would choose to be the owner of half a section of land, and daily contemplate nature, as we tilled the soil, aided in that primitive and noble employment, by our own vigorous children. The dweller in towns and villages may have more of the air and tone of society, and his daughters may keep nearer to the changes of the fashions. But we have little doubt, that, in striking the balance of enjoyment, the latter will be found to be the happier man, and more likely to have a numerous and healthy family.[26]

James L. Machor has shown how much of the discussion of towns in the Mississippi Valley in the early- and mid-nineteenth century endeavored to make their development conform, or appear to conform, to the agrarian myth.[27] In much booster literature towns were portrayed as "destined by nature" to "grow" at a particular location, as "healthy" insofar as their "growth" was founded on the development of the rural hinterland. For example, Daniel Drake in his writings about Cincinnati enfolded his chapter on the town with sections on the region's topography, climate, natural history, geology, and products of the soil.[28]

In some important respects the United States did resemble Australia. If for "Britain" one substitutes "New England," one comes across innumerable very similar references to transplanted enterprise as the driving force behind the founding and building of towns. Frederick Jackson

Turner's essay on "The Significance of the Frontier in American History" and Henry Nash Smith's *Virgin Land* may be set alongside Russel Ward's *The Australian Legend* as demonstrating the evolution of myths connecting the frontier or the bush to themes of national distinctiveness and having little or no place for towns. But the Australian and American processes were fundamentally different. For most of the nineteenth century, as Turner's essay and the U.S. Census Report indicate by bringing it to an end in 1890, the westward expansion of the United States and the "opening up of the frontier" were perceived as ongoing processes, and at every stage cities rapidly rising "in the wilderness" "as if by magic"—to use two of the regularly recurring clichés—were celebrated as part of this momentum, indeed a principal agency in ensuring that it continued. The attempts to integrate cities and towns into the "garden of the West" mythology became increasingly drowned out by the clamor of identification of cities with the fulfillment of America's "manifest destiny." Indeed, much of the rhetoric of "manifest destiny" reads as if derived from the rhetoric regularly employed by boosters to describe the evolution of their cities. As one city after another "rose" in the West, the rapid emergence of advanced urban civilization in the wilderness seemed to be the most dramatic display of the power of the United States to conquer and replace the wilderness. A word that was frequently used to described the relationship of new cities to their hinterland was "empire." Spokane aspired to control what became known as "the Inland Empire." In a book entitled *The Seat of Empire* (1870) Charles Carleton Coffin celebrated the achievements of American westward expansion in passages such as the following:

A few months ago I was on the other side of the globe, where civilization is at a standstill; where communities exist, but scarcely change; where decay is quite as probable as growth; where advancement is the exception, and not the rule. To ride through the streets of St. Paul; to behold its spacious warehouses, its elegant edifices, stores filled with the goods of all lands, the products of all climes,—furs from Hudson Bay, oranges from Messina, teas from China, coffee from Brazil, silks from Paris, and all the products of industry from our own land; to behold the streets alive with people, crowded with farmers' wagons laden with wheat and flour; to read the signs, "Young Men's Christian Association," "St. Paul Library Association"; to see elegant school-edifices and churches, beautiful private residences surrounded by lawns and adorned with works of art,—to see this in contrast with what we have so lately witnessed, and to think that this is the development of American civilization, going on now as never before, and destined to continue till all this wide region is to be thus dotted over with centres of influence and power, sends an indescribable thrill through our veins. It is not merely that we are Americans, but because in this land Christian civilization is attaining the highest development of all time.[29]

Once the "rising" of new cities ceased—and Lawrence H. Larsen argues that the modern pattern of the urban West had become established by the 1880s[30]—this kind of celebration of western cities, and boosterism using these themes, waned. Turner's essay, essentially a throwback to views of western expansion current in the 1830s, largely excluded cities from having a role in it and found distinctive Americanism elsewhere in the western experience. The cowboy image of the West rose to dominance in the era of Theodore Roosevelt and the artists Frederic Remington and Charles M. Russell. The dime novel and the movie and tourist industries vastly reinforced this image. It is only relatively recently that historians such as Richard Wade and John W. Reps have rediscovered the central role which towns and cities had in nineteenth-century perceptions of western expansion.

In Australia, as already noted, Robert Dixon, in a book significantly entitled *The Course of Empire,* argues that there was at one stage in the early nineteenth century, when the Blue Mountains were crossed and settlement began on the interior plains of New South Wales, a perception of expansion that closely resembled Jefferson's Cumberland Gap vision in the United States.[31] But this expansion did not continue. There was to be no similar process of the settling of new territories in an east-west progression. Towns established at or near harbors remained the focus of development for their hinterlands. Unlike in America, new cities did not keep rising in the wilderness and playing a major role in the growth of settlement in their regions.

For most of the nineteenth century Australians' perceptions of their cities oscillated between pride and anxiety. The pride was based on perceptions of what "colonials" had been able to achieve in such a short time. They had built fine cities that were admired by visitors from the Old World as fully the equal of their cities in terms of amenities, fine buildings, etc. It was a form of national pride even if expressed in a form which would much later be satirized in Australia as the "cultural cringe". The anxiety derived from contemporary ideas about social evolution. The direction was right but the pace was abnormal. Was it forced and there-fore dangerously offending against the "laws" of evolution? Or had Australia ever been given the chance to evolve in a "natural" way? Was not its pattern of social evolution artificially inverted and therefore fundamentally flawed from the outset?

This anxiety was kept well subdued for much of the century by the sheer rapidity of development of the big cities and the extent of the marveling at their progress, as well as by the need to suppress doubts in the interests of encouraging investment which would have been deterred had there been serious expression of concern by Australians as to the solidity of their social progress. But the anxiety was always there, not all that far beneath the surface. It manifested itself whenever there was depression and unemployment. At once the debate would, as in the late 1850s in Sydney, focus on the urban question, as there was a perception of a connection between the thousands of unemployed workers and the excessive and "unnatural" development of cities. Unemployment was seen as a manifestation of an artificial maldistribution of population between city and country.

The balance shifted very strongly in favour of pride in the 1880s when there was world-wide acclaim for "Marvellous Melbourne." It swung back even more strongly in the opposite direction in the following decade when depression revealed the rottenness of the foundations of that pride. One can better understand why this happened if one appreciates that what then came to the surface was an anxiety that had been present throughout the development of Australian society in the nineteenth century and was related to widespread assumptions as to the "normal" course which the evolution of a society should take. The "Australian legend" has roots deep in those assumptions and is inadequately understood if analysis of its origins is confined to ideas and influences peculiar to Australia.

Notes

Introduction

1. Richard C. Wade, *The Urban Frontier: Pioneer Life in Early Pittsburgh, Cincinnati, Lexington, Louisville, and St. Louis;* Norman Harper, "The Rural and Urban Frontiers."
2. On this subject see Russel Ward, *The Australian Legend;* John Carroll, ed., *Intruders in the Bush: The Australian Quest for Identity* (Melbourne: Oxford University Press, 1982); and Richard White, *Inventing Australia: Images and Identity, 1688–1980.*
3. Howard J. Nelson, "Town Founding and the American Frontier."
4. For a comment on the state of urban history in the early 1980s, see the essay by David Cannadine in David Cannadine and David Reeder, eds., *Exploring the Urban Past: Essays in Urban History by H. J. Dyos* (Cambridge: Cambridge University Press, 1982), pp. 203–22.
5. Derek Fraser and Anthony Sutcliffe, eds., *The Pursuit of Urban History.*
6. H. J. Dyos, ed., *The Study of Urban History* (London: Arnold, 1976).
7. A selection of his essays and a review of his contributions to urban history are published in Cannadine and Reeder, *Exploring the Urban Past.*
8. See, e.g., Page Smith, *As a City Upon a Hill: The Town in American History;* and Thomas J. Schlereth, "The New England Presence on the Midwest Landscape."
9. There is a developing literature in "new societies" history. Two of the most influential contributions to it are Louis Hartz, *The Founding of New Societies: Studies in the History of the United States, Latin America, South Africa, Canada, and Australia* (New York: Harcourt, Brace & World, 1964); and Donald Denoon, *Settler Capitalism: The Dynamics of Dependent Development in the Southern Hemisphere* (Oxford: Clarendon Press, 1983).
10. Wakefield's most important writings are collected in M. F. Lloyd Prichard, ed., *The Collected Works of Edward Gibbon Wakefield* (Glasgow and London: Collins, 1968).
11. Gunther Barth, *Instant Cities: Urbanization and the Rise of San Francisco and Denver.*
12. For Canada see the works by Alan F. J. Artibise cited in the bibliography.

1. Urban Frontiers

1. Simcoe's plans are documented in E. A. Cruikshank, ed., *The Correspondence of Lieut. Governor John Graves Simcoe, With Allied Documents Relating to His Administration of the Government of Upper Canada,* 3 vols. (Toronto: Ontario Historical Society, 1923–25).

2. This region is surveyed in Malcolm J. Rohrbough, *The Trans-Appalachian Frontier: People, Societies, and Institutions 1775–1850* (New York: Oxford University Press, 1978). "The Urban Dimension" is dealt with in ch. 14.

3. Harry N. Scheiber, "Urban Rivalry and Internal Improvements in the Old Northwest 1820–1860," *Ohio History* (Oct. 1962), 71(3):227–39.

4. There is extensive coverage of the early history of Louisville in Richard C. Wade, *The Urban Frontier: Pioneer Life in Early Pittsburgh, Cincinnati, Lexington, Louisville, and St. Louis.* Perceptions of the town by observers are analyzed in Carl E. Kramer, "Images of a Developing City: Louisville, 1800–1830," and "City with a Vision: Images of Louisville in the 1830s."

5. John Howison, *Sketches of Upper Canada, Domestic, Local, and Characteristic . . .* (Edinburgh and London, 1821), pp. 197–98.

6. Gilbert A. Stelter, "John Galt: The Writer as Town Booster and Builder."

7. John D. Haeger, "Capital Mobilization and the Urban Center: The Wisconsin Lakeports," *Mid-America: An Historical Review* (April–July 1978), 60(2):75–93.

8. For an account of the founding and planning of Madison see John W. Reps, *The Making of Urban America: A History of City Planning in the United States,* pp. 275–77.

9. Lawrence H. Larsen, "Chicago's Midwest Rivals: Cincinnati, St. Louis, and Milwaukee," *Chicago History* (Fall 1976), 5(3):141–51.

10. Scheiber, "Urban Rivalry and Internal Improvements," p. 228.

11. Bayrd Still, "The Growth of Milwaukee as Recorded by Contemporaries," p. 266.

12. Katherine Hart, ed., *Alphonse in Austin: Being Excerpts from the Official Letters Written to the French Foreign Ministry by Alphonse Dubois de Saligny, Chargé d'Affaires of the Kingdom of France to the Republic of Texas with Divers Notes Concerning the Pig War* (Austin: Encino Press, 1967), p. 10.

13. New York *Evening Star,* June 1837, quoted in John G. Gregory, ed., *Southwestern Wisconsin: A History of Old Crawford County* (Chicago: Clarke, 1932), 1:108.

14. Louis Leonard Tucker, "Cincinnati: Athens of the West, 1830–1861."

15. See the reflections on the history of Cairo in Gerald George, "Cairo and Chicago: Cities at the Center," *Chicago History* (Summer 1985), 14(2):38–48.

16. For documentation relating to the founding of Melbourne, see Michael Cannon, ed., *Historical Records of Victoria, Foundation Series, vol. 3: The Early Development of Melbourne* (Melbourne: Victorian Government Printing Office, 1984).

17. The history of the foundation and settlement of South Australia is told in D. Pike, *Paradise of Dissent: South Australia 1829–1857* (Carlton, Victoria: Melbourne University Press, 1967), and A. Grenfell Price, *The Foundation and Settlement of South Australia 1829–1845: A Study of the Colonization Movement, Based on the Records of the South Australian Government and on Other Authoritative Documents* (Adelaide: Preece, 1924).

18. D. N. Jeans, "Official Town-Founding Procedures in New South Wales, 1828–1842," p. 228.

19. For the planning of Detroit see Reps, *The Making of Urban America*, pp. 264–72.

20. John W. Reps, *Cities of the American West: A History of Frontier Urban Planning*, pp. 134–39.

21. J. Rutherford, ed., *The Founding of New Zealand: The Journals of Felton Mathew, First Surveyor-General of New Zealand, and His Wife 1840–1847* (Dunedin and Wellington: A. H. and A. W. Reed, 1940).

22. G. P. de T. Glazebrook, *The Story of Toronto* (Toronto and Buffalo: University of Toronto Press, 1971), pp. 19–23; Edith G. Firth ed., *The Town of York 1793–1815: A Collection of Documents of Early Toronto* (Toronto: Champlain Society, 1962), pp. 10, 22, 30; Cruikshank, *Correspondence of Simcoe*, 1:18, 27.

23. Macquarie to Castlereagh, April 30, 1810, *Historical Records of Australia, Series I: Governor's Despatches to and from England* (1916), 7:269.

24. *Lachlan Macquarie Governor of New South Wales: Journals of His Tours in New South Wales and Van Diemen's Land 1810–1822* (Sydney: Trustees of the Public Library of New South Wales, 1956), p. 40; Frank Crowley, ed., *A Documentary History of Australia, vol. 1: Colonial Australia, 1788–1840* (West Melbourne: Nelson, 1980), p. 212.

25. Brian H. Fletcher, *Ralph Darling: A Governor Maligned* (Melbourne: Oxford University Press, 1984), pp. 173–78.

26. D. Markey, *More a Symbol Than a Success: Foundation Years of the Swan River Colony* (Bayswater, Western Australia: Westbooks, 1977), p. 35.

27. Alan Atkinson, "The Government of Time and Space in 1838," pp. 7–11.

28. Bernard Semmel, *The Rise of Free Trade Imperialism: Classical Political Economy, the Empire of Free Trade and Imperialism 1750–1850* (Cambridge: Cambridge University Press, 1970); John Gallagher and Ronald Robinson, "The Imperialism of Free Trade," in A. G. L. Shaw, ed., *Great Britain and the Colonies 1815–1865*, pp. 142–63 (London: Methuen 1970).

29. *Irish University Press Series of British Parliamentary Papers: Colonies, General. 2: Report from the Select Committee on Disposal of Lands in the Colonies* (1836), *Minutes of Evidence*, 11:46.

30. *Irish University Press Series of British Parliamentary Papers: Colonies, Australia. 2: Minutes of Evidence Taken Before the Select Committee on South Australia* (1841), p. 230.

31. Felix Wakefield, *Colonial Surveying With a View to the Disposal of Waste Land: In a Report to the New-Zealand Company* (London, 1849), p. 26.

32. Herman Merivale, *Lectures on Colonization and Colonies Delivered Before the University of Oxford in 1839, 1840, & 1841 and Reprinted in 1861* (London: Oxford University Press, 1928), p. 421.

33. *Historical Records of Australia, Series I: Governor's Despatches to and from England* (1916), 20:676.

34. *Ibid.,* p. 644 and 21:134.

35. W. H. Miller, *The History of Kansas City, Together With a Sketch of the Commercial Resources of the Country with Which It Is Surrounded* (Kansas City, 1881), p. 6.

36. *The Victorian Hansard* (1859–60), 5:282.

37. Weston Bate, *A History of Brighton* (Carlton, Victoria: Melbourne University Press, 1962), p. 58.

38. "Oculus," *The Home of the Badgers, or a Sketch of the Early History of Wisconsin, with a Series of Familiar Letters and Remarks on Territorial Character and Characteristics, Etc.* (Milwaukee, 1845), pp. 10–11.

39. The history of the major midwestern cities of the mid-nineteenth century and of their relationships with one another is well summarized in Lawrence H. Larsen, "Chicago's Midwest Rivals."

40. Adna Ferrin Weber, *The Growth of Cities in the Nineteenth Century: A Study in Statistics,* p. 1.

41. Sean Glynn, *Urbanisation in Australian History 1788–1900,* pp. 3–5.

42. *Ibid.,* p. 41.

43. Weber, *The Growth of Cities,* p. 1.

44. Theodore Roosevelt, *The Winning of the West* (New York and London: Putnam, 1905), 4:234–37.

2. *The Making of Images of the Urban Frontier*

1. One comes across some evidence of use of booster publications. Here is an extract from a doctor in Madison, Wisconsin, to a friend in 1855: "I will send you a little pamphlet containing the history & Prospects & Destiny of Madison with the hopes of pursuading you to direct your steps up this way instead of going to Keokuk." F. Garvin Davenport and Katye Lou Davenport, eds., "Practicing Medicine in Madison, 1855–57: Alexander Schue's letters to Robert Peter," *Wisconsin Magazine of History* (Sept. 1942), 26(1):81.

2. Charlotte Erickson, *Invisible Immigrants: The Adaptation of English and Scottish Immigrants in Nineteenth-Century America* (Coral Gables, Fl.: University of Miami Press, 1972), p. 35.

3. A major source on this literature and on emigrants' guidebooks in general is Ray Allen Billington, *Land of Savagery, Land of Promise: The European Image of the American Frontier in the Nineteenth Century.*

4. An example of such a publication is Samuel Mossman, *Emigrants' Letters from Australia* (London, 1853). However, it is unusual in that Mossman supplies a critical commentary with advice on how emigrants' letters should be read and a warning that some are fakes.

5. Edgar Langsdorf and R. W. Richmond, eds., "Letters of Daniel R. Anthony, 1857–1862," *Kansas Historical Quarterly* (Spring 1958), 24(1):9–10, 25.

6. Lela Barnes, ed., "An Editor Looks at Early-Day Kansas: The Letters of Charles Monroe Chase," *Kansas Historical Quarterly* (Summer 1960), 26(2):117, 120.

7. For Tocqueville's travels see George Wilson Pierson, *Tocqueville and Beaumont in America* (New York: Oxford University Press, 1938). Siegfried's writings included *Democracy in New Zealand,* first published in French in 1904 and English in 1914. See the new edition by D. A. Hamer (Wellington, New Zealand: Victoria University Press with Price Milburn, 1982). For James Bryce see *The American Commonwealth,* first published in 1888, especially chapter 121, "The Temper of the West," and Edmund S. Ions, *James Bryce and American Democracy, 1870–1922* (New York: Humanities Press, 1970).

8. David A. Shannon, ed., *Beatrice Webb's American Diary 1898* (Madison: University of Wisconsin Press, 1963); D. A. Hamer, ed., *The Webbs in New Zealand 1898: Beatrice Webb's Diary with Entries by Sidney Webb* (Wellington: Price Milburn for Victoria University Press, 1974).

9. For Dickens see *American Notes* (1842) and *Martin Chuzzlewit* (1843). A good modern survey is Michael Slater, ed., *Dickens on America & the Americans* (Hassocks, Sussex: Harvester Press, 1979). For Trollope see *North America* (London, 1862), and *Australia and New Zealand* (Melbourne, 1873). See also Asa Briggs, "Trollope the Traveller," *The Collected Essays of Asa Briggs,* vol. 2: *Images, Problems, Standpoints, Forecasts* (Brighton, Sussex: Harvester Press, 1985), pp. 89–115.

10. Pierson, *Tocqueville and Beaumont in America,* pp. 236–46.

11. Eugene P. Moehring, *Urban America and the Foreign Traveler, 1815–1855* (New York: Arno Press, 1974), p. 66; Glen E. Holt, "St. Louis Observed 'from Two Different Worlds': An Exploration of the City Through French and English Travelers' Accounts, 1874–1889," *Bulletin of the Missouri Historical Society* (Jan. 1973), 29(2):66.

12. Holt, "St. Louis Observed," p. 64.

13. A. D. Jones, *Illinois and the West: With a Township Map, Containing the Latest Surveys and Improvements* (Boston and Philadelphia, 1838), p. 80.

14. J. Richard Beste, *The Wabash: or Adventures of an English Gentleman's Family in the Interior of America* (London, 1855), 2:65–66.

15. Michael Davitt, *Life and Progress in Australia* (London, 1898), p. 173.

16. Edward Dicey, *Six Months in the Federal States* (London, 1863), 2:63, 121.

17. Or else being driven around by townspeople and shown carefully selected sights, as happened to John White when he was given a tour of "the icons of Omaha": the building intended for the state capitol, the baseball ground, "the scalped man of Omaha." John White, *Sketches from America: Part I—Canada; Part II—a Pic-nic to the Rocky Mountains; Part III—The Irish in America* (London, 1870), pp. 229–31. In *Main Street* Sinclair Lewis used a half-hour stroll through Gopher Prairie by the newly arrived Carol Kennicott as the

basis for extensive generalizing by her—and by himself—on the sameness of American towns.

18. Charles Lord Russell of Killowen, *Diary of a Visit to the United States of America in the Year 1883* (n.p.: United States Catholic Historical Society, 1910), p. 66.

19. F. Barham Zincke, *Last Winter in the United States: Being Table Talk Collected During a Tour Through the Late Southern Confederation, the Far West, the Rocky Mountains, &c.* (London, 1868), pp. 180–81. In *Letters from Canada and the United States* (London, 1865), p. 84, George Tuthill Barrett wrote: "I do not know that I have anything particular to say about the city of Chicago itself. . . . all American cities repeat themselves, like the Chinese."

20. Anselm L. Strauss, *Images of the American City*, p. 4.

21. Herbert Hunt, *Tacoma: Its History and Its Builders: A Half Century of Activity* (Chicago: Clarke, 1916), 1:188.

22. *Helena, Montana: Its Past, Present and Future* (Helena, [1891?], pp. 3–6.

23. Maurice O'Connor Morris, *Rambles in the Rocky Mountains: With a Visit to the Gold Fields of Colorado* (London, 1864), pp. 4–5.

24. Klaus H. Burmeister, ed., *Western Canada 1909: Travel Letters by Wilhelm Cohnstaedt* (Regina: Canadian Plains Research Center, University of Regina, 1976), pp. 18, 23.

25. Trollope, *Australia and New Zealand*, p. 251; George Augustus Sala, *America Revisited: From the Bay of New York to the Gulf of Mexico, and from Lake Michigan to the Pacific* (London, 1882), 2:153. John White wrote about his visit to Omaha that, before he was driven around the town, "I had done what no American would do, except under compulsion, namely, explore the town upon foot" (*Sketches from America*, p. 229).

26. Arnold Schrier and Joyce Story, eds., *A Russian Looks at America: The Journey of Alexsandr Borisovich Lakier in 1857* (Chicago and London: University of Chicago Press, 1979), p. 209.

27. Maturin M. Ballou, *Under the Southern Cross or Travels in Australia, Tasmania, New Zealand, Samoa, and Other Pacific Islands* (Boston, [1887]), p. 231.

28. *Sketches of Life in The United States of North America and Texas as Observed by Friedrich W. von Wrede: Compiled by Emil Drescher In Accordance with Journals and Verbal Statements, Cassel, Germany 1844* (Waco, Texas: Texian Press, 1970), p. 38.

29. Trollope, *Australia and New Zealand*, p. 139. For similar appreciative comments on Sydney's streets see Walter Coote, *Wanderings, South and East* (London, 1882), p. 17; Rosamond and Florence Hill, *What We Saw in Australia* (London, 1875), p. 271.

30. See William Darby, *A Tour From the City of New York, to Detroit* (New York, 1819), p. 35.

31. Capt. H. Butler Stoney, *A Residence in Tasmania: With a Descriptive Tour Through the Island, From Macquarie Harbour to Circular Head* (London, 1856), p. 12.

32. For bird's-eye views see the many writings by John W. Reps, e.g., *The*

Making of Urban America: A History of City Planning in the United States; Cities of the American West: A History of Frontier Urban Planning; Cities on Stone: Nineteenth Century Lithographic Images of the Urban West; Views and Viewmakers of Urban America: Lithographs of Towns and Cities in the United States and Canada, Notes on the Artists and Publishers, and a Union Catalog of Their Work, 1825–1925.

33. Davitt, *Life and Progress in Australasia*, p. 114.
34. David Kennedy, Jr., *Kennedy's Colonial Travel: A Narrative of a Four Years' Tour Through Australia, New Zealand, Canada, &c.* (Edinburgh and London, [1876]), p. 363.
35. [A. W. H. Rose], *The Emigrant Churchman in Canada. By a Pioneer of the Wilderness* (London, 1849), 1:170.
36. G. Butler Earp, *The Gold Colonies of Australia, and Gold Seeker's Manual* (London, 1853), p. 68.
37. Olympia Chamber of Commerce, *Olympia: The Capital City of the State of Washington, and the Seat of Government of Thurston County* (Olympia: Recorder Publishing, [1905?]), p. 27.
38. Charles Dudley Warner, *Studies in the South and West With Comments on Canada* (New York, 1889), pp. 265–66.
39. This change is discussed in Graeme Davison, "The Picture of Melbourne 1835–1985."
40. Sir Richard S. Bonnycastle, *The Canadas in 1841* (London, 1841), 1:71–72.
41. *Daily Miners' Express* (Dubuque), Dec. 9, 1852, quoted in Loren Nelson Horton, "Town Planning, Growth, and Architecture in Selected Mississippi River Towns of Iowa, 1833–1860," Ph.D. dissertation, University of Iowa, 1978, p. 101.
42. A. D. Munson, ed., *The Minnesota Messenger, Containing Sketches of the Rise and Progress of Minnesota* (St. Paul, 1855), pp. 17, 45, 47.
43. William M. Thayer, *Marvels of the New West: A Vivid Portrayal of the Stupendous Marvels in the Vast Wonderland West of the Missouri River* (Norwich, Conn., 1877), p. 373. Visitors were indeed so impressed. "In Kansas they parade their public academies on the highest hill in town, and if there is but one good house visible, it is the common school house." William D. Bickham, *From Ohio to the Rocky Mountains: Editorial Correspondence of the Dayton (Ohio) Journal* (Dayton, 1879), p. 21.
44. Munson, *The Minnesota Messenger*, p. 45.
45. Charles Cist, *Cincinnati in 1841: Its Early Annals and Future Prospects* (Cincinnati, 1841), p. 238.
46. A. Lillie, *Canada: Physical, Economic, and Social* (Toronto, 1855), pp. 158–59.
47. Isabella L. Bird, *A Lady's Life in the Rocky Mountains* (Norman and London: University of Oklahoma Press, 1960), pp. 138–39.
48. Bayrd Still, "The Growth of Milwaukee as Recorded by Contemporaries," p. 283.

49. Boston *Chronotype,* quoted in Bayrd Still, *Milwaukee: The History of a City* (Madison: State Historical Society of Wisconsin, 1948), p. 196.

50. John Gates Thurston, *A Journal of a Trip to Illinois in 1836* (Mount Pleasant, Mich.: Cumming, 1971), p. 53.

51. [Atchison, Topeka, and Santa Fe Railroad Company], *The Old and the New. Southwest Kansas As It Was, As It Is, As It Will be* (n. p., n. d.), p. 5.

52. Kate Milner Rabb, ed., *A Tour Through Indiana in 1840: The Diary of John Parsons of Petersburg, Virginia* (New York: Robert McBride, 1920), pp. 312–14.

53. D. H. Pike, "The Diary of James Coutts Crawford: Extracts on Aborigines and Adelaide, 1839 and 1841," *South Australiana* (March 1965), 4(1):14.

54. Davitt, *Life and Progress in Australasia,* p. 113.

55. J. Herbert Roberts, *A World-Tour: Being a Year's Diary, Written 1884–'85* (Liverpool, [1886]), p. 481.

56. Kennedy, *Kennedy's Colonial Travel,* pp. 14–15.

57. Lela Barnes, ed., "North Central Kansas in 1887–1889: From the Letters of Leslie and Susan Snow of Junction City," *Kansas Historical Quarterly* (Autumn 1963), 29(3):279.

58. Schrier and Story, *A Russian Looks at America,* p. 206.

59. Roger W. Lotchin, *San Francisco 1846–1856: From Hamlet to City* (Lincoln and London: University of Nebraska Press, 1979), p. 296.

60. Strauss, *Images of the American City,* p. 156.

61. "The people here [in Sydney] are not even as a rule satisfied with buildings essentially useful and avowedly untasteful; they too often make wild efforts at architectural display, and at one and the same time mar the useful purposes of their buildings, and fall short of aesthetic excellence." Walter Coote, *Wanderings, South and East* (London, 1882), pp. 17–18.

62. Arthur G. Guillemard, *Over Land and Sea: A Log of Travel Round the World in 1873–1874* (London, 1875), pp. 10–11.

63. Hunt, *Tacoma,* 1:329.

64. *Portland, Oregon* (Portland, n. d.), pp. 55–56.

65. Carl Abbott, "Indianapolis in the 1850s: Popular Economic Thought and Urban Growth," p. 295; and *Boosters and Businessmen: Popular Economic Thought and Urban Growth in the Antebellum Middle West.*

66. Don Harrison Doyle, *The Social Order of a Frontier Community: Jacksonville, 1825–70;* Alan F. J. Artibise, "Boosterism and the Development of Prairie Cities, 1871–1913," and *Winnipeg: A Social History of Urban Growth 1874–1914,* pp. 12–15.

67. E. Daniel and Annette Potts, eds., *A Yankee Merchant in Goldrush Australia: The Letters of George Francis Train* (London and Melbourne: Heinemann, 1970), pp. 23–25, 94, 117.

68. Sir William Denison, *Varieties of Vice-Regal Life* (London, 1870), 1:340.

69. William Howitt, *Land, Labour and Gold or Two Years in Victoria: With Visits to Sydney and Van Diemen's Land* (1855; Kilmore: Lowden, 1927), p. 21.

70. Lewis Atherton, *Main Street on the Middle Border,* pp. xv–xvi; Newell Larry Sims, *A Hoosier Village: A Sociological Study With Special Reference to Social Causation* (New York: Columbia University Press, 1912), pp. 81–82.

71. William Kelly, *Life in Victoria or Victoria in 1853, and Victoria in 1858* (London, 1859), p. 160.

72. Howard P. Segal, "Jeff W. Hayes: Reform Boosterism and Urban Utopianism," p. 348.

73. For a survey of these writers see J. Christopher Schnell and Katherine B. Clinton, "The New West: Themes in Nineteenth Century Urban Promotion, 1815–1880."

74. *Documents and Addresses of I. M. Weston While Mayor of Grand Rapids, Mich. 1888–9* (New York, 1889), pp. 63–64.

75. *Helena Illustrated: Capital of the State of Montana* (Minneapolis, 1890), p. 24.

76. Thayer, *Marvels of the New West,* p. 344. Cf. the comments of a modern historian: "the image of the function of a city held by those dominant in city life ultimately determined the form and function of many features of city life. ... Because most cities in North America have emerged in response to economic developments, such as the opening of agricultural or mining districts, the business community—that amorphous group who own and operate business enterprises—has normally determined the course of community development." W. C. McKee, "The Vancouver Park System, 1886–1929: A Product of Local Businessmen," *Urban History Review* (1978), 3:33.

77. John Shaw, *A Gallop to the Antipodes, Returning Overland Through India* (London, 1858), pp. 56–57.

78. Ian Turner, ed., *The Australian Dream: A Collection of Anticipations About Australia from Captain Cook to the Present Day,* pp. 48–49.

79. Stewart Garvie Hilts, "In Praise of Progress: Attitudes to Urbanization in Southwestern Ontario, 1850–1900," Ph.D. dissertation, University of Toronto, 1981, pp. 170, 349–50.

80. James B. Brown, *Views of Canada and the Colonists* (Edinburgh, 1851), p. 289.

3. Old World and New World

1. Adna Ferrin Weber, *The Growth of Cities in the Nineteenth Century: A Study in Statistics,* p. 1.

2. The Chamber of Commerce, Blaine, Washington, *How to Make Money: The City of Blaine* (Blaine, 1891), p. 21.

3. George Wilson Pierson, *Tocqueville and Beaumont in America* (New York: Oxford University Press, 1938), p. 237.

4. "Spirit of our Future Policy," *Australia Felix Monthly Magazine* (June 1849), 1:42–44.

5. On the "symbolic antithesis" of New World and Old World see Cushing Strout, *The American Image of the Old World,* p. 1.

6. F. Eldershaw, *Australia as It Really Is* (London, 1854), p. 47. For a similar comment see Anthony Trollope, *Australia and New Zealand* (Melbourne, 1873), p. 542.

7. However note the quotation from the biography of Truman Marcellus Post in Don Harrison Doyle, *The Social Order of a Frontier Community. Jacksonville, Illinois 1825–70*, p. 1.

8. John Galt, *Lawrie Todd: or, The Settlers in the Woods* (London, [1832], pp. 165–67.

9. *The Autobiography of John Galt* (Philadelphia and Boston, 1834), 2:49–53.

10. Elizabeth Waterston, "Town and Country in John Galt: A Literary Perspective," p. 19; Elizabeth Waterson, "Bogle Corbet and the Annals of New World Parishes," p. 59; Gilbert A. Stelter, "John Galt: The Writer as Town Booster and Builder," pp. 26–27.

11. William H. G. Kingston, *Western Wanderings or, a Pleasure Tour in the Canadas* (London, 1856), 2:26.

12. Rev. Henry Bushnell, *The History of Granville Licking County, Ohio* (Columbus, Ohio, 1889), p. 44.

13. Edward Eggleston, *The Mystery of Metropolisville* (New York, 1884), p. 97. For the difficulties involved in finding out when a town was founded or indeed what "the city-founding process" involved see Howard J. Nelson, "Town Founding and the American Frontier," pp. 9–10.

14. "A Retired Officer of the Hon. East India Company's Service" [T. J. Maslen], *The Friend of Australia; or, a Plan for Exploring the Interior, and for Carrying on a Survey of the Whole Continent of Australia* (London, 1830), pp. 260–69. In *Suggestions for the Improvement of Our Towns and Houses* (London, 1843), Maslen made proposals for the planning of new towns both in Britain and in "our Australian Colonies."

15. Robert Pemberton, *The Happy Colony* (London, 1854), pp. 76, 81, 128.

16. "Melbourne as It Is, and as It Ought To Be," *Australasian* (Oct. 1850), 1:138–39. For laments over the never-to-be-repeated opportunities for building a fine city that were being lost in Melbourne at this time see N. L. Kentish, *Proposals for Establishing in Melbourne, The Capital of Victoria, (Which is Australia Felix,) A Company* (Melbourne, [184?]), pp. 93–95; William Howitt, *Land, Labour and Gold or Two Years in Victoria: With Visits to Sydney; and Van Diemen's Land* (Kilmore: Lowden, 1972), pp. 8, 21.

17. For an example of sensitivity to this on the part of a colonial town planner see W. R. Golding, *The Birth of Central Queensland 1802–1859* (Brisbane: Smith & Paterson, 1966), pp. 195–96.

18. There is extensive comment on this in D. A. Hamer, *The New Zealand Liberals: The Years of Power, 1891–1912* (Auckland: Auckland University Press, 1988).

19. Morton and Lucia White, *The Intellectual Versus the City: From Thomas Jefferson to Frank Lloyd Wright*, pp. 7–19.

20. James L. Machor, "Urbanization and the Western Garden: Synthesizing City and Country in Antebellum America," pp. 421–23. To some extent the

"city of the West" operated more as a metaphor, a "summary concept" of the "characteristic American desire for the best of all possible worlds," than as a reference to geographical location on the frontier. To Emerson "what made American cities Western was not so much their geographical location as their economic and psychological orientation." Michael H. Cowan, *City of the West: Emerson, America, and Urban Metaphor,* pp. 26–34.

21. Charles N. Glaab, "The Historian and the American Urban Tradition."

22. John S. Fisher, *A Builder of the West: The Life of General William Jackson Palmer* (Caldwell, Idaho: Caxton, 1939), pp. 202–3. On the migration of "the East" to "the West," see C. D. Wilber, *The Great Valleys and Prairies of Nebraska and the Northwest,* 3d ed. (Omaha, 1881), pp. 351–52.

23. Daniel S. Curtiss, *Western Portraiture, and Emigrants' Guide: A Description of Wisconsin, Illinois, and Iowa; With Remarks on Minnesota, and Other Territories* (New York, 1852), p. 323.

24. John Martineau, *Letters from Australia* (London, 1869), p. 18.

25. H. H. Hayter, "The Concentration of Population in Australian Capital Cities," *Report of the Fourth Meeting of the Australasian Association for the Advancement of Science* (Hobart, 1892), pp. 542–46.

26. "A Colonist of Twenty Years' Standing, and Late Member of a Colonial Legislature" [C. R. Carter], *Victoria, The British "El Dorado"; or, Melbourne in 1869: Shewing the Advantages of That Colony as a Field for Emigration* (London, 1870), pp. 20–21.

27. Captain Willard Glazier, *Down the Great River* (Philadelphia, 1891), pp. 172–73.

28. Ralph Gregory, "Count Baudissin on Missouri Towns," *Bulletin of the Missouri Historical Society* (Jan. 1971), 27(2):114.

29. For an example see W. H. Scotter, *Ashburton: A History with Records of Town and County* (Ashburton [New Zealand]: Ashburton Borough and County Councils, 1972), p. 60.

30. William Hughes, *The Australian Colonies: Their Origin and Present Condition* (London, 1853), p. 171.

31. Timothy Flint, *Recollections of the Last Ten Years* (1826; New York: Knopf, 1932) p. 39. In a book published in 1813 the Russian Consul-General in Philadelphia compared Russia and the United States with respect to the rapid development of impressive cities—St. Petersburg, Philadelphia, New York—where, little more than a century before, there had been nothing but "impenetrable forests and marshes, inhabited by bears and wolves." Marc Pachter and Frances Wein, eds., *Abroad in America: Visitors to the New Nation 1776–1914,* p. 15.

32. Morris Birkbeck, *Notes on a Journey in America, from the Coast of Virginia to the Territory of Illinois, with Proposals for the Establishment of a Colony of English* (1818: Ann Arbor: University Microfilms, 1968), p. 66.

33. Flint, *Recollections,* p. 43.

34. John Howison, *Sketches of Upper Canada, Domestic, Local, and Characteristic* (Edinburgh and London, 1821), pp. 115–16.

35. C. P. Lucas, ed., *Lord Durham's Report on the Affairs of British North America* (Oxford: Clarendon Press, 1912), 2:212–13.

36. D. McLeod, *A Brief Review of the Settlement of Upper Canada by the U.E. Loyalists and Scotch Highlanders in 1783 . . .* , (Cleveland, 1841), pp. 7–11.

37. Capt. J. E. Alexander, *Transatlantic Sketches; Comprising Visits to the Most Interesting Scenes in North and South America, and the West Indies: With Notes on Negro Slavery and Canadian Emigration* (London, 1833), 2:171–72.

38. W. H. Smith, *Canada: Past, Present and Future, Being a Historical, Geographical, Geological and Statistical Account of Canada West* (Toronto, [1851]), 2:466–70.

39. For an example see N. C. Meeker's letter to the New York *Tribune,* Oct. 11, 1869, quoted in David Boyd, *A History: Greeley and the Union Colony of Colorado* (Greeley, 1890), pp. 17–18. This attitude resurfaces in Sinclair Lewis' *Main Street.*

40. Howison, *Sketches of Upper Canada,* p. 116.

41. Captain Frederick Marryat, *Diary in America* (London: Nicholas Vane, 1960), pp. 114–19. Another traveler who commented on the Rathbun case was William Brown. He found that, when Rathbun was released from jail, "the whole town turned out *en masse,* accompanied with music, flags, and banners, to welcome him home again; and not only this, but every workman in the city contributed one day's wages, every merchant, professional man, shopkeeper, and tradesman, contributed one day's profit, towards starting him again in business." William Brown, *America: A Four-Years' Residence in the United States and Canada . . .* (Leeds, 1849), p. 14.

42. Sandra Martin and Roger Hall, eds., *Rupert Brooke in Canada* (Toronto: P.M.A. Books, [1978]), p. 55.

43. Marryat, *Diary in America,* pp. 133–34.

44. Edward Dicey, *Six Months in the Federal States* (London, 1863), 2:130.

45. C. Hursthouse, *New Zealand, The "Britain of the South": With a Chapter on the Native War, and Our Future Native Policy* (London, 1861), pp. 147–48.

46. A. Russell, *A Tour Through the Australian Colonies in 1839, With Notes and Incidents of a Voyage Round the Globe, Calling at New Zealand and South America* (Glasgow, 1840), p. 167.

47. [W. Shaw], *The Land of Promise; or, My Impressions of Australia* (London, 1854), p. 144.

48. N. S. Shaler, "A Winter Journey in Colorado," *Atlantic Monthly* (Jan. 1881), 47(279):49.

49. Nat Gould, *Town and Bush: Stray Notes on Australia* (London, 1896), p. 25.

50. Graeme Davison, "Sydney and the Bush: An Urban Context for the Australian Legend," pp. 119–22; and "R.E.N. Twopeny and Town Life in Australia," pp. 298–99.

51. Garnet Walch, *Victoria in 1880* (Melbourne, [1881]), pp. 165–66.

52. Percy Clarke, *The "New Chum" in Australia or The Scenery, Life, and Manners of Australians in Town and Country* (London, 1886), p. 26. For criti-

cism of this tendency to compare Melbourne with London see R. H. Horne, *Australian Facts and Prospects* . . . (London, 1859), pp. 195–97.

53. Edward Brown Fitton, *New Zealand: Its Present Condition, Prospects and Resources* (London, 1856), p. 272.

54. A. Lillie, *Canada: Physical, Economic, and Social* (Toronto, 1855), p. 158.

55. Kingston, *Western Wanderings,* 1:viii, 94–95, 117–18.

56. William H. G. Kingston, *How to Emigrate; or, The British Colonists* (London, 1855), p. 40.

57. Eldershaw, *Australia as It Really Is,* p. 47. Cf. this American reference: "Not a few of the citizens of the East express considerable surprise on their first visit to Muscatine at not finding any traces of the barbarism of frontier life." O. G. Jack, *A Brief History of Muscatine* (Muscatine, Iowa, 1870), p. 58.

58. Joyce Neill, ed., *Plum Duff and Cake: The Journal of James Nichols 1874–5* (Christchurch: Pegasus, 1975), p. 133.

59. *Dr Ludwig Leichhardt's Letters from Australia During the Years March 23, 1842, to April 3, 1848* (Melbourne: Pan Publishers, [1944]), pp. 14–18.

60. Thomas Henry Braim, *New Homes: The Rise, Progress, Present Position, and Future Prospects of Each of the Australian Colonies and New Zealand, Regarded as Homes for All Classes of Emigrants* (London, 1879), p. 24.

61. Kingston, *How to Emigrate,* pp. 18, 188.

62. "A Colonist," *Life's Work As It Is; or, The Emigrant's Home in Australia* (London, 1867), pp. v, 18–24. In the story "Emmeline" in Mrs. Charles Clacy, *Lights and Shadows of Australian Life* (London, 1854), 1:23, a similar experience happens to the hero, George, when he reaches Sydney. "Here everything surprised and delighted George; he had expected a straggling, half-built town, and found a city, which, in many respects, may dare to rival our great metropolis, and need not dread the contrast."

63. Bernard Smith, *The Antipodean Manifesto: Essays in Art and History,* p. 86.

64. John F. Carrère, *Spokane Falls Washington Territory, and its Tributary Country* (Spokane Falls, 1889), p. 21.

65. Nathan H. Parker, *The Kansas and Nebraska Handbook, For 1857–8* (Boston, 1857), p. 169. This passage is repeated in James M. Woolworth, *Nebraska in 1857* (Omaha City and New York, 1857), p. 95.

66. Curtiss, *Western Portraiture,* pp. 298–99.

67. Alfred Simmons, *Old England and New Zealand* (London, 1879), pp. 51–52.

68. Rev. James Ballantyne, *Homes and Homesteads in the Land of Plenty: Handbook of Victoria as a Field for Emigration* (Melbourne, 1871), p. 44. For further comment on the effect of Australian cities on the new arrival, see R. E. N. Twopeny, *Town Life in Australia* (London, 1883), p. 1.

69. James B. Brown, *View of Canada and the Colonists* (Edinburgh, 1851), pp. 282–85.

70. Martineau, *Letter from Australia,* pp. 13–14.

71. Captain [John] Henderson, *Excursions and Adventures in New South Wales* (London, 1854), 1:68–69.

72. "An Old Colonist" [W. J. Pratt], *Colonial Experiences; Or, Incidents and Reminiscences of Thirty-Four Years in New Zealand* (London, 1877), pp. 285–86.

73. William D. Bickham, *From Ohio to the Rocky Mountains: Editorial Correspondence of the Dayton (Ohio) Journal* (Dayton, 1879), pp. 70, 83.

74. William Westgarth, *Victoria; Late Australia Felix, or Port Phillip District of New South Wales; Being an Historical and Descriptive Account of the Colony and its Gold Mines* (Edinburgh and London, 1853), pp. 67–68.

75. Charles John Baker, *Sydney and Melbourne; With Remarks on the Present State and Future Prospects of New South Wales, and Practical Advice to Emigrants of Various Classes* (London, 1845), pp. 11–14, 132.

76. Maslen, *The Friend of Australia,* pp. 256–57.

77. Shaw, *The Land of Promise,* p. 10.

78. Samuel Stephens in a letter Feb. 12, 1842, quoted in Ruth M. Allan, *Nelson: A History of Early Settlement* (Wellington: A. H. & A. W. Reed, 1965), p. 140.

79. M. Mortimer Franklyn, *A Glance at Australia in 1880: or, Food from the South* (Melbourne, 1881), p. 30.

80. Josiah Copley, *Kansas and the Country Beyond, on the Line of the Union Pacific Railway, Eastern Division, From the Missouri to the Pacific Ocean* (Philadelphia, 1867), p. 54.

81. On which see Robert G. Athearn, *The Mythic West in Twentieth-Century America.*

82. Joseph T. Holmes, *Quincy in 1857 or Facts and Figures Exhibiting its Advantages, Resources, Manufactures and Commerce* (Quincy, 1857), p. 68.

83. William M. Thayer, *Marvels of the New West: A Vivid Portrayal of the Stupendous Marvels in the Vast Wonderland West of the Missouri River* (Norwich, Conn., 1887), pp. xxxii–v, 329–56.

84. George Albert Boeck, "An Early Iowa Community: Aspects of Economic, Social and Political Development in Burlington, Iowa, 1833–1866," Ph.D., State University of Iowa, 1961, pp. 45–46. For an example of a boosting campaign designed to eradicate this image see Faye Erma Harris, "A Frontier Community: The Economic, Social, and Political Development of Keokuk, Iowa From 1820 to 1866," Ph.D. dissertation, University of Iowa, 1965, p. 117.

85. Quoted in Patrick A. Dunae, *Gentlemen Emigrants: From the British Public Schools to the Canadian Frontier* (Vancouver and Toronto: Douglas & McIntyre, 1981), p. 88.

86. John White, *Sketches From America: Part I—Canada; Part II—A Pic-nic to the Rocky Mountains; Part III—The Irish in America* (London, 1870), pp. 312–13.

87. Willard B. Robinson, "Helena's Fabulous Business Blocks," *Montana* (Jan. 1968), 18(1):44–59.

88. James F. Watkins, "San Francisco," *The Overland Monthly* (Jan. 1870), 4(1):9–23. For the effects of isolation during the Civil War on San Francisco

see Peter R. Decker, *Fortunes and Failures: White-Collar Mobility in Nine-teenth-Century San Francisco* (Cambridge and London: Harvard University Press, 1978), p. 165.

89. Fred H. Taft, *An Empire Builder of the Middle West: Biography of Stephen H. Taft, Minister, Pioneer, Philanthropist, Reformer: A Born Leader of Men: Founder of the Town of Humboldt, Iowa* (Los Angeles: Parker, Stone & Baird, 1929),pp. 88, 115–16.

90. James F. Willard, ed., *The Union Colony at Greeley, Colorado 1869–1871* (Boulder: University of Colorado, 1918), p. 314.

91. George Rex Buckman, "Colorado Springs," *Lippincott's Magazine* (Jan. 1883), pp. 7–8.

92. Irving Howbert, *Memories of a Lifetime in the Pike's Peak Region* (New York and London: Putnam, 1925), pp. 234–36. For comment on this development of an alternative "bumtown" where there is a model "dry" community see Stanley Buder, *Pullman: An Experiment in Industrial Order and Community Planning, 1880–1930* (New York: Oxford University Press, [1967]), pp. 120–23.

93. Quoted in Robert Taft, *Artists and Illustrators of the Old West 1850–1900,* p. 155.

94. A. A. den Otter, *Civilizing the West: The Galts and the Development of Western Canada,* pp. 244–47; Mann, *After the Gold Rush,* pp. 63–67.

95. *The Industries of Tacoma, Washington: Her Resources, Advantages and Facil-ities in Trade, Commerce and Manufactures* ([Tacoma], 1889), pp. 26, 52; *Tacoma; The Western Terminus of the Northern Pacific Railroad* (Tacoma, 1889), pp. 13, 28.

96. R. Edmond Malone, *Three Years' Cruise in the Australasian Colonies* (London, 1854), p. 282.

97. Godfrey Charles Mundy, *Our Antipodes: Or, Residence and Rambles in the Australasian Colonies. With a Glimpse of the Gold Fields* (London, 1857), p. 5. For a similar comment, excepting only the brilliant atmosphere and the vegetation from Sydney's "Englishness," see Rosamond and Florence Hill, *What We Saw in Australia* (London, 1875), p. 271.

98. Franklyn, *A Glance at Australia in 1880,* 179.

99. For an example see Robert R. Dykstra, *The Cattle Towns,* p. 242.

100. Harry C. Freeman, *A Brief History of Butte, Montana: The World's Greatest Mining Camp* (Chicago, 1900), p. 3.

4. Towns and Social Evolution: Perceptions of the Relationship of Towns to the Evolution of New Societies

1. There are many modern editions of the essay. One of the most useful is Ray Allen Billington, ed., *Frontier and Section: Selected Essays of Frederick Jackson Turner* (Englewood Cliffs, N.J.: Prentice-Hall, 1961), pp. 37–62.

2. *Ibid,* pp. 49–50.

3. Notably John W. Reps: *Cities of the American West: A History of Frontier*

Urban Planning, pp. ix–xi, 667; *The Forgotten Frontier: Urban Planning in the American West Before 1890,* pp. 1–2, 143–44, 148–51.

4. For references to towns in the frontier thesis, see Billington, *Frontier and Section,* pp. 37–38, 43, 45–46, 50, 60–61.

5. His father, born in 1832, had been named Andrew Jackson Turner in honor of the president. Ray Allen Billington, *Frederick Jackson Turner: Historian, Scholar, Teacher* (New York: Oxford University Press, 1973), p. 4.

6. Ray Allen Billington, *The Genesis of the Frontier Thesis: A Study in Historical Creativity,* p. 124.

7. Kate Milner Rabb, ed., *A Tour Through Indiana in 1840: The Diary of John Parsons of Petersburg, Virginia* (New York: McBride, 1920), p. 74.

8. J. L. McConnel, *Western Characters or Types of Border Life in the Western States* (New York, 1853), p. 11.

9. *Incidents and Sketches Connected with the Early History and Settlement of the West: With Numerous Illustrations* (Cincinnati, 1854), pp. 7–9, 29.

10. Nathanial Ogle, *The Colony of Western Australia* (London, 1839), p. 111.

11. *Australia Felix Monthly Magazine* (June 1849), 1:16.

12. There is a good account of the history of the idea in James L. Machor, "Urbanization and the Western Garden: Synthesizing City and Country in Antebellum America," pp. 414–15. See also Anselm L. Strauss, *Images of the American City,* p. 161.

13. Billington, *Genesis of the Frontier Thesis,* pp. 33, 67, 113.

14. Robert Dixon, *The Course of Empire: Neo-Classical Culture in New South Wales 1788–1860,* pp. 47–78.

15. Leigh Astbury, *City Bushmen: The Heidelberg School and the Rural Mythology,* pp. 150–57.

16. Billington, *Genesis of the Frontier Thesis,* p. 67.

17. William Hancock, *An Emigrant's Five Years in the Free States of America* (London, 1860), pp. 274–75.

18. *Historical Sketch and Essay on the Resources of Montana; Including a Business Directory of the Metropolis* (Helena: 1868), p. 97.

19. Frank Crowley, ed., *A Documentary History of Australia;* vol. 1: *Colonial Australia, 1788–1840* (West Melbourne: Nelson, 1980), p. 116.

20. James B. Brown, *Views of Canada and the Colonists* (Edinburgh, 1851), p. xi.

21. J. C. Byrne, *Twelve Years' Wanderings in the British Colonies: From 1835 to 1847* (London, 1848), 1:149–50; 2:362.

22. Thomas Cholmondeley, *Ultima Thule; or, Thoughts Suggested by a Residence in New Zealand* (London, 1854), pp. 20–21.

23. W. P. Strickland, ed., *Autobiography of Rev. James B. Finley: or, Pioneer Life in the West* (Cincinnati, 1854), pp. 104–5.

24. J. F. Bennett, *Historical and Descriptive Account of South Australia: Founded on Experience of a Three Years' Residence in that Colony* (London, 1843), p. 23.

25. Cf. the concerned editorial in the *Cheyenne Daily Leader,* April 30, 1870: "A

good farming country around has ever been regarded as a desideradum in the founding of new towns. In this respect, as in others, the history of our town presents an anomaly. Other cities followed civilization—Cheyenne preceded it. Other cities have been created by the surrounding country—Cheyenne must create and develop her rural surroundings." Gilbert Stelter, "The City and Westward Expansion: A Western Case Study," p. 192.

26. Richard C. Wade, *The Urban Frontier: Pioneer Life in Early Pittsburgh, Cincinnati, Lexington, Louisville, and St. Louis.* For Reps see n. 3 above.

27. Norman Harper, "The Rural and Urban Frontiers," *Historical Studies: Australia and New Zealand* (May 1963), 10(40):401–21.

28. David B. Edward, *The History of Texas; or, The Emigrant's, Farmer's, and Politician's Guide to the Character, Climate, Soil and Productions of that Country: Geographically Arranged From Personal Observation and Experience* (Cincinnati, 1836), pp. 35, 51.

29. Sara T. L. Robinson, *Kansas: Its Interior and Exterior Life: Including a Full View of its Settlement, Political History, Social Life, Climate, Soil, Productions, Scenery, etc.* (Boston, 1856), p. 88.

30. Hancock, *An Emigrant's Five Years*, pp. 274–75.

31. L. U. Reavis, *The New Republic, or The Transition Complete, with an Approaching Change of National Empire, Based Upon the Commercial and Industrial Expansion of the Great West; Together With Hints on National Safety and Social Progress* (St. Louis, 1867), pp. 13–14. Similar statements appear in numerous promotional publications of this era, e.g., *City of Winona and Southern Minnesota: A Sketch of Their Growth and Prospects, With General Information for the Emigrant, Mechanic, Farmer, and Capitalist* (Winona, 1858), pp. 3–4.

32. "Emigration," *Western Journal* (Jan. 1849), 3(4):211–12.

33. "Towns and Statistics of Minnesota," *Western Journal* (May 1851), 6(2): 103–4.

34. James M. Woolworth, *Nebraska in 1857* (Omaha City and New York, 1857), pp. 16–17.

35. *Reminiscences of General William Larimer and of his Son William H. H. Larimer: Two of the Founders of Denver City* (Lancaster, Pa.: private circulation, 1918), p. 24.

36. *Sidney's Emigrant's Journal* (Dec. 21, 1848), 1(12):90.

37. Wilson Nicely, *The Great Southwest, or Plain Guide for Emigrants and Capitalists, Embracing a Description of the States of Missouri and Kansas* (St. Louis, 1867), pp. 68–69. For a later comment on the change from the Daniel Boone type of pioneer who disliked "crowding" to the pioneer who "hailed with joy the advent of new settlers and the upbuilding of a little market town in the neighborhood," see Theodore Roosevelt, *The Winning of the West* (New York and London: Putnam, 1905), 4:234–37.

38. Barry Broadfoot, *The Pioneer Years 1895–1914: Memories of Settlers Who Opened the West* (Markham, Ont.: Paper Jacks, 1978), p. 243.

39. J. M. S. Careless, "Some Aspects of Urbanization in Nineteenth-Century

Ontario," in F. H. Armstrong, K. A. Stevenson, and J. D. Wilson, eds., *Aspects of Nineteenth-Century Ontario* (Toronto: University of Toronto Press, 1974), p. 70.

40. Wayne Griswold, *Kansas, Her Resources and Developments or the Kansas Pilot Giving a Direct Road to Homes for Everybody* (Cincinnati, 1871), pp. 27–28. For similar concern regarding premature urban development in Iowa, see H. B. Turrill, *Historical Reminiscences of the City of Des Moines, Ia.* (Des Moines, 1857), pp. 106–11.

41. W. David McIntyre, ed., *The Journal of Henry Sewell 1853–7* (Christchurch: Whitcoulls, 1980), 1:138.

42. C. P. Lucas, ed., *Lord Durham's Report on the Affairs of British North America* (Oxford: Clarendon Press, 1912), 2:239.

43. Donald Winch, *Classical Political Economy and Colonies* (London: G. Bell, 1965), p. 136.

44. H. B. Turrill, *Historical Reminiscences,* made the best of a bad job by telling emigrants that at least they had large urban markets already made and available to them.

45. William Hutt, *Emigration and Colonization: A Speech Delivered at a General Meeting of the National Colonization Society, June, 1830, By William Hutt, Esq.* (London, 1832), pp. 4–11.

46. John Galt, *Bogle Corbet* (Toronto: McClelland and Stewart, 1977), p. 65; Gilbert A. Stelter, "John Galt: The Writer as Town Booster and Builder," pp. 17–43.

47. Galt, *Bogle Corbet,* p. 66.

48. Page Smith, *As a City Upon a Hill; The Town in American History;* Richard Lingeman, *Small Town America: A Narrative History 1620–The Present,* pp. 15–103.

49. Quoted in Eli Thayer, *A History of the Kansas Crusade: Its Friends and Its Foes* (New York, 1889), p. 119. Compare the commendation of the French and Spanish practice of founding towns and villages first in the Mississippi valley as "nuclei of civilization" in *Western Journal* (March 1850), 3(6):385.

50. Richard Charles Mills, *The Colonization of Australia (1829–42): The Wakefield Experiment in Empire Building* (London: Sidgwick and Jackson, 1915), p. 328.

51. June 29, 1836. *Irish University Press Series of British Parliamentary Papers: Colonies, General. 2: Report from the Select Committee on Disposal of Lands in the Colonies, 1836,* p. 110.

52. R. N. Ghosh, "Malthus on Emigration and Colonization: Letters to Wilmot-Horton," *Economica* (1963), N. S., 30:59.

53. *New South Wales Legislative Council, Votes and Proceedings, 1843: Report from the Select Committee, on the Crown Land Sales Act, 1843,* p. 10.

54. *Ibid.,* p. 11. William C. Foster, *Sir Thomas Livingston Mitchell and His World 1792–1855: Surveyor General of New South Wales 1828–1855* (Sydney: Institution of Surveyors, New South Wales, 1985), pp. 346–47.

55. William J. Patterson, *Some Plain Statements About Immigration, and Its*

Results: Submitted at Annual Meeting of Dominion Board of Trade, Held at Ottawa, January 17th, 1872 (Ottawa, 1872), p. 1; Florence B. Murray, ed., *Muskoka and Haliburton 1615–1875: A Collection of Documents* (Toronto: Champlain Society, 1963), p. 295.

56. Leo A. Johnson, "Ideology and Political Economy in Urban Growth: Guelph, 1827–1927," Gilbert A. Stelter and Alan F. J. Artibise, eds., *Shaping the Urban Landscape: Aspects of the Canadian City—Building Process*, p. 31.

57. Hazell Udell, *A History of Gingin 1830 to 1960* (Gingin, Western Australia: Shire of Gingin, 1980), p. 78.

58. *History of Crawford County and Ohio* (Chicago, 1881), p. 346.

59. Rev. C. B. Boynton and T. B. Mason, *A Journey Through Kansas; With Sketches of Nebraska: Describing the Country, Climate, Soil, Mineral, Manufacturing, and Other Resources: The Results of a Tour Made in the Autumn of 1854* (Cincinnati, 1855), p. 211.

60. David Boyd, *A History: Greeley and the Union Colony of Colorado* (Greeley, 1890), pp. 33–34.

61. *Ibid.;* Johnson, "Ideology and Political Economy," p. 31.

62. *Irish University Press Series of British Parliamentary Papers: Colonies, Australia. 2: Minutes of Evidence Taken Before the Select Committee on South Australia* (March 26, 1841), p. 229.

63. Martin Sullivan, *Men & Women of Port Phillip* (Sydney: Hale & Iremonger, 1985), p. 25.

64. "Although men may lay out a town, and commence building it, yet it cannot prematurely be forced into existence. It must have a back settlement to support it. The merchant and mechanic cannot sell, unless there are inhabitants to buy." A. A. Parker, *Trip to the West and Texas* (Concord, N. H., 1835), p. 158.

65. Simcoe to Lord Dundas, June 21, 1794, E. A. Cruikshank, ed., *The Correspondence of Lieut. Governor John Graves Simcoe, With Allied Documents Relating to His Administration of the Government of Upper Canada* (Toronto: Ontario Historical Society, 1923–25), 2:284.

66. Dorchester to Simcoe, Oct. 7, 1793, *ibid.*, p. 83.

67. Boyd, *A History: Greeley and the Union Colony*, p. 34.

68. Galt, *Bogle Corbet*, p. 66.

69. Adam Fergusson, *Practical Notes Made During a Tour in Canada, and a Portion of the United States, in MDCCCXXXI* (Edinburgh, 1833), pp. 278–79. See also Johnson, "Ideology and Political Economy," pp. 33–35; and Clarence Karr, *The Canada Land Company: The Early Years: An Experiment in Colonization 1823–1843* (Toronto: Ontario Historical Society, 1974).

70. Galt, *Bogle Corbet*, pp. 65–67.

71. Boyd, *A History: Greeley and the Union Colony*, p. 81.

72. *Ibid.*, pp. 82–83.

73. James F. Willard, ed., *The Union Colony at Greeley, Colorado 1869–1871* (Boulder, 1918), p. 287.

74. Boyd, *A History: Greeley and the Union Colony*, pp. 81–82.

75. *Ibid.*, pp. 159, 185.
76. Cf. James Bonwick's 1873 novel, *The Tasmanian Lily,* which was designed to encourage migration to Tasmania. It shows that, by taking a farm near Hobart, one can enjoy the benefits of urban life as well: "The wife can get in to her shopping . . . I can learn the news by an easy trot." Ian Turner, ed., *The Australian Dream: A Collection of Anticipations About Australia from Captain Cook to the Present Day,* p. 81.
77. The New Zealand situation is described in Stevan Eldred-Grigg, *A Southern Gentry: New Zealanders Who Inherited the Earth* (Wellington: A. H. & A. W. Reed, 1980).
78. Andrew Picken, *The Canadas* (London, 1832), pp. 347–48.
79. William Bridges, *The Colonization of British America* (London, 1848), pp. 14–16.
80. *Ibid.*, pp. 5–6. For a similar proposal see "An Officer of Rank, Nearly Twenty Years Resident in Canada" (Alexander W. Light), *A Plan for the Systematic Colonization of Canada, and All Other British Colonies* (London, 1850), pp. 7–52.
81. D. N. Jeans, "Official Town-Founding Procedures in New South Wales, 1828–1842."
82. Francis Fuller, *Five Years' Residence in New Zealand; or, Observations on Colonization* (London and Edinburgh, 1859, pp. 73–75.
83. Glenelg to Governor Bourke, April 13, 1836, Francis Peter Labilliere, *Early History of the Colony of Victoria, From Its Discovery to Its Establishment as a Self-Governing Province of the British Empire* (London, 1878), 2:135.
84. Byrne, *Twelve Years' Wanderings,* 1:149–50, 191–94.

5. Towns and Social Evolution: The Growth of Towns

1. Charles N. Glaab, "The Historian and the American Urban Tradition"; "Visions of Metropolis: William Gilpin and Theories of City Growth in the American West"; "Jesup W. Scott and West of Cities"; James L. Machor, "Urbanization and the Western Garden: Synthesizing City and Country in Antebellum America," pp. 415–17; Patrick E. McClear, "Logan U. Reavis: Nineteenth Century Urban Promoter"; J. Christopher Schnell and Katherine B. Clinton, "The New West: Themes in Nineteenth Century Urban Promotion, 1815–1880"; Lawrence H. Larsen, *The Urban West at the End of the Frontier,* pp. 111–14.
2. "J. W. S.," "The Great West," *De Bow's Review* (July 1853), 15(1):50–53; "Westward the Star of Empire," *ibid.* (Aug. 1859), 27(2):125–36; J. W. Scott, "Internal Trade," *The Hesperian* (Nov. 1838), 2(1):47. His ideas influenced the writers in *The Western Journal:* note especially M. Tarver, "The Growth of Cities in the United States"; *Western Journal* (March 1851), 5(6):283–87.
3. W. H. Withrow, *Our Own Country: Canada Scenic and Descriptive* (Toronto, 1889), p. 438.

4. Robert Dixon, *The Course of Empire: Neo-Classical Culture in New South Wales 1788–1860,* pp. 14–17.
5. For comment on this see Anselm L. Strauss, *Images of the American City,* pp. 19–20.
6. [I. J.] Benjamin, *Three Years in America 1859–1862* (Philadelphia: Jewish Publication Society of America, 1956), 1:120.
7. Estelline Bennett, *Old Deadwood Days* (New York: J. H. Sears, 1928), pp. 3–4, 7–8.
8. Edward D. Mansfield, *Memoirs of the Life and Services of Daniel Drake, M. D., Physician, Professor, and Author; with Notices of the Early Settlement of Cincinnati and Some of its Pioneer Citizens* (Cincinnati, 1855), pp. 49, 130.
9. "Wichita has passed the period of traditional history. References to small beginnings and pioneer efforts are now matters of pleasant remembrance." Andrew A. Hensley, ed., *Wichita: An Illustrated Review of its Progress and Importance* (n. p., 1886), p. 18.
10. "Contrary to all recognised principles of progress . . . we find that in Port Pirie the stone age . . . follows upon the wooden . . . This fact is due no doubt to the peculiar situation of the town and the hurried circumstances of its foundation—no stone being nearer than eight miles and the early settlement requiring buildings to be run up quickly and cheaply. Now that the population is becoming less nomadic this characteristic of wooden buildings is becoming less marked, and people are turning their attention to structures of more substantiality." Port Pirie *Gazette* (1878), quoted in Nancy Robinson, *Reluctant Harbour: The Romance of Pirie* (Jamestown, S.A.: Nadjuri Australia, [1976]), pp. 148–49. On materials used at different stages in town developments see Anthony Trollope, *Australia and New Zealand* (Melbourne, 1873), p. 551.
11. W. Fraser Rae, *Newfoundland to Manitoba Through Canada's Maritime, Mining, and Prairie Provinces* (New York, 1881), p. 198.
12. George Flower, *History of the English Settlement in Edwards County Illinois, Founded in 1817 and 1818, by Morris Birkbeck and George Flower* (Chicago, 1882), p. 60.
13. J. G. Kohl, *Travels in Canada, and Through the States of New York and Pennsylvania* (London, 1861), 1:247, 2:14.
14. Jerome C. Smiley, ed., *History of Denver With Outlines of the Earlier History of the Rocky Mountain Country* (Denver: Times-Sun, 1901), pp. 218, 459.
15. Nevin O. Winter, *A History of Northwest Ohio* (Chicago and New York: Lewis, 1917), 1:489.
16. Alfred Sorenson, *Early History of Omaha; or, Walks and Talks Among the Old Settlers* (Omaha, 1876), p. 43.
17. Henry Cornish, *Under the Southern Cross* (Madras, 1880), p. 278.
18. J. Richard Beste, *The Wabash: or Adventures of an English Gentleman's Family in the Interior of America* (London, 1855), 1:249. The people of Madison seem to have been rather sensitive about the size of their town.

When David Thomas visited it in 1816, he was not very impressed. His companion asked a local "how long this *little town* had been laid out? . . . assuming all the majesty of repulsive greatness, he exclaimed 'I hope you don't call this a *little town.'*" David Thomas, *Travels Through the Western Country in the Summer of 1816* (Auburn, N.Y. 1819), p. 117.

19. D. W. Meinig, *The Great Columbia Plain: A Historical Geography, 1805–1910* (Seattle: University of Washington Press, 1968), p. 227.

20. Examples are two books boosting Quincy, Illinois: Joseph T. Holmes, *Quincy in 1857 or Facts and Figures Exhibiting its Advantages, Resources, Manufactures and Commerce* (Quincy, 1857), p. 12; and Pat H. Redmond, *History of Quincy, and Its Men of Mark, or Facts and Figures Exhibiting Its Advantages and Resources, Manufactures and Commerce* (Quincy, 1869), p. 6.

21. Anthony Trollope, *North America* (New York: Knopf, 1951), p. 126. Another traveler who makes this comment about New World towns is Maturin M. Ballou, *Under the Southern Cross or Travels in Australia, Tasmania, New Zealand, Samoa, and Other Pacific Islands* (Boston, 1887), pp. 228–29. An Australian periodical acknowledged that Australians received the benefit of the mother country's "improvements in civilization and social institutions." *The Atlas* (Oct. 16, 1847), 3:151, 498.

22. Fredrika Bremer, *The Homes of the New World: Impressions of America* (New York, 1853), 2:135.

23. John Gates Thurston, *A Journal of a Trip to Illinois in 1836* (Mount Pleasant, Mich.: John Cumming, 1971), p. 21.

24. Bayard Taylor, *Eldorado, or Adventures in the Path of Empire* (New York: Knopf, 1949), p. 226.

25. Charles Dudley Warner, *Studies in the South and West: With Comments on Canada* (New York, 1889), p. 191.

26. E. A. Horsman and Lillian Rea Benson, eds., *The Canadian Journal of Alfred Domett: Being an Extract from a Journal of a Tour in Canada, the United States and Jamaica 1833–1835* (London, Ont.: University of Western Ontario, 1955), p. 22.

27. Robert Dawson, *The Present State of Australia: A Description of the Country, Its Advantages and Prospects with Reference to Emigration* (London, 1830), p. 47.

28. Rolf Boldrewood, *Old Melbourne Memories* (London, 1896), p. 1.

29. Cf. the 1872 and 1884 engravings of Winnipeg, and the commentary on them, in Withrow, *Our Own Country*, pp. 432–34.

30. Cornish, *Under the Southern Cross*, pp. 88–89.

31. William Kelly, *Life in Victoria or Victoria in 1853, and Victoria in 1858 Showing the March of Improvement Made by the Colony Within Those Periods, in Town and Country, Cities and the Diggings* (London, 1859), p. 268.

32. William Westgarth, *Victoria and the Australian Gold Mines in 1857; with Notes on the Overland Route from Australia, Via Suez* (London, 1857), p. 4.

33. Thomas M'Combie, *Australian Sketches: The Gold Discovery, Bush Graves, &c., &c.* (London, 1861), p. 103.

34. Ralph Gregory, "Count Baudissin on Missouri Towns," *Bulletin of the Missouri Historical Society* (Jan. 1971), 27(2):114.

35. John Regan, *The Emigrant's Guide to the Western States of America; or, Backwoods and Prairies* (Edinburgh, n. d.), p. 222.

36. Sandra Martin and Roger Hall, eds., *Rupert Brooke in Canada* (Toronto: P.M.A. Books, 1978), p. 98.

37. W. E. Adams, *Our American Cousins: Being Personal Impressions of the People and Institutions of the United States* (London and Newcastle-on-Tyne, 1883), pp. 34–35.

38. R. Therry, *Reminiscences of Thirty Years' Residence in New South Wales and Victoria: With a Supplementary Chapter on Transportation and the Ticket-of-Leave System* (London, 1863), p. 357.

39. James S. Ritchie, *Wisconsin and Its Resources; with Lake Superior, Its Commerce and Navigation* (Philadelphia and Chicago, 1857), pp. 262–65.

40. Westgarth, *Victoria and the Australian Gold Mines in 1857,* pp. 4–5.

41. George Wilson Pierson, *Tocqueville in America* (Garden City, N.Y.: Anchor Books, 1959), p. 431.

42. Rev. John Kirkwood, *An Autumn Holiday in the United States and Canada* (Edinburgh, 1887), pp. 217–18.

43. In his *Essay on Ranke's History of the Popes,* T. B. Macaulay prophesied a time "when some traveller from New Zealand shall, in the midst of a vast solitude, take his stand on a broken arch of London Bridge to sketch the ruins of St. Paul's."

44. B. I. Coleman, ed., *The Idea of the City in Nineteenth-Century Britain* (London and Boston: Routledge & Kegan Paul, 1973).

45. Stow Persons, "The Cyclical Theory of History in Eighteenth Century America," *American Quarterly* (Summer 1954), 6(2):147–63; David Lowenthal, "The Palace of the Past in the American Landscape."

46. Quoted in Lowenthal, "The Place of the Past," p. 93.

47. Michael H. Cowan, *City of the West: Emerson, America, and Urban Metaphor,* p. 32.

48. Rae, *Newfoundland to Manitoba,* p. 199. Cf. the fear of a Kingston newspaper that the town would become "a 'deserted village,' notwithstanding the many advantages it possesses; while the forests of the West produce new ones [towns] daily like mushrooms." *Kingston Chronicle and Gazette,* July 11, 1835, quoted in Brian S. Osborne, "Kingston in the Nineteenth Century: A Study in Urban Decline," J. David Wood, ed., *Perspectives on Landscape and Settlement in Nineteenth Century Ontario* (Toronto: McClelland and Stewart and the Institute of Canadian Studies, 1975), p. 161.

49. S. J. B., "The Future Progress of Ohio," *Western Monthly Review* (1830), 3:334.

50. Mansfield, *Memories of the Life and Services of Daniel Drake,* pp. 234–34.

51. Carl E. Kramer, "Images of a Developing City: Louisville, 1800–1830," p. 185.

52. *Ibid.,* p. 183.

53. Carl E. Kramer, "City with a Vision: Images of Louisville in the 1830s," pp. 449–51.

54. Allen J. Share, *Cities in the Commonwealth: Two Centuries of Urban Life in Kentucky,* pp. 28–31.

55. *The Western Messenger* (May 1838), 5(2):112–20.

56. Henry D. Shapiro and Zane L. Miller, eds., *Physician to the West, Selected Writings of Daniel Drake on Science & Society,* p. 64.

57. Mansfield, *Memoirs of the Life and Services of Daniel Drake,* p. 78.

58. Thomas, *Travels Through the Western Country,* p. 143.

59. Carl David Arfwedson, *The United States and Canada in 1832, 1833, and 1834* (New York and London: Johnson Reprint, 1969), 2:1–2.

60. Gregory, "Count Baudissin on Missouri Towns," p. 115.

61. Thomas Ashe, *Travels in America, Performed in 1806* (London and Newburyport, 1808), p. 181.

62. Mansfield, *Memoirs of the Life and Services of Daniel Drake,* p. 118.

63. John W. Reps, *Cities of the American West: A History of Frontier Urban Planning,* p. 206.

64. For example, W. R. Holloway, *Indianapolis: A Historical and Statistical Sketch of the Railroad City* (Indianapolis, 1870), p. 17; *The Evergreen State Souvenir Containing a Review of the Resources, Wealth, Varied Industries and Commercial Advantages of the State of Washington* (Tacoma and Seattle, 1893), p. 8.

65. J. L. McConnel, *Western Characters or Types of Border Life in the Western States* (New York, 1853), p. 11.

66. Benjamin, *Three Years in America,* pp. 120–21.

67. Samuel Bowles, *Across the Continent: A Summer's Journey to the Rocky Mountains, the Mormons and the Pacific States, with Speaker Colfax* (Springfield, Mass., and New York, 1866), p. 160.

68. Robert G. Athearn, *The Coloradans* (Albuquerque: University of New Mexico Press, 1976), p. 85.

69. Pierson, *Tocqueville in America,* p. 135.

70. Trollope, *Australia and New Zealand,* p. 142.

71. Morton Price, *A Theatrical Trip for a Wager! through Canada and the United States* (London, 1861), pp. 60–69, quoted in Edwin C. Guillet, ed. *The Valley of the Trent* (Toronto: Champlain Society, 1957), p. 418.

72. Nathaniel Hawthorne, *Tales, Sketches, and Other Papers* (Boston and New York, 1883), pp. 18–19.

73. Wilson Nicely, *The Great Southwest, or Plain Guide for Emigrants and Capitalists, Embracing a Description of the States of Missouri and Kansas* (St. Louis, 1867), p. 67.

74. M'Combie, *Australian Sketches,* p. 238.

75. Alfred Brunson, *Prairie du Chien: Its Present Position and Future Prospects* (Milwaukee, 1857), p. 11.

76. Hensley, *Wichita,* p. 18.

77. Mansfield, *Memoirs of the Life and Services of Daniel Drake,* pp. 233–34.
78. Cole Patrick Dawson, "Yankees in the Queen City: The Social and Intellectual Contributions of New Englanders in Cincinnati, 1820–1850," Ph.D. dissertation, Miami University, Oxford, Ohio, 1977.
79. Mansfield, *Memoirs of the Life and Services of Daniel Drake,* p. 269.
80. For Vaughan see Andrew Lees, *Cities Perceived: Urban Society in European and American Thought, 1820–1940* (Manchester: Manchester University Press, 1985), pp. 45–47, 68; and Coleman, *The Idea of the City,* pp. 87–94.
81. "Great Cities," *Putnam's Monthly Magazine* (March 1855), 5:254–63.
82. On Scott's ideas see the references in nn. 1 and 2 above and also *A Presentation of Causes Tending to Fix the Position of the Future Great City of the World in the Central Plain of North America* (Toledo, 1876).
83. "Emigration," *Western Journal* (Jan. 1849), 3(4):215–16.
84. "Chicago in 1856," *Putnam's Monthly Magazine* (June 1856), 7:606–13.
85. Herman Kogan, " 'Grander and Statelier than Ever . . . ,' " p. 236.
86. E. J. Goodspeed, *History of the Great Fires in Chicago and the West* (New York, 1871), pp. xiii–xiv.
87. Kogan," 'Grander and Statelier than Ever . . . ,' " p. 236.
88. John J. Pauly, "The Great Chicago Fire as a National Event."
89. William Bross, *Chicago and the Sources of Her Past and Future Growth* (Chicago, 1880), p. 3.
90. Charles N. Glaab, "The Historian and the American Urban Tradition," p. 24.
91. L. U. Reavis, *Saint Louis: The Future Great City of the World* (St. Louis, 1870), pp. 13, 35–37; McLear, "Logan U. Reavis."
92. Gregory, "Count Baudissin on Missouri Towns," p. 117; McLear, "Logan U. Reavis," pp. 574–77.
93. J. S. Buckingham, *The Eastern and Western States of America* (London and Paris, n. d.), 2:435.
94. A contemporary comment on Winnipeg, quoted in Alan F. J. Artibise, *Winnipeg: A Social History of Urban Growth, 1874–1914,* p. 15.
95. Edward Dicey, *Six Months in the Federal States* (London, 1863), 2:111.
96. *The Old and the New: Southwest Kansas As It Was, As It Is, As It Will Be* (Atchison, Topeka & Santa Fe Railroad Company, c. 1877), p. 7.
97. Hensley, *Wichita,* p. 16.
98. A. Theodore Brown, *Frontier Community: Kansas City to 1870* (Columbia: University of Missouri Press, 1963), p. 116.
99. Glaab, "Visions of Metropolis."
100. [S. H. Goodin], "Cincinnati, Its Destiny," Charles Cist, *Sketches and Statistics of Cincinnati in 1851* (Cincinnati, 1851), pp. 309–20.
101. Sally Graham, *Pioneer Merchant: The Letters of James Graham 1839–54* (South Yarra: Hyland House, 1985), p. 41.
102. Diary of W. J. Douglas, 1892, National Library of Australia (Canberra), MS 1629/1.

103. Arnold Schrier and Joyce Story, eds., *A Russian Looks at America: The Journey of Alexsandr Borisovich Lakier in 1857* (Chicago and London: University of Chicago Press, 1979), p. 175.

104. *Helena Illustrated: Capital of the State of Montana* (Minneapolis, 1890), p. 5. For another example see *Rise and Progress of Minnesota Territory* (St. Paul, 1855), 4:12.

105. *Early & Authentic History of Omaha*, p. 2.

106. "Wall Street Looks at the Agricultural Northwest," *Minnesota History* (Summer 1952), 33(2):68.

107. David Boyd, *A History: Greeley and the Union Colony of Colorado* (Greeley, 1890), p. 81.

108. John Francis McDermott, ed., *Travels in Search of the Elephant: The Wanderings of Alfred S. Waugh, Artist, in Louisiana, Missouri, and Santa Fe, in 1845–1846* (St. Louis: Missouri Historical Society, 1951), p. 45.

109. John S. Wright, *Chicago: Past, Present, Future* (Chicago, 1868), pp. v–xii.

110. *The Commerce of Kansas City in 1886 with a General Review of Its Business Progress* (Kansas City, 1886), p. 7.

111. James M. Woolworth, *Nebraska in 1857* (Omaha City and New York, 1857), pp. 86–87.

112. Glaab, "Visions of Metropolis."

113. Wayne Griswold, *Kansas: Her Resources and Developments or the Kansas Pilot Giving a Direct Road to Homes for Everybody* (Cincinnati, 1871), p. 35.

114. Julian Ralph, *Our Great West: A Study of the Present Conditions and Future Possibilities of the New Commonwealths and Capitals of the United States* (New York, 1893), p. 315.

115. Charlotte Erickson, *Invisible Immigrants: The Adaptations of English and Scottish Immigrants in Nineteenth-Century America* (Coral Gables, Fl.: University of Miami Press, 1972), pp. 126–27.

116. Schrier and Story, *A Russian Looks at America*, p. 174.

117. Charles Richard Weld, *A Vacation Tour in the United States and Canada* (London, 1855), pp. 99–100.

118. William Rees, *Description of the City of Keokuk, Lee County, Iowa* (Keokuk, 1854), p. 5; Sorenson, *Early History of Omaha*, p. 20; William Henry Bishop, *St. Louis in 1884* (California: Outbooks, 1977), p. 3.

119. Kate Milner Rabb, ed., *A Tour Through Indiana in 1840: The Diary of John Parsons of Petersburg, Virginia* (New York: McBride, 1920), pp. 101–2.

120. Cist, *Sketches and Statistics*, pp. 310–13.

121. N. B. Ashby, *The Riddle of the Sphinx* (Des Moines, 1890), p. 130, quoted in Mildred Throne, "The Grange in Iowa, 1868–1875," *Iowa Journal of History* (Oct. 1949), 47(4):311.

122. Nicely, *The Great Southwest*, pp. 71–72.

123. Willoughby M. Babcock, "The St. Croix Valley as Viewed by Pioneer Editors," *Minnesota History* (Sept. 1936), 17(3):285. Cf. the obsession of

William Gilpin and others with finding the great "Central City" of the continent—or "Centropolis," as Gilpin called it (Glaab, "Visions of Metropolis"). Gilpin was excited by St. Louis after his first visit there at the age of twenty-one: "Just look at her position on the map of North America —Exactly in the *centre* of the territory of the Union, where the navigable arteries unite. This will be, one day not far off, the seat of government and the great Heart of the Great Valley" (Thomas L. Karnes, *William Gilpin: Western Nationalist,* p. 32). L. U. Reavis saw St. Louis as the future central city of the world (*Saint Louis,* pp. 36–37). The Kansas City newspaper editor and booster, Robert Van Horn, tried to combine centrality with an end to the westward movement: "the herald of civilization has . . . fixed upon the rock-bound bay of the Missouri and Kansas as the last great seat of the wealth, trade, and population in the westward march of commerce toward the mountain basins of the Mississippi and Pacific. If men will only study topography the problem is solved. . . . Kansas City stands on the extreme point of western navigation—it is *the* west of commerce; beyond *us* the west must come to us overland. I say again—the west at last is found." W. H. Miller, *The History of Kansas City, Together With a Sketch of the Commercial Resources of the Country with which it is Surrounded* (Kansas City, 1881), p. 79.

124. An even greater prize was the location of the state capital (St. Louis aspired for many years to become the nation's capital). Cf. the *Minneapolis Tribune,* Feb. 28, 1869: "The location of a State Capital has far more influence than many suppose in determining immigration. The tendency of population is to radiate from and circle round a center, like the planets in the solar system." Neil B. Thompson, "A Half Century of Capital Conflict: How St. Paul Kept the Seat of Government," *Minnesota History* (Fall 1973), 43(7):246.

125. See, for example, D. Knight and S. Burrows, "Centrality by Degrees: A 19th Century Canadian's Measurement for Central Location."

126. For comment on the use of maps as boosting tools see Charles Gordon Mehaffey, "Changing Images of the Cutover: A Historical Geography of Resource Utilization in the Lake Superior Region, 1840–1930," Ph.D. dissertation, University of Wisconsin–Madison, 1978, pp. 409–10.

127. For a Canadian example of a town's aspiration to have this image as "the great center of attraction and radiation," see Leo A. Johnson, "Ideology and Political Economy in Urban Growth: Guelph, 1827–1927," in Gilbert A. Stelter and Alan F. J. Artibise, eds., *Shaping the Urban Landscape: Aspects of the Canadian City-Building Process,* p. 41.

128. Cf. Ignatius Donnelly's vision for his city of Nininger, in Ralph L Harmon, "Ignatius Donnelly and His Faded Metropolis," *Minnesota History* (Sept. 1936), 17(3):264.

129. Alphonso Taft, *A Lecture on Cincinnati and her Rail-Roads: Delivered Before the Young Men's Mercantile Library Association, January 22, 1850* (Cincinnati, 1850), p. 52.

130. James H. Madison, "Businessmen and the Business Community in Indianapolis, 1820–1860," Ph.D. dissertation, Indiana University, 1972, p. 94.

6. Antipodean Patterns of Urban Development

1. Robert Dixon, *The Course of Empire: Neo-Classical Culture in New South Wales 1788–1860,* pp. 79–119.
2. Barrie Drummond Dyster, "The Role of Sydney and the Roles of Its Citizens in New South Wales, 1841–1851," M.A. dissertation, University of Sydney, 1965, p. 4.
3. Charles Griffith, *The Present State and Prospects of the Port Philip District of New South Wales* (Dublin, 1845), p. 20. Yet later in the book (p. 70) he himself urges migrants to stay in Melbourne for a while and take their time deciding where to settle.
4. [Edward Wilson], *Rambles at the Antipodes: A Series of Sketches of Moreton Bay, New Zealand, the Murray River and South Australia, and the Overland Route* (London, 1859), p. 5.
5. *Legislative Assembly, New South Wales, 1859–60: Votes and Proceedings: Report from the Select Committee on the Condition of the Working Classes of the Metropolis,* pp. 99, 20.
6. Quoted in J. M. Richmond, "Country Town Growth in South-Eastern Australia: Three Regional Studies, 1861–1891," Ph.D. dissertation, Australian National University, 1969, p. 11. For the British criticism of developments in Australia see this thesis and Craufurd D. W. Goodwin, *The Image of Australia: British Perception of the Australian Economy from the Eighteenth to the Twentieth Century,* p. 94.
7. T. A. Coghlan, *The Wealth and Progress of New South Wales 1886–87* (Sydney, 1887), p. 140.
8. Francis Adams, *The Australians: A Social Sketch* (London, [1893]), pp. 25, 204.
9. *The Bulletin* (May 6, 1882), 9(119):1–2.
10. Henry Tudor, *Narrative of a Tour in North America* (London, [1834]), 1:280.
11. John Costley, "Ten Years' Progress," *Canadian Monthly and National Review* (Jan. 1874), 5(1):5–6.
12. H. H. Hayter, "The Concentration of Population in Australian Capital Cities," *Report of the Fourth Meeting of the Australasian Association for the Advancement of Science* (Hobart, 1892), pp. 545–46.
13. The most recent and best biography is D. W. A. Baker, *Days of Wrath: A Life of John Dunmore Lang* (Melbourne: Melbourne University Press, 1985).
14. John Dunmore Lang, *An Historical and Statistical Account of New South Wales: Including a Visit to the Gold Regions, and a Description of the Mines; With an Estimate of the Probable Results of the Great Discovery,* 3rd ed.

(London, 1852), 2:164–68, 317–18. It was at this time that Daniel Drake's biographer reported that Drake "said, after all his observation and experience, that he thought the moral dangers to youth in the country, were greater than in the city." Edward D. Mansfield, *Memoirs of the Life and Services of Daniel Drake, M.D., Physician, Professor, and Author; with Notices of the Early Settlement of Cincinnati and Some of its Pioneer Citizens* (Cincinnati, 1855), p. 40.

15. John Dunmore Lang, *Phillipsland; or the Country Hitherto Designated Port Phillip: Its Present Condition and Prospects, as a Highly Eligible Field for Emigration* (Edinburgh, 1847), pp. 54–55, 108–9; Lang, *Cooksland in North-Eastern Australia* (London, 1847), pp. 104–7. See also the article in his journal, probably by himself: *The Colonist* (Feb. 5, 1835), 1(6):43–44.

16. On Westgarth see the essay by Geoffrey Serle in Geoffrey Serle and Russel Ward, eds., *Australian Dictionary of Biography* (Carlton, Victoria: Melbourne University Press, 1976), 6:379–83.

17. William Westgarth, *Personal Recollections of Early Melbourne & Victoria* (Melbourne and Sydney), pp. 21–22.

18. William Westgarth, *Victoria and the Australian Gold Mines in 1857; With Notes on the Overland Route from Australia, Via Suez* (London, 1857), pp. 86–87; Westgarth, *Victoria; Late Australia Felix, or Port Phillip District of New South Wales* (Edinburgh and London, 1853), pp. 63–64.

19. William Westgarth, *The Colony of Victoria: Its History, Commerce, and Gold Mining; Its Social and Political Institutions; Down to the End of 1863: With Remarks, Incidental and Comparative, Upon the Other Australian Colonies* (London, 1864), pp. 108–13.

20. For an example see Dyster, "The Role of Sydney," p. 141.

21. *Report from the Select Committee on the Condition of the Working Classes*, pp. 28–29.

22. Westgarth, *Victoria and the Australian Gold Mines*, p. 86.

23. Westgarth, *The Colony of Victoria*, pp. 109–10.

24. John Gershom Greenhough, *Towards the Sunrising; or, A Voyage to the Antipodes* (London: Stockwell, 1902), p. 120; Henry Demarest Lloyd, *Newest England: Notes of a Democratic Traveller in New Zealand, With Some Australian Comparisons* (New York: Doubleday, Page, 1903), pp. 243–44.

25. James Anthony Froude, *Oceana or England and her Colonies* (London, 1886), pp. 212–13.

26. Alexander Hill, *A Run Round the Empire* (London, 1897), p. 140; E. Brodie Hoare, *Impressions of New Zealand* (Christchurch, 1887), p. 505.

27. John Bradshaw, *New Zealand of To-Day (1884–1887)* (London, 1888), p. 360.

28. James Coutts Crawford, *Recollections of Travel in New Zealand and Australia* (London, 1880), pp. 278–79.

29. Hayter, "Concentration of Population," pp. 542–44.

30. C. P. Lucas, ed., *Lord Durham's Report on the Affairs of British North America* (Oxford: Clarendon Press), 2:146.

31. "Present Population and Future Prospects of the Western Country," *Western Monthly Review* (Oct. 1827), 1:331.

32. "The Author of 'Austria As It Is'" [Charles Sealsfield], *The Americans as They Are; Described in a Tour Through the Valley of the Mississippi* (London, 1828), p. 14.

33. M. Tarver, "The Growth of Cities in the United States," *Western Journal* (March 1851), 5(6):283–87. See also the article in which he calls for the embellishment of western cities: "Civic and Rural Embellishment," ibid. (Nov. 1851), 7(2):75–79.

34. Daniel Pratt Baldwin, *How States Grow* (Logansport, Ind., 1880), pp. 25–27, 36.

35. Roy Jenkins, *Truman* (London: Collins, 1986), p. 38.

36. Sinclair Lewis, *Babbitt* (New York: New American Library, n. d.), pp. 98–100, 149, 151–54.

37. Westgarth, *The Colony of Victoria*, pp. 112–13.

38. Hayter, "Concentration of Population," pp. 545–47.

39. S. B. Sutton, ed., *Civilizing American Cities: A Selection of Frederick Law Olmsted's Writings on City Landscapes*, pp. 34–38.

40. Adna Ferrin Weber, *The Growth of Cities in the Nineteenth Century: A Study in Statistics*, p. 1.

41. Rev. Dr. Scott, *A Lecture Delivered Before the Mercantile Library Association of San Francisco, on the Influence of Great Cities, in Musical Hall, June 16th, 1854* (San Francisco, 1854), pp. 5–6, 16.

42. L. U. Reavis, *Saint Louis: The Future Great City of the World* (St. Louis, 1870), p. 9.

43. Ralph Mansfield, *Analytical View of the Census of New South Wales For the Year 1841; With Tables Showing the Progress of the Population During the Previous Twenty Years* (Sydney, 1841).

44. Goodwin, *The Image of Australia*, p. 93. On the use of organic imagery to discuss towns see Graeme Davison, "The City as a Natural System: Theories of Urban Society in Early Nineteenth Century Britain," in Derek Fraser and Anthony Sutcliffe, eds., *The Pursuit of Urban History*, pp. 349–70.

45. Lang, *An Historical and Statistical Account*, 2:164–67.

46. *The Bulletin* (May 6, 1882), 9(119):1.

47. Anthony Trollope, *Australia and New Zealand* (Melbourne, 1873), p. 448.

48. Coghlan, *Wealth and Progress of New South Wales 1886–87*, pp. 136–40.

49. T. A. Coghlan, *The Wealth and Progress of New South Wales 1889–90* (Sydney, 1890), p. 409.

50. T. A. Coghlan, *The Wealth and Progress of New South Wales 1894* (Sydney, 1896), p. 889.

51. T. A. Coghlan, *A Statistical Account of the Seven Colonies of Australasia, 1897–8* (Sydney, 1898), pp. 60–61.

52. Colin Roderick, ed., *Henry Lawson: Autobiographical and Other Writings 1887–1922*, vol. 2 of *Collected Prose* (Sydney: Angus and Robertson, 1972), pp. 11–13.

53. Coghlan, *Wealth and Progress of New South Wales 1886–87*, pp. 138–40.

54. Bayrd Still, "Milwaukee, 1870–1900: The Emergence of a Metropolis," *Wisconsin Magazine of History* (Dec. 1939), 23(2):143–45.

55. Richard Tangye, *Reminiscences of Travel in Australia, America, and Egypt* (London and Birmingham, 1883), p. 101; G. H. Reid, *An Essay on New South Wales, The Mother Colony of the Australias* (Sydney, 1876), p. 142.

56. *The Bulletin* (May 20, 1882), 9(121):1–2; " 'Capricornus,' 'Labour' and Immigration," *The Australian* (1878–79), 1:193–98.

57. Coghlan, *Wealth and Progress of New South Wales 1886–87*, pp. 136–37.

58. W. H. Hall, *The Official Year Book of New South Wales 1904–5* (Sydney: Government of the State of New South Wales, 1906), p. 630.

59. Cf. Thomas Spence's evidence: *Report from the Select Committee on the Condition of the Working Classes*, p. 55.

60. *Irish University Press Series of British Parliamentary Papers: Colonies, General. 2: Report from the Select Committee on Disposal of Lands in the Colonies* (1836), 11:177–78.

61. This summary of arguments is based on evidence given to numerous committees, chiefly of the New South Wales Legislative Assembly: the Select Committee on the Condition of the Working Classes of the Metropolis, 1859–60; the Select Committee on the Present State of the Colony, 1865 (*Votes and Proceedings*, 1865); the Select Committee on the Unemployed, 1866 (*Votes and Proceedings*, 1866); the Select Committee on Assisted Immigration, 1880 (*Votes and Proceedings*, 1879–80). Also used were reports of committees of the New South Wales Legislative Council: the Select Committee on the Petition From Distressed Mechanics and Labourers, 1843 (*Votes and Proceedings*, 1843); the Select Committee on Immigration, 1843 (*ibid.*); the Select Committee on Distressed Labourers, 1844 (*Votes and Proceedings*, 1844).

62. Andrew Picken, *The Canadas* (London, 1832), p. 287; Joseph Bouchette, *The British Dominions in North America; or a Topographical and Statistical Description* (London, 1831),2:234. For an Australian call for government action to help migrants leave the cities, see *The Colonist* (Jan. 22, 1835), 1(4):25.

63. William H. G. Kingston, *How to Emigrate; or, The British Colonists* (London, 1855), 35, 188–92.

64. D. A. Hamer, *The New Zealand Liberals: The Years of Power 1891–1912* (Auckland: Auckland University Press, 1988), pp. 65–66; Adams, *The Australians*, pp. 204–6.

65. Coral Lansbury, *Arcady in Australia: The Evocation of Australia in Nineteenth Century Literature*.

66. Coghlan refers to it in *Wealth and Progress . . . 1895–6*, p. 497, as does Hall in *Official Year Book . . . 1904–5*, p. 631. For an early example of refusal to believe that pastoralism and concentration of population in a city went together, see "An Australian Colonist," *The Resources of Australia* (London, 1841), p. 26. But pro-"squatter" interests argued that only extensive pastor-

alism could provide a strong financial support for cities and towns: *Sydney Herald*, April 5, 1839, March 23, 1840, Feb. 16, 1841.

67. *The Victorian Hansard*, 8:498.

68. *Report from the Select Committee on the Conditions of the Working Classes*, p. 20.

69. *Hamilton Spectator*, April 18, 1862, quoted in J. M. Powell, *The Public Lands of Australia Felix: Settlement and Land Appraisal in Victoria 1834–91 With Special Reference to the Western Plains* (Melbourne: Oxford University Press, 1970), p. 104. Cf. the following verdict on the land reform panacea: "It is a curious fact how little the cry of the 'three acres and a cow' seems to affect the people. They will flock to large towns. In England they all go to London. It is the same in America. Land is to be had in abundance, but, nevertheless, the town offers greater inducements than the country." J. Ewing Ritchie, *An Australian Ramble or A Summer in Australia* (London, 1890), p. 120. That land reform was not the cure for overcrowding in cities was also noted by George R. Parkin, "Australian Cities: The Anglo-Saxon in the Southern Hemisphere," *Colonial Century* (March 1891), p. 690. It continued to be the case, as in the 1840s, that a high proportion of propagandists for closer agricultural settlement "were unrepentantly residents of the town." Dyster, "The Role of Sydney," p. 19.

70. This is a major issue in the debate between Russel Ward and his critics. See Russel Ward, "The Australian Legend Re-visited," pp. 172–73.

71. D. A. Hamer, "Towns in Nineteenth-Century New Zealand," pp. 13–15.

72. David Kennedy, Junior, *Kennedy's Colonial Travel: A Narrative of a Four Years' Tour Through Australia, New Zealand, Canada, &c.* (Edinburgh and London, 1876), p. 27.

73. Lang, *Historical and Statistical Account*, 2:164–68.

74. Charles Lindsey, *The Prairies of the Western States: Their Advantages and Their Drawbacks* (Toronto, 1860), pp. 40–41, 70. A decade earlier M. Tarver had written an article about St. Louis giving reasons why it was certain to become the principal city on the Mississippi. Once a town had become established in its growth, "and progressed far beyond its competitors," it was highly unlikely that they could ever again seriously challenge it, "for capitalists never risk their money in building up towns that are overshadowed by their neighbors. . . . The town that has fallen behind in its growth, is compelled to contend not only against the active capital and enterprise of its more prosperous neighbor; but against the value of the grounds and improvement which it contains also; for these constitute a basis or fixed capital, on which money or credit may be obtained at pleasure. And from these, and other causes of like nature, there is not an instance, perhaps, in all history, where a large town has lost its business by reason of a smaller one having grown up within its neighborhood and influence" ("St. Louis—Its Early History," *Western Journal*, Feb. 1849, 2(2):84–85).

75. Josiah Hughes, *Australia Revisited in 1890, and Excursions in Egypt, Tasmania, and New Zealand* (London, 1891), p. 176.

76. Coghlan, *Wealth and Progress . . . 1895–6,* p. 497.
77. Richmond, "Country Town Growth," pp. 5–7, 409–11, 429; Don Garden, *Hamilton: A Western District History* (North Melbourne: Hargreen, pp. 63, 69–70.
78. Richmond, "Country Town Growth," p. 430.
79. Lang, *Phillipsland,* pp. 54–55; *The Colonist* (Feb. 5, 1835), 1(6):43–44.
80. Edward Jenks, *The Government of Victoria (Australia)* (Melbourne, 1897), pp. 381–83.
81. Rev. James Ballantyne, *Homes and Homesteads in the Land of Plenty: Handbook of Victoria as a Field for Emigration* (Melbourne, 1871), p. 46. Cf. Westgarth's use of Melbourne to illustrate Victoria's progress in *The Colony of Victoria,* p. 6.
82. Legislative Assembly, New South Wales, *Votes and Proceedings 1879–80,* p. 5; *Progress Report from the Select Committee on Assisted Immigration,* p. 49.
83. See Waldemar Bannow who, in *The Colony of Victoria Socially and Materially* (Melbourne, 1896), set out to write about the whole of Victoria in order to encourage people to leave the overcrowded cities yet spends much time dwelling on Melbourne's fascinations as a "metropolis."
84. E. Carton Booth, *Another England: Life, Living, Homes, and Homemakers in Victoria* (London, 1869), p. 268.
85. Catherine Helen Spence, *Clara Morison* (Adelaide: Rigby, 1971), pp. 272–73.
86. *Report from the Select Committee on the Condition of the Working Classes,* pp. 14–15.
87. Lansbury, *Arcadia in Australia.* For comment on the failure of Australia's country towns to match the Old World image of the village, see *The Bulletin* (May 20, 1882), 9(121):1–2: "the chief features in the landscape are the pound with a thicket of Bathurst burrs, a dead horse, and a pile of empty bottles."
88. H. W. Bunbury, *Early Days in Western Australia* (1930), pp. 61–64, quoted in J. T. Gilchrist and W. J. Murray, eds., *Eye-Witness: Selected Documents from Australia's Past* (Adelaide: Rigby, 1968), p. 47. The tendency of "small places" to remain "small" was sometimes attributed to the quarrelsome character of their inhabitants. Donald S. Garden, *Albany: A Panorama of the Sound from 1827* (West Melbourne: Nelson, 1977), p. 103.
89. J. Y. Walker, *The History of Bundaberg: A Typical Queensland Agricultural Settlement* (Sydney: Dryden Press, 1977), p. 85. See also James Dixon, *Narrative of a Voyage to New South Wales and Van Dieman's Land, in the Ship Skelton, During the year 1820* (Edinburgh, 1822), p. 47; Robert Dawson, *The Present State of Australia; A Description of the Country, Its Advantages and Prospects with Reference to Emigration* (London, 1830), p. 47. For the destruction of community in small towns through the onset of "social distinctions," see also E. H. Hallack, *Our Townships, Farms, and Homesteads: Southern District of South Australia: Comprising a Series of 25 Articles written for the "S. A. Register" and "Adelaide Observer"* (Adelaide, 1892), p. 29. Of

course, a similar pattern often developed in towns in other countries. One local history tells of how in Lafayette, Indiana, "with the expanding fortunes of some worthy citizens of our growing town, there appeared to be mixed a slight leven of aristocracy, which some feared might in time, if not checked, create heart-burnings and jealousies in the community, by establishing castes and grades in social life, based more upon wealth than merit." A course of lectures on "Flunkeysim" was organized, and that "completely cured the growing distemper." Sandford C. Cox, *Recollections of the Early Settlement of the Wabash Valley* (Freeport, N.Y.: Books for Libraries Press, 1970), p. 83. The "democratic" character of American frontier towns was often emphasized. See Lewis Atherton, *Main Street on the Middle Border*, pp. 100–3. For an example see John Regan, *The Emigrant's Guide to the Western States of America; or, Backwoods and Prairies* (Edinburgh, [1843]), pp. 197–99.

90. D. N. Jeans, "Fiction and the Small Town in the United States: A Contribution to the Study of Urbanisation."

91. Quoted in Morton and Lucia White, *The Intellectual Versus the City: From Thomas Jefferson to Frank Lloyd Wright*, pp. 126–27.

7. Time and Space on the Urban Frontier

1. Anselm L. Strauss, *Images of the American City*, pp. 18–19.

2. George Augustus Sala, *America Revisited: From the Bay of New York to the Gulf of Mexico, and from Lake Michigan to the Pacific* (London, 1882), 2:153.

3. William Howitt, *Land, Labour and Gold or Two Years in Victoria: With Visits to Sydney and Van Diemen's Land* (Kilmore: Lowden, 1972), p. 22.

4. Arnold Schrier, "A Russian Observer's Visit to 'Porkopolis'—1857," *Cincinnati Historical Society Bulletin* (Spring 1971), 29(1):39.

5. Frederick J. Jobson, *America and American Methodism* (London, 1857), pp. 297–98.

6. John Askew, *A Voyage to Australia & New Zealand* (London, 1857), p. 158.

7. "Illinois in Spring-Time," *Atlantic Monthly* (Sept. 1858), 2:488.

8. Othman A. Abbott, *Recollections of a Pioneer Lawyer* (Lincoln: Nebraska State Historical Society, 1929), p. 122.

9. J. Max Clark, *Colonial Days* (Denver: Smith-Brooks, 1902), pp. 29–31.

10. Charles Hooton, *St. Louis' Isle, or Texiana; With Additional Observations Made in the United States and in Canada* (London, 1847), pp. 7–11.

11. J. H. Beadle, *The Undeveloped West; or, Five Years in the Territories* (Philadelphia: [1873]), p. 122.

12. Denton J. Snider, *The St. Louis Movement in Philosophy, Literature, Education, Psychology with Chapters of Autobiography* (St. Louis: Sigma, 1920), pp. 14–15, 70–78.

13. "Cities and Parks: With Special Reference to the New York Central Park," *Atlantic Monthly* (April 1861), 7:418.

14. Wilson Nicely, *The Great Southwest, or Plain Guide for Emigrants and Capi-*

talists, *Embracing a Description of the States of Missouri and Kansas* (St. Louis, 1867), p. 71.

15. For examples see "Garryowen" (Edmund Finn), *The Chronicles of Early Melbourne 1835 to 1852: Historical, Anecdotal and Personal* (Melbourne, 1888), 1:117; Douglas M. Gane, *New South Wales and Victoria in 1885* (London, 1886), p. 55; and Henry T. Davis, *Solitary Places Made Glad: Being Observations and Experiences for Thirty-Two Years in Nebraska* (Cincinnati, 1890), p. 166.

16. L. U. Reavis, *Saint Louis: The Future Great City of the World* (St. Louis, 1870), p. 134; Snider, *The St. Louis Movement*, pp. 82–88.

17. John Howison, *Sketches of Upper Canada, Domestic, Local, and Characteristic: To Which Are Added, Practical Details For the Information of Emigrants of Every Class; and Some Recollections of the United States of America* (Edinburgh, 1821), pp. 115–16.

18. Quoted in G. P. de T. Glazebrook, *The Story of Toronto* (Toronto and Buffalo: University of Toronto Press, 1971), p. 58.

19. "Wall Street Looks at the Agricultural Northwest," *Minnesota History* (Summer 1952), 33(2):65–66.

20. Nils William Olsson, ed., *A Pioneer in Northwest America 1841–1858: The Memoirs of Gustaf Unonius* (Minneapolis: University of Minnesota Press, 1950), 2:142.

21. Ralph Gregory, "Count Baudissin on Missouri Towns," *Bulletin of the Missouri Historical Society* (Jan. 1971), 27(2):114.

22. Sala, *America Revisited,* 2:154–55.

23. Charles Dudley Warner, *Studies in the South and West with Comments on Canada* (New York, 1889), p. 195.

24. E.g., William Morris, *Letters Sent Home: Out and Home Again by Way of Canada and the United States* (Swindon, n. d., [the letters were written in 1874]), p. 204.

25. See James B. Brown, *Views of Canada and the Colonists* (Edinburgh, 1851), pp. 175–76; Catherine Helen Spence, *Clara Morison* (Adelaide: Rigby, 1971), p. 17.

26. Arthur G. Guillemard, *Over Land and Sea: A Log or Travel Round the World in 1873–1874* (London, 1875), pp. 19–20. Incongruity in Melbourne was often commented on: see Anthony Trollope, *Australia and New Zealand* (Melbourne, 1873), p. 252; John Shaw, *A Gallop to the Antipodes, Returning Overland Through India* (London, 1858), p. 56; Waldemar Bannow, *The Colony of Victoria Socially and Materially* (Melbourne, 1896), p. 10; Henry Cornish, *Under the Southern Cross* (Madras, 1880), p. 93.

27. "Another Glimpse of the Future," *Illinois Monthly Magazine* (Sept. 1831), 1:566. For a vision of incongruities swept away by fire and replaced by uniformity, see Joseph N. Balestier, *The Annals of Chicago* (Chicago, 1846), p. 11.

28. J. Richard Beste, *The Wabash: or Adventures of an English Gentleman's Family in the Interior of America* (London, 1855), 1:i.

29. Carl Abbott, "Boom State and Boom City: Stages in Denver's Growth," *Colorado Magazine* (Summer 1973), 50(3):215; John White, *Sketches from America: Part I—Canada; Part II—A Pic-nic to the Rocky Mountains; Part III—The Irish in America* (London, 1870), pp. 312–13.

30. Arnold Schrier and Joyce Story, eds., *A Russian Looks at America: The Journey of Alexsandr Borisovich Lakier in 1857* (Chicago and London: University of Chicago Press, 1979), p. 175. Of course, guidebooks were often "out-of-date" in the opposite direction, in their description of the great cities of the future as though they already existed. See William Hancock, *An Emigrant's Five Years in the Free States of America* (London, 1860), pp. 255–56.

31. Anthony Trollope, *North America* (New York: Knopf, 1951), p. 126.

32. Edward Dicey, *Six Months in the Federal States* (London and Cambridge, 1863), 2:63–64.

33. T. H. Gladstone, *The English in Kansas or Squatter Life and Border Warfare* (Lincoln: University of Nebraska Press, 1971), p. 137.

34. Orion Clemens, *City of Keokuk in 1856: A View of the City, Embracing Its Commerce and Manufactures, and Containing the Inaugural Address of Mayor Curtis, and Statistical Local Information* (Keokuk, 1856), p. 4.

35. For a typical comment of this kind see "Hopeful," *"Taken In"; Being, A Sketch of New Zealand Life* (London, 1887), pp. 177–78.

36. William Fairfax, *Handbook to Australasia: Being a Brief Historical and Descriptive Account of Victoria, Tasmania, South Australia, New South Wales, Western Australia, and New Zealand* (Melbourne, 1859), p. cxxvii.

37. James Ballantyne, *Homes and Homesteads in the Land of Plenty: Handbook of Victoria as a Field for Emigration* (Melbourne, 1871), p. 47.

38. J. S. Buckingham, *The Eastern and Western States of America* (London and Paris, n. d.), 2:351. For other comments on the mounds at Circleville and their fate see Thomas, *Travels Through the Western Country*, p. 94; Bernhard, Duke of Saxe-Weimar Eisenach, *Travels Through North America, During the Years 1825 and 1826* (1828), 2:148–49. For another traveler's comments on the attitude to the past revealed in the destruction of mounds see Thomas Ashe, *Travels in America, Performed in 1806* (London and Newburyport, 1808), pp. 181–82. For other accounts of destruction of mounds see Thos. J. Summers, *History of Marietta* (Marietta, Ohio: Leader Publishing, 1903), 304–5; M. H. Dunlop, "Curiosities Too Numerous to Mention: Early Regionalism and Cincinnati's Western Museum," *American Quarterly* (Fall 1984), 36(4):527.

39. This attitude to relics can be seen beginning before the buildings even were relics. See David Thomas' comments in 1816 on the modest jail, built of hewn logs, in Madison, Indiana: "though these buildings neither shine much in topographical description, nor add to the beauty of these villages, yet posterity, from such specimens will learn with interest the simplicity of new founded empires; for in a few years these will be only *remembered*" (*Travels*

Through the Western Country in the Summer of 1816, Auburn, N.Y., 1819, p. 117).

40. Julian Ralph, *Our Great West: A Study of the Present Conditions and Future Possibilities of the New Commonwealths and Capitals of the United States* (New York, 1893), p. 315.
41. Lyle W. Dorsett, *The Queen City: A History of Denver* (Boulder, Colo.: Pruett, 1977), pp. 31–32, 97.
42. Estelline Bennett, *Old Deadwood Days* (New York: J. H. Sears, 1928), p. 8.
43. *Chicago in 1860; A Glance at its Business Houses* (1860), p. 126.
44. Walter L. Creese, *The Crowning of the American Landscape: Eight Great Spaces and Their Buildings* (Princeton: Princeton University Press, 1985), p. 209.
45. *Collection of Nebraska Pioneer Reminiscences Issued by the Nebraska Society of the Daughters of the American Revolution* (Cedar Rapids, Iowa: Torch Press, 1916), pp. 303–4.
46. Cited in David Lowenthal, "The Place of the Past in the American Landscape," p. 91.
47. Augustus [F.] Harvey, *Sketches of the Early Days of Nebraska City, Nebraska Territory, 1854–1860* (Saint Louis, 1871), pp. 29–30.
48. Lowenthal, "The Place of the Past in the American Landscape," pp. 90–95.
49. Joseph Schafer, *The Winnebago–Horicon Basin: A Type Study in Western History* (Madison: State Historical Society of Wisconsin, 1937), pp. 280, 295.
50. Ben Casseday, *The History of Louisville, From Its Earliest Settlement Till the Year 1852* (Louisville, 1852), p. 203. For other references to recovery after fire see A. Timbrell, "There and Back; or, Two Years in Queensland," *Colonial Monthly* (Sept. 1867–Jan. 1868), 1:377–78; Brown, *Views of Canada,* p. 284; Harry H. Hook and Francis J. McGuire, *Spokane Falls Illustrated* (Minneapolis, 1889), p. 58. For a discussion of the tendency to regard fires as a blessing, see Ray Allen Billington, *Land of Savagery Land of Promise: The European Image of the American Frontier in the Nineteenth Century,* pp. 210–11.
51. Herman Kogan, " 'Grander and Statelier than Ever . . .' "
52. Henry Sienkiewicz, *Portrait of America* (New York, 1959), quoted in Paul M. Angle, ed., *Prairie State: Impressions of Illinois, 1763–1967, By Travelers and Other Observers* (Chicago and London: University of Chicago Press, 1968), p. 393.
53. *Wyandotte County and Kansas City, Kansas: Historical and Biographical* (Chicago, 1890), p. 426.
54. George E. Loyau, *The Gawler Handbook* (Adelaide, 1880), p. 26.
55. C. Gavan Duffy, "Port Phillip: A Preliminary Chapter in the Political History of Victoria," *Melbourne Review* (Oct. 1876), 4:385.
56. M. Tarver, "St. Louis—Its Early History," *Western Journal* (Feb. 1849),

2(2):83–84. For similar sentiments see a letter written by a congressman who was an early Illinois pioneer and quoted in John H. Thurston, *Reminiscences, Sporting and Otherwise, of Early Days in Rockford, Ill.* (Rockford, 1891), p. 44.

57. L. U. Reavis, *Saint Louis: The Future Great City of the World* (St. Louis, 1871), p. 127.

58. John B. Read, ed., *Resources of Butte* (Butte, 1895), p. 16.

59. Casseday, *History of Louisville*, pp. 13–14.

60. William Westgarth, *The Colony of Victoria: Its History, Commerce, and Gold Mining; Its Social and Political Institutions; Down to the End of 1863* (London, 1864), p. 10.

61. Buckingham, *Eastern and Western States,* 3:148.

62. Alphonso Taft, *A Lecture on Cincinnati and her Rail-Roads: Delivered Before the Young Men's Mercantile Library Association, January 22, 1850* (Cincinnati, 1850), pp. 28–29. Delight in "anticipating the future" is also defined as an American characteristic in Tarver, "St. Louis—Its Early History," p. 84.

63. Lawrence Oliphant, *Minnesota and the Far West* (Edinburgh and London, 1855), p. 144.

64. John Gates Thurston, *A Journal of a Trip to Illinois in 1836* (Mount Pleasant, Mich.: John Cumming, 1971), p. 33.

65. "Wall Street Looks at the Agricultural Northwest," pp. 65–66.

66. Chas. H. Allen, *A Visit to Queensland and Her Goldfields* (London, 1870), p. 111.

67. Henry Tudor, *Narrative of a Tour in North America* (London, 1834), 1:186.

68. Caroline Matilda Kirkland, *A New Home or Life in the Clearings* (New York: Putnam, 1953), p. 52.

69. Dan Elbert Clark, "Some Episodes in the Early History of Des Moines," *Iowa Journal of History and Politics* (April 1915), 13(2):197–99.

70. Oliphant, *Minnesota and the Far West,* p. 145.

71. Francis Jameson Rowbotham, *A Trip to Prairie-Land Being a Glance at the Shady Side of Emigration* (London, 1885), pp. 22–27.

72. Frances Trollope, *Domestic Manners of the Americans* (New York: Knopf, 1949), p. 39.

73. Dicey, *Six Months in the Federal States,* 2:114.

74. "A Retired Officer of the Hon. East India Company's Service" (T. J. Maslen), *The Friend of Australia; or, a Plan for Exploring the Interior, and for Carrying on a Survey of the Whole Continent of Australia* (London, 1830), p. 267.

75. *The Autobiography of John Galt* (Philadelphia and Boston, 1834), 2:54.

76. Cf. the quotation from a contemporary publication inviting the reader to "fill, in your imagination," the plat and acquire "the outline and shadow of the picture, that will in reality ornament Tom Elliott's town site [Elliott, North Dakota] in the near future," in John W. Reps, *Cities of the American West: A History of Frontier Urban Planning,* pp. 545–47.

77. Gladstone, *The Englishman in Kansas,* p. 142.

78. Kate Milner Rabb, ed., *A Tour Through Indiana in 1840: The Diary of John Parsons of Petersburg, Virginia* (New York: McBride, 1920), p. 144.
79. Emily Pfeiffer, *Flying Leaves from East and West* (London, 1885), p. 121.
80. Frank Thomas Bullen, *Advance Australasia; A Day-to-Day Record of a Recent Visit to Australasia* (London: Hodder and Stoughton, 1907), p. 242.
81. Sala, *America Revisited,* 2:153–54.
82. Raymond Stanley, ed., *Tourist to the Antipodes: William Archer's "Australian Journey, 1876–77"* (St. Lucia: University of Queensland Press, 1977), p. 17.
83. Alexander Begg, *Practical Hand-Book and Guide to Manitoba and the North-west* (Toronto, 1877), p. 99.
84. Derek Whitelock, *Adelaide 1833–1976: A History of Difference* (St. Lucia: University of Queensland Press, 1977), p. 28.
85. Colin Kerr, *"A Excellent Coliney": The Practical Idealists of 1836–1846* (Adelaide: Rigby, 1978), p. 106.
86. "A Squatter" (E. Lloyd), *A Visit to the Antipodes: With some Reminiscences of a Sojourn in Australia* (London, 1846), pp. 85–86.
87. T. Horton James, *Six Months in South Australia* (London, 1838), pp. 33, 90.
88. Robert Harrison, *Colonial Sketches: or, Five Years in South Australia, with Hints to Capitalists and Emigrants* (London and Newcastle-on-Tyne, 1862), pp. 32–35.
89. Rosamond and Florence Hill, *What We Saw in Australia* (London, 1875), p. 48. For comment on the contrast between the present and the anticipated metropolitan future as reflected in a plan, see also White, *Sketches From America,* pp. 229–30.
90. Sala, *America Revisited,* 2:153–54.
91. James, *Six Months in South Australia,* p. 90.
92. Anthony Forster, *South Australia: Its Progress and Prosperity* (London, 1866), p. 84.
93. Gladstone, *The Englishman in Kansas,* p. 145.
94. *Sidney's Emigrant's Journal* (Dec. 21, 1848), 1(12):89–90.
95. Edith G. Firth, ed., *The Town of York 1793–1815: A Collection of Documents of Early Toronto* (Toronto: Champlain Society, 1962), p. 23.
96. J. G. Kohl, *Travels in Canada, and Through the States of New York and Pennsylvania* (London, 1861), 2:16–17.
97. Frederick Law Olmsted, *A Journey Through Texas; or, A Saddle-Trip on the Southwestern Frontier* (New York, 1857), pp. 5–6.
98. John Ernest Tinne, *The Wonderland of the Antipodes; and Other Sketches of Travel in the North Island of New Zealand* (London, 1873), p. 43.
99. Godfrey Charles Mundy, *Our Antipodes: Or, Residence and Rambles in the Australasian Colonies: With a Glimpse of the Gold Fields* (London, 1857), p. 95; Mary Stuart Boyd, *Our Stolen Summer; The Record of a Roundabout Tour* (Edinburgh and London, 1900), p. 96.
100. Olsson, *A Pioneer in Northwest America,* 2:143.

8. The Town in the Garden

1. Letters by an unknown author, published in the *Minnesota Pioneer*, Nov. 8 and 15, 1849, and quoted in Willoughby M. Babcock, "Steamboat Travel on the Upper Mississippi in 1849," *Minnesota History* (March 1926), 7(1):60.

2. Laurence Oliphant, *Minnesota and the Far West* (Edinburgh and London, 1855), p. 257.

3. "A Colonist," *Life's Work As It Is; or, The Emigrants Home in Australia* (London, 1867), pp. 20, 84.

4. Edward Dicey, *Six Months in the Federal States* (London and Cambridge, 1863), 2:53.

5. Sándor Forkas Bölöni, *A Journey to North America* (1838), quoted in Marc Pachter and Frances Wein, eds., *Abroad in America: Visitors to the New Nation 1776–1914*, p. 49.

6. George Wilson Pierson, *Tocqueville and Beaumont in America* (New York: Oxford University Press, 1938), pp. 236–37.

7. William Oliver, *Eight Months in Illinois With Information to Immigrants* (Newcastle upon Tyne, 1843; Chicago: Walter M. Hill, 1924), p. 27.

8. George Henry, *The Emigrant's Guide, or Canada As It Is* (Quebec, n.d.), p. 118.

9. Joaquin Miller, "A Ride Through Oregon," *The Overland Monthly* (April 1872), 8(4):307.

10. [Edmund Flagg], *The Far West: or, A Tour Beyond the Mountains* (New York, 1838), reprinted in R. G. Thwaites, ed., *Early Western Travels 1748–1846* (Cleveland: Arthur H. Clark, 1906), pp. 27, 241.

11. *Ibid.*, p. 202.

12. Frederick Law Olmsted, *A Journey Through Texas; or, a Saddle-Trip on the Southwestern Frontier* (New York, 1857) p. 5.

13. [C. R. Carter], *Victoria, The British "El Dorado"; or, Melbourne in 1869. Showing the Advantages of That Colony as a Field for Emigration* (London, 1869), p. 181.

14. Nils William Olsson, ed., *A Pioneer in Northwest America 1841–1858: The Memoirs of Gustaf Unonius* (Minneapolis: University of Minnesota Press, 1950), 1:152.

15. J. G. Kohl, *Travels in Canada, and Through the States of New York and Pennsylvania* (London, 1861), 2:18–19.

16. John Dunmore Lang, *An Historical and Statistical Account of New South Wales* (London, 1852), 2:279.

17. Paul de Rousiers, *American Life* (Paris and New York, 1892), pp. 131–32.

18. For comments on "illusory décors," see Stephen Fender, *Plotting the Golden West: American Literature and the Rheotoric of the California Trail* (Cambridge: Cambridge University Press, 1981), p. 108; Lady Barker, *Station Life in New Zealand* (Auckland: Golden Press, 1973), p. 18; W. David McIntyre, ed., *The Journal of Henry Sewell 1853–7* (Christchurch: Whitcoulls, 1980), 1:186–87.

19. Almon Gunnison, *Rambles Overland: A Trip Across the Continent* (Boston, 1884), pp. 86–87.
20. John M. White, *The Newer Northwest* (St. Louis, 1894), pp. 41–42.
21. Ferdinand Roemer, *Texas with Particular Reference to German Immigration and the Physical Appearance of the Country: Described Through Personal Observation* (San Antonio: Standard Printing, 1935), pp. 97; Captain Frederick Marryat, *Diary in America* (London: Nicholas Vane, 1960), p. 119.
22. Gunnison, *Rambles Overland,* p. 86.
23. Anna Brownell Jameson, *Winter Studies and Summer Rambles in Canada: Selections* (Toronto: McClelland and Stewart, 1965), p. 52.
24. G. H. Haydon, *Five Years Experience in Australia Felix* (London, 1846), 1:54–55.
25. "A Squatter" [E. Lloyd], *A Visit to the Antipodes: With Some Reminiscences of a Sojourn in Australia* (London, 1846), p. 84.
26. G. E. Bell to Edwin R. Bell, Sept. 29, 1843 (Chicago Historical Society collections), quoted in G. Thomas Tanselle, "Herman Melville's Visit to Galena in 1840," *Journal of the Illinois State Historical Society* (Winter 1960), 53(4):377.
27. See Charles Fenno Hoffman, *A Winter in the West, by a New Yorker* (New York, 1835), pp. 40–41.
28. For comment on this see James T. Lemon, *The Best Poor Man's Country: A Geographical Study of Early Southeastern Pennsylvania* (Baltimore and London: Johns Hopkins University Press, 1972), pp. 98–109.
29. See the description of Virgil, Ohio, in John Regan, *The Emigrant's Guide to the Western States of America; or, Backwoods and Prairies* (Edinburgh, n.d.), p. 60. See also the description of settlement near Melbourne in [W. Westgarth], *Commercial and Statistical Report on the Colony of Port Phillip, New South Wales* (Melbourne, 1844), p. 1.
30. Coral Lansbury, *Arcady in Australia; The Evocation of Australia in Nineteenth-Century English Literature.*
31. "A Late Resident" [Francis Fairplay], *The Canadas as They Now Are* (London, 1833), p. 41.
32. Lang, *An Historical and Statistical Account,* 2:258.
33. Henry T. Newton Chesshyre, *Canada in 1864: A Hand-Book for Settlers* (London, 1864), pp. 35–36.
34. Cf. the comment in "A Citizen of the World" [James Boardman], *America, and the Americans* (London, 1833), pp. 126–27.
35. Pierson, *Tocqueville and Beaumont in America,* p. 246.
36. "American and European Scenery Compared," *The Home Book of the Picturesque, or American Scenery, Art, and Literature* (1832), p. 69, quoted in Cushing Strout, *The American Image of the Old World* (New York: Harper & Row, 1963), p. 97. On Cooper see also Marvin Meyers, *The Jacksonian Persuasion* (Stanford: Stanford University Press, 1957).
37. Daniel S. Curtiss, *Western Portraiture, and Emigrants' Guide: A Description of Wisconsin, Illinois, and Iowa: With Remarks on Minnesota, and Other*

Territories (New York, 1852), p. 321. On the New England village ideal see Thomas J. Schlereth, "The New England Presence on the Midwest Landscape," p. 133.

38. James L. Machor, "Urbanization and the Western Garden: Synthesizing City and Country in Antebellum America," and *Pastoral Cities: Urban Ideals and the Symbolic Landscape of America;* Leo Marx, *The Machine in the Garden: Technology and the Pastoral Ideal in America;* Thomas Bender, *Toward an Urban Vision: Ideas and Institutions in Nineteenth-Century America,* pp. 14, 77–79.

39. William Darby, *A Tour From the City of New-York, to Detroit* (New York, 1810), p. 23.

40. For an example of the "town in the garden" image, see Hopkins Rowell, *The Great Resources, and Superior Advantages of the City of Joliet, Illinois,* (Joliet, 1871), p. 20.

41. Richard Howitt, *Australia Historical, Descriptive, and Statistic: With an Account of a Four Years' Residence in That Colony: Notes of a Voyage Round the World; Australian Poems, &c* (London, 1845), p. 118.

42. For an example of this theme in transition see [John Hinchcliffe], *Historical Review of Belleville, Illinois, From Early Times to the Present, With a Glance at Its Business, Present and Prospective* (Belleville, 1870), p. 78. Discussion of this theme by historians may be found in P. R. Proudfoot, "Arcadia and the Idea of Amenity"; Miles Fairburn, "The Rural Myth and the New Urban Frontier: An Approach to New Zealand Social History, 1870–1940," *New Zealand Journal of History* (April 1975), 9(1):3–21; Graeme Davison, *The Rise and Fall of Marvellous Melbourne,* pp. 137–55; Kenneth T. Jackson, *Crabgrass Frontier: The Suburbanization of the United States,* pp. 45–86.

43. Mary Hoban, *Fifty-One Pieces of Wedding Cake: A Biography of Caroline Chisholm* (Kilmore, Victoria: Lowden, 1973), p. 337.

44. Kohl, *Travels in Canada,* 1:249.

45. John Robert Godley, *Letters From America* (London, 1844), 1:112–13.

46. E.g., J. W. F. Blundell, *Early Days of a Colony; or, A Ramble Near Melbourne* (n.p., n.d.), (pamphlet in Mitchell Library), p. 393.

47. Anthony Trollope, *Australia and New Zealand* (Melbourne, 1873), p. 28.

48. John Kennedy, Junior, *Kennedy's Colonial Travel: A Narrative of a Four Years' Tour Through Australia, New Zealand, Canada, &c.* (Edinburgh and London, 1876), p. 34.

49. Chester A. Loomis, *A Journey on Horseback Through the Great West, in 1825* (New York, n.d.), p. 25.

50. Lawrence H. Larsen, *The Urban West at the End of the Frontier,* pp. 47–60; John W. Reps, *Cities of the American West: A History of Frontier Urban Planning.*

51. Richard C. Wade, *The Urban Frontier: Pioneer Life in Early Pittsburgh, Cincinnati, Lexington, Louisville, and St. Louis,* pp. 27–30; M. G. Upton, "The Plan of San Francisco," *Overland Monthly* (Feb. 1869), 2(2):131–37.

52. William Howitt, *Land, Labour and Gold or Two Years in Victoria: With Visits to Sydney and Van Diemen's Land* (1855; Kilmore: Lowden, 1972), p. 8.

53. Examples include San Francisco and Kansas City in the United States and Wellington and Dunedin in New Zealand. For comment on the Dunedin situation see A. H. McLintock, *The History of Otago: The Origins and Growth of a Wakefield Class Settlement* (Dunedin: Otago Centennial Historical Publications, 1949), pp. 423–24.

54. Capt. H. Butler Stoney, *A Residence in Tasmania: With a Descriptive Tour Through the Island, From Macquarie Harbour to Circular Head* (London, 1856), p. 17.

55. J. Rutherford, ed., *The Founding of New Zealand: The Journals of Felton Mathew, First Surveyor-General of New Zealand, and his Wife, 1840–1847* (Dunedin: A. H. & A. W. Reed, 1940), p. 197.

56. Reps, *Cities of the American West,* pp. 565–68.

57. "Melbourne As It Is, and As It Ought To Be," *The Australasian* (Oct. 1850), 1:137–46.

58. D. N. Jeans, *An Historical Geography of New South Wales to 1901,* pp. 110–12.

59. John Dunmore Lang, *Phillipsland; or the Country Hitherto Designated Port Phillip: Its Present Condition and Prospects, as a Highly Eligible Field for Emigration* (Edinburgh, 1847), pp. 183–84.

60. C. E. Sayers, ed., *Earle's Port Fairy: A History by William Earle, First Published at the Gazette Office, Port Fairy, 1896* (Olinda, Victoria: Olinda Public Relations, 1973), pp. xvii–xviii.

61. J. S. Buckingham, *The Eastern and Western States of America* (London and Paris, n.d.), 2:351.

62. William Westgarth, *Victoria; Late Australia Felix, or Port Phillip District of New South Wales; Being an Historical and Descriptive Account of the Colony and its Gold Mines* (Edinburgh and London, 1853), pp. 64–65.

63. William Westgarth, *The Colony of Victoria: Its History, Commerce, and Gold Mining; Its Social and Political Institutions; Down to the End of 1863: With Remarks, Incidental and Comparative, Upon the Other Australian Colonies* (London, 1864), pp. 92–93.

64. *The Industries of Tacoma, Washington: Her Resources, Advantages and Facilities in Trade, Commerce and Manufactures* (Tacoma, 1889), p. 26. *Tacoma: The Western Terminus of the Northern Pacific Railroad* (Tacoma, 1889), p. 13.

65. Fender, *Plotting the Golden West,* pp. 18, 28.

66. F. Lancelott, *Australia As It Is: Its Settlements, Farms, and Gold Fields* (London, 1852), 2:204–5.

67. Charles Richard Weld, *A Vacation Tour in the United States and Canada* (London, 1855), p. 9. For the removal of "wilderness" from new towns see Gunther Barth, *Instant Cities: Urbanization and the Rise of San Francisco and Denver,* pp. 92–127.

68. Elizabeth Waterston, "Towns and Country in John Galt: A Literary Perspective," *Urban History Review/Revue d'histoire urbaine* (June 1985), 14(1):17–22.

69. *The Autobiography of John Galt* (Philadelphia and Boston, 1834), 2:53.

70. John Galt, *Lawrie Todd: or, The Settlers in the Woods* (London, [1832]), pp. 165–67.

71. Pat Hayward, ed., *Surgeon Henry's Trifles: Events of a Military Life* (London: Chatto and Windus, 1970), pp. 232–33.

72. *History and Directory of Kent County, Michigan, Containing a History of each Township, and the City of Grand Rapids* (Grand Rapids, 1870), p. 114.

73. *Lecture on the "West"; Delivered by Special Request, at the Tremont Temple, Boston, Mass., February 24, 1858, by Hon. George B. Sargent, Mayor of Davenport, Iowa* (Davenport, 1858), pp. 3–5.

74. J. Douglas Stewart and Ian E. Wilson, *Heritage Kingston* (Kingston: Queen's University, [1973]), p. 131.

75. See the account of Vancouver, British Columbia, in the extracts from W. H. H. Murray, *Daylight Land* (1888), in James Doyle, ed., *Yankees in Canada: A Collection of Nineteenth-Century Travel Narratives* (Downsview, Ont.: E. C. W. Press, 1980), pp. 212–15.

76. Frank Crowley, ed., *A Documentary History of Australia*, vol. 2: *Colonial Australia 1841–1874* (West Melbourne: Nelson, 1980), p. 57; Russel Ward, *The Australian Legend*, p. 79; Jeans, *Historical Geography of New South Wales*, 298–99.

77. Joseph Pickering, *Inquiries of an Emigrant: Being the Narrative of an English Farmer From the Year 1824 to 1830* (London, 1832), p. vi.

78. C. P. Lucas, ed., *Lord Durham's Report on the Affairs of British North America* (Oxford: Clarendon Press, 1912), 2:239, 256.

79. Susanna Moodie, *Roughing it in the Bush or Forest Life in Canada* (Toronto: McClelland and Stewart, [1970]), p. 237.

80. Susanna Moodie, *Life in the Clearings* (Toronto: Macmillan 1959). This is a reprint of the 1853 edition of *Life in the Clearings Versus the Bush.*

81. E. S. Dunlop, ed., *Our Forest Home Being Extracts From the Correspondence of the Late Frances Stewart* (Montreal: Gazette Printing and Publishing, 1902), p. 83.

82. Douglas M. Gane, *New South Wales and Victoria in 1885* (London, 1886), p. 144.

83. Rev. H. Berkeley Jones, *Adventures in Australia, in 1852 and 1853* (London, 1853), p. 71.

84. Margaret Kiddle, *Caroline Chisholm* (Carlton, Victoria: Melbourne University Press, 1969), p. 72.

85. *New South Wales Legislative Council: Votes and Proceedings, 1843: Report From the Select Committee on Immigration*, pp. 17, 39.

86. *New South Wales Legislative Council: Votes and Proceedings, 1849: Minutes of Evidence Taken Before the Select Committee on Crown Lands*, p. 4.

87. *Legislative Assembly, New South Wales: Votes and Proceedings, 1859–60: Report from the Select Committee on the Condition of the Working Classes of the Metropolis,* pp. 3–4, 25, 94, 105–7, 115–17, 128. Balmain is an inner-city suburb of Sydney on the west side of Darling Harbour, The Rocks where the settlement of Sydney originated being on the east side. It is accessible by a five to ten minutes' ferry ride from Circular Quay. The North Shore is similarly close—on the northern end of the Sydney Harbour bridge. Waverley is a suburb just south of Bondi beach on the seacoast south of Port Jackson. It is about 8 kilometers from the inner city.

88. *New South Wales Parliamentary Debates,* First Series, 2:1806.

89. James Dixon, *Narrative of a Voyage to New South Wales, and Van Dieman's Land, in the Ship Skelton, During the Year 1820: With Observations on the State of These Colonies, and a Variety of Information, Calculated to be Useful to Emigrants* (Edinburgh, 1822), p. 73.

90. [Caroline Chisholm], *Female Immigration Considered, in a Brief Account of the Sydney Immigrants' Home* (Sydney, 1842), pp. 13, 89.

91. *The Sydney Herald,* Dec. 4, 1841.

92. Charles Wentworth Dilke, *Greater Britain: A Record of Travel in English-Speaking Countries* (London, 1885), p. 296.

9. Towns and the Evolution of "Civilization"

1. Laurence Oliphant, *Minnesota and the Far West* (Edinburgh and London, 1855), p. 159.

2. For examples see Morris Birkbeck, *Notes on a Journey in America, from the Coast of Virginia to the Territory of Illinois, with Proposals for the Establishment of a Colony of English* (London, 1818), p. 78; Carl David Arfwedson, *The United States and Canada in 1832, 1833, and 1834* (New York and London: Johnson Reprint, 1969), 2:1–2: Thomas Henry Braim, *A History of New South Wales, From its Settlement to the Close of the Year 1844* (London, 1846), 2:306; [C. R. Carter], *Victoria, The British "El Dorado"; or, Melbourne in 1869: Shewing the Advantages of that Colony as a Field for Emigration* (London, 1870), pp. 10–11; *The Sydney Herald,* Oct. 24, 1842; Frank Crowley, ed., *A Documentary History of Australia,* vol. 1: *Colonial Australia, 1788–1840* (West Melbourne: Nelson, 1980), p. 171; Carl Abbott, *Boosters and Businessmen: Popular Economic Thought and Urban Growth in the Antebellum Middle West,* p. 150.

3. "A Colonist," *Life's Work As It Is; or, The Emigrant's Home in Australia* (London, 1867), pp. 23–24. For a similar description of Adelaide see J. F. Bennett, *Historical and Descriptive Account of South Australia: Founded on the Experience of a Three Years' Residence in that Colony* (London, 1843), p. 18. Horace Earle applied the theme generally to Australian urban development in *Ups and Downs; or, Incidents of Australian Life* (London, 1861), p. vii.

4. Earle, *Ups and Downs,* p. vii.
5. James B. Brown, *Views of Canada and the Colonists* (Edinburgh, 1851), p. 23.
6. C. Gavan Duffy, "Port Phillip: A Preliminary Chapter in the Political History of Victoria," *Melbourne Review* (Oct. 1876), 4:385.
7. E.g., *Records of the Castlemaine Pioneers* (Adelaide: Rigby, 1972), p. 65.
8. *The New British Province of South Australia; or A Description of the Country* (London, 1835), p. 124.
9. John Elmsley to Mary Elmsley, Dec. 10, 1827, in Edith G. Firth, ed., *The Town of York 1815–1834: A Further Collection of Documents of Early Toronto* (Toronto: Champlain Society, 1966), pp. 318–19.
10. *The A.B.C. of Colonisation: In a Series of Letters. By Mrs. Chisholm* (London, 1850), 1:31.
11. Eugene E. Snyder, *Early Portland: Stump-Town Triumphant: Rival Townsites on the Willamette 1831–1854* (Portland: Binford & Mort, 1984), p. 46.
12. See the pleasure at the early transformation of Fremantle expressed in George Fletcher Moore, *Diary of Ten Years Eventful Life of an Early Settler in Western Australia; and Also a Descriptive Vocabulary of the Language of the Aborigines* (London, 1884), p. 150.
13. See the descriptions of Cobourg and London, Ontario, in Brown, *Views of Canada and the Colonists,* pp. 175–76, 282–85.
14. Bernard Smith, *The Antipodean Manifesto: Essays in Art and History,* p. 86.
15. "Three Hundred Years Hence," *Illinois Monthly Magazine* (Nov. 1830), 1:52–54.
16. "Another Glimpse of the Future," *Illinois Monthly Magazine* (Sept. 1831), 1:565–66.
17. See John Graves Simcoe to the Duke of Portland, Oct. 23, 1794, urging "the increase of Towns, the want of which occasions the barbarous manners & roving tendency of the Subjects of the United States." E. A. Cruikshank, ed., *The Correspondence of Lieut. Governor John Graves Simcoe, With Allied Documents Relating to His Admininstration of the Government of Upper Canada* (Toronto: Ontario Historical Society, 1925), 3:142; A. L. Strauss, *The Contexts of Social Mobility: Ideology and Theory,* p. 27.
18. Archibald Michie, *Readings in Melbourne; With an Essay on the Resources and Prospects of Victoria, for the Emigrant and Uneasy Classes* (London, 1879), p. 153.
19. *How and Where to Get a Living: A Sketch of "The Garden of the West"; Presenting Facts Worth Knowing Concerning the Lands of the Atchison, Topeka & Santa Fe Railroad Co., in Southwestern Kansas* (Boston, 1876).
20. J. C. Byrne, *Twelve Years' Wanderings in the British Colonies: From 1835 to 1847* (London, 1848), 1:157–58, 191–94.
21. *The New British Province of South Australia,* p. 124.
22. Donald Winch, *Classical Political Economy and Colonies* (London: G. Bell, 1965), p. 166.

23. D. W. Meinig, *On the Margins of the Good Earth: The South Australian Wheat Frontier 1869–1884;* Michael Williams, *The Making of the South Australian Landscape: A Study in the Historical Geography of Australia.*

24. *Legislative Assembly, New South Wales: Votes and Proceedings, 1865; Minutes of Evidence Taken Before the Select Committee on the Present State of the Colony,* pp. 60–75.

25. J. M. Powell, *The Public Lands of Australia Felix: Settlement and Land Appraisal in Victoria 1834–91, With Special Reference to the Western Plains* (Melbourne: Oxford University Press, 1970), p. 95.

26. Thomas Bender, *Toward an Urban Vision: Ideas and Institutions in Nineteenth-Century America,* p. 10; Marvin Meyers, *The Jacksonian Persuasion: Politics and Belief* (Stanford: Stanford University Press, 1957).

27. Richard Hildreth, *Despotism in America: An Inquiry into the Nature, Results, and Legal Basis of the Slave-Holding Systems in the United States* (Boston, 1854), p. 139.

28. For New England missionary attitudes to the West see Rush Welter, *The Mind of America 1820–1860,* pp. 309–11.

29. Quoted in John S. Wright, *Chicago: Past, Present, Future* (Chicago, 1868), p. 273.

30. Cole Patrick Dawson, "Yankees in the Queen City: The Social and Intellectual Contributions of New Englanders in Cincinnati, 1820–1850," Ph.D. dissertation, Miami University, Oxford, Ohio, 1977.

31. Theodore Gerrish, *Life in the World's Wonderland: Illustrated: A Graphic Description of the Great Northwest, From St. Paul, Minnesota, to the Land of the Midnight Sun* (Biddeford, Maine, 1887), pp. 136–37, 165.

32. *The New States: A Sketch of the History and Development of the States of North Dakota, South Dakota, Montana, and Washington, with Map and Illustrations* (New York and Chicago, 1889), pp. 51–52.

33. See Meyers, *The Jacksonian Persuasion.*

34. Quoted in Martin Sullivan, *Men & Women of Port Phillip* (Sydney: Hale & Iremonger, 1985), p. 25.

35. Simcoe to Henry Dundas, June 30, 1791, Cruikshank, *Correspondence of Simcoe,* 1:27.

36. *Ibid.,* p. 18.

37. The outstanding practitioner of this type of boosterism was Daniel Drake, for whom see Henry D. Shapiro and Zane L. Miller, eds., *Physician to the West: Selected Writings of Daniel Drake on Science & Society;* and Richard C. Wade, *The Urban Frontier: Pioneer Life in Early Pittsburgh, Cincinnati, Lexington, Louisville, and St. Louis,* pp. 155–57.

38. Louis Leonard Tucker, "Cincinnati: Athens of the West, 1830–1861."

39. E. H. Coombe, *History of Gawler 1837 to 1908* (Gawler: Gawler Institute, 1908), p. 347.

40. For some Australian examples see Keith Swan, *A History of Wagga Wagga* (Wagga Wagga, 1970), p. 68; Janette Nolan, *Bundaberg: History and People* (St. Lucia: University of Queensland Press, 1978), p. 191; J. Y. Walker, *The*

History of Bundaberg: A Typical Queensland Agricultural Settlement (Sydney: Dryden Press, 1977), p. 191. See also D. Whitelock, *The Great Tradition: A History of Adult Education in Australia* (St. Lucia: University of Queensland Press, 1977); Weston Bate, *Lucky City: The First Generation at Ballarat 1851–1901* (Carlton, Victoria: Melbourne University Press, 1978), pp. 239–40; A. Wesson, "Mechanics' Institutes in Victoria," *Australian Journal of Adult Education* (1972), p. 12.

41. Brown, *Views of Canada and the Colonists*, p.285. On the London mechanics' institute see Nancy Z. Tausky and Lynne D. Di Stefano, *Victorian Architecture in London and Southwestern Ontario: Symbols of Aspiration*, pp. 211–14.

42. Kate Milner Rabb, ed., *A Tour Through Indiana in 1840: The Diary of John Parsons of Petersburg, Virginia* (New York: McBride, 1920), p. 327.

43. A. de Q. Robin, *Charles Perry, Bishop of Melbourne: The Challenges of a Colonial Episcopate, 1847–76* (Nedlands: University of Western Australia Press, 1967), pp. 165–66; C. H. S. Matthews, *A Parson in the Australian Bush* (1908; Adelaide: Rigby, 1973), pp. 26, 52; William Bell, *Hints to Emigrants; In a Series of Letters From Upper Canada* (Edinburgh, 1824), p. 103.

44. William Darby, *A Tour From the City of New-York, to Detroit* (New York, 1810), p. 190.

45. *Maclehose's Picture of Sydney; and Strangers' Guide to New South Wales for 1839* (Sydney, 1839; St. Ives: Ferguson, 1977), p. vi. For similar sentiments expressed in a private letter see *Dr. Ludwig Leichhardt's Letters From Australia During the Years March 23, 1842, to April 3, 1848* (Melbourne: Pan Publishers, 1944), p. 17.

46. Melbourne, 1881. See the famous 1934 postage stamp depicting an aborigine looking at Melbourne's modern skyline: Jim Davidson, ed., *The Sydney-Melbourne Book*, p. 228.

47. J. C. Myers, *Sketches on a Tour Through the Northern and Eastern States, The Canadas & Nova Scotia* (Harrisonburg, 1849), pp. 112–13.

48. Sir Richard S. Bonnycastle, *The Canadas in 1841* (London, 1841), 1:148.

49. *The Minnesota Messenger, Containing Sketches of the Rise and Progress of Minnesota* (Saint Paul, 1855), p. 11.

50. Gunther Barth, *Instant Cities: Urbanization and the Rise of San Francisco and Denver*, pp. 201–2.

51. Don H. Doyle, *Nashville in the New South 1880–1930* (Knoxville: University of Tennessee Press, 1985), pp. 13–14.

52. Ralph L. Harmon, "Ignatius Donnelly and his Faded Metropolis," *Minnesota History* (Sept. 1936), 17(3):264.

53. William Kelly, *Life in Victoria or Victoria in 1853, and Victoria in 1858 Showing the March of Improvement Made by the Colony Within Those Periods, in Town and Country, Cities and the Diggings* (London, 1859), p. 37.

54. See Alfred Brunson, *Prairie du Chien: Its Present Position and Future Prospects* (Milwaukee, 1857), p. 5.

55. *Rise and Progress of Minnesota Territory* (Saint Paul, 1855), p. 39. For

similar sentiments about a town in Ohio see W. D. Root, *Sandusky in 1855: City Guide and Business Directory* (Sandusky, 1855), pp. 13–15.

56. [Edward Wilson], *Rambles at the Antipodes: A Series of Sketches of Moreton Bay, New Zealand, the Murray River and South Australia, and the Overland Route* (London, 1859), p. 23.

57. Richard Howitt, *Australia: Historical, Descriptive, and Statistic: With an Account of a Four Years' Residence in That Colony: Notes of a Voyage Round the World; Australian Poems, &c.* (London, 1845), pp. 118, 185–87.

58. Herbert Hunt, *Tacoma: Its History and Its Builders: A Half Century of Activity* (Chicago: S. J. Clarke, 1916), 1:133. Cf. the description of Indians at St. Paul in J. W. Bond, *Minnesota and its Resources* (Chicago, 1857), pp. 112–14.

59. Allan M. Nixon, *Inglewood Gold: Gold Town of Early Victoria 1859–1982* (Greensborough, Victoria: Sundowner Press, 1982), p. 37.

60. John S. Fisher, *A Builder of the West: The Life of General William Jackson Palmer* (Caldwell, Idaho: Caxton, 1939), p. 239.

61. F. Lancelott, *Australia As It Is: Its Settlements, Farms, and Gold Fields* (London, 1852), 2:204–5.

62. *Collection of Nebraska Pioneer Reminiscences Issued by the Nebraska Society of the Daughters of the American Revolution* (Cedar Rapids, Iowa: Torch Press, 1916), pp. 141–42.

63. George Conrad Petersen, *Palmerston North: A Centennial History* (Wellington: A. H. & A. W. Reed, 1973), pp. 109–10.

64. See Edward Wilson's description of the blacks in Brisbane as "not greatly deteriorated by contact with that civilisation which we cavalierly acknowledge to be their death warrant" (*Rambles at the Antipodes*, p. 23). For the argument that indigenous peoples must be expelled because of the corrupting effect on them of urban life see Howitt, *Australia*, p. 198.

65. See Barth, *Instant Cities*, pp. 125, 197.

66. Rabb, *A Tour Through Indiana in 1840*, p. 135.

67. H. J. Jones, *From Bush to Borough: Official Souvenir 1906–1956 Commemorating the Golden Jubilee of the Borough of Levin* (Borough of Levin: Levin, 1956), p. 11.

68. See, for example, the quotations in Malcolm J. Rohrbough, *The Trans-Appalachian Frontier: People, Societies, and Institutions 1775–1850* (New York: Oxford University Press, 1978), pp. 277–78; and Evelyn Stokes, *A History of Tauranga County* (Palmerston North: Dunmore Press, 1980), pp. 283–85.

69. Derek Whitelock, *Adelaide 1833–1976: A History of Difference* (St. Lucia: University of Queensland Press, 1977), pp. 59, 185.

70. Lancelott, *Australia As It Is*, 2:205.

71. Colin Kerr, *"A Exelent Coliney." The Practical Idealists of 1836–1846* (Adelaide: Rigby, 1978), p. vii.

72. Don Garden, *Hamilton: A Western District History* (North Melbourne: Hargreen, 1984), p. 116.

73. Frank Eliel, *Our Little Town: Dillon, Montana: Reflections and Reminiscences Recorded by Frank Eliel* (n.p. 1925), p. [8].

74. John Mortimer Murphy, *Rambles in North-Western America From the Pacific Ocean to the Rocky Mountains* (London, 1879), p. 142.

75. Charles Wentworth Dilke, *Greater Britain: A Record of Travel in English-Speaking Countries* (London, 1885), p. 80.

76. *Letters, Written by John Kingman, While on a Tour to Illinois and Wisconsin, in the Summer of 1838* (Hingham, 1842), p. 25. For other examples of revulsion from Indians in the streets see A. A. Parker, *Trip to the West and Texas* (Concord, N.H., 1835), pp. 35–36; and Tocqueville's reaction as described in George Wilson Pierson, *Tocqueville and Beaumont in America* (New York: Oxford University Press, 1938), p. 148.

77. James Kingston, *The Australian Abroad: Branches from the Main Routes Round the World* (Melbourne: 1885), pp. 203–4; Frank Thomas Bullen, *Advance Australasia; a Day-to-Day Record of a Recent Visit to Australasia* (London: Hodder and Stoughton, 1907), pp. 247–49.

78. Frank Crowley, ed., *A Documentary History of Australia, vol. 2: Colonial Australia 1841–1874* (West Melbourne: Nelson, 1980), p. 17.

79. E. M. Curr, *Recollections of Squatting in Victoria* (Melbourne, 1883), p. 20.

80. Richard Broome, *Aboriginal Australians: Black Response to White Dominance 1788–1980* (Sydney: Allen & Unwin, 1982), p. 66.

81. Beverley Nance, "The Level of Violence: Europeans and Aborigines in Port Philip, 1835–1850," *Historical Studies* (Oct. 1981), 19(77):543–44.

82. R. H. W. Reece, *Aborigines and Colonists: Aborigines and Colonial Society in New South Wales in the 1830s and 1840s* (Sydney: Sydney University Press, 1974), pp. 4–17.

83. Robin Fisher, *Contact and Conflict: Indian-European Relations in British Columbia, 1774–1890* (Vancouver: University of British Columbia Press, 1977), pp. 111–15.

84. *Durango As It Is* (Durango, 1892), pp. 98–99.

85. Mary Quayle Innis, ed., *Mrs. Simcoe's Diary* (Toronto: Macmillan, 1978), p. 72.

86. Ray Allen Billington, *The Genesis of the Frontier Thesis: A Study in Historical Creativity,* pp. 10–12.

87. Godfrey Charles Mundy, *Our Antipodes: Or, Residence and Rambles in the Australasian Colonies: With a Glimpse of the Gold Fields* (London, 1857), p. 5.

88. John Askew, *A Voyage to Australia & New Zealand* (London and Cockermouth, 1857), pp. 82–86.

89. Rosamond and Florence Hill, *What We Saw in Australia* (London, 1875), pp. 267, 301. Aborigines were literally made "marginal" people. See also Donald S. Garden. *Albany: A Panorama of the Sound from 1827* (West Melbourne: Nelson, 1977), p. 179. The margins were being ever pushed outwards. Cf. *Rise and Progress of Minnesota Territory,* p. 6, on St. Paul in 1855: "From Third Street rearward, for the most part, the primeval forest

still rose up in its beauty and grandeur, and the Indian stalked to and fro among the cabins of the settlers, as if the day of his greatness, and the substance of his power were not gone."

90. John Dunmore Lang, *An Historical and Statistical Account of New South Wales* (London, 1852), 2:279.

91. William Westgarth, *Personal Recollections of Early Melbourne & Victoria* (Melbourne and Sydney, 1888), pp. 14–15. For a last corroboree see Rob Charlton, *The History of Kapunda* (Melbourne: Hawthorn Press, 1971), p. 62.

92. Alfred Simmons, *Old England and New Zealand* (London, 1879), pp. 51–52, 72–73.

93. Bonnycastle, *The Canadas in 1841,* 1:149.

94. Henry Capper, *Capper's South Australia* (London, 1839), pp. 57–58.

95. Barth, *Instant Cities,* pp. 201–2. H. Craig Miner, *Wichita: The Early Years 1865–80* (Lincoln and London: University of Nebraska Press, 1982), pp. 102, 165.

96. Murphy, *Rambles in North-Western America,* p. 143. On the "local black" see David Kennedy, Jr., *Kennedy's Colonial Travel: A Narrative of a Four Years' Tour Through Australia, New Zealand, Canada, & c.* (Edinburgh and London, 1876), p. 43.

97. R. C. Seaton, *Six Letters From the Colonies* (Hull, 1886), pp. 54–55.

10. The Urban Frontier and the Development of Myths of National Identity

1. John S. Wright, *Chicago: Past, Present, Future* (Chicago, 1868), pp. 108–10.

2. I. E. Quastler, *The Railroads of Lawrence, Kansas, 1854–1900: A Case Study in the Causes and Consequences of an Unsuccessful American Urban Railroad Program* (Lawrence, Kan.: Coronado Press, 1979), pp. 38–39.

3. On Canada see Stewart Garvie Hilts, "In Praise of Progress: Attitudes to Urbanization in Southwestern Ontario, 1850–1900," Ph.D. dissertation, University of Toronto, 1981.

4. William Westgarth, *Half a Century of Australasian Progress: A Personal Retrospect* (London, 1889), pp. 58–59.

5. Thomas Henry Braim, *A History of New South Wales, From its Settlement to the Close of the Year 1844* (1846), 2:277–78, 310.

6. Charles John Baker, *Sydney and Melbourne* (London, 1845), p. 19.

7. [J. Marshall], *Twenty Years' Experience in Australia* (London, 1840), p. 18.

8. W. J. Woods, *A Visit to Victoria* (London, 1886), p. 13.

9. Samuel Mossman and Thomas Banister, *Australia Visited and Revisited: A Narrative of Recent Travels and Old Experiences in Victoria and New South Wales* (London, 1853), p. 206.

10. [C. R. Carter], *Victoria, The British "El Dorado"; or Melbourne in 1869:*

Shewing the Advantages of that Colony as a Field for Emigration (London, 1870), p. 53.

11. For an account of what happened at this time see Graeme Davison, *The Rise and Fall of Marvellous Melbourne.* The trend from pride to shame is traced by J. B. Hirst in "The Pioneer Legend," pp. 17, 32.

12. John Freeman, *Lights and Shadows of Melbourne Life* (London, 1888), pp. 15, 18.

13. *Argus,* March 26, 1890, quoted in J. M. Powell, "The Land Debates in Victoria, 1872–1884, Leases versus Freeholds: A Preparation for Henry George," *Journal of the Royal Australian Historical Society* (1971), 56(4):277.

14. M. Clark, ed., *Sources of Australian History* (London: Oxford University Press, 1957), p. 592.

15. Russel Ward, *The Australian Legend.*

16. Douglas M. Gane, *New South Wales and Victoria in 1885* (London, 1886), pp. 40–41.

17. Edward Kinglake, *The Australians at Home: Notes and Anecdotes of Life at the Antipodes Including Useful Hints to Those Intending to Settle in Australia* (London, [1892]), p. 134.

18. See, for example, Graeme Davison, "Sydney and the Bush: An Urban Context for the Australian Legend," Carroll, *Intruders in the Bush,* pp. 109–30; Richard White, *Inventing Australia: Images of Identity 1688–1980,* pp. 85–109; and Leigh Astbury, *City Bushmen: The Heidelberg School and the Rural Mythology.*

19. For Lawson on urban romanticization of the bush see Colin Roderick, ed., *Henry Lawson: Autobiographical and Other Writings 1887–1922,* vol. 2 of Collected Prose (Sydney: Angus and Robertson, 1972), pp. 32–36.

20. Judith M. Woodward, "Urban Influence on Australian Literature in the Late Nineteenth Century," *Australian Literary Studies* (Oct. 1975), 7(2):120–21.

21. Quoted from *The Bulletin,* Dec., 8, 1900, in Ian Turner, ed., *The Australian Dream: A Collection of Anticipations about Australia from Captain Cook to the Present Day,* p. 247.

22. Vance Palmer, *The Legend of the Nineties,* p. 49.

23. Doug Owram, *Promise of Eden: The Canadian Expansionist Movement and the Idea of the West 1856–1900,* p. 136. For attitudes to the cities of the Canadian West see also R. Douglas Francis, "Changing Images of the West," pp. 636–37; and "From Wasteland to Utopia: Changing Images of the Canadian West in the Nineteenth Century," pp. 190–91.

24. George Altmeyer, "Three Ideas of Nature in Canada, 1893–1914," pp. 23–25; David C. Jones, " 'There is Some Power About the Land'—The Western Agrarian Press and Country Life Ideology."

25. The classic work on this subject is Henry Nash Smith, *Virgin Land: The American West as Symbol and Myth* (Cambridge: Harvard University Press, 1970).

26. *Western Monthly Review* (Oct. 1827), 1:331.

27. James L. Machor, "Urbanization and the Western Garden: Synthesizing

City and Country in Antebellum America," and *Pastoral Cities: Urban Ideals and the Symbolic Landscape of America.*

28. Henry D. Shapiro and Zane L. Miller, eds., *Physician to the West: Selected Writings of Daniel Drake on Science & Society.*

29. Charles Carleton Coffin, *The Seat of Empire* (Boston, 1870), pp. 17–18.

30. Lawrence H. Larsen, *The Urban West at the End of the Frontier.*

31. Robert Dixon, *The Course of Empire: Neo-Classical Culture in New South Wales 1788–1860,* pp. 79–82.

Select Bibliography

This list is designed to provide a guide to secondary literature in which there is significant discussion of nineteenth-century ideas on towns and of the major influences on the formation and application of those ideas, e.g. boosterism.

General

Briggs, Asa. *Victorian Cities.* Harmondsworth: Penguin Books, 1968.

Fraser, Derek and Anthony Sutcliffe, eds. *The Pursuit of Urban History.* London: Arnold, 1983.

Harper, Norman. "The Rural and Urban Frontiers." *Historical Studies: Australia and New Zealand* (May 1963), 10(40):401–21.

Lees, Andrew. *Cities Perceived: Urban Society in European and American Thought, 1820–1940.* Manchester: Manchester University Press, 1985.

Powell, J. M. *Mirrors of the New World: Images and Image-Makers in the Settlement Process.* Canberra: Australian National University Press, 1978.

Weber, Adna Ferrin. *The Growth of Cities in the Nineteenth Century: A Study in Statistics.* Ithaca: Cornell University Press, 1963.

Australia and New Zealand

Astbury, Leigh. *City Bushmen: The Heidelberg School and the Rural Mythology.* Melbourne: Oxford University Press, 1985.

Atkinson, Alan. "The Government of Time and Space in 1838." *The Push From the Bush: A Bulletin of Social History Devoted to the Year of Grace, 1838* (July 1981), 9:1–19.

Barrett, John. "Melbourne and the Bush: Russel Ward's Thesis and a La Trobe Survey." *Meanjin Quarterly* (Dec. 1972), 31(4):462–70.

Bolger, Peter. "The Changing Image of Hobart." In J. W. McCarty and C. B. Schedvin, eds., *Australian Capital Cities: Historical Essays,* pp. 159–70. Sydney: Sydney University Press, 1978.

Cannon, Michael. *Life in the Cities.* Melbourne: Nelson, 1975.

Cannon, Michael, ed. *Vagabond Country: Australian Bush & Town Life in the Victorian Age: By The Vagabond (John Stanley James, "Julian Thomas").* Melbourne: Hyland House, 1981.

Cooper, Roslyn Pesman. "Some Italian Views of Australia in the Nineteenth

Century." *Journal of the Royal Australian Historical Society* (Dec. 1984), 70(3):171–93.

Davidson, Jim, ed. *The Sydney-Melbourne Book*. Sydney: Allen & Unwin, 1986.

Davison, Graeme. "The Picture of Melbourne 1835–1985." In A. G. L. Shaw, ed., *Victoria's Heritage: Lectures to Celebrate the 150th Anniversary of European Settlement in Victoria*, pp. 12–36. Sydney: Allen & Unwin, 1986.

—— "R. E. N. Twopeny and Town Life in Australia." *Historical Studies* (Oct. 1974), 16(63):292–305.

—— *The Rise and Fall of Marvellous Melbourne*. Carlton, Victoria: Melbourne University Press, 1979.

—— "Sydney and the Bush: An Urban Context for the Australian Legend." In John Carroll, ed., *Intruders in the Bush: The Australian Quest for Identity*, pp. 109–30. Melbourne: Oxford University Press, 1982.

De Vries-Evans, Susanna. *Historic Sydney as Seen by Its Early Artists*. North Ryde, N.S.W.: Angus & Robertson, 1987.

Dixon, Robert. *The Course of Empire: Neo-Classical Culture in New South Wales 1788–1860*. Melbourne: Oxford University Press, 1986.

Flower, Cedric. *The Antipodes Observed: Artists of Australia 1788–1850*. South Melbourne: Sun Books, 1975.

Gilbert, Alan. "The Roots of Anti-Suburbanism in Australia." *Australian Cultural History* (1985), 4:54–70.

Glynn, Sean. *Urbanisation in Australian History*, 2d ed. West Melbourne: Nelson (Australia), 1975.

Goodwin, Craufurd D. W. *The Image of Australia: British Perception of the Australian Economy from the Eighteenth to the Twentieth Century*. Durham, N.C.: Duke University Press, 1974.

Hamer, D. A. "Impressions of Wellington." *Onslow Historian* (1984), 14(2):3–13.

—— "Towns in Nineteenth-Century New Zealand." *New Zealand Journal of History* (April 1979), 13(1):5–24.

Hirst, J. B. *Adelaide and the Country 1870–1917: Their Social and Political Relationship*. Carlton, Victoria: Melbourne University Press, 1973.

—— "The Pioneer Legend." In John Carroll, ed., *Intruders in the Bush: The Australian Quest for Identity*. Melbourne: Oxford University Press, 1982.

Jeans, D. N. *An Historical Geography of New South Wales to 1901*. Sydney: Reed Education, 1972.

—— "The Impress of Central Authority upon the Landscape: South-Eastern Australia 1788–1850." In J. M. Powell and M. Williams, eds., *Australian Space, Australian Time: Geographical Perspectives*. Melbourne: Oxford University Press, 1969.

—— "Official Town-Founding Procedures in New South Wales, 1828–1842." *Journal of the Royal Australian Historical Society* (Dec. 1981), 67(3):227–37.

—— "Territorial Divisions and the Locations of Towns in New South Wales, 1826–1842." In J. M. Powell, ed., *The Making of Rural Australia: Environ-*

ment, Society and Economy: Geographical Readings, pp. 47–58. Melbourne: Sorrett, 1974.

Lansbury, Coral. *Arcady in Australia: The Evocation of Australia in Nineteenth-Century English Literature.* Carlton, Victoria: Melbourne University Press, 1970.

Lawson, Ronald. "The 'Bush Ethos' and Brisbane in the 1890's." *Historical Studies* (April 1972), 15(58):276–83.

McCarty, J. W. and C. B. Schedvin, eds. *Australian Capital Cities: Historical Essays.* Sydney: Sydney University Press, 1978.

Meinig, D. W. *On the Margins of the Good Earth: The South Australian Wheat Frontier 1869–1884.* Chicago: Rand McNally, 1962.

Neutze, Max. "City, Country, Town: Australian Peculiarities." *Australian Cultural History* (1985), 4:7–23.

Palmer, Vance. *The Legend of the Nineties.* Melbourne: Melbourne University Press, 1963.

Proudfoot, P. R. "Arcadia and the Idea of Amenity." *Journal of the Royal Australian Historical Society* (June 1986), 72(1):3–18.

Roe, Jill. "Historiography in Melbourne in the Eighteen Seventies and Eighties." *Australian Literary Studies* (Oct. 1969), 4(3):130–38.

Roe, Michael. "The Australian Legend." *Meanjin Quarterly* (Sept. 1962), 21(3):363–66.

Saclier, Michael and Shirley A. Storrier. "As Others Saw Us." *Journal of the Royal Australian Historical Society* (Sept. 1965), 51(3):213–48.

Seddon, George and David Ravine. *A City and Its Setting: Images of Perth, Western Australia.* Fremantle: Fremantle Arts Centre Press, 1986.

Smith, Bernard. *The Antipodean Manifesto: Essays in Art and History.* Melbourne: Oxford University Press, 1976.

Turner, Ian, ed. *The Australian Dream: A Collection of Anticipations About Australia from Captain Cook to the Present Day.* Melbourne: Sun Books, 1968.

Ward, Russel. *The Australian Legend.* Melbourne: Oxford University Press, 1966.

—— "The Australian Legend Re-visited." *Historical Studies* (Oct. 1978), 18(71):170–90.

White, Richard. *Inventing Australia: Images and Identity, 1688–1980.* Sydney: Allen & Unwin, 1981.

Williams, Michael. *The Making of the South Australian Landscape: A Study in the Historical Geography of Australia.* London: Academic Press, 1974.

Woodward, Judith M. "Urban Influence on Australian Literature in the Late Nineteenth Century." *Australian Literary Studies* (Oct. 1975), 7(2):115–29.

Canada

Altmeyer, George. "Three Ideas of Nature in Canada, 1893–1914." *Journal of Canadian Studies* (Aug. 1976), 11(3):21–36.

Artibise, Alan F. J. "Advertising Winnipeg: The Campaign for Immigrants and

Industry, 1874–1914." *Historical and Scientific Society of Manitoba, Transactions* (1970–71), 3(27):75–106.

—— "Boosterism and the Development of Prairie Cities, 1871–1913." In R. Douglas Francis and H. Palmer, eds., *The Prairie West: Historical Readings,* pp. 408–34, Edmonton: Pica Pica Press, 1985.

—— "Exploring the North-American West: A Comparative Urban Perspective." *American Review of Canadian Studies* (1984), 14(1):20–43.

—— *Gateway City: Winnipeg in Documents, 1873–1913.* Winnipeg: University of Manitoba Press, 1979.

—— *Winnipeg: A Social History of Urban Growth, 1874–1914.* Montreal: McGill-Queen's University Press, 1975.

Bell, Michael. *Painters in a New Land: From Annapolis Royal to the Klondike.* Toronto: McClelland and Stewart, 1973.

Burant, J. *Artists of the Canadian Frontier.* Toronto: Dundurn Press, 1985.

Den Otter, A. A. *Civilizing the West: The Galts and the Development of Western Canada.* Edmonton: Alberta University Press, 1981.

Doyle J. *North of America: Images of Canada in the Literature of the United States, 1775–1900.* Toronto: E. C. W. Press, 1984.

Firth, Edith G. *Toronto in Art: 150 Years Through Artists' Eyes.* Toronto: Fitzhenry and Whiteside, in cooperation with the City of Toronto, 1983.

Francis, R. Douglas. "Changing Images of the West." In R. Douglas Francis and Howard Palmer, eds. *The Prairie West: Historical Readings,* pp. 629–49. Edmonton: Pica Pica Press, 1985.

—— "From Wasteland to Utopia: Changing Images of the Canadian West in the Nineteenth Century." *Great Plains Quarterly* (Summer 1987), 7:178–94.

Jones, David C. " 'There is Some Power About the Land'—The Western Agrarian Press and Country Life Ideology." *Journal of Canadian Studies* (Fall 1982), 17(3):96–108.

Kerr, D. C. "Saskatoon 1910–1913: Ideology of the Boomtime." *Saskatchewan History* (1979), 32:16–28.

Knight, David B. and Susan Burrows. "Centrality by Degrees: A 19th Century Canadian's Measurement for Central Location." *Canadian Cartographer* (1975), 12:109–20.

Owram, Doug. *Promise of Eden: The Canadian Expansionist Movement and the Idea of the West, 1856–1900.* Toronto: University of Toronto Press, 1980.

Reid, Dennis. *"Our Own Country Canada": Being an Account of the National Aspirations of the Principal Landscape Artists in Montreal and Toronto 1860–1890.* Ottawa: National Gallery of Canada, 1979.

Stelter, Gilbert A. "John Galt: The Writer as Town Booster and Builder." In Elizabeth Waterston, ed., *John Galt: Reappraisals,* pp. 17–43. Guelph: University of Guelph, 1985.

Stelter, Gilbert A. and Alan F. J. Artibise, eds. *The Canadian City: Essays in Urban History.* Toronto: Macmillan of Canada, 1979.

—— *Shaping the Urban Landscape: Aspects of the Canadian City-Building Process.* Ottawa: Carleton University Press, 1982.

Swainson, Donald. "Chronicling Kingston: An Interpretation." *Ontario History* (Dec. 1982), 74(4):302–33.

Tausky, Nancy Z. and Lynne D. Di Stefano. *Victorian Architecture in London and Southwestern Ontario: Symbols of Aspiration.* Toronto: University of Toronto Press, 1986.

Waterston, Elizabeth. "Bogle Corbet and the Annals of New World Parishes." In Elizabeth Waterston, ed., *John Galt: Reappraisals,* pp. 57–62. Guelph: University of Guelph, 1985.

—— "Town and Country in John Galt: A Literary Perspective." *Urban History Review/Revue d'histoire urbaine* (June 1985), 14(1):17–22.

Wood, J. David. "Grand Design on the Fringes of Empire: New Towns for British North America." *Canadian Geographer* (1982), 26(3):243–55.

The United States

Abbott, Carl. *Boosters and Businessmen: Popular Economic Thought and Urban Growth in the Antebellum Middle West.* Westport, Conn.: Greenwood Press, 1981.

—— "Civic Pride in Chicago, 1844–1860." *Journal of the Illinois State Historical Society* (Winter 1970), 63(4):399–421.

—— "Indianapolis in the 1850s: Popular Economic Thought and Urban Growth." *Indiana Magazine of History* (Dec. 1978), 84(4):293–315.

Athearn, Robert G. *The Mythic West in Twentieth-Century America.* Lawrence: University Press of Kansas, 1986.

—— *Westward the Briton.* New York: Scribner's, 1953.

Atherton, Lewis. *Main Street on the Middle Border.* New York: Quadrangle, 1966.

—— "The Midwestern Country Town—Myth and Reality." *Agricultural History* (July 1952), 26(3):73–79.

Barth, Gunther. *Instant Cities: Urbanization and the Rise of San Francisco and Denver.* New York: Oxford University Press, 1975.

—— "Metropolism and Urban Elites in the Far West," In Frederick Cople Jaher, ed., *The Age of Industrialism in America: Essays in Social Structure and Cultural Values,* pp. 158–87. New York: Free Press; London: Collier-Macmillan, 1968.

Belcher, Wyatt Winton. *The Economic Rivalry Between St. Louis and Chicago 1850–1880.* New York: Columbia University Press, 1947.

Bender, Thomas. *Community and Social Change in America.* Baltimore and London: Johns Hopkins University Press, 1982.

—— *Toward an Urban Vision: Ideas and Institutions in Nineteenth-Century America.* Lexington: University of Kentucky Press, 1975.

Berger, Max. *The British Traveller in America, 1836–1860.* Gloucester, Mass.: Peter Smith, 1964.

Billington, Ray Allan. *The Genesis of the Frontier Thesis: A Study in Historical Creativity.* San Marino, Calif.: Huntington Library, 1971.

—— *Land of Savagery, Land of Promise: The European Image of the American Frontier in the Nineteenth Century.* New York and London: Norton, 1981.

Boorstin, Daniel. *The Americans: The National Experience.* New York: Vintage Books, n. d.

Brooks, John G. *As Others See Us: A Study of Progress in the United States.* New York: Macmillan, 1908.

Burchell, Robert A. "The Loss of a Reputation; or, The Image of California in Britain Before 1875." *California Historical Quarterly* (Summer 1974), 83(2):115–30.

Cowan, Michael H. *City of the West: Emerson, America, and Urban Metaphor.* New Haven and London: Yale University Press, 1967.

Cronon, William J. "To Be the Central City: Chicago, 1848–1857." *Chicago History* (Fall 1981), 10(3):130–40.

Dondore, Dorothy A. *The Prairie and the Making of Middle America: Four Centuries of Description.* Cedar Rapids, Iowa: Torch Press, 1926.

Dorsett, Lyle and Mary Dorsett. "Rhetoric Versus Realism: 150 Years of Missouri Boosterism." *Bulletin of the Missouri Historical Society* (Jan. 1972), 28(2):77–84.

Doyle, Don Harrison. *The Social Order of a Frontier Community: Jacksonville, Illinois, 1825–70.* Urbana: University of Illinois Press, 1978.

—— "Social Theory and New Communities in Nineteenth-Century America." *Western Historical Quarterly* (Apr. 1977), 8(2):151–66.

Duis, Perry R. "Chicago Chronicles." *Chicago History* (Winter 1985–86), 14(4):56–67.

Dykstra, Robert R. *The Cattle Towns.* New York: Atheneum, 1976.

—— "Town-Country Conflict: A Hidden Dimension in American Social History." *Agricultural History* (Oct. 1964), 38:195–204.

Glaab, Charles N. "The Historian and the American Urban Tradition." *Wisconsin Magazine of History* (Autumn 1963), 47(1):12–25.

—— "Jesup W. Scott and a West of Cities." *Ohio History* (Winter 1964), 73(1):3–12.

—— *Kansas City and the Railroads: Community Policy in the Growth of a Regional Metropolis.* Madison: State Historical Society of Wisconsin, 1962.

—— "Visions of Metropolis: William Gilpin and Theories of City Growth in the American West." *Wisconsin Magazine of History* (Autumn 1961), 45(1):21–31.

Goldfield, David R. "Pursuing the American Dream: Cities in the Old South." In Blaine A. Brownell and David R. Goldfield, eds., *The City in Southern History: The Growth of Urban Civilization in the South.* Port Washington, N. Y., and London: Kennikat Press, 1977.

—— *Urban Growth in the Age of Sectionalism: Virginia, 1847–1861.* Baton Rouge and London: Louisiana State University Press, 1977.

Hales, Peter B. *Silver Cities: The Photography of American Urbanization, 1839–1915.* Philadelphia: Temple University Press, 1984.

Hamer, D. A. "Time, Space and the Western Town." *Australian Journal of American Studies* (July 1981), 1(2):15–24.

Herron, Irma Honaker. *The Small Town in American Literature.* New York: Haskell, 1971.

Hine, Robert V. *Community on the American Frontier: Separate but Not Alone.* Norman: University of Oklahoma Press, 1980.

Holt, Glen E. "St. Louis Observed 'from Two Different Worlds': An Exploration of the City through French and English Travelers' Accounts, 1874–1889." *Bulletin of the Missouri Historical Society* (Jan. 1973), 29(2):63–87.

Hudson, John C. *Plains Country Towns.* Minneapolis: University of Minnesota Press, 1985.

Jackson, John Brinckerhoff. *The Southern Landscape Tradition in Texas.* Fort Worth: Amon Carter Museum, 1980.

Jackson, Kenneth T. *Crabgrass Frontier: The Suburbanization of the United States.* New York and Oxford: Oxford University Press, 1987.

Jakle, John. *Images of the Ohio Valley: A Historical Geography of Travel, 1790–1860.* New York: Oxford University Press, 1977.

Jeans, D. N. "Fiction and the Small Town in the United States: A Contribution to the Study of Urbanisation." *Australian Geographical Studies* (Oct. 1984), 22(2):261–74.

Johnson, Hildegard Binder. *Order Upon the Land: The U.S. Rectangular Land Survey and the Upper Mississippi Country.* New York: Oxford University Press, 1976.

Karnes, Thomas L. *William Gilpin: Western Nationalist.* Austin and London: University of Texas Press, 1970.

Kogan, Herman. " 'Grander and Statelier than Ever . . .'." *Chicago History* (Fall 1971), 1(4):236–44.

Kramer, Carl E. "City with a Vision: Images of Louisville in the 1830s." *Filson Club History Quarterly* (Oct. 1986), 60(4):427–52.

—— "Images of a Developing City: Louisville, 1800–1830." *Filson Club History Quarterly* (April 1978), 52(2):166–90.

Lauer, Jeanette C. and Robert H. Lauer. "St. Louis and the 1880 Census: The Shock of Collective Failure." *Missouri Historical Review* (Jan. 1982), 76(2):151–63.

Larsen, Lawrence H. *The Urban West at the End of the Frontier.* Lawrence: Regents Press of Kansas, 1978.

Lemelin, Robert. *Pathway to the National Character 1830–1861.* Port Washington, N.Y., and London: Kennikat Press, 1974.

Lewis, Lloyd. *John S. Wright: Prophet of the Prairies.* Chicago: Prairie Farmer, 1941.

Lewis, Lloyd and Henry Justin Smith. *Chicago: The History of Its Reputation.* New York: Harcourt, Brace, 1929.

Lewis, Robert. "Frontier and Civilization in the Thought of Frederick Law Olmsted." *American Quarterly* (Fall 1977), 19(4):385–403.

Lingeman, Richard. *Small Town America: A Narrative History 1620–The Present.* Boston: Houghton Mifflin, 1980.

Lowenthal, David. *The Past Is a Foreign Country.* Cambridge: Cambridge University Press, 1985.

—— "The Place of the Past in the American Landscape." In David Lowenthal and Martyn J. Bowden, eds., *Geographies of the Mind: Essays in Historical Geosophy: In Honor of John Kirtland Wright,* pp. 89–118. New York: Oxford University Press, 1976.

Luckingham, Bradford. "Agents of Culture in the Urban West: Merchants and Mercantile Libraries in Mid-Nineteenth Century St. Louis and San Francisco." *Journal of the West* (April 1978), 17(2):28–35.

McDermott, John Francis. *The Lost Panoramas of the Mississippi.* Chicago: University of Chicago Press, 1958.

Machor, James L. *Pastoral Cities: Urban Ideals and the Symbolic Landscape of America.* Madison: University of Wisconsin Press, 1987.

—— "Urbanization and the Western Garden: Synthesizing City and Country in Antebellum America." *South Atlantic Quarterly* (Autumn 1982), 81(4):413–28.

McLear, Patrick E. "John Stephen Wright and Urban and Regional Promotion in the Nineteenth Century." *Journal of the Illinois State Historical Society* (Nov. 1975), 68(5):407–20.

—— "Logan U. Reavis: Nineteenth Century Urban Promoter." *Missouri Historical Review* (July 1972), 66(4):567–88.

Marx, Leo. *The Machine in the Garden: Technology and the Pastoral Ideal in America.* London: Oxford University Press, 1967.

Meinig, D. W. *Imperial Texas: An Interpretive Essay in Cultural Geography.* Austin: University of Texas Press, 1969.

Mesick, Jane L. *The English Traveller in America, 1785–1835.* New York: Columbia University Press, 1922.

Moehring, Eugene P. *Urban America and the Foreign Traveler, 1815–1855.* New York: Arno Press, 1974.

Nathan, Marvin R. "Classical Architecture and Vigilantes in Gold Rush San Francisco." *Journal of American Culture* (Spring 1982), 5:100–6.

Nelson, Howard J. "Town Founding and the American Frontier." *Association of Pacific Coast Geographers Yearbook* (1974), 36:7–23.

Pachter, Marc and Frances Wein, eds. *Abroad in America: Visitors to the New Nation 1776–1914.* Reading, Mass.: Addison-Wesley, in association with the National Portrait Gallery, Smithsonian Institution, 1976.

Pauly, John J. "The Great Chicago Fire as a National Event." *American Quarterly* (Winter 1984), 36(5):668–83.

Reps, John W. *Cities of the American West: A History of Frontier Urban Planning.* Princeton: Princeton University Press, 1979.

—— *Cities on Stone: Nineteenth Century Lithograph Images of the Urban West.* Fort Worth: Amon Carter Museum, 1976.

—— *The Forgotten Frontier: Urban Planning in the American West Before 1890.* Columbia and London: University of Missouri Press, 1981.

—— *The Making of Urban America: A History of City Planning in the United States.* Princeton: Princeton University Press, 1965.

—— *Views and Viewmakers of Urban America: Lithographs of Towns and Cities in the United States and Canada, Notes on the Artists and Publishers, and a Union Catalog of their Work, 1825–1925.* Columbia: University of Missouri Press, 1984.

Repson, Richard L. *Britons View America: Travel Commentary, 1860–1935.* Seattle: University of Washington Press, 1971.

Rifkind, Carole. *Main Street: The Face of Urban America.* New York: Harper & Row, 1977.

Robinson, Willard B. "Helena's Fabulous Business Blocks." *Montana* (Jan. 1968), 18(1):44–59.

Ross, Steven J. "Industrialization and the Changing Images of Progress in Nineteenth-Century Cincinnati." *Queen City Heritage* (Summer 1985), 43(2):3–24.

Schlereth, Thomas J. "The New England Presence on the Midwest Landscape." *The Old Northwest: A Journal of Regional Life and Letters* (Summer 1983), 9(2):125–42.

Schnell, J. Christopher. "Chicago Versus St. Louis: A Reassessment of the Great Rivalry." *Missouri Historical Review* (April 1977), 71(3):245–65.

Schnell, J. Christopher and Katherine B. Clinton. "The New West: Themes in Nineteenth Century Urban Promotion, 1815–1880." *Bulletin of the Missouri Historical Society* (Jan. 1974), 30(2):75–88.

Segal, Howard P. "Jeff W. Hayes: Reform Boosterism and Urban Utopianism." *Oregon Historical Quarterly* (Winter 1978), 79(4):345–58.

Shapiro, Henry D. and Zane L. Miller, eds. *Physician to the West: Selected Writings of Daniel Drake on Science & Society.* Lexington: University Press of Kentucky, 1970.

Share, Allen J. *Cities in the Commonwealth: Two Centuries of Urban Life in Kentucky.* Lexington: University Press of Kentucky, 1982.

Sibley, Marilyn M. *Travelers in Texas, 1761–1860.* Austin: University of Texas Press, 1967.

Siegel, Adrienne. *The Image of the American City in Popular Literature 1820–1870.* Port Washington, N. Y., and London: Kennikat Press, 1981.

Slotkin, Richard. *The Fatal Environment: The Myth of the Frontier in the Age of Industrialization, 1800–1890.* Middletown, Conn.: Wesleyan University Press, 1986.

Smith, Page. *As a City Upon a Hill: The Town in American History.* Cambridge, Mass., and London: M.I.T. Press, 1966.

Snider, Denton J. *The St. Louis Movement in Philosophy, Literature, Education, Psychology with Chapters of Autobiography.* St. Louis: Sigma, 1920.

Stelter, Gilbert. "The City and Westward Expansion: A Western Case Study." *Western Historical Quarterly* (April 1973), 4(2):187–202.

Still, Bayrd. "The Growth of Milwaukee as Recorded by Contemporaries." *Wisconsin Magazine of History* (Mar. 1938), 21(3):262–92.

Stoehr, C. Eric. *Bonanza Victorian: Architecture and Society in Colorado Mining Towns.* Albuquerque: University of New Mexico Press, 1975.

Strauss, Anselm L. *The American City: A Sourcebook of Urban Imagery.* London: Allen Lane, 1968.

—— *The Contexts of Social Mobility: Ideology and Theory.* Chicago: Aldine, 1971.

—— *Images of the American City.* New York: Free Press of Glencoe, 1961.

Strout, Cushing. *The American Image of the Old World.* New York: Harper & Row, 1963.

Sutton, S. B., ed. *Civilizing American Cities: A Selection of Frederick Law Olmsted's Writings on City Landscapes.* Cambridge, Mass., and London: M.I.T. Press, 1979.

Taft, Robert. *Artists and Illustrators of the Old West 1830–1900.* New York: Scribner's, 1953.

Tucker, Louis Leonard. "Cincinnati: Athens of the West, 1830–1861." *Ohio History* (Winter 1966), 75(1):10–25.

Tyler, Ron. *Visions of America: Pioneer Artists in a New Land.* London: Thames and Hudson, 1983.

Volkman, Nancy J. "Landscape Architecture on the Prairie: The Work of H. W. S. Cleveland." *Kansas History* (Summer 1987), 10(2):89–110.

Wade, Richard C. *The Urban Frontier: Pioneer Life in Early Pittsburgh, Cincinnati, Lexington, Louisville, and St. Louis.* Chicago and London: University of Chicago Press, 1959.

Welter, Rush. *The Mind of America 1820–1860.* New York and London: Columbia University Press, 1975.

White, Morton and Lucia White. *The Intellectual Versus the City: From Thomas Jefferson to Frank Lloyd Wright.* Oxford: Oxford University Press, 1977.

White, William A. "Tradition and Urban Development: A Contrast of Chicago and Toronto in the Nineteenth Century." *The Old Northwest* (Fall 1982), 8(3):245–72.

Index

Cattle ranchers, 109
Cemeteries, 123, 126, 170-71
Census, American, 1890, 37, 94, 139
Centers, city, 70; towns as, 137-38
"Central City," search for, 261n123
Centralization, Australian, 141-45,
 152-53, 159-60
Central Park, New York City, 192
Central place theory, 4, 132
Chadwick, Edwin, 121
Chesshyre, Henry T. Newton, on
 compensating for lack of church
 spires in Canadian wilds, 190
Cheyenne, Wyo., 89; needs to "develop her rural surroundings," 250-
 51n25
Cheyenne Daily Leader, 250-51n25
Chicago, Ill., 54, 149, 162; as Baptist
 headquarters, 210; boom and crash
 of 1837, 21-22; cemeteries in, 170-
 71; as a coming "world city," 129;
 Great Fire (1871), 130, 172;
 growth of, 22, 34; incongruities in,
 167; moral deficiencies of, 129-30;
 newness of, 172; origins of, 18, 21;
 other towns aspired to be like, 166;
 out-of-dateness of guidebook to,
 168; population of, vs. that of St.
 Louis, 165; position in the West,
 135-37; "resolute and occupied air"
 of crowds, 164; revival after 1871
 fire, 130, 172; rivalry with other cities, 13, 23; Wright and future of,
 134, 166
*Chicago and the Sources of Her Past
 and Future Growth,* 130
Chicago: Past, Present, Future
 (Wright), 134, 166
Chicago Tribune, 133; 1882 visit to
 Duluth of correspondent, 166, 175
Chilicothe, Ohio, decay predicted, 125
Chisholm, Caroline: escorted young female migrants up country, 202-3;
 plans for settlement of Australian in-

terior, 206; on working-people's
 cottages in Melbourne, 192-93
Cholmondeley, Thomas, 96
Christchurch, N.Z., 78, 147; "Englishness" of, 46; founding of, 7
Churches: lack of in interior of Australia, 212; in landscapes of Old and
 New Worlds, 191
Cincinnati, Ohio, boosting of, 19-20,
 53; as center of religious and "civilizing" influence in the West, 127-
 28, 210; coming of railroad to, 138;
 Dicey on arrival at, 185; Drake and,
 19, 114, 127-28, 230; in 1857, 163;
 Flint on, 70-71; founding of, 18;
 growth of, 33-34; impossibility of
 depicting as a whole, 51; rapid rise
 of, 117; tendency of people to dwell
 on "great hereafter," 175; Mrs.
 Trollope and, 24, 49, 177, 212; as
 Tyre or Athens of the West, 123
Circles, Goodin's theory of evolution
 via, 132, 136
Circle maps, 137-38
Circleville, Ohio, ancient mound at,
 169, 196-97
Cist, Charles, as booster, 20, 53, 136,
 174
Cities, large: in Australia, 13, 16, 140-
 61, 227; in Canada, 229
"City," use of in names of American
 towns, 115, 165
"City of the West," as metaphor,
 245n20
Civilization: contrasted with "frontier
 barbarisms," 188-89; contrasted
 with "wilderness," 184-86, 193; encroachment on wilderness, 189,
 200; replacing wilderness, 206-7;
 towns as agencies for spread of, 207-
 12, 217, 231; towns representing
 advance of, 204
Civil War, American, 9
Clark, J. Max, on Greeley, Colo., 164

Clarke, Percy, 77

Classical names and analogies, 123, 176

Clay, Henry, 22

Clemens, Orion, *City of Keokuk in 1856,* 168

Cleveland, Ohio, 72; founding of, 18; growth of, 19-20, 22

Cody, William F., *see* "Buffalo Bill"

Coffin, Charles Carleton, celebrated achievements of American westward expansion, 231

Coghlan, T. A.: analysis of Australian population statistics, 150-52, 154; on Australia's urban population, 141; on predominance of large cities in Australia, 151-53, 158

Cohnstaedt, Wilhelm, 47

Collins, David, 95

Colonial Magazine, 203

Colonial Office, 7, 28, 30

Colonial Reformers, 28

Colonies: concentration as basis for development, 102; evolution of, 93; Greek, 101-2; town-based, 101-8

Colonization: Chisholm on, 206; concentration and, 103-4, 111; Galt and, 102; planning of, 15; role of towns in, 100-8; Wakefield on, 103; Wakefieldian, 29-30, 101-6

Colonizing companies, Wakefield on the role of, 29

"Colonist, A," *Life's Work As It Is* (1867), 80, 184, 204

Colorado, 36, 39, 47, 69, 126

Colorado City, relationship to Colorado Springs, 89

Colorado Springs: as "anti-frontier" town, 88-9; Palmer's vision for, 69; Ute Indians and, 216

Columbia River, 32

Comfort, Texas, 33

Commerce of Kansas City in 1886, The, 134

Community, towns as, 104

Competitiveness among towns, 11-13

Concentration: Adelaide's plan and, 180; and colonization, 101-4, 106, 111-12; and provision of towns, 103-4

Concentration of population in cities: in Australia, 16, 38-39, 141-48, 150-53; Weber on, 38-39

Condorcet (Marquis de), 93

Conservation: of historic buildings, 170; of wilderness, 200

Constantinople, 130

Convicts: fear of in Australia, 203; in novels set in Australia, 228; sent to Australia, 19

Cooper, James Fenimore: on presence of churches in European vs. American towns, 191; on towns as "centres of exertion," 211

Copley, Josiah, 85, 88

Cornish, Henry, 115

Corroborees, 215, 218, 221-23

Costley, John, 142

Cottages in Melbourne, 192-93

Council Bluffs, Iowa, 35

"Country," "city" and, 157, 193, 230

Country towns: agitation for land reform in Australia and New Zealand, 157; between "city" and "country," 157; weakness of in Australia, 38, 159

County seats, striving of towns to become, 23, 137, 149

Cowboy cult, 232

Cowboy image of the West, 1

Crawford, James Coutts, Australia vs. New Zealand urban development, 147

Crèvecoeur, Hector St. John de, 68

Cricket in Australia, 32, 223

Crockett, Davy, 92

"Cultural baggage," 15

"Cultural imperialism," 208

Kames, Lord, 93
Kansas: colonization of in 1850s, 97-98; development of towns in, 100; devising a railroad strategy for, 225; free-soil colonization of, 102, 105, 210; migration to southwestern, 208; new type of pioneer in, 100; promotion of, 135; settlement of, 34-35; struggle in over slavery, 97-98; towns in, 1857, 41-42; townsite speculation in, 35
Kansas City, Kans., treatment of past at, 172
Kansas City, Mo.: centrality of, 261n123; growth of, 35, 134; origins of, 22
Kansas League of Cincinnati, 105
Kansas-Nebraska Act, 35
Kaskaskia, Ill., 18
Kelly, Ned, 95
Kelly, William, on Melbourne's growth, 118, 215
Kennedy, David: on Echuca, Vict., 193; on view from Hamilton Mountain, 50; visits Geelong, 157; visits Melbourne, 56
Kennedy, Paul, 120
Kennicott, Carol, 162
Kentucky, 139; settlement, 18; urban development, 39
Keokuk, Ill., address by mayor, 1856, 168-69
Kilbourn, Byron, on Milwaukee, 23
Kinglake, Edward, on novels set in Australia, 228
Kingston, Ont.: fear of its becoming a "deserted village," 257n48; growth, 20; improvement, 200; Indians in streets, 220
Kingston, William H. G.: on Canadian towns, 78; on migrants' reaction to colonial towns, 79-80, 155
Kirkland, Caroline Matilda, on sites of new towns in Michigan, 176
Kirkwood, John, 120, 122

Kohl, J. G.: on Bytown (Ottawa), 193; on changes in names of towns, 115; on Toronto, 182, 187
Kramer, Carl E., 122

Lafayette, Ind., "Flunkeyism" in, 268n89
Lakier, Alexsandr: on America enthusiasm for towns, 57; on Cincinnati in 1857, 163; on out-of-date Chicago guidebook, 168; on rapid growth of American towns, 132-33; on rise of cities in the West, 136; in St. Louis, 48
Lancaster, Nebr. (Lincoln, Nebr.), 35
Lancelott, F.: on aborigines of Adelaide, 218; on parklands at Adelaide, 198
Land and Emigration Commissioners, and creation of towns in colonies, 30
Land monopoly, 155-56
Land reform, as a panacea, 266n69
Landscape, Americans and, 198
Lang, Dr. John Dunmore: on concentration of population in Sydney, 141, 151; on grand names given to villages, 187; influenced by Vaughan's *Age of Great Cities,* 144, 150; on moral advantages of concentrating population in large cities, 144-45, 159, 212; on plan given to Portland, Vict., 196; preference for aboriginal names for towns, 221; wished for villages on banks of Brisbane River, 190; as writer and commentator on Australia, 143-44
Lansbury, Coral, on Arcadian myth, 161
La Platte City, Nebr., 99
Larimer, William, acquired land in Nebraska, 99
Larsen, Lawrence H., 232
Lawrence, Kans., 35; center of free-soil colonization, 103; in 1857, 42